Boundaries of the City

Boundaries of the City

The Architecture of Western Urbanism

Alan Waterhouse

UNIVERSITY OF TORONTO PRESS
Toronto Buffalo London

© University of Toronto Press Incorporated 1993
Toronto Buffalo London
Printed in Canada
ISBN 0-8020-0538-1

Printed on acid-free paper

Canadian Cataloguing in Publication Data

Waterhouse, Alan
  Boundaries of the city : the architecture of
western urbanism

  ISBN 0-8020-0538-1

  1. City planning – Europe – History. 2. Architecture
– Europe – History. 3. Urbanization – Europe –
History. I. Title.

NA9183.W37 1993   711'.4'094   C93-094070-9

This book has been published with the help of a grant from the Social Science Federation of Canada, using
funds provided by the Social Sciences and Humanities Research Council of Canada. Publication was also
assisted by a generous grant from the University of Toronto Women's Association.

For Sandra

Contents

Illustrations

Acknowledgments

I wish to express my gratitude to two agencies for their generosity in supporting the research upon which the book is based. Both the Alexander von Humboldt-Stiftung of Bonn–Bad Godesberg and the Social Sciences and Humanities Research Council of Canada gave me a base in Europe, at the Lehrstühl für Städtebau und Regionalplanung of the Technische Universität in Munich. From such a place, inspired by the wise counsel of Professor Gerd Albers, researching the cities of Germany, France, Greece, Turkey, and Italy has been, for me, an especially gratifying pursuit.

Because so many ideas in this book have flowed from conversations with people who love cities, I wish to thank my students and colleagues at the University of Toronto; in particular I owe much to the friendship of Professor John Hitchcock and Professor Shoukry Roweis, as I do to that of the late Professor Hans Blumenfeld. I am also grateful to Professor Imre Koroknay, who, in providing many of the illustrations, has let me take advantage of his gifts as an artist and connoisseur of cities.

Finally, special thanks are due to Beverley Beetham Endersby, Michael Mather, Irene Wilk, and Robin Waterhouse, all of whom, in their different ways, were invaluable when it came to piecing the manuscript for this book together.

Alan Waterhouse
Toronto

Introduction

The human imagination, social forms, the constructed city – these are the axes we shall consider. How do the first two intersect with the other?

The central character in Hermann Hesse's spiritual autobiography *Gertrud* is a man called Kuhn. This name, which translates as 'boldness,' or 'daring,' stands for everything Kuhn lacks but wishes he had. Lohe, the perspicacious schoolmaster in the story, tells him: 'individualism or imaginary loneliness ... has insinuated itself into your imagination; you are isolated; no one troubles about you and no one understands you.' Hesse wrote that piece in 1910, at a time and place I deal with in the closing chapters of this book. That was a year of prophecy, when a callow avant-garde began signalling to a world seduced by thoughts of progress how Kuhn's affliction would spread through the West, and span the century. Hesse's protagonist, one would now say, was quintessentially urban, wrestling with that disquiet born of two minds, regretting the sacrifice entailed in keeping humanity at arm's length in order to fathom and cope with its bewildering ubiquity; for, all the while, Kuhn's refuge 'demands something that has to be subtracted from the enjoyment of life.'

We continue to live this dilemma, recognizing its embodiment, perhaps more than did Hesse's contemporaries, in a metropolitan landscape as hyperactive and unfocused as the modern spirit. The landscape itself, shredded by xenophobia, works back on the dilemma and deepens it further, insisting on a price for insularity; the price is a solitariness we long to escape, but cannot avoid getting caught up in the centrifuge of modern urbanism as it spins other lives away from our own into inaccessible zones.

One asks, naturally enough, about the place of disparity, fed selectively by technology and affluence, in this scheme of things, and whether the centrifugal urge is a constant in urban history or something new. The past, after all, resounds with evidence of the connection between money and that unhappiness surely manifested in an extreme aversion to propinquity. The type described by Lucretius in *De Rerum Natura* (iii, 1053) seems no less than an unreflective (and therefore more familiar) version of Kuhn: 'There is a weight on their minds, and a mountain of misery lies on their hearts ... For each, not knowing what he wants, seeks always to change his place, as if he could drop his burden. There is one who, bored to death at home, goes forth every now and then from his palace; but feeling no better abroad, suddenly returns. Off he courses, driving his nags to his country house in head-long haste ... He has hardly crossed the threshold when he yawns, or seeks oblivion in a heavy sleep, or even hurries back to the city. So each man flees from himself.'

But if the flight from oneself surfaces in the flight from others, ancient Rome was never monopolized by this affliction, as we can discern from the binary organization of its landscape. Latium had its walled-in enclaves; but the urban quarters were vibrant with humanity, not excluding whole parts of the Esquiline and the Oppian where monied people lived, as were the Roman and Imperial fora no less so, accretions woven over centuries into equally venerable plebeian neighbour-hoods like the Vicus Tuscus and the Vicus Jugarius; processional solemnity had its own precincts, yet they were thrown into sharp relief by the intrusion of Trajan's markets, and all was shaped around an interdependent life we can scarcely imagine, let alone experience. The nostalgic are bound to ask, too, when reading the many stories of friendships that grew out of chance encounters in the streets and at the great public festivals, or of famous walks by men like Horace and Martial, who relished that city's porosity and human dis-play, whether the best part of such a life is not recoverable. But the integrative spirit of antiq-uity was sustained by an ideology we cannot, and perhaps should not want to replicate. The *res publica*, together with its medieval reincar-nation in *communitas*, represented a tran-scendent arc holding its individual subjects together, and, like all such things, was doubt-less a curse as well as a blessing. Nor does the integrative spirit account for a large dose of intractability, even shapelessness, in the urbanism of antiquity and the Middle Ages; nostalgia always works selectively in remi-niscing about events, as Horace himself saw in deriding the *laudator temporis acti* – the praiser of past times – 'If some god offered to take you back to those days, you would refuse every time.'

Nevertheless, ideologies come and go, and history is not exhausted by giving an account of them and nothing else. Are they not, in a sense, opportunistic constructs feeding para-sitically off this latency and that, embedded in human consciousness? The cult of individual-ism, no less than a belief in mutualism, re-quires an explanation preceding that of poli-tics, which describes but seems unable to account for the recurrent dialectic of the two. Hermann Hesse heard Socrates and countless others express a paradox when he wrote: 'constantly I point ... to the blessed motley of this world, but equally constantly bring to mind the fact that at the basis of this motley lies a unity.'

In voicing this perennial contradiction, Hesse was content to let it be; if, to him, cohesiveness had individuality as an omni-present shadow, each surfaced harmlessly in the content of his prose, in dialogue and reflection on the human condition. Others more concerned with deeds than words enjoy no such distance from events, and are obliged to structure and restructure the dialectic as it weaves its way through quotidian life. As archaeologists know well, the practices of urbanism, whereby cities are arranged ac-cording to what passes for reason, have a story to tell as illuminating as any text about the way in which humans have encountered na-ture and each other, or turned away from them, in the course of daily life; the settle-ments of the past may be ciphers of propa-ganda born of some political will or other, but do they not also reveal a large residue made up of everyday habits and imaginative wayward-ness that fall through the ideological net, to be embodied in constructed banalities and, if not masterpieces, then plenty to admire on occa-sion? Those occasions have, none the less, not figured prominently of late; for, while the unity Hesse saw may still live in the imagina-tion, it no longer seems able to find a place outside texts and dreams, to colour the urban landscape. We did not contrive this calamity; by a quirk of circumstance surely engineered by no one, its forms work their way into consciousness and action to fashion an insularity unparalleled in history, one whose fall-out, in the subversive manner of Kuhn's distress, withers true individuality.

The modern promise that sanctioning the pursuit of self-interest brings freedom is mocked by the uncrossable boundaries surrounding every territory of modernity's own ubiquitous cipher, the metropolis. That the metropolis ends up far removed from the motives that bring it into being is the greatest denial of that promise, and proof too of urbanism's disintegration. For the past century, urbanism has been wielded according to what has been called the public interest, an idea shaped by the regulatory, distributive, and occasional redistributive tasks of the state. Quite unlike the *res publica*, this interest, grounded in empiricism, has failed to reach beyond those aggregates of private interest by which its accomplishments are measured. Urban politics, like other pursuits of the state, now passes muster according to head counts; so public planning, while claiming to serve the common good, cannot extricate itself from a utilitarian reason whose objective is the welfare of individuals. The offspring of an idea once powerful enough to turn the minds of citizens outwards to the city, impelling them to articulate its landscape in recognition of each other and the cosmos, now serves only to darken the shadow of inwardness.

Recently, Nathan Glazer and Mark Lilla, in *The Public Face of Architecture* (ix–xvi), called for the introduction of educational programs to cultivate 'taste and civic awareness' as a first step in re-establishing a truly public domain in the city. The sceptic might reasonably claim that qualities such as these can only remain bloodless in the absence of a more fundamental moral orientation that makes us again interact with the world around. Do not architects and urbanists face a difficulty in advocating tasteful forms – reworking a divided habitat with images of the classical and the picturesque, or threading whole quarters with networks of convivial streets and squares

– if public and private behaviour continue to be monopolized by self-absorption? The answer to such a question is far from simple, although this book attempts to provide one.

Merely to placard the past, as Horace implied, takes little courage and bears no fruit; but the past offers more than a warehouse of forms, to be picked through and discarded as we choose: the forms themselves were manifestations of a practical reason that depended upon, and in turn ordered, the experience of life, and they could not be separated from that experience as its inert by-products. On the contrary, the constructed city *informed* life like nothing else – at one level, it was a source of data certainly, to be assimilated in a detached manner according to one's taste and civic awareness, but, at another, the city invaded the senses with an immediacy over which the discerning mind had no control; the citizen may volunteer to read the city as one would a text, but choice evaporates when the urban quarters press against awareness. In this sense nothing has changed; places do not persuade us of their presence, but insist. If this presence is no longer the product of practical reason, but an intended or inadvertent consequence of some less admirable mechanism, it does not lose its power to inform life; no exegesis needs tell us which metropolitan streets and wastelands are malevolent, nor does experiencing them leave anyone untouched. True, familiarity might well modify our judgment of such places, but their fundamental character remains intact to become lodged in memory and the subconscious, there affecting our competence to engage the landscape and its people.

What, then, can history provide in the way of practices that would be valid today? The history of architecture and city planning places taste and civic awareness at its normative centre, with good reason. Who refuses to believe that illustrious cities were the work of informed and rational minds; or to dream that urban places, if only in some distant future, will again be realms of exquisite beauty and shared pleasure, domains where the community of citizens can stand, as Lucretius once said, amid the majesty of things? But recall, too, how that great Epicurean took account of the 'man who flees from himself'; he, rest assured, is also a historical constant, and a symbol of those myriad forces that, in countering urbanism's common cause, give to the latter its peculiar status as a half-realized endeavour, neither art nor anarchy. Should not history take account of him in the building of cities, especially given his pervasiveness in the contemporary landscape? In so doing the chronicle would enter into quotidian life, to discover why taste and civic awareness have only seldom occupied the centre of urban experience; instead, we encounter something more banal but just as arcane – namely, the territorial imperative. Here the material resources of the city – its infrastructure, architecture, and terrain – are garnered and articulated into countless shades of privacy, giving rise to the boundaries along which urbanism's dialectic has been played out since the beginning. The processes whereby these boundaries are fashioned display a remarkable historical resiliency despite the versatility which always enables them to signal the manifold character of urban life. Their double-sidedness also envelops this life, affecting those who lead it with the immediacy described above, here cutting them off from each other, and there, more felicitously, bringing them together.

What follows are some reflections arising out of my research on the formation of urban boundaries and the part they play in everyday life. In this volume I deal, with some necessary exceptions, with certain events in the history of European city building up to and including the birth of modernism at the beginning of our own century, to form a chronicle of sorts which has no pretence to comprehensiveness. The scenes described mostly concern the perennial opposition between human insularity and a stubborn aspiration for the complementary of things, creating tensions which I believe give urbanism its special character, one normally bereft of the harmonies one expects to see in great artistic and architectural enterprises. The reader should not be too annoyed, therefore, to find scant attention paid to some of the more graceful accomplishments of European urbanism. I hardly mention Periclean Athens, or the Imperial German towns, and baroque Rome is passed over lightly; I say virtually nothing about mercantile Amsterdam or London, and barely mention Spain. My excuse is that, while these places exhibit what I seek, it is always enmeshed with localized, extraordinary material admirably covered elsewhere, and that my selection still avoids the obscure. I deal with such places as Pergamum and Priene, the crowded armatures of ancient Rome and her colonial towns, half-finished projects in medieval Florence and Siena, the suburbs of neoclassical Paris, and the industrial quarters of Berlin, then finally wrestle with modernism's crucible, located not coincidentally in the hinterland of the German city; the whole builds a platform to an analysis of the contemporary metropolis contained in a second volume.

Nobody gets away with wrapping the breathtaking complexity of city building into a simple package, because one is confronted at every turn with exceptions to some rule or other. Nevertheless, I have tried to string this book together around two conceptual themes, which are explained in Part I, and illustrated in Part II, while hastening to add that, if these themes add up to an idea, they do not amount to a theory; selective history, after all, denies that possibility. One theme tries to capture the citizen's city, rather than that of the discerning analyst. The citizen becomes immersed in a labyrinth of symbols and constructed facts, tantalized by, often afflicted by an architecture of boundaries that can signal sanctuary or incarceration, in domains where fantasy coexists with alienation and, not least, in a phenomenal world where speed and light promise escape from the tedium of closed boundaries. The analyst may discern all this, but from a distance, through a veil of connoisseurship or with a scepticism that dismisses the banal and the capricious as of little account.

The second theme I try to fold into the first by situating urbanism, not within the institutional confines of planning – for the practices covered in these pages have more of a quotidian basis than one suggesting institutional order – but in the boundary zones dividing the city into territories and also marking the frontier incursion into nature. Here I treat architecture as a constituent of boundaries, and consider how it and the city have been shaped through time by alliances of self-interest acting against the natural order and against those who aspire to the complementarity of things. Political economy enters the picture, because the second theme lends itself – perhaps too well – to this subject; all divisions of the terrain, nearly all constructions, involve third parties whose welfare is also invested in boundary articulation.

The most striking evidence to emerge from all this is a historical resilience in practices many might think are very recent. First, to have believed a few years ago, before the advent of environmentalism, that city planning ought to follow rules embodied in the natural world would have been tantamount to believing in witchcraft. Yet the seeds of environmentalism, far from taking root in latter-day activism, were first planted at the dawn of consciousness, then nurtured by a morality identical to what sustained the urbanism of antiquity. Not only were the clan and the city once integral to a god-filled landscape, but the very exercise of rationality made *res natura* the supreme exemplar for *res publica*. Cicero, in *De Re Publica* (iii, 22), voices the practical reason of countless generations in proclaiming that 'true law is right reason in agreement with nature, world-wide in scope, unchang-

ing, everlasting.' He was advocating, not some Rousseauesque idyll, but a society whose structures were shaped by that same reverence our ancestors once felt when contemplating the natural world. If this reverence flourished in times past by making a virtue out of necessity, banishing insecurity and loneliness by creating an ideology whose forms were ritual, pageantry, and certain acts of construction, so be it. Once again nature grows insistent, and, Cicero would claim, in turning our attention outwards to the welfare of the countryside, we encounter each other.

Yet this harmonizing ethic has been enmeshed with and confronted by a very different reality, one we have the nerve to call postmodern, but which, in fact, spans the history of urbanism. I am referring to a recurrent abrogation of any central organizing principle in order to defy the authority of money, reason, and politics, mostly by men who are young, unattached, and unmanageable. Here, an ambiguous poetry suffuses the dialectic, revealing, beneath the facts of social formation, the arcane structures of human restlessness. In antiquity the king having 'cast his net' would connote an act of city planning. This net, orthogonally conceived, often oriented towards divine features in the landscape, endures as an organizing principle of urbanism down to our time. But its boundaries are rarely absolute and nowhere stable. As we shall see, the constructed world yields to several kinds of order; the king can never lay claim to them all because his enemies, ever watchful, prowl the interstices of the city, waiting to penetrate the architecture protecting the rule-governed domain.

PART ONE

Elements of the Boundary Idea

CHAPTER ONE

Expressive Meanings, Ancient and Modern

The Source of Urban Boundaries

Readers of the *Iliad* will know that one of Homer's favourites was the lame god Hephaestus. On Olympus, only he had neither beauty nor swiftness; his every move was agonizing to him, his deformations an insult to the eye. Yet he alone could take lifeless material, metal and stone, and give to it the very things fate had denied him: unparalleled beauty. Through his work, his countless shining images of the chase and the dance, Hephaestus could transform himself, astonishing even the Olympian pantheon when showing them the perfect identity of his interior self and the artefacts he forged.

Hephaestus, as a god, could do more or less as he liked. But human reason, especially after Socrates, treated gifts such as those displayed by Hephaestus with contempt; mortals were not supposed to meddle with nature's materials but to contemplate their unparalleled excellence *in situ*. In *Politics* (1333a), for instance, Aristotle sets down how one should pursue the good life, in which reflecting on nature as given is the best of deeds, an idea that returns to us today with a vengeance. The same theme recurs down through history: that humans could never hope to match what has

been divinely endowed, and should refrain from producing anything at all, was a doctrine not limited to Aristotle, or to Plato, who trashed Homer in the *Republic* and despised whatever was considered necessary or useful. A millennium and a half later, in the second part of his *Summa Theologiae*, Thomas Aquinas saw beauty and truth only in God's cosmos, and warned against admiring those things made by human hands. Today, in the minds of many, nature returns to her untouchable state.

Neither Attic philosophy nor medieval scolasticism had much time for *homo faber*, whose putative exemplar happened to be Hephaestus. But the old philosophers went even farther; having libelled production, they then asserted the identity of contemplation and *stillness*. The activity of work required movement, and moving about deflected the mind from its proper focus, which was meant to be unshakeably fixed on the eternal given. So Hephaestus, whom Homer and the Olympians loved the most, ended up being doubly condemned as one who devalued nature twice over, having made of it an instrument to display the character of speed.

Stillness, inactivity, contemplation – it seems these things again infuse the good life, and are taken up for the sake of nature herself. Activity, work, movement have become conceits, according to many, and considered antithetical to nature's cause. So *homo faber* recovers a reputation handed him by Greek and scholastic philosophy: the vulgar artificer intent on pillage, at whose hand 'all property was destroyed in the process of appropriation, all things devoured in the process of their production and the stability of the world undermined in a constant process of change.'[1] Who today dare doubt the truth of Hannah Arendt's observation? Above all, the activity of city building, of all *homo faber*'s works, the one whose product is farthest from the idea that brings it into being, presses against all things stable, catching them in a giant centrifuge to spin out an awful landscape in perpetual motion. Aristotle, one might say, now has the last word.

But even his intellectual foreground depended on a material havoc wrought behind the scenes by slavery, shifting around the landscape of Attica with the axe, the shovel, and the hammer. How, then, is it possible to reconcile this philosopher's abhorrence of work, or Plato's dream of stability and permanence with city building, with Homer's volatile epic? The question probably has no answer, although think of the latter's description of Achilles' shield; its purpose was warfare, but Homer does not dwell on this. In fact, the usefulness of things does not figure prominently in the *Iliad*. Materials, spears, tools, chariots, armour, ships, cities – all are described in terms of their power, their speed or beauty, but hardly ever as utilitarian objects. Similarly, processes of reification – the conversion of natural materials into these objects – are generally magical and ritualized, viewed as integral to the poet's narrative flow, rather than as technical events: 'He cast imperishable bronze on the fire, and some tin and precious gold and silver. Then he put a great anvil on the stand and gripped a strong hammer in one hand and a pair of tongs in the other.'[2] Hephaestus's toil becomes an extension of those other transformations that suffuse the

narrative: characters take their lead from the elusive god Proteus, adopting disguises, changing shape or personality by wiliness and magic.

When Homer does deritualize work, he makes of it a scruffy procedure, but only as a cipher for impending trouble. Alarmed by a high rampart built by the Achaean army, Poseidon informs his brother Zeus: 'Have you seen that the long-haired Achaeans have thrown a wall round their ships and dug a trench along it, without offering the proper sacrifices to the gods? People will talk about this wall of theirs as far as the light of Dawn is spread; and the wall that I and Phoebus Apollo built with such labour for King Laomedon will be forgotten.' Zeus was indignant with his brother. 'Imperial Earthshaker,' he said, 'your misgivings are absurd. Leave it to other gods less powerful and resolute than you to be alarmed at this contraption; and rest assured that wherever the light of Dawn is spread, yours is the name that will be held in honour' (Book VII)[3] (Fig. 1.1). Homer, not given to dealing in ambiguous shades of meaning, makes a forthright distinction: Hephaestus is transformed from beast to beloved through his kind of work, whereas the Achaeans can expect nothing but trouble, which they get when Hector breaches their wretched wall. The difference between what we would now call imbuing procedures and objects with aesthetic content and merely throwing together a 'contraption' was to Homer what separated the nobility of life from ignominious death. Clearly for him there are two species of *homo faber*; only one descends from Hephaestus. To contemplate the world as given and to act upon it may be different, but not necessarily antithetical things, which gives Homer's view a sophistication even Attic philosophy appears to lack.

Consider, too, the question of motility. Homer and the Greeks in general (or at least those who were not Plato or Aristotle) instantly associated movement with brightness, and this composite carried to them meanings of exquisite beauty. For instance, Homer de-

1.1   Poseidon, brother of Zeus, father of Proteus. Archetypal divider of the world. Fourth century B.C. bronze; National Archaeological Museum, Athens

scribes Hera's chariot thus: 'So Hera, Queen of Heaven and Daughter of mighty Cronos, went off to put the golden harness on her horses, while Hebe deftly got her chariot ready by fixing the two bronze wheels, each with eight spokes, on the ends of the iron axle-tree. The felloes of the wheels were made of imperishable gold, with bronze tires fitted on the rims – a wonderful piece of work – while the naves that rotate on each axle are of silver. The car itself has a platform of gold and silver straps tightly interlaced, with a double railing round it, and a silver shaft running out from the front' (Book v).[4]

The *Iliad* is filled with such associations of speed, light, and beauty, like the blazing chariot of Zeus, Achilles' silver bow, bright-eyed Achaeans, glittering javelins, the flaming golden manes of warhorses, and the bronze flashing on the breast of Idomeneus as he ran. Whatever Homer admired shone, as it were, with the light of speed, and we know this admiration was shared by his fellow Greeks: Their word *phainesthai* means both 'to appear' and 'to shine forth' (Fig. 1.2).

Attic philosophy, in contrast, particularly what Plato had to say, seems totally at odds with the *Iliad*. Plato's ideal combined stability and permanence, substituting the measures, standards, and limits of his Theory of Forms for Homer's volatile images. Plato admired a predictable world divided by uncrossable boundaries, whereas the *Iliad*'s very theme concerns a storming of city walls, a deed mirrored all through the text in violence, but also in the character of work, speed, and blazing light, where protagonists pass swiftly among the heavens, Earth, and Homer's wine-dark sea, contemptuous of every obstacle and stricture except fate itself.

Does not the oscillation between Plato's and Homer's domains parallel the circuit of human life, and also define the urban land-scape? But to claim that the essence of every city lies on the precarious axis joining one domain to the other is not enough; in one sense cities constitute the very material from which the axis is formed, because they are articulated to reconcile these extremes by bringing into play the astonishing dialectic of boundaries. Only fate rules in a totally accessible world, which has no matrix to give actions the predictable outcome human reason deems necessary. So both temporal and spatial stability, within which actions shed their transience and take on regularity, depend on the presence of boundaries of one kind or another; in a sense, they are the instrument of historical continuity and its sign, rendering visible that human penchant for a predictable life by displaying the permanence and significance with which boundaries are often endowed. But boundaries can also be more and less than this. They define, according to their nature, the manner in which the individual and collective come to terms with the world around. Myriad forms of benevolence, in-wardness, fear, gregariousness, and dominance colouring how we relate to the world are signalled, then reinforced by the disposi-tion and character of boundaries. In the stand-ardized, unchanging landscape implied in the *Republic* and the *Statesman*, boundaries are necessarily inviolable, affected neither by con-templation nor by the discourse of the agora. In the *Republic* (420), Plato remarks that the philosopher-king makes his city as a sculptor

1.2   Figure from the Tower of the Winds, Athens, first century B.C.

his statue, revealing his clear preference for cities whose boundaries are literally carved in stone, possessing the durability and immobility of monoliths. By contrast, the 'bright-eyed' Achaeans bivouac in the Ionian fields, speaking and thinking, if at all, only about tomorrow's assault on Priam's stronghold, whose outer boundary is the battle front.

Between the bivouac camp and the petrified outlines of the philosopher-king's *polis* lies an infinity of boundary conditions, each distilled from the urban territorial ebb and flow. But territoriality manifests itself less from the actual occupancy of space than from the articulations formed along its edges, so, as we do Agamemnon's golden cup, we know the contents by experiencing the container.

Urbanism too is the working out of boundaries, making cities into a vast middle ground embodying truces between the agents of circumvallation and assault. The city, through the dialectic of its boundaries, is the instrument whereby each absolute is tempered by the other, creating the rich stew we call urban life, whose events oscillate between the predictable and the volatile. Plato gets to meet Homer, not in the philosopher-king's sculptured *polis*, or on the Ionian field, but in cities the world over.

What is the nature of this urban-boundary dialectic? It is not one that ascends easily towards synthesis. We shall see, by witnessing the building of cities such as Pergamum, Rome, Siena, Paris, and Berlin, its peculiar combination of power and instability, and how it fashions local circumstances into patterns that are everywhere unique, and nearly everywhere incomplete. We shall also note that, while the surveyor and the legislator play indispensable parts, they rarely occupy the foreground. Instead, boundaries are the place where urbanism and architecture join and divide in a process that, like the making of Achilles' shield, is sometimes felicitous, although more often we end up with a dangerous contraption or countless remnants of unfinished work. Should one have hoped, in company with Aristotle, and without in any sense suggesting that the boundary dialectic is played out according to individual will, that it should have been the cultivated person and not the specialist in charge?

For all the manifest complexity and mutations of recent history, even now much can be discovered about our urban landscape by returning to that time when a few fledgling settlements faced a hostile world. Plato's dream of immutable structures was his intellect's defence, perhaps, against the fourth-century tempest sweeping Attica aside, just as Homer's lyricism half a millennium before gave his threadbare audience, conscious only of their stretch of Illyrian shore, the power of flight. At the beginning two kinds of nostalgia were stirred in the urban crucible.

Plato's kind, dominated by his doctrine of the Idea, of a pure and ideal order uncontaminated by the bestiality of the senses, has its metaphor, to repeat, in the sculpted *polis*. Let us suppose without having to speculate too much – Plato never referred explicitly to this point – that the philosopher-king imposes his will by placing restrictions on his subjects' powers of movement, in the double sense of restricting both circulation and work. Discourse certainly would be encouraged, as would *practice*, although the latter, to Plato and Aristotle, included the freedom to know and to choose, but not to alter the world as given through work.[5] Notice, then, that the free life of the *polis* did not extend to restructuring the *polis* itself; its very stones limited, and therefore imposed a large measure of predictability on what we ourselves would call practice. The everlasting purity of the sculptured *polis* would, therefore, be guaranteed by petrifying its enclosures and subdivisions at the start, leading Plato to exclude

them from the realm of mutability wrought by his own beloved dialectic. His ideal *polis* is telling in another way: the act of hewing stone carries with it a profoundly expressive meaning of impermeable weight, which not only emphasizes the aura of finality, but evokes a picture of unambiguous obstruction as well. Plato chose his metaphor well; its boundaries are not designed to encourage either the citizen conspirator or the horde outside.

Compare this unlikely citadel of Reason with Homer's equally impossible landscape and recall the character and actions of those intent on savaging the walls of Troy. Reason, that handmaid of predictability, finds no foothold in a landscape such as this. Remember, too, the close, even overlapping association of speed, luminescence, magical transformation, and work, and the dual nature of work itself, which Homer nicely encapsulates in Achilles' shield and the Achaean contraption. These qualities the poet deploys against Priam's stronghold in this epic contest of action versus inertia. Morality as we know it is barely evident in the ensuing struggle; there are few rules, and no politics. Instead, all kinds of boundaries fall to brilliant lights shining across the landscape; they give way to high velocity and are pierced by far-seeing eyes, and their protectors succumb to wily disguises or to the artefacts wrought by divine Hephaestus.

There have been occasions in history – no more than a few – when cities were divided and surrounded by boundaries approaching the impassability of Plato's. As we shall see, the Sumerian inhabitants in Ur of the Chaldees, for instance, came close to being incarcerated within their city's boundaries. Now and again the dogmatic pursuit of a single Idea has been embodied in the hard and fast geometry of some plan that mercifully, in most instances, remained on paper. We can excuse some of their perpetrators, including Plato, on grounds of inadvertency; of not paying enough attention to the ramifications of what they propose. Otherwise, the city as a prison house has not been prominent in urban history, although Michel Foucault thought otherwise. At the other extreme, given that we might define cities according to some specified density of boundaries – although I shall refrain from doing so – Homer's world is scarcely present outside, and even inside, the purely nomadic state. The Sahel settlements of the Fali peoples, however, represent a case worth being considered, as it will be shortly.

It follows that our two polar opposites represent theoretical absolutes rather than empirical examples; each is a jewel of the imagination, the dream of rational, predictable existence versus that magic landscape ruled by fate alone. Do not the realities of human propinquity colouring urbanization's unfolding exhibit neither purity for the very reason that cities are formed to allow us to partake of both? Hovering above urbanization's alleged material *telos* – and increasingly brought into contradiction with it – lie the dual imperatives driving human life which Plato and Homer first brought into sharp relief. Reckless flight through a magic realm, sanctuaries of foreseeable events – humanity seeks to move between them, and they come together on their common ground, the city. In the city we partake of their mutant strains, here mesmerized by the luminescence, hazards, kinesis, and fantasy of the streets, theatre, and festivals; there retreating into the sanctuaries of the daily round which encompass family life and work.

The modern metropolis, no less than the city-state of antiquity, feeds off and displays this Janus-faced condition, its destiny tied to the rigours of sustaining two antithetical landscapes in one place. There, urbanism takes over, working and reworking the city's productivity to forge boundaries, unstable alliances, territorial hierarchies. Inevitably, the original purities infiltrate across mutual boundaries and cross-fertilize to form vestige hybrids: structures of communal order extend from the household to tame a once-reckless domain, while conspiracy and invasion haunt the sanctuaries. The boundaries of the city, meanwhile, catalyse and mirror this incessant dialectic, still absorbing into their fabric those countless, archaic remnants from a binary past.

Poetry and Construction

If cities are still built from archaic remnants, then the materialist explosion of Western civilization and, with it, the alleged collapse of urbanism in this century must be shrouded in a bewildering array of metaphors, many of which obstinately echo the accumulations of history. Despite the fantastic alteration of urban economies, the successive rejection and reincarnation of methods and styles, the traumas accompanying an upheaval in real estate's supply and demand, and the monstrous scale of land conversion and redevelopment, some old essences persist. We barely recognize them because what was once intuitively understood must now be explained away in an alien language of political, economic, and administrative rationality. Yet the essences are not and never were hidden; they are surface phenomena, exposed for all to see, for how else could they be a crucial part of urban experience (Figs 1.3 and 1.4)?

It is not necessary to dredge up some theory of immutable human nature in support of these recurrences. Yet the appropriation of terrain, and the practices whereby the relationship to otherness is stamped into boundary construction, seem instinctual. Moreover, each epoch must make the best of what is handed down from history, and the most millennial flowering in cultural expression pushes in vain against the ultimate limits of imagination. The limits may be distant, but they exist nevertheless, and are rather more constraining when it comes to the building of a city than when a poem is written. But we know that even poetry feeds off itself, that each piece of writing from Homer's to any being penned at this moment is essentially a rewriting. Could it also be that, with city building, all the canonical treatises and Platonic models; the classicisms and Gothic fantasies; the purist purges and strident manifes-

1.3   Aerial view of the Don Valley, Metropolitan Toronto. The administered landscape, shaped by a boundary hierarchy but rooted in recollections of an idyllic past

1.4   The lower Don Valley, Metropolitan Toronto. Boundaries of seclusion, exclusion, and invasion

tos; the appeals to rational method, ideology, social justice, and even efficiency are somehow connected through their constructed consequences? We cannot invoke some persistent classicism by way of explaining why this is so. In architecture and in the arrangement of cities, as in literature, classical forms are necessarily arbitrary, however insistent and recurrent they may be. Classicism is a manifestation of what precedes it, and it is the latter that we seek to discover and to understand.

I have chosen to do so by committing the minor heresy of treating all boundary forms and their meaningful content as *purposeful*, a strategy that, outside the realm of architecture and urbanism, but still within the broad sphere of art, would surely be unacceptable. To enquire into the purpose of most art would not be a happy exercise, for I happen to agree with the philosophers that the very *uselessness* of art is its saving grace. Even though the ensuing pages do not concern urbanism primarily as an art, I feel obliged, nevertheless, to waylay possible accusations of aestheticism by pointing out the obvious: that uselessness in the case of art means the opposite of a thing to be discarded and ignored, for there is truth in the slogan that art is the medium that informs life as nothing else does. I do not know whether what is called the marginalization of art today can be attributed to our alleged inability to distinguish between usefulness and the possession of worth. These may be superannuated thoughts, but I raise them in passing in order to differentiate the purpose of urbanism from the possession of worth in 'higher' forms of art. What I hope will become apparent is that, while architecture and urbanism can and often do inform life – having something to say about life that is worth knowing, although not in precisely the fashion of the other arts – their boundary purpose lies elsewhere. In a way, as we shall see, this purpose is at the same time more banal and more robust than art's worth, having to do with certain ancient, but imperishable associations between the individual and

nature and society. Whether we like it or not, therefore, it cannot be said that whatever is left over, after all the functional requirements that go into the act of building have been met, is an opportunity for artistic indulgence. In the first place, as any architect or urbanist knows very well, disentangling the 'essential' from the 'non-essential' is practically impossible. No design or planning process, however simple, proceeds in a unidirectional manner through a perfectly disaggregated and hierarchically arranged set of things to be resolved. In this respect, no thanks are due to the rather modest advances made, after two or three decades of effort, in the application of problem-solving mathematics and computerization to city-building procedure. As we shall see, urban boundaries are made up of fragments, often disjointed, shapeless, inchoate, and, like human perception itself, highly ambiguous. I leave it to others to decide whether this condition is regrettable, while pointing out the possibility that order may sometimes come disguised as chaos.

Second, I hope to show that a part of what is sometimes called the 'art' of architecture is not a residue but an essence of building that connects it to urbanism, a matter placing the once widely held belief that form should follow function in a peculiar light. In any case, like many others I do not believe that – apart from a few, necessarily undistinguished exceptions – architectural functionalism was ever practised according to the letter. When it comes to urbanism, however, it is not so easy to be unequivocal, especially as the term itself remains rather obscure, a matter that will need to be addressed along with some other imprecisions.

Urbanism and Dialectics

I feel obliged to offer an explanation of my use of the word *urbanism*, rather than continue to bandy it about, knowing full well that the word could have as many meanings as users. At one exteme it is a term that great student of the city Henri Lefebvre hesitated to use, convinced that it surreptitiously implied an entity or essence he believed did not exist. The reader thus might conclude that the term as used here means 'urban planning,' as it often does in texts translated from the French. But this is not quite the case, because I would like to reserve the term 'urban planning' to denote a practice of which urbanism is sometimes but not always a part. It is the part that planning shares with architecture, because, in these pages at least, urbanism has to do with construction, or more precisely with the arrangement of construction to achieve a certain character that I call *urban*.

Practitioners in the know will now wonder, why not use the category 'urban design' and have done with it? I can only suggest that they refer to the 1984 compendium of that name by David Gosling and Barry Maitland;[6] there they will discover a categorial feast running from soup to nuts. I imply no criticism; the authors are astute enough to know that, until we can really come to grips with this fashionable term, and we have still to do so, inclusiveness is by far the best policy. Moreover, it has to be said that the term 'design' has its own connotations, suggesting comprehensiveness, intellectual detachment from its subject, and a short distance between intention and outcome. Only very rarely, we shall see, do these things – or *can* these things – be brought to play in boundary formation. I am not all that far from Louis Wirth's classic definition, in *Urbanism as a Way of Life*,[7] but, however deplorable it is to shut off one body of knowledge from another, the present subject is a kind of practice that arises from some of the ways of life documented by Wirth (often lamentably so), although it cannot be described as such.

Defining an urban character, one might think, is not in the least problematic. Does not everyone nowadays agree that a combination of relatively intensive land use, high lot coverage, mixtures of commercial and residential activities, dense infrastructures, streets and squares thronged with people, and so on constitutes an urban character? And is not a non-urban character to be expected not only from woods and fields, but also from garden cities, Corbusian towers, Frank Lloyd Wright's Broadacre proposal, industrial parks, suburban neighbourhoods, and exurban communities? This accumulation of examples, however, leaves the puzzle intact, because each set suffers from great internal disparity, bringing us not much closer to understanding the essential character of what is or is not urban than if we had taken a single empirical dimension, like population density. Urban character, like its human equivalent in a Rembrandt portrait, cannot be discerned by scrutinizing the parts, so the search must lead to some unifying theme. The analogy of portraiture might suggest that this theme is somehow distant from the events of everyday life, of interest only to the aesthetically minded. So of what good is all this character anyway when we know beyond a doubt it does not determine human behaviour and well-being? Why trouble with cosmetics when there are far weightier urban questions to deal with?

The reader need only reflect for a moment on his or her own experience to understand the vacuity of these last two questions. The substitution of an old dogma (that urban character determines) for a new dogma (that urban character is but a neutral backdrop to social activity) leads nowhere. There exists a vast and, for the most part, untrodden ground between these extreme positions that contains an important truth: we are neither at the complete mercy of urban settings nor indifferent to them; rather, we act upon them and react to them in ways that can be described only as *dialectical*. This tedious word is one that must be employed rather frequently in what follows, for it has no reliable substitute; nevertheless, one ought to remember that it was treated with contempt from the start, following its alleged 'invention' by Zeno of Elea, as connoting an abstract disputation that was devoid of practical value. I shall try to avoid at least the more common abuses of the term, namely, its employment as a cover-up for vacillation or lack of commitment to an idea, or an overcommitment to a certain political philosophy.

In a nutshell, I put forward here but two basic ideas, without in any sense claiming to have found the key to most of the mysteries surrounding the subject: that architecture and urbanism are and always have been dialectical practices, whence comes their uniqueness and unbreakable association with each other; and that, to a surprising extent, the working out of what happens to be dialectical is a prerational or suprarational operation occurring along urban boundaries (Figs 1.5 and 1.6).

It almost goes without saying that there is no novelty in explaining and even advocating artistic and social behaviour from a dialectical corner. Nineteenth-century Romanticism thrived on dialectics, and volumes have been written, reaching well back before Hegel, on the higher synthesis that accrues from the confrontation of metaphysical opposites. Plato used the dialectic to search for the form shared by entities of the same category, connecting them with the 'Idea of the Good' (*Republic*, vii), although he regarded all arts (and sciences) as inferior to the dialectic, which proceeds 'by means of forms, through forms, to forms.' Much more recent, and in architecture, the commentaries of Sir John Summerson on Viollet-le-Duc and the Gothic cathedral one recalls with admiration.[8] I shall certainly refer to some of this kind of work, and in doing so, it will be apparent that I am attracted to a few, although by no means all,

1.5   Theodore J. Musho, *Monday in Easter Week*. Pen and ink, 1961. One manifestation of an uncompleted dialectical process in urbanism. Solid objects are perceived as fluid, shifting, and transparent to reveal their interdependence and that of the life they contain.

1.6   Entrance to the Castelnuovo, Naples, fifteenth century. A double signal common to the urban dialectic. The archetypal fortress sheds its skin.

the special meanings given to dialectics by Hegel. Whether or not these meanings have equal validity outside the present subject I do not know, but their pertinence to the act of city building is more than incidental.

Hegel took from the critical philosophy of Kant and the Greeks to argue that the relation between logic, nature, and the mind (*Geist*), together with their method of exposition, are dialectical. All thinking – 'the discourse of the soul with itself' – Hegel considered dialectical, containing within itself an initial opposition that becomes reconciled in a higher synthesis. Even the latter is ultimately opposed, because of what Hegel claimed were the two aspects of any process: the positive aspect of growth, from which emerges the new; and the negative aspect of rejection, whereby the old is discarded. The negative aspect of thought therefore rejects its own achievement; ultimately, by a circular route, thinking reaches a synthesis which is identical with its starting-point, except that all that was once implicit is now made explicit. It is my contention that dialectical thought, although not precisely as construed by Hegel, because urban boundaries rarely ascend to full synthesis, is made strikingly manifest in architecture and urbanism. *In particular, that if they possess an essence or a purpose, then it will be found in the negation that they carry within, turning the overwhelming presence of construction into special kinds of absence* (Fig. 1.7).

Whoever claims to explain everything explains nothing, so let it be said right away that factors other than the one mentioned above are at work. It was Hegel, no less, who saw history as the embodiment of rational will; architecture and the building of cities, in the best instances, are the fruits of conscious practical reason, which many would claim to be closer to logic than dialectics. While conceding a great deal, we must also say that much of what passes for reason in architecture and urbanism is, in fact, abstract, rationalistic, and arbitrary, as many others have shown. That still leaves artistry, for who could deny that great buildings, even the occasional city,

1.7 Philip Johnson, Architect's House, New Canaan, Connecticut, 1941. The radical forms of high modernism (or the absence thereof) reveal a recurrent aspiration in boundary formation.

are more poetic than dialectical, and that they defy all analysis? Most of all, the dialectic suggests a plateauing, a shifting of events towards ultimate outcomes, whereas the boundary dialectic is often partial, fragmented, incessant, an undermining of certainties and prescribed forms.

As we shall see, however, this does not mean that the dialectic always frustrates the pursuit of desired ends; urbanism is replete with in-between states, with boundary zones, thresholds, domains of passage from one realm to the next, all of which have their source in the conduct and ritual of everyday life. The *liminal* domain threads its way through the constructed city, the embodiment of double meanings and the place where space and time shift backwards and forwards just as they do in the contemplation of life's passage (Fig. 1.8).

In contradiction to all this, it has not gone unnoticed that a peculiarity of much professional life is the tendency to transmit ideas with an aura of great certitude, and it must be said that architects and planners have not been left behind in this respect. I leave it to someone else to delve into the reasons why, but ideas and proposals having to do with the constructed world are presented to a verbal accompaniment that too often borders on take-it-or-leave-it bombast. One might think that the hard sell is just a modernist affair, but no more than a cursory inspection of Vitruvius would be enough to dispel such an illusion.

The fact is that *verbal* reasoning in architecture and urbanism has nearly always tended to be the opposite of dialectical, which makes it impossible to trace one of the major themes of this book from those intentions that have been written down. Any history or theory based on whatever architects have penned would call up a story of passionately held ideals in which a near-squalid contempt for the work of others does not figure least. With this in mind, I am not alone in having to depend rather more on the veracities to be found in what builders have drawn and constructed and to regard with a certain suspicion whatever they have said and written. Be that as it may, nobody gets away with denying that untempered rhetoric has indeed found its way into actual construction; we are literally surrounded by accumulations of unyielding 'statements.' But the point I intend to make is that whenever this happens, architecture and urbanism – as un-

derstood here – have not been deficient, but simply absent (Fig. 1.9).

Nevertheless, there is enough dialectical architecture produced by the most irritating writers – one need only think of Le Corbusier – to suggest that dialectics originates less in conscious reasoning than in the crevices of subconsciousness. Moreover, once produced, it appears that dialectical architecture and urbanism are not recognized as such, but as something of a lower order – *mimesis*, a style, a form, a type, a relationship – all of which, I would claim, do not precede the dialectical purpose but are wittingly or unwittingly deployed to serve it. In a crucial sense, this purpose is a manifestation of that part of the self which yields to the presence of others, compromising what would otherwise be an impossible narcissism. Yet many would vehemently oppose such an idea, perceiving the ancient city and modern metropolis as instruments of unbridled exploitation, monopolized by an opportunism that rewards only self-interest, leaving alienation and the pillage of the natural world in its wake. My point is that they are half right, and that their very

1.8   Francesco di Giorgio (attrib.), *Ideal City,* late fifteenth century. Berlin-Dahlem Museum. The city as a continuous threshold, an in-between place leading forwards and backwards in time and space

1.9   Modern Paris. The ubiquitous undialectical landscape

anguish springs from an awareness and the possibility of an entirely different world.

The Primary Structures of Urbanism

Over the past few years, many astute observers have been disseminating the increasing and depressing belief that the metropolitan landscape is nothing more than a supreme repository of ideology, one that 'naturalizes and dehistoricises a historically created reality.'[9] Is the constructed world in its entirety, then, but a mask and a decoy, hiding absolute truths residing in structures of power, soothing away any suspicion that life is enveloped by institutions, or by universal co-optation to those intent on pillaging the biosphere? If so, how is this incubus to be confronted? If at all, we are told, then only by a certain branch of critical history I prefer to call *reductive*, which claims to conduct its analysis outside the 'fictive reality' of its subject-matter – the constructed metropolis – to 'constitute the discourse of the architecture under study in so far as it is structured by relations invested in institutions and historically determined myths.'[10] According to this view of things, we are nowhere near – and may never reach – the stage of advancing architectural and urban propositions that are truly purged of ideological insidiousness.

I want to take issue with this now-pervasive view not because it is utterly false – it is not – but because of its panlogism – the reduction of practices occurring within dialectically driven history to a single logic of cause and effect. Reductive history treats construction as an object of suspicion, as though the metropolis were but a product of malign intent. But the false start of reductive history is its own reliance on myth: its belief that urban formation is indeed the subject of intention, whether that of some despot or other or one that originates within structures of bureaucratic, corporate, and professional power. But if this were indeed so, such intentions would depend in their entirety on consciously held knowledge of an urban future whose malleability is complete. The metropolis as an instrument of the dominant classes thus overextends the undeniable possibility that they may manipulate its construction; that possibility, however, is not monopolized by selfish reason, nor by rationality of any kind. In a way, cities do possess a quasi-natural existence all their own, an existence that demystifying analysis may yet illuminate, but, in my view, cannot terminate. Whether mystery *should* everywhere be opposed by reason depends, of course, on how each is defined.

What, then, is urbanism if it is not the consequence of focused, action-oriented consciousness? Let us trace, via the heresy of what will be shown to be recurrent, the impulse that precedes rationality in the sphere of city building.

Northrop Frye, in his last book, *Words with Power*, wrote of myths as 'an interconnected body of significant stories that a society needs to know'; in *The Raw and the Cooked*, Claude Lévi-Strauss showed 'not how men think in myths, but how myths operate in men's minds without their being aware of the fact.'[11] Each is referring to the here and now, as well as to remoteness in time and space. Quite unlike the mendacity attributed by reductive historians to myth formation, *mythopoeia*, to Lévi-Strauss, is a form of historical reconstruction whose necessary purpose is the organizing of life and human perceptions. A large part of the core of these reconstructions bears directly on our boundary theme because what is confirmed and reconfirmed with remarkable consistency through the study of *mythopoeia* is the universal attribution of *oneness* to the self and the host of objects comprising the world. Oneness, it goes without saying, can be a troublesome concept if taken to mean an absence of differentiation or the bending of the self to some imposed authority; certainly not every myth is devoid of such insidiousness, and we shall examine instances where this distorted concept brings a homogeneous, brutalizing landscape in its wake. But the evidence from *mythopoeia* displays an entirely different universe, one saturated with paradox, ambiguity, and negation, existing at some distance from the political and economic forces operating within the society. Boundaries, in such a universe, become primary; their facts and symbols partition the terrain, not to shut out one way of life from another, but to signal the simultaneous presence of diversity and oneness in the same entity.

Through the epochs, architecture and urbanism owe a debt to such things, as I hope to show. But the debt is scarcely intellectual; here we sense some deeper region of human consciousness at work, and are obliged to use history to bring it to the surface. However, the region first must be given a name. Here I choose to avoid an excursion into the minefield of competing views on the netherworld of the mind by referring to an especially pertinent, representative one, namely, that of Ernst Cassirer.

Cassirer's reflections on *mythopoeia* led him to conclude that the attribution of oneness is an *Urphänomen*, in Goethe's sense that, like the phenomena of spatiality and temporality, it can have no explanation. Cassirer called it *expressive meaning*: 'the being that is represented in perception confronts us not as a reality of things, of mere objects, but as a kind of presence of living subjects ... The farther we trace back perception, the greater the predominance of the "thou" over the "it."'[12] Knowledge, then, could never initially be 'about' the world because it appears to us in the first instant of perception not as an 'it' but as an expressive community of life. 'For the reality we apprehend is in its original form not a reality of a determinate world of things, originating apart from us (ie having no relationship to us); rather, it is the certainty of a living efficacy that we experience.'[13]

Experience originates not in observation, but from *interaction* with a world that expresses itself as an embodied subject. Nature and culture become separate spheres only when perception passes this 'sympathetic' stage to become observational-theoretical, or practical-manipulative.[14] So the passage from sympathetic to disinterested perception always contains a moment of profound disappointment, one that Plato referred to in *The Sophist*: 'The isolation of everything from everything else means a complete abolition of all discourse, for any discourse we can have owes its existence to the weaving together of forms.'[15]

Here, at the most fundamental level, the articulation and division of space permeates human consciousness. In a world viewed sympathetically, spatial proximity strengthens the force connecting separate things. While things affect other things because they are substantially one, and this belonging together means that any part can affect the whole, being *close together* increases the sense of oneness. The feeling of being close together, of course, depends on more than spatial proximity; distance can be either dissolved or stretched to virtual infinity by intervening boundaries and the expressive meanings they happen to carry; or, just as important to our theme: 'The part does not merely represent the whole, or the specimen its class; they are identical with the totality to which they belong; not merely as mediating aids to reflective thought, but as genuine presences which actually contain the power, significance, and efficacy of the whole.'[16] Just as the Greek Apollo inhabited every laurel, and Zeus every oak, so was the Mexican corn goddess Chicomecóatl present in every kernel, and so too could special places or things assume the complexity of the cosmos and the city.

Of what relevance are these old tales, when the hyperactive and unfocused consciousness of modernism seems to have driven the mythic mind underground for ever? While some cities of antiquity and constructions of primitive man may have been conceived, not as objects, but as embodiments of oneself, who could claim the survival of such mythic efficacy beyond the Enlightenment? But if expressive meaning is indeed an *Urphänomen*, it might be suppressed, but can be no more subject to erosion than can spatiality. Can it really be claimed that, if not the Enlightenment, then the revolutionary idolatry of form, technique, and function under modernism purged construction of expressive meaning? Not according to Cassirer, who takes issue with Heidegger on the power of expressive meaning; because symbolic pregnancy is *in* the nature of things, it cannot be mere sensory psychological content, subject to the interpretations of a being (*Dasein*): 'There is, finally, a breaking away (of meaning) from the merely ontological, without actually tearing the bond with it.'[17] Nor is expressive meaning only an epiphenomenon of things, as the existentialists might claim it to be; that is, with transitory character, tied to the historical, pragmatic dimensions of life. Rather, expressive meaning possesses an intersubjective validity, *Geltung*, that is not limited to finite experience. This stratum of expression precedes history and interpretation; it is subject neither to formation nor to transformation by the intellect, whose concerns are the different (but not higher) planes of representation and pure significance.[18]

Merleau-Ponty takes up Cassirer's thesis with approval in his work *Phenomenology of Perception*: 'Cassirer clearly has the same aim when he takes Kant to task for having most of the time analyzed only an "intellectual sublimation of experience", when he tries to ex-

press through the notion of symbolic pregnancy, the absolute simultaneity of matter and form.'[19] So the world Cassirer speaks of is not composed just of images perceived from a distance, but of something intrinsically powerful in nature – and, one might say, in the constructed world: 'Where the meaning of the world is still that of pure expression, every phenomenon discloses a definite "character", which is not merely deduced or inferred from it but which belongs to it immediately. It is itself gloomy or joyful, agitating or soothing, pacifying or terrifying.'[20] The beginning of human awareness is therefore an existential, not an intellectual responsiveness. Things are initially threatening or friendly in character; they press upon experience with an immediate sense of the subject being acted upon. Perception has a kind of helpless, passive side, whether confronted by whatever is familiar and sheltering, or inaccessible and repugnant (Figs 1.10 and 1.11).

Both R.H. Hook and Alfred Lorenzer have remarked on the close similarity between Cassirer's work and that underlying psychoanalysis. Hook refers to the translation whereby the expressive symbolism of dreams is raised to the representational symbols of discourse, noting that dream images are formed by processes quite different from those applied to interpretation. The latter depend on conscious penetration to the roots of symbolic formation.[21] Such consciousness belongs, according to Lorenzer, to the 'secondary process' of Freud, who distinguished between it and a 'primary process' whereby the concentration, absence of contradiction, intensity, and free association of dream content are formed.[22]

But reductive history does not operate through this primary process; it completely neglects expressive meaning to deal only with the interpretation of consciously intended images in construction. Ideological content can be derived only from some kind of (supposedly subversive) ratiocination that is alien to mythic thought. What, then, is 'primary' in the constructed world? Must we immediately

1.10   Town centre, Tapiola, Finland. Modest architecture, shaped into a sheltering garden wall

1.11   Ludwig Hilberseimer, perspective for a housing estate (from *Grossstadt-Architektur*, 1927)

exclude all the consequences of rational design – the styles and Platonic models, the invocations of Pure Form? Not at all, because, even if we concede the possibility that such secondary processes might be a cloak to ideology, they always carry a primary subtext. The latter is not far removed from what Hegel, in the *Phenomenology of Mind*, called *Wesen* (essence). His phenomenology is not concerned with history, but with the study of the essential, and Cassirer states more than once how his own conception of expressive meaning rests on Hegel's phenomenology.[23] There is no replacement through history of the *Urphänomen* by the representative symbolism of language or science; as John Krois explains, rational thought cannot be regarded as some higher, evolved form of mythic 'thought,' which, being derived from action, is a misleading designation.[24] 'It is not mere observation but action which constitutes the center from which man undertakes the intelligent organization of reality.'[25] The designation 'image' to connote the perceived phenomenon of what is expressive is equally misleading; such an 'image' cannot be sensory data because it is not so much 'seen' or 'looked at' as *felt*. It can be *striking* or *move* us emotionally.[26] Cassirer recognized this absence of 'data' as crucial in mythic awareness: 'A whispering or rustling in the woods, a shadow darting over the ground, a light flickering on the water: all these are demonic ... only very gradually does this pandemonium divide into separate and clearly distinguishable figures.'[27] Here, we come very close to urbanism, which deals in expressive meanings like this. Once the pandemonium divides, urbanism dissolves into sources of data, for analysis, criticism, aesthetic appreciation; but by then we have lost what we all share.

It follows from the nature of mythic awareness that while the primary process which brings it to life can readily be conceived as working prior to those perceptions based on observation, what is observed might also be the constitua of what we primarily feel. How does this apply to urban boundaries? Consider John Ruskin's favourite wall, the principal façade of the Doge's palace in Venice, which he describes as 'an oblong, elongated to the eye by a range of thirty-four small arches, and thirty-five columns, while it is separated by a richly canopied window in the centre.'[28] Yet these closely studied elements taken together *contain*, prior to what is apparent through attention, a unitary character remarkably reminiscent of Cassirer's 'demonic pandemonium,' as Ruskin himself is aware:

mighty masses, vigorous and deep, of shadow mingled with its surface. And among the first habits that a young architect should learn, is that of thinking in shadow, not looking at a design in its miserable liny skeleton; but conceiving it as it will be when the dawn lights it, and the dusk leaves it; when its stones will be hot, and its crannies cool; when the lizards will bask on the one, and the birds build in the other. Let him design with a sense of cold and heat upon him; let him cut out the shadows, as men dig wells in unwatered plains ... all that he has to do must be done by spaces of light and darkness; and his business is to see that the one is broad and bold enough not to be swallowed up by twilight, and the other deep enough not to be dried like a shallow pool by a noon-day sun.[29] (Fig. 1.12)

Ruskin is referring here to expressive meaning, to that primary, pre-aesthetic condition that *strikes* him as a forceful, living presence. Only subsequently are scrutiny, analysis, the critical faculties necessary to aesthetic and other interpretations brought into play, whereupon what is expressive in the Venetian façade becomes an object of data and appreciation.

It follows that the source of what is striking cannot be neatly isolated from the object of interpretation; they are the same constitua of the natural and constructed worlds. With respect to subjective experience, however, we can identify two levels of reception, namely, the *expressive* and the *interpretable*, while maintaining the unity of the perceived source. Thus our initial sense of a threatening, benign,

1.12   Bernardo Rossellino, Piazza Pia II, Pienza, 1462

or familiar construction depends on more than the raw distribution of mass, colour, and shadow in the urban landscape; we can also sense how these raw constitua are modulated, without subjecting them to scrutiny.

Consider the analogy of Impressionist painting, and its crucial distinction from both the earlier Pre-Raphaelite school and that of the later Parisian Cubists. Claude Monet's *Le Bassin aux nymphéas* (1899) captures – no more and no less – the full power of the expressive meaning contained in the wooded river landscape of Giverny. Monet is not inviting us to study his landscape but to *enter into it* with complete and instant awareness of its essential properties: the enclosing foliage, a raft of lilies framed by water reeds, the arc of a footbridge in filtered sunlight (Fig. 1.13). Now contrast this scene – which Monet appears to have absorbed at a glance – with John Everett Millais's *Blind Girl* (1878). This canvas is an accumulation of minute detail, from the rain-soaked eyelashes of the girl to the anatomical particulars of the farm animals occupying the middle ground (Fig. 1.14). For Millais, a flower is not a splash of colour but a specific member of a species; yet Monet's depiction is no less complete, because, for him, the *impression* conveys a far more compelling reality.

Such an impression, the embodiment in paint of expressive meaning, is no more abstract than *Blind Girl*, however; if the latter is a painstaking record of a particular place, the former is not more ambiguous when it comes to showing us *this* landscape and no other. The essences that Cassirer insisted lay at the heart of expressive meaning similarly adhere to particular places or events, and are of an entirely different sort from the universal order that was later sought by the Parisian Cubists. For instance, Fernand Léger's *Trois Visages* (1926) is a near reversal of Impressionism in that he depicts the imposition of abstract reasoning upon the perceived world to reveal, not the latter's qualities, but the structures of the mind, made visible through the composition of pure form (Fig. 1.15).

1.13   Claude Monet, *Bassin aux nymphéas*, 1899. Musée d'Orsay, Paris

1.14   J.E. Millais, *Blind Girl*, 1878. Birmingham City Art Gallery

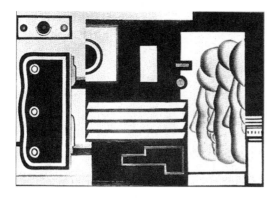

1.15   Fernand Léger, *Trois Visages*, 1926. Private collection

In case someone might conclude that this attribute of Cubism is precisely analogous to the abstract shapes of twentieth-century urbanism, let me just mention for now that there is danger in overinterpreting the similarities deemed to exist between Cubism and architectural modernism.[30] Impressionism, by contrast, is not only the depiction of many kinds of expressive meaning but the key to *what* is sensed most strongly in the urban landscape. To be exposed to the urban landscape is to be, in short, acted upon; only then may we choose to detach ourselves from it, in order to observe.

Imagining Unity: Connecting to History the Dissolution of Space

As man's consciousness drew him apart from the great concourse of unselfconscious nature from which he was emerging, he was bound to turn to look at nature, and having contemplated it seek to explain what he saw, to affect it for his own ends, and finally to regard it with awe and reverence and a desire for reunion – Jacquetta Hawkes.[31]

I have referred to the call by Glazer and Lilla for a reawakening of taste and civic consciousness in urbanism; in a sense, these things form but a cultivated surface to that universal attribution of oneness that Cassirer and others discover in mythic awareness, and only at this deeper level do the boundaries of the city and nature merge into a single, problem-charged domain. Today, the alarm that greets the plunder of ecosystems is fuelled by an increasing scientific certainty of human irrationality. Every act of environmental degradation erodes our own chance of survival, and this we know from the painstaking accumulation of empirical evidence. But who would deny that our objections are driven not only by the precariousness of our own continuing existence, but also by what have been called aesthetic and altruistic feelings towards nature? The depletion of species and the scars on the Earth are morally appalling as well as suicidal.

In so far as morality enters the picture, we reinvoke feelings probably as ancient as humankind itself, to judge by evidence culled from archaeology, old documents, and the vestiges of pre-urban ritual. In antiquity every taking from nature had to be sanctioned by the gods, for it involved a desecration of one sort or another. Even the tilling of fields in ancient Etruria wounded the Earth, and was preceded by ritual acts of apology. In the Maori culture, to chop a tree was to sever nature's limb, which demanded a ceremonial, healing procedure whose source was a mythical story of regret and arboreal rebirth.[32] But if the use of the plough and the axe violated a hallowed world, so did construction, inducing the Witoto and Bora peoples of Columbia even now to build their *malocas* as the stylized crouching down of a human being, thereby ameliorating what to them constitutes an intrusion into a god-made landscape. Their concept, indeed, embodies in the relationship of the walls, their covering, and of all the supported and unsupported elements a restoration of the entire equilibrium of nature and the clan which suffered disturbance by the act of building.[33] Here we witness a striking, pervasive idea: any building's outer skin is a boundary zone whose very material cuts off one presence from another; the obligation to *work* this material – to fix its location with great deliberation; to chisel and shape its planes, apertures, and thresholds in order to disguise one expressive meaning as its opposite – is deeply rooted in moral consciousness (Figs 1.16 and 1.17).

The depth of emotion associated with construction can be sensed in the frequency with which human sacrifice was involved to expiate the desecration brought about by digging, shovelling, cutting. The Old Testament tells how Malik (Moloch), the god of first-born sons, was usually the recipient in the meticulous bloody ceremony marking the laying of a foundation stone. Such acts were not only religious, but a reminder that magic and a highly developed imagination suffused practical life. Man discovered himself *in* the universe because nature was full of a man-like consciousness, having a purposive life that at times attained the demonic. Many ancient and contemporary instances have been documented in which offerings are made to the Earth by way of atonement for the digging that precedes construction. In Plutarch's *Life of Romulus,* the account of Remus's death at the hand of his brother for showing contempt at the latter's design of the Roman walls is probably a reminiscence about the ritual slaying that often accompanied the building of things. Rossana Lok, in her recent study of the house in Tzinacapan, a village in the highlands of Puebla, writes of the placement of offerings beneath the hearth and corners; this ritual is part of an elaborate system of beliefs whereby the house is understood as a microcosm.[34] Reverence shown to nature would in like manner often be extended to the clan, each being perceived as an equally intrinsic part of the cosmos and possessing such attributes of subjectiveness that made separating from either anathema. Nature, clan, and the self were a unity transcending the intervention of space, time, and constructed boundaries, a conviction often made visible in, and reconfirmed by, the spatial organization of the settlement and in architectural work down to the last detail.

1.16   Johann Balthasar Neumann, entrance to Vierzehnheiligen pilgrimage church, Franconia, 1743–72

1.17   Frank Lloyd Wright, Kaufmann House, Bear Run, Pennsylvania, 1936

Of the innumerable such instances known, few have been so closely documented as the villages of the Fali peoples of Cameroon. Here, the concept of sustaining that crucial equilibrium between opposites is ubiquitous, and Jean-Paul Lebeuf's account shows how the absence of social or political stratification among the Fali leaves the unifying expressive meaning of their constructions virtually un-contaminated by material intervention. Each Fali clan forms an extended family whose settlement consists of an enclosed group of circular, conically roofed huts and granaries disposed around one or more covered court-yards (Fig. 1.18). Their founding myth nar-rates how four tribes with ancient common roots from north, south, east, and west came together in reunion, a parable that is embod-ied in the quadripartite division of the settle-ment; but in extraordinary fashion the divi-sion is then dissolved by subordinating it and its various constructions to the iconic form of a single human body (Fig. 1.19). In another founding legend two cosmic eggs, those of the tortoise and the toad, created the universe through their balanced correspondence, an act signified by a further twofold division of the land into settled and unsettled parts; of society into two corresponding groups; and of each dwelling into a binary symbol. This feeling for a dialectical world is the basis of further differentiation, whereby everything real is accounted for and held in place by the congruent oscillation of contradictory oppo-sites, creating a pervasive equilibrium meant to sustain the complementary of things (Fig. 1.20).

Remarkably, in the Fali imagination, noth-ing is static: artefacts and territorial patterns revolve according to codes of internal and external reciprocity. Each house depends on a dynamic relationship to the human/tortoise form of the settlement and is itself divided in two parts, the one revolving round the other: the female cylindrical walls and the male roof cone. Similar correspondences govern the car-dinal points and the existence of large features in the landscape, which in turn are reciprocal with the spatial articulation of the whole village, including the anthropomorphic, toad/tortoise mimesis of architectural detail.[35]

No mere aesthetic urge can explain the imposition of such a highly developed coher-ence upon the world. To the Fali, cosmos and subject are an entity, so the distancing brought about by construction and everyday mobility is immediately dissolved in a counteracting spatial expression. Only the intricacy of this symbolic system makes it unusual: far less common seem to be instances in pre-urban societies where some kind of unitary expres-sion in spatial organization is absent. Our understanding of the full significance of this practice is still incomplete, because many of the forms that constitute unitary spatial ex-pression are often culture specific, requiring an interpretation that is possible only from a deep understanding of the society in all its uniqueness. However, we are now beginning to realize that this great formal diversity is held together by certain recurrent themes of expressive meaning, which are the manifesta-tion of a widely shared basis of significance and intent.[36]

There seems little doubt that the high level of symbolic complexity evident in the Fali world is the fruit of their long-standing famil-ial social structure. The bonds between indi-vidual, clan, and environment were nurtured without those political digressions that have beset – and often impoverished – spatial ex-pression elsewhere. Enrico Guidoni has pointed out how both the unifying and divi-sive expressive power of spatial organization can be exploited for political ends in hierarchi-cally structured societies. What he does not acknowledge, however, is the dependence of this process of appropriation upon the pre-existing *Urphänomen* of expressive meaning – the fact that power élites seem incapable of inventing *de novo* systems of architectural and territorial division that are not grounded

1.18   View of a Fali village, Cameroon (from J.P. Lebeuf, *L'Habitation des Fali*, 1961)

in some prior sense of what is unitary, benign, threatening, or familiar. This is strikingly evident in the physical arrangement of the ancient city-states of Sumer. They were theocracies, each built by a god to remain literally his property. Nippur belonged to Enlil, Ur to Nannar, Uruk to Anu.[37]

The god's right to plunder and transform his own landscape distinguishes the Sumerian cities from the reticent, interactive settlements described above, although the precise nature of the deities' sanctions, working through their chosen human agents, was a source of

great deliberation and preoccupation. Practically the only written work preserved from the Akkad period is concerned almost exclusively with the ritual of temple building. Gudea, the pious ruler of Lagash around 2200 B.C., was instructed in a dream by the city's god Ningirsu to construct a temple in his honour, but misinterpreted the dream. The text narrates, at considerable length, the true meanings of the dream – the awesome appearance of Ningirsu, his attendant servants and heroes, Gudea's consultation with the goddess Nasche and his fervent assurance to Ningirsu

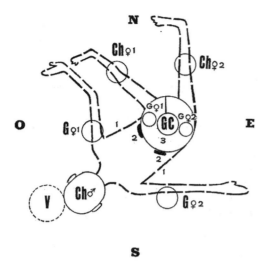

1.19 Anthropomorphism in the layout of a Fali settlement. 1: Flanks of a male turned to the right, facing the earth; 2: clavicle; 3: abdomen; the genitals are represented by the central granary [GC]; Ch: chamber; G: granary; V: vestibule (from Lebeuf)

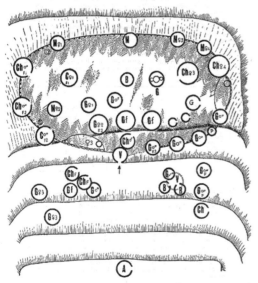

1.20 Dwelling of a Fali patriarch. B: Livestock pen; C: Kitchen; Chc: couple's chamber; Che: children's chamber; Chfa: eldest son's chamber; Chfr: brother's chamber; Chh: host's chamber; Fs: oven; G: granary; Gf: son's granary; M: grindstone; P: chicken house; R: storehouse; V: vestibule (from Lebeuf)

that his temple would indeed be built according to his wishes.

The hymnal narrative continues by describing how the king instructed the people of Lagash, who responded enthusiastically. The city first had to be purified ethically and morally, so all the inhabitants who were considered unclean were banished. Then, following more omens, oracles, sacrifices, and prayers, Gudea set about the heroic and exacting task of constructing the Temple of Ningirsu. At this point the narrative takes up, in lengthy, repetitive, and obscure detail, the story of Gudea's task. Once completed, the temple was ritually cleansed for the ceremony preceding habitation by the god and his wife, and a group of minor deities appointed to care for the temple. The narrative ends by describing the final celebratory banquet, and a paean of praise for the temple and the divine couple now ensconced within.[38]

Clearly, with a god as architect, there would be none of the compromise between edifice and setting that characterizes, say, Fali, Etruscan, or Maori construction. Much of what we know about Sumerian life in its later, autocratic phase reveals how urban physical arrangement, far from sustaining a unitary spirit, can be an impediment to human freedom and association. Samuel Kramer, the distinguished translator of Sumerian poetry, writes: 'Sumerian thinkers, in line with their world view, had no exaggerated confidence in man and his destiny. They were firmly convinced that man was fashioned of clay and created for one purpose only: to serve the gods ... Life, they believed, is beset with uncertainty and haunted by insecurity ... When [man] dies, his emasculated spirit descends to the dark, dreary nether world, where life is but a dismal and wretched reflection of earthly life.'[39]

Every aspect of daily life was codified, circumscribed by a labyrinth of laws, injunctions, prohibitions, taxes, and punishments. Sumerian poetry is made up largely of sermons, and speaks of injustice, cynicism, and self-aggrandizement.[40] The *Hymn to Enlil* boasts of Nippur, 'the city – its face is awesome fear and splendour … Where the word of the father is heeded; where the son humbly fears his mother.'[41] Above all, the gods, through their agents the kings and priests, held an entire population in virtual captivity.

The god's house lay inside the walls of the city, but within its *temenos*, a whole quarter set aside for the divine ruler, walled off from the rest behind a massive enclosure, and accessed only via monumental gates (Fig. 1.21). The divine house, or *ziggurat*, took on the shape and scale of a mountain, and was raised on a platform to enable the god to oversee his subjects and territory (Fig. 1.22). Homage could be paid only vicariously, via an elaborate body of priests who alone were allowed to approach the god in his *temenos*. Minor gods, in effect members of the divine retinue, were assigned their own houses located in subordinate positions against but inside the *temenos* walls.[42] At Ur, in the Third Dynasty, the great gods, members of the Sumerian pantheon who owned other cities, were also represented, but in monumental

houses located outside the city proper. Kings, divinely appointed as earthly representatives of the deity, occupied a palace raised on a platform against, but outside the *temenos*. As for the remainder of the city, it was devoid of any systematic organization, comprising a tangled labyrinth of one- and two-storey dwellings packed at high density into the confines of the walled precinct. It would be difficult to conceive of a more *Foucauldian* setting, so steeped in absolutism that the distribution of power could be utterly maintained by architecture and *its* distribution. Only a god had the sanction to thrust such an uncompromising presence upon the universe, to reorder the visible world as a constant reminder of the inescapable servitude due to him. An incantation from the Third Dynasty echoes the purpose of Sumerian architecture: 'Around the ancient track marched, rank on rank, the army of unalterable law.' Around 2100 B.C., when the great ziggurat was built by Ur-Nammu, the earthly representative of the god Nannar, every event in human life was codified and administered by an army of

1.21   Reconstruction of the *temenos* of Ur, ca 2100 B.C.

1.22   Remains of the ziggurat at Ur

priests, whose more pleasant tasks included inflicting violent punishment upon infant transgressors.

Consider the urban elements of this system, whose expressive meaning surely signals the simultaneous presence of despotism and insecurity: Ur occupied the highest point in an otherwise level terrain, on a hill further elevated by the rubble of prior settlements. The ziggurat, whose terraces were planted with trees to reconfirm the name 'Hill of Heaven,' according to Leonard Woolley must have been clearly visible to any farmer working the fields of the plain twenty-four to thirty-two kilometres away.[43] Its walls were battered inwards, and non-functional buttresses accentuated the impression of great height. The walls also bulged outwards in a slight, but perceptible entasis to emphasize the ziggurat's visual power. A great oval rampart eight metres high with a steeply sloping outer face surrounded the city, and it was here that King Ur-Nammu built his defensive wall 'like a mountain' in the Third Dynasty (Fig. 1.23). Inside, an artificial terrace measuring 250 by 175 metres formed the base of the *temenos*, raised above everything else and shut off behind a massive bulwark of mud brick. Within this enclosure, access to the first sanctuary was limited to three monumental stepped ramps, each converging from the platform below to a single portal constricting entry to the holy of holies at the highest terrace of the ziggurat. Symmetry, that most static of architectural conventions, everywhere clinches the sense of permanence, inviolability, and stasis. The city was altogether a masterly instrument of domination and subordination, a threatening, eternal system of spatial locks, barriers, points of control, and surveillance based on a primal space matrix of higher/lower and inside/outside (Fig. 1.24).

Clearly, Ur and the Fali village represent two extremities of expressive meaning in urban boundary arrangement. The anti-dialectical world of fear manifested in the Sumerian city stands in stark contrast to the complicated reciprocity that dissolves distance to place every feature of the Fali territory in dynamic apposition. But while mutant forms of each case echo through history, it would be wrong to reduce their existence and diversity to the single dimension of political ideology. They depend on attributes of spatiality preceding ideology in all its manifestations, lying at the root of practical reason and having to do with our deep sense, always hovering in the background, of an interdependent world. One's

1.23   The archetypal wall. Remains of the ziggurat ramps

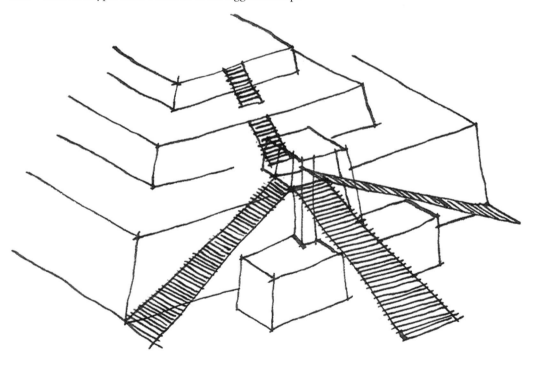

1.24   The ziggurat at Ur. System of access ramps and gates (after Lenzen)

instinct, then, is to pass judgment on Ur as aberrant, even without knowledge of whichever theocratic principles seem to have governed its formation.

So ideological appropriation still leaves expressive meaning intact, as Claude Lévi-Strauss demonstrates again and again, most notably in his famous study of the Tsimshian Indians of British Columbia. They simultaneously employ several codes to bring out a homology between *natural* opposites (empyrean sky/chthonian earth, high/low, mountains/sea, upstream/downstream, winter/summer) and *sociological or economic* opposites (filiation/reliance, endogamy/exogamy, hunting/fishing, abundance/dearth). Their environment as it *should* be is thus re-created in the imagination, a re-creation that cannot be traced to the mundane politics of subordination and dominance.[44]

Expressive Meaning and the Arrangement of Urban Space

What are these attributes of expressive meaning so crucial to urban-boundary formation? The example of Ur can readily be understood through the metaphor *incubus*: that malign spirit which descends to trap and weigh down the sleeping person. The Sumerian city encumbered the landscape and its human life by exploiting our strongest intuitions about construction, namely, the certainty of its power to *wall off* and to *wall in*, of its *preponderance* and *permanence*. The walls of Ur were virtually unadorned, and symmetry forces their uncompromising size and weight incessantly upon the attention. The birthplace of literacy – a wide and empty plain – was transformed in the second millennium before Christ into a claustrophobic penance forever confined by architecture and incantation.

If the incubus in boundary formation is all too recognizable, not just at Ur but, as we shall see, in the modern metropolis, what of the other, more felicitous extreme? No convenient metaphor comes immediately to mind in contemplating the Fali village, a puzzle which, in fact, gives the clue to its fundamental char-

acter. No element of the village, including the village itself, can be understood as an entity because nothing less than the whole Fali universe possesses the quality of wholeness. They have given this ancient idea a form reminiscent of the utmost modernity by conjuring away the forces that anchor the location of objects in space, thereby shedding their objectiveness. But, in being moved by more powerful forces joining everything into a single subject, objects also shed their weight, and in the process symbolically *disencumber* the place occupied by the village, leaving the landscape as it once was. This complicated sleight of hand erases precisely those qualities of construction used by the Sumerian hierarchy to evoke their version of *timor Dei*: walling off, walling in, preponderance, and permanence. Instead, by a refined act of the imagination, the desert landscape of the Sahel is able to reabsorb the village as a dynamic, ephemeral tissue. In a word, it becomes boundaryless.

But this is not the whole story; although the Fali enclosures, territories, and huts relinquish their status as independent objects, the granaries set within the village form a special case because each represents the mythical ark that descended from the sky, containing the seeds of all plant life. Consequently, they are accorded a pivotal dual status in this oscillating landscape: like everything else, the granaries are intrinsic to the whole, but they also act as the fulcra about which the elements of the village rotate, thereby endowing them with a unique iconic significance. The granary therefore simultaneously *represents* the cosmos while *being integral* to it. This dual role is made visible through the remarkable inventiveness expended on granary architecture. Each conforms to a basic type – a round jar raised off the ground and moulded in successive layers to the height and rough proportions of a man. The jar is internally divided to hold many different types of grain, and decorated externally in an endless variety of anthropomorphic or toad/tortoise patterns (Fig. 1.25). The Fali idea of binarism, then, reveals how a single edifice can symbolize subordina-

1.25   Fali granary. A cosmic icon (from Lebeuf)

tion to a transcendent living entity whose metaphor is the edifice itself. We shall return to this theme – the erasure of boundaries by inverting the symbols that adhere to separate things – in chapter 3.

Obviously, it takes a remarkable imagination to conceive thus of spatiality in the pursuit of unification: territory is divided in order to express oneness, but construction possesses a purposive life of its own, its meaning dissolves boundaries; it is partial and disembodied, yet can embody entirety. But what may seem to us to be a hallucinated phenomenon turns out to be the opposite: the product of a kind of suprarationality keeping what is supremely important to Fali life in the foreground.

If Sumerian space is weighed down by an incubus, then Fali spatiality is rather like Proteus. This ancient deity of the sea who knew everything past, present, and future had the power of assuming whatever shape he pleased, and was incapable of being pinned down. Herodotus narrates how this son of Poseidon came to be regarded by the Orphic mystics as symbolizing the original matter out of which the universe was made. His person, constantly in flux like the sea itself, shifted from one form to another in a masterly display of illusion and elusiveness. Yet, through all the metamorphoses, the god remained essentially himself – all-knowing, dynamic, *protean*. The protean landscape, then, denies its own permanence, materiality, and immobility precisely in order to proclaim the validity of its presence in a boundless, interdependent world.

CHAPTER TWO

The Narrative of Boundary Architecture

The Dialectical Archetype

Remember the arguments by which it has been proved that the world is, as it were, one city or community – Marcus Aurelius[1]

How could the incubus and Proteus, hoary metaphors born out of the fears and fantasy of childhood, possibly be relevant to contemporary urbanism? Do we not try to purge action of such things, filtering history itself from planning by subjecting it to the strictures of institutional reason? Are not real estate economies intrinsic to this reason, modelling cities for better or worse according to the rules of the market-place? Subjecting urban development to rules of one sort or another seems, after all, to be the primary purpose of planning, which seeks to play one regularizing system off against another. But to what end? The question must be raised, but I can provide no answer; perhaps it has no satisfactory answer. While one might point to the various objectives often set down in modern plans – comprehensiveness, allocating land and public services for future growth, protecting valued resources, and so on – they all depend on the stipulation of boundaries. This act, as we have seen, precipitates chains of events having

very little to do with such objectives because boundary effects cannot be governed by regularization. Even Plato, that master rule maker, recognized very clearly how impossible it was to perceive the higher purpose just by contemplating the regularization of life that he advocated. By contrast, our dual metaphors reveal, in their seemingly antithetical ways, the inextricable nature of their means and ends as embodied in the respective boundary conditions of Ur and the Fali settlement. Because these boundaries – the walls, ramps, gates, and monuments – do not merely contain the life led within but are integral to it, and therefore possess great significance, they become far more than just instruments of some 'higher' purpose. If, however, I as a planner fail to recognize this bond, tracing only an abstract pattern of lines on a map, then in failing to see the consequences of my actions, I sabotage the pursuit of prescribed ends. In Part II we shall see just how pervasive is this latter tendency in practice, filling the history of urbanism with unfinished beginnings and wayward fragments; nevertheless, we shall also see that these things have their own kind of order, and are more indispensable than any set of rules. The expressive meaning of cities, then, the commonplace character that strikes and invades the senses in an instant, must be somehow wedded to the slow, deliberate reflection needed to bring cities into being in the first place. Urbanism, in this sense, is an analogue of the twofold nature of the human mind. What are the dimensions of this bond, and how do we situate the enterprise of urbanism around it?

Perhaps the most pertinent message from Kant is entered in his *Critique of Judgement*: there are no reasonable rules governing the use of rules. Even when we know everything knowable, we still depend on the ability to recognize what the Greeks called the *kairos*: knowing when to speak and in which manner. But the *kairos* cannot be understood or assimilated by reference to rules, to Aristotle's science, or to the *techne*; it is a part of practical reason and therefore inextricably bound up with notions of the good. In the *Phaedrus* (280) Plato jokes about the tragedian and musician who have learned all the rules of their trade, but cannot write or perform. Even more pertinent is the analogy he advances in the *Statesman* (305e), where political craft is akin to artistry in weaving, in that each must weave opposing factors into a unity, from an acute sense of what constitutes the good in life. Urbanism, one might add, surely belongs in such company, because its dialectic must be driven by something not unlike the *kairos*.

The *kairos*, knowing when and how to deliver what is factually known, is the enduring link between the *techne*, with their precisely teachable skills, and political ethics. This means, as I implied in chapter 1, that we must locate the source and content of moral affairs in city building to discover what cannot be assimilated by rules. Now one could fill a library with works on this subject, which has agitated urban and architectural polemicists since Vitruvius first put pen to paper. To my knowledge, however, they invariably are concerned with construction as a rule-governed, aesthetic artefact, whereas expressive meaning occupies a rather different realm of consciousness. Is this realm a seat of morality?

Here we face a formidable question. What is the point, said Rousseau, in his challenge to the rationalist condescension of the Enlightenment, in claiming legitimacy for constructing a whole philosophy of ethics if each of us is endowed *a priori* with natural moral consciousness? If we are born with the remarkable ability to distinguish precisely between the slightest shades of right and wrong, then of what conceivable use is moral instruction? It was Kant who first confronted this question, but we must turn in contrary fashion to his critic Hegel, who gave out that art was no longer the highest form of truth, and that architecture was the least of arts, to enlighten us about a question that is of the greatest importance to architecture. For Hegel devised the antithesis of empirical social science, namely, the doctrine of the objective spirit. Through the latter, he was able to topple Kant's version of moral inwardness and self-certitude that was so vital to the Enlightenment idea of the autonomy of the self. In its place, he put the objective life structures that bind individuals together. The consciousness of the individual is overtaken by a common reality that is to be discovered in these structures, from which alone flows the moral position. Not surprisingly, Hegel's speculative doctrine, especially as expounded in his *Phenomenology of the Spirit*, has been attacked for its reactionary implications and metaphysical basis, although not decisively so. Hans-Georg Gadamer, for instance, points to Hegel's demonstration that a true sense of self – that is, of being certain of oneself – cannot be reached by being subjected to and assimilating what is alien. Both the slave *and* the master suffer within a structure of domination.

The latter point should bring to mind the case of Ur. But the constructions of urbanism form a rather different category from the institutional structures meant by Hegel; nevertheless, the evidence discussed in chapter 1 suggests that boundary 'objectness' cannot be neatly severed from the human relationships and ways of life that articulate it in the first place. Like nature herself, boundaries are pervasive, value-laden, and invasive, so we should expect that those things having to do not only with enclosure, but also with morality – the recognition of others, the suppression of self-interest – are somehow contained within them. Echoing Cassirer's thoughts on expressive meaning, Leroi-Gourhan remarks, in *Le Geste et la Parole*, how 'the foundation of man's moral and physical comfort is the wholly animal perception of the perimeter of security, of the close refuge, or of the socializing rhythms.'[2] Let us open this issue by examining the elements from which urban boundaries are made, namely, architectural forms.

The location of the source of morality would not be a matter of indifference to architectural discourse provided it could be substantiated that architecture is *about* morality. Now there are several ways in which this may be the case. In the first place, the morality of a building may be read *in front of* the architecture through expressive meaning; we might instantly recognize (but not necessarily assimilate) the intended message, which is often complex. Consider the illustrious case of Abbot Suger's enlargement of the basilica of St Denis, of which the narthex was consecrated in 1140. The west front, and particularly the upper choir with its rear ambulatory and cluster of chevets (1144), are justly regarded not only as a masterpiece, but also as the very crucible of Gothic architecture, setting the course of ecclesiastical building throughout northern Europe for the next three hundred years (Fig. 2.1).

We know a great deal about Abbot Suger, his life, his intentions at St Denis, and the extent of his participation in erecting the fabric, because he wrote several texts about this operation. We know, for instance, that he was greatly influenced by the metaphysics of John the Scot, whereby 'it is impossible for our mind to rise to the imitation and contemplation of the celestial hierarchies unless it relies upon that material guidance which is commensurate to it.' For Suger, this meant that the

2.1   Choir of St Denis Abbey Church, Paris, 1140–4

most divine material – the House of God on Earth – should become immaterial, through the intervention of light: 'The material lights, both those which are disposed by nature in the spaces of the heavens and those which are produced on earth by human artifice, are images of the intelligible lights, and above all of the True Light itself.'[3] Thus we are asked, by contemplating a virtual etherealization of the whole St Denis choir from vault to crypt through a veil of light, to perceive and act, if not upon a moral, then upon a religious injunction that is not at all straightforward, but that can be grasped immediately in the presence of the architecture. 'And bright is the noble edifice which is pervaded by the new light'[4] (Fig. 2.2).

It could be claimed, with some reason, that precisely because the religious injunction in question is concerned with the element of light, architecture is supremely equipped to bring it so immediately to our attention by increasing height; enlarging windows; reducing walls to

2.2   Ceiling of St Mary Redcliffe, Bristol, 1400

slender piers, or massive vaults to delicate clusters of ribs; and so on. But what of other ethical messages – freedom, justice, and truth, for instance? Here, it must be admitted that, with respect to what can be read in front of the text, architecture is relatively inarticulate. Relatively complex as well as subtle and deep shades of intended meaning are generally absent in the constructed landscape, so moral injunctions tend to be moralizing and rather obvious, revolving around the often over-stated equivalence of truth and beauty, or justice and grandeur, or structural, functional, and human honesty. We confront an entirely different story when considering what lies *behind* the text, in the camouflaged places where architecture and the character of whole urban boundaries no longer moralize, but, like body language, *inadvertently* reveal meanings that reflect a different, sometimes opposite morality to that displayed in front. Now these meanings may be expressive and banal, instantly invading the senses, for instance, with evidence of rampant social injustice; think of the lucid urban landscapes of poverty and extreme wealth which afflict the metropolitan experience (Figs 2.3 and 2.4). Alternatively, complicated procedures of exegesis might be necessary to uncover what is hidden when confronted with certain manipulative images in the modern metropolis. I deal with this question – the question of the *detractive*, ideological purpose of architecture – later on.

But there exists a more durable level of morality than that of religious injunction, which happens to find expressive meaning in the airy tissue of St Denis, and which brings us to one of the very roots of urbanism. In order to inspire thoughts of God, the spectacular

2.3   Gustav Doré, *Over London – by rail*, 1872

2.4   Abandoned housing in Belfast; the 'Weetabix' project

display at St Denis must strike us instantaneously with its own magical presence; a moment later, as close scrutiny and admiration take over, this experience becomes aesthetic. But the magic of that first instant depends in its entirety on the sense of metamorphosis – of bringing countless tons of inert materials to life, transmogrifying the character of stone, vaporizing solid matter into a kinetic, luminescent tissue. So feelings of flight and of wizardry mingle with Abbot Suger's call to witness the divine presence; but these feelings are also connected to a morality that precedes, supersedes, and in all likelihood inspired the abbot's doctrine: to return God's landscape to its pristine state by conjuring the St Denis choir away. This same morality, mediated and often neutered by rules, devalued by politics and self-interest, threads its way through the history of urbanism in countless manifestations of the ways in which we recognize nature's and humanity's existence. More than anywhere else this morality finds expressive meaning in the location and articulation of boundaries; the material facts of St Denis separate the profane from the divine, requiring a dematerializing act not unlike the erasure of boundaries that reunites members of the Fali settlement. The moral basis of urbanism thus has to do with closing the distance placed between the self and the world around by the adulterating facts of construction. In other words, urbanism can be a referring back to this world and to the self in a gesture of respect, atonement, reconciliation, and apology for violating an *a priori* order by constructing boundaries. In this sense, urbanism is construction in the poetic guise of what is being alienated; truly an apologetic wolf in sheep's clothing (Fig. 2.5).

Archetypal Form and Archetypal Content

In the beginning environment was a moving ocean. It is becoming. From this becoming the human personality detaches itself to affirm itself in the face of it. The person does it as it might;

that is, by modelling environment in its own image, according to both individual and generalized characteristics. But for this very reason it does it almost regretfully, and nurturing deep within itself the nostalgia of the union, of the intimate fusion with becoming which had enveloped it; being constantly pulled by these two forces: The need to affirm and the need to deny itself, the human personality always finds itself wanting when confronted with the wholeness of becoming – E. Minkowski[5]

According to the preceding section, a simple, not to say simple-minded principle seems to emerge when articulating the boundaries of the city: they should be open, convivial, welcoming. But, if we recall the encapsulation of urban life described at the beginning of the previous chapter – that dialectic oscillating between the worlds of Homer and Plato – then our principle seems more at home in a theme park than in the city. The full power of the mythic past ranges across the spectrum of human experience and aspiration, so we shall witness how all this is still caught up in the practice of urbanism, despite official words to the contrary.

We have implied that the veritable chorus of those who mourn the loss of the old rituals, the old meanings that were the main part of architecture and city building, depends on two suppositions. The first has to do with a belief in a theory of history applied to all forms of social relations and cultural production, including architecture and urbanism – namely, that they are historically constituted. Thus the monumental structure of the contemporary city, according to Joseph Rykwert, is but an analogue of a pathological social condition.[6] As such, architectural meaning is said to be monopolized by the material production, distribution, and consumption that drive the capitalist metropolis. Architecture, then, inescapably represents the urban function – or malfunction – as it never did before.

Second, we are said to live in the age of disbelief. All those mimetic references of the old architecture are now demythologized: di-

2.5   Hiding the unacceptable materiality of construction. Temple of Antoninus and Faustina. From Andrea Palladio, *Four Books of Architecture*, Book 4, ch. IX, 1570

vine nature, God, the celestial harmonies and earthly reconciliations, *mathesis* – all have succumbed to scientific rationalism. We may continue to build recurrent forms, to make architecture out of architecture, but with no hope of resurrecting former meanings. All that remains is nostalgia, display, ironies, information, mere accessories to the 'realities' of structure and function. The ancient rites and rituals that accompanied the locating of a *templum*, the fixing in space of the site, the boundaries and walls of the city itself, the invocation of divine sanction to build, the purifying of land to be enclosed and roofed, the lowly status once given to functionality – all have come to naught.[7]

Or so it seems. But does what we happen to believe or disbelieve as rational beings, or whatever is historically conditioned, exhaust the human foundations upon which the creation and reception of cities are built? We have yet to come to terms with the workings of some important corners of collective and individual consciousness.

Suppose we turn the arguments of rational criticism around. The rituals and acts of *mimesis* that accompanied both the constructions of Greek and Roman antiquity and those of the Middle Ages were sanctioned by shared beliefs that we tend to assume were then stable and inviolable. But, for whatever reason, our perception of the myths upon which these beliefs were founded is itself, in a sense, mythical. The Homeric works, for instance, are a kind of snapshot of a single moment of legends that happen to have their own rather complex evolutionary history. They, like all other myths, were not 'fixed' in an obscure, preliterate epoch and handed down unchanged through the millennia. *They* were historically conditioned, each recipient society adapting the stories according to then current needs and circumstance.

In fact, scepticism about the canonical power of myths goes back much farther than many critics would have us believe, to the scientific enlightenment of late classical antiquity. What has been called the post-mythic

consciousness of the Stoics led them to allegorize Homer: the adultery of Zeus and Leto was no longer an unbridled sexual act but the union of power and wisdom. The Gods were suddenly *moral*, and remained so for as long as was didactically necessary.[8] It is worth while remembering that if even Homer could be so interpreted, then the content of *all* myths as absolute can immediately be called into question. Think of Auerbach's famous commentary on Homer's resistance to being misunderstood because of 'the need of the Homeric style to leave nothing which it mentions half in darkness and unexternalized ... to represent phenomena in a fully externalized form, visible and palpable in all their parts, and completely fixed in their spatial and temporal relations. The Homeric style knows only a foreground, only a uniformly illuminated, uniformly objective present.'[9] Mythical truths probably were always contentious, and the supposedly rock-hard sources of architectural meaning were rarely regarded as absolute. The same scepticism was certainly applied throughout the Christian epoch to the divinity of nature, despite its supremacy as the subject of artistic mimicry; that God made nature, but did not make it holy, was closer to official biblical truth. Nor were unofficial opinions about God's work absent; think of those blasphemies and erotica carved for all to see on the *misericordia* of the finest cathedrals.

Perhaps we are guilty only of the reflexive exaggeration that accompanies the loss of every beloved object, but it does seem that the eighteenth-century Enlightenment neither initiated the questioning of myths nor finished them off once and for all. We are not even certain that the object of conventionalized reference in architecture existed in the mythically based values that could be consciously held and articulated, despite the assertions of theorists like Plato, Aristotle, and Vitruvius. All we know for sure is that if architecture imitated anything, it imitated other architecture. When Iktinos, the alleged architect of the Temple of Apollo at Bassae (ca 430–400 B.C.), introduced his highly evolved Ionic half-capitals into the interior of his temple, he was not mimicking *de novo* the plant and animal forms from which the Order was originally derived. Instead, in all likelihood, his conscious point of departure was the Ionic capital he had already used on the Parthenon. The design at Bassae thus began with an established *architectural* model, rather than with nature herself, a model that was modified in response to the peculiar relationship that otherwise would have occurred between the canted volutes, the architrave, and the projecting buttress to which the Order was applied.[10] Iktinos's success, we can assume, was measured by his ability to resolve circumstances like these while leaving the Order intact. That he could do so with poetic grace is beyond question, but who would wish to say that such grace derives from the *mimesis* of nature as opposed to that of prior architectural conventions? Nevertheless, the answer to this question would shed only a dim light on the expressive meaning of the Greek temple – a matter to be considered below.

If the ancients were not quite so beholden to the culturally fusing, transcendent idea as we have often been led to believe (and the same argument can be made for the Medieval and Renaissance mind), neither does the converse follow that contemporary architecture is ruled by anti-mythical reason. Historical categorism of this sort begins to break down, for instance, when we turn from the concept of myth to that of near-myth. Walter Abell, in *The Collective Dream in Art*, draws a comparison between a 'primitive' effort to come to terms with a phenomenon of nature – namely, a volcanic eruption in 1780 on the Nass River that traumatized members of the Haida Indian nation of British Columbia, leading them to carve their great Eagle's Nest totems – and the origins of Picasso's famous painting *Guernica* (1937). The totem imagery and *Guernica* are representations of a collective shock precipitated by violent circumstances, but Picasso, working as an imaginative individual, was able to summon up so powerful a representation of the event that others recognized it as an embodiment of the horror that erupted around the world:

In all these respects the painting is cousin to the myths. But it differs from them with regard to the last ... condition ... essential to the birth of a complete myth. It operates within a *differentiated* mentality instead of an *undifferentiated* one. The tension image remains subject to our power of rational discrimination and therefore fails to attain hallucinatory reality. Instead of confusing it with the outward world, we say that it *expresses* or *symbolizes* our reactions to certain aspects of that world. In this respect it corresponds, not to the true dream, but to the daydream as normally circumvented by reason. Cultural tension imagery which is thus circumvented might be described as *near myth* or, if we apply the analogy of the daydream, as day myth.[11]

If we are prepared to find a place for daydreams, near-myths, myths, and even hallucinations in the worlds of religion and most art, it is only because these worlds have now been hermetically sealed from supposedly rational everyday life, and accorded an inferior status. However, in architecture, and especially the administered discipline of planning, any concept presented as the fruit of unreason would be a distinct embarrassment. Professionalism itself thrives on the ability to distinguish fact from fancy. What it hides, none the less, are the unplumbed layers from which so much professional discourse emerges; concepts and precepts like comprehensiveness, function and structure, even efficiency, let alone community, harmony, unity, proportion, and beauty. Abell reminds us about the extent to which, despite our best efforts, the workings of the prerational mind cannot be contained: 'The distinction between the myth and the near myth in any culture is neither fixed nor clear. Instead of a sharp line of demarcation between the two, we find a shifting zone of intermixture. As the daydream of the individual fluctuates from lesser to greater reality in response to changing relations between reason and emotion in the dreamer, so myth and near myth fluctuate into each other in the complicated mental atmosphere of a culture.'[12] Here again we confront the power of indeterminacy, not just in art but in everyday life, of a protean, liminal world that marks the shift from one state to the next, and one that figures, too, in countless threshold zones where the boundaries of the city take their cue from the quotidian momentum.

Architecture and Recurrence

If urbanism has to do with the recognition, displayed in the character of boundaries, of the manner in which the self is related to the world around, what value does urbanism retain in the contemporary metropolis, that contraption seemingly designed to sustain inwardness and to exploit whatever lies outside the self? I have referred to the debasement of *civitas* into something we now call the public interest, which happens to be little more than an aggregate of self-interests. Who today would join Socrates in claiming more reason to be grateful to the community than to his parents? Does this not reduce urbanism to a set of empty gestures, a hopeless pastiche devoid of any central significance, or, worse, to something approaching the incarcerating boundaries inflicted on Ur?

A moment's reflection shows that, precisely because of the metropolitan condition, if indeed urbanism is tied to the kind of moral questions discussed above, and surfaces through expressive meanings that precede rational thought, then its validity remains intact whatever the nature of practice. So as the mind turns away from the modern landscape, it instantly recognizes the continuing truth of *philopolis* described more than two millennia ago by Pericles in his funeral speech: 'We play our part in the community as free men, both in public life and also in everyday life, because we avoid mutual suspicion; we are not angry with our neighbour if he enjoys himself, nor do we indulge in resentment which, though

not harmful, is unpleasant to observe.'[13] This description of the good life has its own landscape, not far removed from that of fifth-century Attica and reincarnated many times since, perhaps most recently in the impossibly boundaryless region of Kevin Lynch's *Place Utopia* (1981), whose inhabitants are tolerant of, but not indifferent to one another.[14]

If this theme is recurrent, we should be able to recognize it beneath the layers of local and historical conditioning, and to recognize there the ubiquitous interplay of a predictable life governed by rules with its antithesis, brought into play along the boundaries of cities. Recurrence – a controversial subject often confused with historical determinism – has been most widely discussed in the areas of classicism and language, so it might be worth while finding out if urbanism is somehow related to these topics. All three, it is true, are patterned by shifts in historical context, but they are also subjects of the imagination, which brings to mind Henri Lefebvre's rhetorical question: 'Is not the fabric of the imaginary woven from threads of remembrance and therefore of recurrence?'[15] Because buildings form the constituents of urban boundaries, let us again turn our attention to architecture.

Edwin Lutyens sensed the force of prerationality in writing of the classical architectural Orders: 'They have to be so well digested that there is nothing but essence left … the perfection of the Order is far nearer nature than anything produced on impulse and accident-wise. Every line and curve the result of force against impulse through the centuries.'[16]

Are the classical Orders, having embellished urban boundaries since antiquity, the enduring expression of the quasi-natural character of the objective spirit? Lutyens's digestion refers to a rational act of judgment, so that, while the Order may be near nature, its perfection is not derived from nature-in-itself, but from the painstaking avoidance of naturalism in the process of imitation. An unwillingness to bow down completely while paying homage to nature is the sign of the contemplative mind that we recognize immediately in stylistic convention. Nature may be the subject of classical *mimesis*, but the accomplishment is ours. The Orders were the first fully realized expression of the dialectic occurring between humans and their landscape that set Western architecture on a course from which it has rarely deviated. But it would be a mistake to imagine, in contemplating the beauty set down in those great canonical texts of Vitruvius and Vasari, in Alberti's *De Re Aedificatoria*, or in Palladio's *I Quattro Libri dell'Architettura*, that classical immutability lies in the precise forms and syntagmatic relationships of base, pediment, column shaft, capital, entablature, and pediment; or even in the location and subtleties of mouldings, entasis, echinus, volute, acanthus, and triglyph. What we examine with such pleasure is indeed an essence, but one to which the authors have given particular forms and several layers of localized meaning. The canonical works are *techne*, rule books prepared for the articifers of building on the properties of foundations, metal, timber, sand, and lime. When they are this way, we can make no essential distinction between, say, Palladio's instruction to fell timber 'in autumn, or during the winter season, in the wane of the moon; for then the trees recover the vigour and solidity that in spring and summer were dispersed among the leaves and fruit'[17] and his precise injunctions respecting the formal disposition of ornament: 'The *metope*, or space between triglyph and triglyph, ought to be as broad as it is high. The cornice must be a module and one sixth in height, and divided into five parts and a half, two of which are given to the cavetto and ovolo. The caveto is less than the ovolo by the width of its listello. The remaining three parts and a half are to be given to the corona or cornice, which is vulgarly called *gocciolatoio*, and to the gola or cima recta and reversa'[18] (Fig. 2.6).

What we read, and often overinterpret in such competencies, is not the classical essence of architecture, but Palladio's (or Vitruvius's) particular worked-out version of an unex-

2.6   Working out an unexplained first condition. Andrea Palladio, Doric Order, *Four Books of Architecture*, Book 1, ch xv, 1570

plained first condition. Palladio begins and ends with the axiom that architecture is an 'imitatrix of nature,' which must contain nothing that is alienating to her. But the usual assumption of dogmatic nature takes no heed of the dialectic that Palladio himself (probably subconsciously) engaged in to produce his Veneto masterpieces. Must we paraphrase Kant to explain this omission by saying that architecture is an art hidden in the depths of the human soul, and it will always be difficult to extract the true mechanism from nature to lay it open before our eyes?

It would certainly be unwise to underestimate this difficulty, but I will make the claim that, if there exists an absolute knowledge in architecture, then a part of it will not to be discovered in the arbitrary choices that produced what are known as the classical canons, but in the boundary purpose that underlies them. As I hope to demonstrate in Part II, it also underlies practically the whole course of Western architecture, a torch that was only just kept alight through the Romanesque and Carolingian, that was not extinguished in the twelfth century at St Denis but, on the contrary, was given a new breath of life, to illuminate the great ecclesiastical fabrics of the Middle Ages. Brunelleschi and Borromini guaranteed its passage up to the nineteenth century, to make a mockery of the ensuing stylistic partisanship. Even modernism, which believed itself purged of all history, could not avoid it. Even today, the age of neo-rationalism, decisionism, the gaff that architectural essence exists in stripped-down classicism, the hopeless reincarnation of ossified formalism, the debasement of the metropolitan landscape to images and pastiches, we can just perceive, here and there, the flicker of urbanism that propelled the architecture of antiquity.

To continue the search for this purpose we shall need to make a loose analogy, but no more, with the field of literature. A.J. Greimas attempts to lay bare the consistencies that are common, at a deep structural level, to seemingly diverse forms of narrative.[19] He does so by a process of systematic condensation of the mutual relations occurring between typical narrative roles, and by the establishment of a system of rules governing the transposition of these relations. We should be wary, of course, in our analogy, of overinterpreting the term 'structure.' Precisely because that term is borrowed from architecture in the first place, we should not be too hasty in supposing that architecture possesses an equivalent sort of 'deep structure' to that of language. In linguistic analysis, 'structure' refers to the immanent relations that hold between the system of signs that constitute a language. The text is treated as a kind of 'wordless, authorless' object that can be explained (but not understood, for there is nothing to understand) by the specific combinations of oppositions between the con-

stitutive semiotic units. Since each sign can be defined *only* in its relation to and dependence on others, there are no absolute terms.

At a superficial level, there are, no doubt, seductive parallels to be drawn between linguistic and architectural structure, provided we limit the comparison to the 'technical' systems such as the load-bearing and load-transmitting elements in building. In a sense, architectural structure is the field of the engineer, who can legitimately exclude all intended external value reference from his work. But can the built structure, as in language, be considered an object of scientific investigation devoted exclusively to its own internal relations? Each structural unit can certainly be defined and determined by its role relative to that of others within the system of which it is but a part. But this kind of parallel is not at all helpful because, in architecture, as opposed to language, there is always a residue of 'signs' that are not related to each other by immutable structural rules. The residue, moreover, is normally far greater than the rule-governed structural core. Think of the innumerable ways whereby integral and superimposed loads can be transmitted from roofs, floors, and screens through beams, columns, and bearing walls to foundations. Consider, too, the fundamental *structural* differences among trabeated, triangulated, arched, domed, and paraboloid forms. Only in a highly indirect sense can each system be considered equivalent to a separate but related language: what connects them is not a deep intrinsic structure but a universal set of forces such as gravity operating within nature itself. The logic of architectural structure is not, as in language, internally and autonomously derived; on the contrary, it must answer to an infinitely variable set of externally imposed conditions (Fig. 2.7). Nor can it be claimed that the *elements* of architectural structure are equivalent to linguistic signs, each of which is but an arbitrary convention that can be changed by purely accidental events occurring in history. For this reason, linguistic analysis is able to treat them relationally rather than sub-

2.7   Andrea Palladio, Staircase at Chambor, *Four Books of Architecture*, Book 1, ch. XXVIII, 1570

stantively. But no such arbitrariness characterizes the choice of elements in architectural structure: the selection of a specific type of post-tensioned beam is a rational act that is highly constrained by its structural purpose within the ubiquitous imperatives of available material means.

So far our comparison with language has been limited to only one of several architectural systems, the one that seems closest to linguistic structure. Similar reservations could be put forward when considering the other systems that are answerable to natural forces: the mechanical and electrical servicing networks, for instance. But our distant analogy breaks down completely when we turn from the signifying to the symbolic purpose of language. Metaphysical reference in architecture *can* be determined according to certain structural rules – think of the structural expressionism of the Chicago School and the Russian Constructivists – or to quasi-structural rules, as one way to regard the classical Orders. However, we must assume that the willingness to subject architectural design to these rigours is a matter of making a choice from a wide range of stylistic options. Language, however, is pregiven, with a signifying purpose that architecture does not usually possess, so that, in its infinite variety, language must retain the structural rules that makes it socially accessible. Even poetry, which Roland Barthes tells us is a critique of language itself, is composed, not in some metalanguage, for there can be no metalanguage of language, but in conformity to the rules of linguistic structure. Architecture, like all art, in contrast, derives its concepts from outside itself – namely, from the practice of life and our attitudes towards it – so Alan Colquhoun is correct in asserting the existence of an architectural metalanguage.[20] We bring these practices and values to bear in the making of architecture, whereas, in speech, they can be defined and uttered only through a pregiven language.

Now these practices and values seem to be historically contingent, so eighteenth- and nineteenth-century rationalism failed in its attempt to search for architectural absolutes in various structurally based and geometrically based Platonic models. Without the kind of immutability that governs deep structure in language, architecture seems destined to be historically relative, a matter that has exercised architectural discourse since the Enlightenment. If we are free to choose, then we may choose in principle according either to contemporaneity or to historical precedent, as we wish. Architecture, then, at first glance seems destined to be, at best, the product of the free artistic will acting upon some rationalized, but entirely temporary consensus.

It must follow that such a consensus cannot be of the same order as the stylistic injunctions set down in the canonical texts of Alberti or Palladio. Those masters were blessed with an age practically devoid of ethical and aesthetic equivocation, so, for them, the classical Orders must have possessed the same pregiven status in architecture as language had in everyday life. The Orders needed no rationalization, being self-evidently rational. Modern consensus, however, is grounded in ideologies of one sort or another, and therefore subject to critique. This applies whether a consensus develops about architectural process, such as functionalism; or the aesthetic consequent–ialism recently espoused by the Martin Centre for Architectural and Urban Studies at Cambridge; or about typological architectural paradigms, like the Corbusian *objets-types* and more recently those of the various European neorationalist schools. We have obviously reached a stage in history when the forging (or imposing) and dissolving of consensus is invariably partial. (The fact that consensus is also often regionally localized seems to disturb no one; on the contrary, it is welcomed as a sign of cultural integration *somewhere*.)[21]

Architectural practice, then, seems to occupy a hopeless relativistic sphere. But our discussion has dealt only with the search for a system of rules governing the choice of a process or a formal repertoire. However, the *significance* of these things, the meanings they take on in everyday life, is our primary concern. In this regard we must recall construction's underlying effect, which I referred to in the previous chapter as extending the distance between the self and the world around; architecture's purpose is to close this distance, and it is precisely here that architecture and literature coincide.

Architectural Narrative

So, at this point, we return to literature, not to pursue further a not-too-helpful structural analogy, but to confront the very difficulties that the linguistic structuralists themselves encounter in attempting to incorporate narrative within structure. What is at stake is the unavoidable tendency within structuralist criticism to assign the elements of narrative time to the level of surface structure, because of the essentially *achronic* nature of deep grammar. Structure in language is concerned exclusively with immanent relations that are non-successive, so the large diachronic residue, namely, the narrative itself, cannot be taken into account except by treating it as a manifestation. Greimas himself conceded as much: 'the whole narrative would be reduced to … simple structure if there did not remain a diachronic residue, under the form of a functional pair, confrontation versus success … which cannot be transformed into an elementary semic category.'[22] Moreover, the successive nature of narrative, its dramatic form, 'can be interpreted as the inversion of an initial situation, roughly described as the rupture of an order, for the sake of a terminal situation which is conceived as the restoration of order.'[23] Hence an achronic reading of the text is unable to absorb the elements of the plot, which takes the form of a *quest* of one sort or another, one that gives the uncertainty to narrative literature and without which *nothing would actually happen*. The plot, therefore, cannot properly be construed as a mere surface manifestation (a 'placarding') of immanent structural transformations. Paul

Ricoeur, in particular, questions the priority given to deep structure that inductive structuralism demands, and wonders whether a reversal would not be more appropriate, whether the so-called deep level is nothing more than an ideal projection of an essentially narrative operation.

At first sight such a reversal – the raising to eminence within textual analysis of what appears to be its wayward, subjective component – seems subversive, for while there are rules that always guarantee the unity of linguistic structures, no such rules seem to prevail over the diachronic residue. What is fiction if not spontaneous inventiveness? Indeed, what captures and holds the attention of the reader is an outcome that cannot be predicted from the unfolding of the plot, so does not the author begin to work the narrative of every successful text *de novo*?

Actually, this seems doubtful; if, even within *genres*, an infinite variety of plot, character, and reference seems to be quite within the capability of language and human inventiveness, in fact we know this is not the case. Each 'new' story is but a working over of sedimented literary conventions. Poetry, says Northrop Frye, 'can only be made out of other poems; novels out of other novels. Literature shapes itself.'[24]

Does architecture shape itself? At one level, this can hardly be questioned. Who would doubt that copying is the norm rather than the exception? An adjustment here, a modification there according to circumstance – is not the sameness of contemporary architecture the consequence of substituting ready-made images for imaginative invention? Or, more forgivable perhaps, is not the recurrence of classicism and other typologies the sure sign of the continuing strength of sedimented traditions? But Frye does not mean this kind of thing when he writes of *archetypes* as the nuclei of literary conventionalization. An archetype is what makes written art fundamentally communicable *as art* rather than factual or historical narrative; we are able to recognize an epic, a poem, a novel *as such* by its reference back to the categories and subcategories that give order to the prior world of literary convention.

Before jumping to a dangerously seductive conclusion, we need to acknowledge, at this point, the essential difference between the literary archetype, on the one hand, and the Orders, Platonic models, and *objets-types* of architecture, on the other. Frye's insight was revelatory, a discovery illuminating the formal narrative unity of a seemingly diverse tradition, an insight with considerable implications for literary analysis and criticism. The Orders, models, and types, however, do not possess this kind of analytical distance from practice; they are normative injunctions, heuristic guides to everyday practical work. They forfeit any claim to intrinsic archetypal character because none of them is self-evidently superior to the rest, a situation requiring an act of persuasion on the part of their proponents. In other words, none of them tells its own story, and the story behind the forms is what we are looking for. Consider the rhetoric that invariably accompanies each and every injunction to return to some primordial type, the verbal exertion required to convince us about the supposed association between pure geometry and architectural essence. In effect, we are asked (or told) to believe in a tradition that is reinvented with each exhortation, telling us very little about the story flowing out of this connoisseur's architecture, and virtually nothing about its relationship to human per-

ception and socially held values that are a feature of the literary archetype.

For instance, certain rationalists have proffered the plane, the void, the cube, the sphere; yet none of these elementary forms is *architecturally* primordial as the Purists imagined. On the contrary, they exchanged history for a set of meanings derived from the total identification of form with content, which became one fundamental hallmark of modernism itself (Fig. 2.8). In this sense, architectural ideals suffer a kind of reduction based on the quite unwarranted assumption that the birthplace of architecture is the rational selection of forms whose narrative becomes relegated to a second-order manifestation. But, even in the best instances, a large gap separates conscious intention and effect, a gap that is rarely taken up in criticism, because too often we judge modern architecture according to its own rationalization, as if the latter were an *episteme*, thereby misdirecting our attention away from the narrative core, the real seat of archetypal categories in literature, architecture, and urbanism.

Architectural Discourse and Expressive Meaning

No claim can be made that the rational selection and assembly of forms in architectural practice is an invalid exercise; on the contrary, Ruskin has shown us that these forms are the elements of expressive meaning, which, in

2.8   Ludwig Hilberseimer, Housing Estate (from *Grossstadt-Architektur*, 1927)

turn, produces urbanism. But if the forms monopolize analysis and practice, then urbanism, which deals in expressive meanings, becomes an accidental by-product, giving us a landscape filled with unintended quests that fall through the net of architectural discourse. In doing so, this discourse tends to deal, not in matters affecting everyday life, but in connoisseurship. Architecture's boundary purpose evaporates into irrelevance. In a 1978 essay, that astute critic Alan Colquhoun provides an illustration of the extent to which architectural scholarship, then as now, has distanced itself from the quotidian. It contains his favourable assessment of various buildings designed by Michael Graves, in which he inserts some program notes from the architect himself: 'The design of a guest house addition is given to focus ... attention on the perceptual elements of a building, the wall surfaces, and the spaces they describe ... The plan is as a conceptual tool, a two-dimensional diagram or notational device, with limited capacity to express the perceptual elements which exist in three-dimensional space.'[25] Colquhoun then goes on to analyse Graves's work according to these 'perceptual elements,' namely, planes, solids, and voids. In the case of Graves's 'early phase,' the 1972 Gunwyn Ventures Building at Princeton, for instance, 'the space of the office is complex, with various penetrations through three stories. A hatch to the second floor office projects over one of these voids. Its wafer-thin work-top is carried on a bracket attached to the column on the *opposite* side of the void, which thus reaches out to receive an unexpected but hardly onerous burden and at the same time provides the hatch with a frame which it has borrowed from the nearby tubular balustrade at floor level'[26] (Fig. 2.9).

All of this suggests that admirable close observation of the empirical kind favoured by the younger John Ruskin. The building is presented as a composition whose architectural content is, for the most part, locked into a display of abstract forms. External reference seems not to be the fundamental architectural theme, but a residue: 'Most of the columns are

2.9   Michael Graves, Gunwyn Ventures Building, Princeton, NJ, 1972

circular, but when they occur in a wall they turn into pilasters and merge with the wall surface above. All these fragments and transpositions have a local, internal logic of their own. Their shock effect is a result of the way they undermine expected hierarchies. The fragments are differentiated by means of colour, for the most part brilliant, but intermixed with grass greens, sky blues and flesh pinks. Just as these colours suggest elements of nature, so does the metaphorical play of functional elements have anthropomorphic, and sometimes surreal, overtones relating mechanical functions to our own bodies and making us question reality.'[27]

Apart from this fairly prosaic and indirect metaphorical occurrence, Graves's references, according to Colquhoun, are to other works whose source, in turn, is not strictly

2.10   Michael Graves, Plocek House, façade, Warren, NJ, 1977–8

'architectural.' In this phase they are chiefly those of the machine references of Le Corbusier and the Italian fascist Terragni. It is at this point that a certain amount of counter-productive erudition, on the part of architect and critic, takes over and appears to govern the enterprises of both production and critical reception. Michael Graves's work is presented as an imaginative mimesis of a world of prior work, but one that seems to consist solely of a pregiven formal repertoire – albeit 'non-architectural' – upon which the imagination imposes new relations that are almost entirely immanent.

This is no less the case in Graves's later phase, in which abstract motifs give way to a different but still pregiven repertoire, one made up of 'perceptual elements' to which are attached a set of meanings that are now deemed to be internal to architecture itself. Beginning with the pivotal Claghorn House of 1974 and culminating in the 1978 Plocek 'Keystone House,'

traditional figures are introduced as quotations and fragments, as were the functionalist motifs of the earlier work. Because these figures already exist in our memory, and because they are ornamental and not structural, they can be transposed, split up, inverted or distorted, without losing their original meanings. The chief sources of this 'metalanguage' are Italian Mannerism, eighteenth century Romantic Classicism, and the

later Beaux-Arts. But in developing a language of ornament which is simple and allows for repetition, Graves has recourse to the language of Art Deco – that 'debased' style which tried to unite the more decorative aspects of Cubism with a remembered tradition of architectural ornament.[28] (Fig. 2.10)

In a sense, Graves's personal transition is not unlike a chronological inversion of the paradigmatic shift that occurred seventy years earlier between Peter Behrens's corporeal Berlin AEG turbine plant (1908) and Walter Gropius's etherealized factory at Alfeld (1911) (Figs 2.11 and 2.12). This shift heralded a crucial change in urban-boundary formation, and will be examined in some detail in chapter 9. While Graves's abstract planes, having no density of their own, seem merely to 'placard' the spaces they contain, the later Keystone House, emphasized by the weight of the appliquéd motifs, intrudes upon the landscape, asserting a rather dogmatic human presence in Graves's subsequent work. Now Behrens's referents are not 'architectural,' in the sense meant by Colquhoun, namely, a set of motifs recognizable by their association with this or that style. There are virtually no classical, mannerist, or Beaux-Arts reminiscences in Behrens's AEG Turbinenfabrik. In fact it is precisely this absence of stylistic reference that distinguishes Behrens's factories from those of the Ludwig Loewe firm built

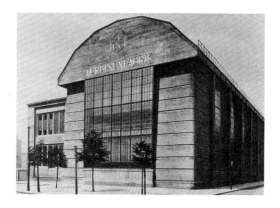

2.11   Peter Behrens, Turbine factory, Berlin, 1908

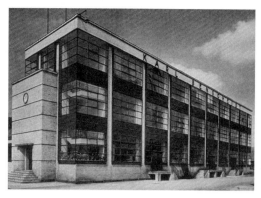

2.12   Walter Gropius, Fagus-Werk, Alfeld, 1911.
Administrative block

at the same time and located next door on Berlin's Huttenstrasse. But there is a powerful kinship of expressive meaning between Graves's later work – most notably in the Portland City Hall – and the industrial oeuvre of Peter Behrens, one that does not underlie the motival references but, on the contrary, strongly subordinates them.

I am referring to their shared expressive meaning of *animality*. There is as much of the sphinx in the Keystone House as there is of stylistic reference. The house reclines, half concealed by the sloping terrain into which it is set. It possesses a head – the main portal – whose broken arch is a pair of ears and the door a mouth. But the portal also takes on the character of a whole cat: now, a sitting figure guarding the flanks of a larger feline whose single paw protects the terrace dominated by the cleft, eyed head of the west elevation. The house *sprawls*, yet gives the definite illusion of being able to *spring* to life. The striated, horizontal lines may predominate along the base, but they are everywhere held in tension by opposing structures of columns, pilasters, and mullions, which rise through and hold the anatomical weight of the house in suspension. All animal references are highly conventionalized, but are never hidden. They cannot be read beneath the surface of architectural detail because they do not comprise an internal

essence; instead, they are aggregated into a visible assembly, to become the most telling unifying characteristic of the whole edifice (Fig. 2.13).

I leave it to the reader to pick out the forms of Behrens's Turbinenfabrik that give it an overriding animal-like quality. This time, the animal stands, and its shape is more archaic than that of the Keystone House. Why should a building be made to resemble an ominous animal? Not, it should be said immediately, because the architects were afflicted with a gratuitous urge to imitate nature. I suggest, rather, that, in bringing the buildings to life in this way, we are reminded simultaneously of imminent *movement* and eventual threat. In each case, the landscape the building occupies becomes metaphorically encumbered, completely unlike the boundaries of the Fali and at St Denis. But what of the Gunwyn Ventures Building and the Alfeld factory? Here the story is more complicated, and a full explanation must await the closing chapters. For now, consider their crucial similarity of expressive meaning, despite their differences; reducing their materiality to virtually nothing erases all signs of an ominous presence, thereby enabling them to be absorbed into the foreground. *Mimesis*, as we shall see, in its rich and infinite variety, has this underlying character, one connected to a fundamental pur-

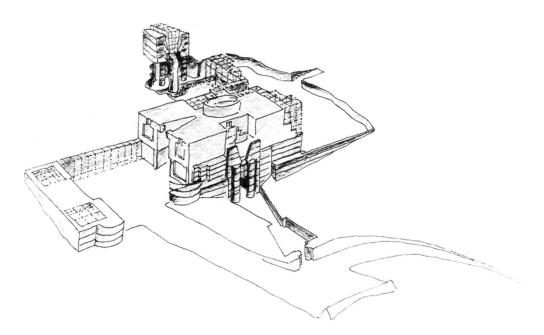

2.13   Plocek House, axonometric

pose of urbanism, whereby the damaged natural and social orders are reconstituted at a different, sometimes higher plane.

Foreground Moves to Background

Injecting life into inanimate things is one of the commonplaces in art history, and hardly commands the serious attention of the connoisseur; but urbanism's arena is expressive meaning, which works at the level of the commonplace, and demands no special knowledge of its recipient, although its making is quite another matter. Bringing inert materials to life, for instance, can force them upon our attention to the point of aggressiveness, but can also, by wielding a different skill, make them retreat from the foreground. The quality of self-effacement described above figures prominently in the discussion of boundary practices contained in Part II, and the evidence is strong – think of the Fali village – that such special kinds of absence are associated both with moral behaviour and with the

kind of boundaryless world described by Homer. I make no claim that this association will everywhere be supported by empirical analysis of actual social relations; nevertheless, I do claim that it signals the presence of social aspiration and, like the *kairos*, of agreement about ways of life and ways of doing things. Here we must shift the analytical scale up a notch from individual works to detect how such agreements can transcend the passage of time and material circumstances to figure prominently in the landscape of a culture.

Consider a half-truth about the English – that they possess a reticent character; does this alleged trait find its way into their architecture and urbanism? A few years ago Nikolaus Pevsner took on the difficult task of defining the peculiar Englishness of English art. He did so believing in that aesthetic theory which gives prominence to geography and history in the determination of artistic production. According to this belief, if we can recognize something uniquely French in the work of the

2.14   Ceiling, Alcock's Chapel, Ely Cathedral, 1486

Abbot Suger and Renoir, then we can trace a different kind of consistency across centuries of English art. What Pevsner concludes is that the English have a fascination for linear art, a propensity whose origins go back to the Book of Kells. The English line reaches an apogee in the intricacies of Gothic Decorated tracery, then enters the protracted tedium of the Perpendicular style (Fig. 2.14). William Blake, Fuseli, and the Pre-Raphaelites are masters of the curved line, as are the Glasgow School duo of Thomas Mackmurdo and Charles Rennie Mackintosh.

According to Pevsner, English linear art stems partly from the foul climate of that country; cloud, fog, mist, and rain reduce the visual effectiveness of sculptural mass, which is at its best when displaying sunlit contours and shadowed recesses.[29] But there seems to be another reason behind the English aversion

to sculptural solidity, one that is much closer to our present theme. In deciphering eighteenth-century portraiture, Pevsner writes: 'the English portrait also keeps long silences, and when it speaks, it speaks in a low voice, just as the Englishman does to this day, and as indeed the muffled sound of the English language seems to demand. Or, to put it differently, the English portrait conceals more than it reveals, and what it reveals it reveals with studied understatement ... There could be no better way of characterizing the portraits of Reynolds and Gainsborough: temperance, smoothness, judiciousness, moderation.'[30] Pevsner is not alone in thinking that England 'has never been happy with the Grand Manner.' 'Reticence or taciturnity' is an aspect of English character, and even passionate Hamlet is made to say that whatever is overdone 'cannot but make the judicious grieve.'

2.15   J.M.W. Turner, *Chichester Canal*, ca 1828. Tate Gallery, London

This thesis is not without its problems. Pevsner does not account for Henry Moore's interpretation of the human form as a wind-eroded landscape, and his book predates the aggression, not to say pugnaciousness of so much British art, architecture, and social life in the sixties, seventies, and eighties. Yet his broader truths still seem to hold, especially when considering the disembodied paintings of David Hockney or Francis Bacon, and, as far as Henry Moore is concerned, his drawings at least seem to fit Pevsner's characterization of the English. Portrayal, to the English, is so often the art of the muted presence; whether we consider the atmospherics of Constable's clouds and Girtin's sepias, Turner's phantasmagoria, or the 'blot' landscapes of Cozens, nature's essence usually comes through as blurred, smudged, not quite in focus – real but not realistic (Fig. 2.15).

This penchant for the reluctant presence passes over into urbanism and especially architecture, which, with landscape design, has been considered by some the finest art of the English. Britain has a superabundance of the picturesque, the quirkily illogical, the eccentric in the way of buildings, but their common theme seems to be one of self-effacement. This technique of self-effacement works when constructed mass is broken down to its constituent parts by great patterns of lines, angles, and screens. The architectural screen is a favourite English idiom, a bit of sleight of hand to conceal what the logicians insist should be emphasized. The screened façade, for instance, is typically English; at Lincoln cathedral the Norman west front once 'logically' displayed the aisled nave that lay behind, until its thirteenth-century conversion into a wider screen with no organic connection to the building. Similar screened façades were built at Wells, Ely, and Salisbury, and internal screens, like the famous reredos at Winchester, came later. If the screen hides the building, then something has to hide the screen, and here the English fascination for the intricately patterned wall takes over. The great fronts at Lincoln, Wells, and Salisbury

2.16   Wells Cathedral, West Front, 1230–1435

are made diaphanous by interlacing lines of closely spaced half niches, mock colonnettes, and blank arcades. Whole grids of curved, horizontal, and vertical members obscure the wall, transforming its mass to a fancy tissue, a screen in front of a screen (Fig 2.16).

Inside, even structural logic and economy give way to the urge to obscure the pressure and vulgar presence of constructed weight. At Lincoln, the normally serious job of supporting the stone vault in the choir turns into a crazy game. What begins as a straightforward quadripartite vault ends as a densely woven cloak of short lierne ribs, so that structural rationality is completely eclipsed. Line crosses line at close intervals, blithely ignoring point loads and paths of transmitted weight, turning cumbrous stone into a trellis of twigs.

If structural weight is dissolved by line, the anatomy of the English cathedral and parish church has undergone a further kind of decomposition. Instead of the sort of compactness that characterizes the short-limbed body of French ecclesiastical fabrics, in England each major component – the porch, chapter house, transepts, nave, and chancel – extend away from the central choir, so the church reads as a loosely assembled kit of parts. The typical English cathedral is very long but, as at Salisbury and Winchester, divided laterally by internal screens, so the spectator experiences it piece by piece. Externally, the frequent projecting cubes of the double transepts and porches to north and south similarly divide up the experience of the whole at close quarters (Fig. 2.17). Only from a distance – and some-

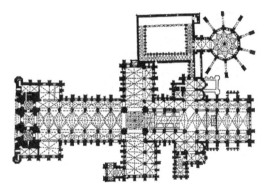

2.17   Lincoln Cathedral, Plan, 1192–1280

times the cathedral was set into a verdant precinct to permit middle-distant views of the building – can one appreciate the whole edifice. But, as Constable's painting of Salisbury Close reveals, from such a distance the cathedral is already enveloped by trees and sky, both muting its dominance and increasing the sense of ethereality.

The boundaries of the countryside itself once echoed – or were echoed by – the loose assemblies of linear shapes characterizing English architecture. In the Midlands particularly, medieval landscape division seems haphazard, as though territorial ownership were of little account. Maurice Beresford, in his survey of lost villages, notes how extensive was the terrain reclaimed by cooperative labour, held in communal ownership and distributed according to an 'open field' system.[31] Before the massive enclosure movement of the eighteenth century, whereby land became reassembled into large blocks of pasture whose ownership was confirmed by walls, hedges, and fences, the countryside used to be patterned by clusters of unbounded furlong strips, each in turn lined by the ridge-and-furrow method of ploughing. Because, as Penelope Lively has shown, reclamation work proceeded selectively, depending on which areas could be cleared or drained with relative ease, the furlongs were thrown together in no apparent order;[32] so the landscape evolved into a congeries of lines from horizon to horizon (Fig. 2.18).

All this adeptness is but a part of the stunningly variable theme of moderating the impact of boundaries on the senses. Certainly the English repertoire of linearism, of screens, of decomposition, hardly exhausts their technique. Robert Adam, as Pevsner also reminds us, was a Scot who was educated in Italy, but a genius notwithstanding when it came to the art of disembodying buildings. His was partly a reaction, quite widespread in Europe by the 1760s, against the bombast of late Baroque and Rococo decoration.[33] Adam's masterpieces are his famous interiors, crafted from graceful ellipses, low-relief modelling, and delicate colours. To enter the salon of Osterley Park, Middlesex (1766–73), is to take one's spatial cues as much from the echo of footsteps as from visual evidence; the walls and ceiling, even the floor simply drifts at the edge of one's attention. Their reticent beauty emerges only when we fasten the eye on their surface. The oval reliefs of the ceiling float like clouds, the largest of which is reflected on the floor as if in a pool. The reliefs and pilasters barely interrupt the palest of wall planes. So close are Adam's interiors to the margin of self-effacement that the person with a taste for the resolute might call them insipid. But they are more than just redeemed by the graceful marks of the most demanding hand (Fig. 2.19).

The reticence of Adam was applied at an urban scale in the organization of eighteenth-century London. In 1776, John Gwynn remarked that 'London is ... without the least pretension to magnificence or grandeur.'[34] More like Amsterdam than Paris or Rome, London had no – nor would it ever have – large gestures, royal axes, expressions of imperial or ecclesiastical dominance. A part of this modesty had to do with English politics as well as the difficulty of disengaging large spaces from the tangle of streets; Trafalgar Square with its monument, fountain, and National Gallery, extracted from a group of stables near Charing Cross, are better accoutrements to a spa town than symbols of a heroic national event (Fig. 2.20).

2.18   Dixton Manor, Vale of Evesham, showing partial enclosure. Anon., eighteenth century. Cheltenham Art Gallery

2.19   Robert Adam, Osterley Park, Middlesex. Entrance Hall, ca 1766

2.20   London, aerial perspective, 1851. Bibliothèque Nationale, Paris

2.21   John Nash, Chester Terrace, Regent's Park, London, 1885. One step up, two steps back from the public domain

If English architecture and urbanism verge on the bland by carrying the modesty principle almost too far, the best of it stops well short of denying a place for the individual. Indeed the kind of crankiness and eccentricity that keep on appearing in places like the Lincoln choir vaults, Port Madoc, the Archigram cartoons and topiary gardens are the best demonstration that construction need not be just socially expressive or theoretically correct. But the very exceptionality of examples like these reveals the power of what is sometimes called architectural context but is really architectural essence. If we judge architecture by its *fittingness*, we still refer to the large number of ways employed in ameliorating the intrinsic spoiling effects of raw building upon equilibria pre-existing in nature and social life (Fig. 2.21).

Architecture, in such instances, is a kind of metaphorical salvage operation whose reticences and amusements, elegant postures and transparencies are a symbolic reassurance against the deharmonizing rudeness of pick, shovel, and bulldozer. They reassure the instigator and the occupant, as well as those on the outside, that the empirical facts of change have been symbolically anchored in a prior world whose boundaries, wherever assaulted, demand restoration.

CHAPTER THREE

Self-Interest and Reciprocity

The Urbanism of Self-Interest

So far in this discussion, emphasis has been placed on the role of the human imagination in urbanism, especially on how it orients memory, creativity, and perception towards homage and respect, or to an enchanted, accessible world. We have suggested, too, that this imagination is connected instinctively to moral questions, pursuing, through the way in which urban landscapes are arranged, a return to that integrative state before men and women separated themselves from nature, and from other people, behind constructed boundaries.

But what of that other side to dialectical urbanism we sometimes equate with rationality, which seeks to set down rules and backs away from the fanciful and protean? Is it not also involved, as many now believe, and as Plato and Aristotle would have claimed, with the way in which we relate to the world around? No doubt this is true, as their advocacy of the interdependent life of the *polis* shows; yet they also advocated the *polis* as an instrument of individual fulfilment, each recognizing within himself the legitimacy of personal aspiration. Nowadays, this aspiration seems to have evolved into an irreducible core

of self-interest, even when coming to terms with that amalgam of other self-interests our society prefers to call the public good; but however mediated historically, self-interest constitutes the archetypal second pole of urbanism. It manifests itself, in extreme cases, in the appropriation and closing of urban boundaries, nurturing material gain, power over others, or a predictable inner life by forming territorial divisions that are reinforced, in turn, with impermeable architecture. Ways of life dominated by various forms of self-interest – which is certainly not what Plato or Aristotle had in mind – have their own landscapes, whose expressive meanings range between those of the cities of ancient Sumeria and vast expanses of the modern metropolis. While its antithesis – protean urbanism – by its very character cannot be fitted simply into categories, we encounter fewer difficulties locating the nature of self-interest. Because it manifests itself in the appropriation of material things, whether for their own sake, for purposes of subjugation, or to sustain inwardness in its various forms, its pursuit underlies certain assumptions on which classical and neoclassical economics are based, so we have a ready-made source of knowledge to illuminate this less attractive side of urbanism.

It might be claimed, of course, that wherever self-interest does not primarily seek material gain, then economics is of limited analytical value. In one sense this happens to be true, in that politics and psychology may provide better lessons in what motivates the will to power displayed at Ur, for instance, or the urge we all share to find solitude, and privacy for one's family. My concern, however, rests with how such motives come to be manifested in the urban landscape, and, without exception, they are linked by strategies of territorial appropriation and the construction of impermeable boundaries. These strategies, while varying in detail, are constrained, in the final analysis, by what an economist would call the efficiencies of resource allocation, efficiencies that happen to display a remarkable lack of diversity in their underlying logic, as will become apparent in the following chapters. This logic is here illustrated by referring to a ubiquitous historical condition – namely, the city as a competitive market-place for urbanism's resources, a market-place dominated, in this case, by the activities of landowners and builders.

The pertinent material things the city has to offer are its public resources, land, and the boundaries between them. To a considerable extent – some would say to a complete extent, although it does not matter here – the private wealth that can be gleaned from urban land depends upon the intensity and quality of the public resources serving it. Networks of public spaces in particular, together with the infrastructures they contain, form a primary source of variation in the intensity of abutting construction, and are thus a major source of variation in the character of intervening boundaries (Fig. 3.1). Expressed in very sim-

3.1   Intensity of non-residential development across the New York region. From a 1965 inventory by the Tri-State Transportation Commission

3.2   A street in the centre of Salzburg. Intensive development and strongly defined boundaries

3.3   A view of suburban North York, Metropolitan Toronto. While building height varies, intensity remains low, and boundary definition is ambiguous.

ple terms, wherever these networks are well endowed with infrastructure, as they generally are in central urban locations, self-interest works to ensure that unregulated construction intensity is high and the intervening boundaries strongly defined and articulated (Fig. 3.2). Conversely, peripheral locations, where public resources are usually relatively deficient, tend not to exhibit the tightly packed conditions associated with centrality, so development is generally *extensive* and boundary definition more ambiguous (Fig. 3.3). Of course the private urge to appropriate public resources, land, and boundaries varies not only from location to location but also historically, through temporal changes in the local demand for these things relative to their supply.

A fuller explanation than this will be necessary to understand how self-interest works as a dynamic force acting upon urbanism's history, and one will be offered shortly. For now, it should be clear that this force runs perpendicular to the myth-laden complementarities and metamorphoses described above by imposing upon the city, often through highly selective alliances with other self-interests, hierarchies of exclusive territory. Recall that the character this imposition takes on originates primarily in certain relationships between public space, construction intensity on land, and intervening boundaries, induced by the provision of infrastructure (Fig. 3.4). For simplicity's sake I shall refer to these relationships as *intensive* or *extensive*, and as *mechanical*. They possess, in the first place, a

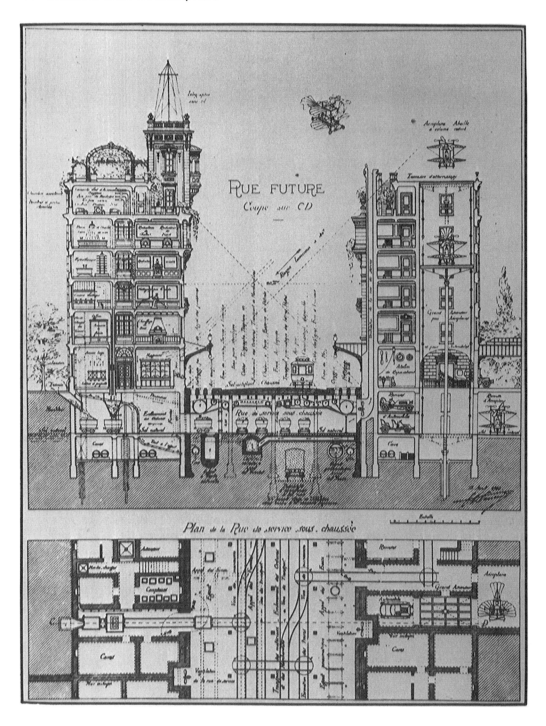

3.4   Eugène Hénard, Street of the Future. From *Études sur les transformations de Paris*, 1903. Intensive mechanical relations induced by infrastructure and characterized by high construction intensity and a clear division between public and private space

3.5 Nineteenth-century housing in Cologne. Street architecture constrained and shaped by intensive mechanical relations

3.6 Philip Johnson, Architect's House, New Canaan, Connecticut, 1941. An architecture that is feasible only where completely disengaged from the site boundaries

quasi-natural character whereby a large part of the condition of urbanism is affected by them. Second, mechanical relationships often usurp local traditions, styles, and myth-laden practices, which enables us to recognize underlying similarities between, to use an intensive example, the *insulae* assemblies of fourth-century Rome and thirteenth-century Florence, as well as their more recent counterparts in industrial Berlin and the 'railroad' tenement districts of New York's Lower East Side. At the other extreme, extensive mechanical relationships work in a more or less recurrent and characteristic fashion on the low intensity of suburban and exurban patterns. In most cases, it will become apparent how architectural invention, far from being an autonomous activity, must take its cues from the ubiquitous imperatives of mechanical relationships (Figs 3.5 and 3.6).

In a sense, then, these relationships constitute the second archetypal force in urban-landscape formation, although there are many occasions when their presence can be revealed only by a kind of exegesis. On these occasions, they work dialectically with inte-

grative and architectural ideas, ancient practices, and statutory controls imposed upon urban boundaries, each affecting the others to produce an outcome often far from predictable and rarely stable. Later on we shall consider, for instance, how this dialectic worked upon the chains of public facilities called *armatures* in Imperial Roman cities, and how similar chains were only half-realized in the face of boundary competition in medieval Italy. We shall see, too, how a dramatic alteration of mechanical relationships from intensive to extensive that was induced by the fifteenth-century demographic decline in Europe, almost by default provided both the opportunity to apply new architectural theories and the softening boundaries necessary to usher in the practices of Renaissance urbanism. Then we shall examine how these relationships have figured more recently, moulding the core and suburbs of eighteenth-century Paris in characteristic ways; and finally, how, by affecting the invention of architectural modernism and its newer variants, they work upon the landscapes of the contemporary metropolis.

The Mechanical City

The pole of self-interest as manifested in urban-landscape formation does not, of course, contain the full range of Hellenic philosophy's discourse on the *polis*. Nevertheless, among other things, that discourse was concerned with the idea of bringing together like-minded men in one place, and structuring the *polis* accordingly. The principle of setting up such closed precincts for a select and privileged few is one point of contact between those ancient conversations and the practice of urbanism. But another aspect of self-interest must be added that was inimical to Greek thought: the subjugation of nature and the city to the cause of material gain. Nowadays we tend to conceive of this phenomenon as the self-interest of private property working against a putative public interest; but our own conception of the public as an aggregation of self-interests is crucially different from the Greek *philopolis*, the *res publica* of Roman civilization, or the *communitas* of medieval and Renaissance cultures: they were all blessed with an instinctive feel for coherence that found its way into ways of life, laws, and city building, often transcending the sum of individual actions and demands. Our amnesia in this respect impoverishes the practice of contemporary urbanism, but it inadvertently provides us with a form of analysis that brings the roots of extreme self-interest to the surface, letting us see the logic that underlies mechanical relations and their effect on urban-boundary formation.

The character of boundaries, as I mentioned above, is conditioned by competition between self-interests for the appropriation of the city's material things, and then articulated according to variation within the networks of public resources we call infrastructure. This articulation depends, in the first instance, on decisions having to do with development intensity, which can be defined for now as the amount of construction allocated to any given unit of land. This definition, it should be pointed out, does not take into account the fact that construction is the consequence of deploying units of capital and labour to land, which in practice are allocated to produce amounts of construction that vary considerably according to its quality (Fig. 3.7). Given that most statutory controls over intensity deal in quantities rather than qualities, the regulation of private development is far from complete, but this matter will be taken up later.

The articulation of urban intensity can be studied in a number of ways, but because our theme concerns the division and subjugation of the landscape for material ends, it would be helpful to consider private development as a kind of commodity, voided of its intrinsic value, and produced, distributed, and consumed according to some simple economic laws. A good place to start would be a consideration of the analogy of manufacturing production.

If we lump together capital and labour in manufacturing as a single production factor, then intensity can be measured by the number of manufactured units produced on each unit of land. Allen Scott has shown that firms engaging in intensive production would tend to locate on land commanding a high (differential) rent, even when a shift to intensification entails an increase in the unit cost of production. In this way Scott helps to explain the incidence of intensity gradients and land-use differentiation in cities.[1]

According to Scott, firms that increase their input of land to produce a fixed number of manufactured commodities would tend to migrate away from an urban centre. Conversely, a decrease in land inputs to produce this fixed number would precipitate a shift *towards* the centre. This continues to occur until land rents adjust to increases or decreases in demand, and the cost advantages of migration become temporarily neutralized. The propensity to migrate is, of course, affected by the assessment of changes in all production and transportation costs; if total costs increase by shifting to a more or less intensive technique, an increase that cannot

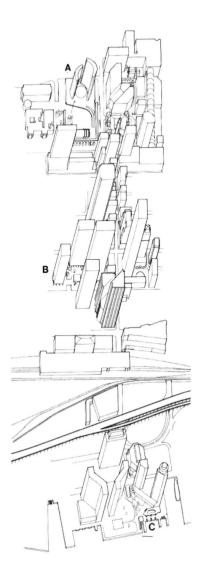

3.7 An administered landscape, downtown Toronto, axonometric of Bay Street. A: New City Hall; B: Bank headquarters; C: Harbour. Many of the boundaries in this intensively developed area are suburban in character. The City Hall, like many institutional buildings, was exempt from market-driven conditions. The bank headquarters were constrained by an evolving system of regulation that began, in the 1960s, by prohibiting the occupancy of site boundaries by construction. Development of the harbour took place on a largely empty (quasi-suburban) terrain, encouraging the construction of a set of detached, free-form structures.

be recouped by raising prices, then in spite of savings in land rent, no shift occurs. However, should total costs decrease by undertaking this shift, then migration might be pronounced and widespread. This would occur, for instance, when public investment in transportation or other facilities alters the pattern of attraction across the region.

Now, if we consider architecture to be a commodity – that is, if buildings are understood to be profit-generating units of accommodation, the production of which is affected by the costs of land, capital, and labour – then firms wishing to build these commodities would also be affected by the conditions of production mentioned above, but with one obvious and crucial difference. Accommodation units are not, like other commodities, transported to the market, but are sold (or rented) *at the place of manufacture*: they are constructed, as it were, in the market-place – the city – and its characteristics tend to monopolize the firm's behaviour. For instance, in being tied to the market-place, given the general relationship between the intensity of production and differential land rent, the amount of capital and labour – the level of intensity – that such firms deploy to each land unit is fixed within certain limits (Fig. 3.8). In principle, the producers of architectural commodities enjoy the same freedom of location within the network of public resources as other producers, because, given the source of variation in land rent, their prices can be adjusted to the buyer's transport costs. However, if the non-land (capital and labour) production costs increase because of the necessity to shift to higher levels of intensification, then these added costs can be recouped with some impunity by price increases only when competitive producers in the same location are also affected by largely fixed levels of intensification. It is thus possible to conceive of a land market of highly differentiated rents which are adjusted over time to enable landowners to appropriate what are called 'excess' development profits, thereby sustaining more or less equal levels of builder's profit throughout the

3.8   Extensive mechanical relations. Intensity levels are fixed, not by regulation, but by the general relationship between production intensity and differential land rent. Boundary formation and everyday life, in this case of a Metropolitan Toronto suburb, become homogenized over a wide area.

market. The migration of development capital within this market occurs through attempts by builders to earn excess profit themselves before rent adjustments are made in the destination area, a migration accompanied by shifts in intensification as capital moves between zones of differential land rent. It follows that, should the builder manage to gain control over a large territory in the destination area, he would have greater chances to control rent adjustments (Fig. 3.9).

Now any change in intensification normally affects the non-land costs of production for each accommodation unit, so that adaptations become necessary either to remain competitive should these costs increase, or to capture excess profit should they decrease.

Consider, for instance, the case of large-scale housing production. Under private mar-

ket conditions, in principle the average rent in a given location would tend to decline as the number of units increases (whether measured as square metres of habitable space or as dwelling units). This change occurs for two reasons: first, there will be an effect of monopolistic competition, perhaps slight, because the demand for units, however high in the location, is eventually limited, so that as supply becomes augmented, the market price (or rent) for those units may tend to decline; second, and more significant, with a fixed input of land, which is the normal condition of development, the *quality* of each unit under varying intensity conditions does not remain constant. Usually, each unit in a relatively intensive development is worth less to the builder. This change in value occurs because of congestion effects on site: each additional

3.9   Scarborough City Centre, Metropolitan Toronto, in the late 1970s. The suburban nucleus of a major single-ownership assembly prior to the onset of 'comprehensive' intensification. Its boundaries were widely drawn to capture internal control over function, built form, and rent.

unit reduces the amenity of the remainder, but also those of nearby competitors, by reducing privacy and daylight, increasing noise levels, reducing exclusive access to site facilities, and so on. Nowadays there are also detrimental symbolic effects that are part of the reduced status associated with living in high-density districts. So, again, the builder's inclination would be to capture and control as large a territory as possible in order to internalize the above externalities as well as realize economies of scale (Figs 3.10 and 3.11).

We should bear in mind that these effects of added density are far from universal or unidirectional. For instance, certain complexities enter the picture that are related to the amenity value of expensive items like underground parking or elevators, whose fixed costs can be more feasibly distributed among relatively large numbers of units. Nevertheless, it is clear that the revenue-generating potential of each commodity unit – the dwelling – changes significantly with variation in the numbers constructed in each production round on a fixed amount of land. Only by enjoying control over very large amounts of land can this condition be alleviated, which sets in motion the propensity to shape the landscape into an effective market-place by stipulating its boundaries; otherwise, even taking account of the complexities referred to above, a downward pressure is exerted upon marginal revenue by each additional unit.

The marginal costs to the builder at first decline steeply with increasing intensity, revealing a dual initial effect of intensification. First, the high initial cost of acquiring serviced land, paying consultants, and seeking approv-

3.10   Stuyvesant Town and Peter Cooper Village, New York City. (Thomas Airviews, courtesy Metropolitan Life Insurance Co.)

als is distributed among a larger number of units; second, certain benefits of joint production and maintenance begin to take effect. Shared party walls, floors, roofs, foundations, access, and various service systems tend to reduce marginal costs at first, although not in a continuous way. Above a certain intensity, however, marginal costs begin to shift upwards, reflecting a relative decline in the advantages of joint production and the onset of certain additional costs associated with dense construction: the need to switch to a more sophisticated structural system; extra costs entailed in lifting materials above grade; perhaps the necessity for high-speed elevators, more robust foundations, additional levels of underground parking, more complex architectural forms – all add to unit cost at the margin (Fig. 3.12).

According to this kind of analysis, for the builder the optimum number of units can be identified by that point where marginal costs equal marginal revenue, an intersection which is also supposed to identify price, although many other factors are usually brought to this decision, among which are public-policy issues related to levels of construction quality, subsidy, and the incidence of regulatory controls. All of this shows the virtual impossibility of considering the dwelling unit as fixed in price, type, and use value quite independently of project and area-wide characteristics. Nor is unit variation attributable only to scale or intensity. Construction costs and unit type and quality can vary substantially with site configuration; architectural form, including height, bulk, and the location of units relative to each other; and a host of off-site activities. This applies as much to non-residential as to residential architecture: for instance, no proper understanding of the economic feasibility of space units in an office building or factory is possible if the pronounced effects of adjacent activities, site configuration, and the whole building are ignored.

In the case of architectural commodities then, more often than not the whole market-

3.11   Toronto Dominion Centre, Toronto

place – the urban landscape – determines the part, which complicates the task of conducting analysis based on economic theory working outwards from a constant unit of production. More pertinent for our story is the fact that commodity producers – the builders – realize that too, which leads them to try to appropriate, shape, and divide, through acquisition, local alliances, and regulatory guarantees, as much of their market-place as possible.

It should be apparent that the migration, land appropriation, and intensification described above are not just modern events; ever since networks of public resources have varied internally to affect rent levels in private land markets, a phenomenon going back at least to Republican Rome, this mechanism has been in place. But the mechanism reaches beyond the simple distribution of building intensities to affect the way in which the market-place is divided up, in other words, the articulation of intervening boundaries.

For instance, urban land division and acquisition generally proceed according to a certain geometrical logic which, particularly

3.12   Housing in Richmond, London. The limits of building technology and organization place limits on levels of intensification and boundary formation.

in high-land-rent locations, works to mini-mize the private costs entailed in accessing networks of public infrastructure. In other words, there exists a tendency for private owners to reduce site frontage on these net-works to no more than would be required for infrastructural access and internal function-ing; in economics parlance this is the tendency to exploit to the point of congestion scarce public goods that are fixed in price. This factor, working in combination with the urge to reduce costs further by engaging in joint production – for instance, by sharing the costs of constructing walls that occupy flanking site boundaries between adjacent owners – leads, in the absence of countervailing public regula-tion, to frontage saturation. Referring back to our theme, this propensity explains those in-stances where intervening boundaries are ap-propriated and walled off at high intensities (Fig. 3.13).

An extreme instance of this propensity is exemplified in those infamous railroad tene-ment districts which, during a period of forty years, beginning in the 1830s, filled large parts of Lower and Midtown Manhattan. From four to six storeys high, the tenement occupied nearly all of a site about eight metres wide from the street line to a narrow rear yard, usually three metres deep, permitting daylight and ventilation to penetrate feebly at the front and back. Widely described and condemned as a primitive artefact of human degradation, the railroad tenement in fact represented the ingenious culmination – or nadir – of an accelerating tendency both in Europe and in the United States to capture the vast housing markets created by the needs of an inmigrant

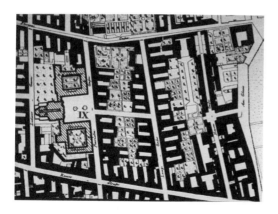

3.13 Vienna, District VIII, 1828. A central location in the process of intensifying by rear lot infill. A continuous street perimeter has already been established by exploiting the narrow lot pattern and joint production of the party walls. The institutional building is exempt from this development logic, and displays a different kind of boundary.

urban poor. In this case, the presence of a large, impoverished market, spatially captive at high densities because of the great intensity of infrastructure and industrial production in Lower Manhattan, enabled builders to devise and propagate the ultimate refinement in low-cost building commodities. For this reason the elements of the railroad tenement are worth close scrutiny; they are the clearest expression we have in recent times of unmediated self-interest shaping the market-place by urban-boundary articulation (Fig. 3.14).

We have noted that normally, with each increase in intensity – that is, for each unit of accommodation or construction capital and labour added to a fixed unit of land – the producer earns a discount until land rents rise to the level at which the discount is almost completely appropriated by the landowner. The amount of the discount earned on added units diminishes as intensity increases beyond the point of increasing returns to scale. Thus, beyond this point, the propensity to add units decreases with each additional level of intensification, a matter which, in a competitive

land market, leads to further adjustments in land rent. With time, districts of homogeneous rent are established, in which development is characterized by relatively fixed amounts of capital per unit of land. In the case of Lower Manhattan, however, the extreme centralization of manufacturing, commerce, and housing attracted by public infrastructures of one kind and another led to the investment of very large amounts of building capital in land and highly intensive mechanical relations. Because the captive demand consisted of largely poor households, residential capital was used to construct large areas of low-quality space whose unit cost continued to decline at the margin while prices did not.

Second, we have noted that where intensity is high, the tendency to congest fixed-cost public infrastructure generates a lot arrangement whereby the amount of land served by a given street frontage can be maximized. This tendency is essentially the urge on the part of producers to earn discounts on frontage costs and fosters the narrow, deep lots and continuous street boundaries that were characteristic of the railroad tenement districts. The original sixteen metre–by–thirty-two metre lots were divided into eight-metre-wide parcels so the tight lot dimensions seriously constrained the internal organization of the tenements. This arrangement, nevertheless, enabled the builder to provide access – although congested – to expensive public infrastructure for large numbers of people at a low, fixed cost to himself. But doing so entailed dividing up his market-place in a certain way, then reinforcing the boundaries by blanketing them in intensive construction (Fig. 3.15).

By contrast, at places on the public-resources network where land rents are relatively low – for example in the hinterland of the perimeter zones – the urge to appropriate boundaries in this way declines. As infrastructure value and price decline with distance from the centre, so do land rents, levels of intensity, and the propensity to saturate frontages, all of which produce landscapes with that characteristic expressive meaning we in-

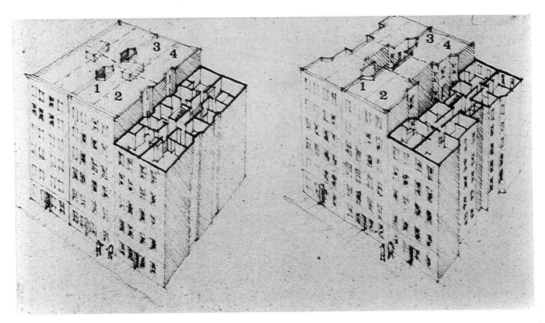

3.14   Old-Law (pre-1890) and New-Law tenements built in New York. Each floor in both types houses four families. The New-Law tenement marks an early shift, in this case induced by regulation, away from contiguous architecture.

stantly recognize as suburban. Moreover, in locations like this, any effects spilling over from one self-interest to the others – such as congestion and various residues of propinquitous life found in high-intensity areas – also decline because extensive mechanical relations leave boundaries largely unoccupied. It is therefore no coincidence that modern public regulation of the urban landscape, in seeking, as the economists would say, to internalize all externalities, has fostered the incidence of suburban mechanical relations, even at the centre, by limiting levels of intensity, prohibiting boundary occupation, and reducing the scarcity of public-resources networks by increasing their supply at the periphery – in other words, encouraging outward migration to a newly serviced hinterland. Urbanism, ways of life and human relatedness, and nature herself are caught up and rearranged in the process.

Essentially, this is the chain of effects whereby architecture and urban boundaries are affected by mechanical relations. As the chain is historically transformed by major changes in the urban land market, which might occur through demographic decline or sustained inmigration, increases in land supply resulting from infrastructural expenditure, the scale of assembly, and the imposition of statutory controls, then we can expect certain consequent architectural transformations to occur along with changes in boundary articulation. It is also the case that the urge to maximize profit in building-commodity production influences not only the intensity of development but also its location. It seems most likely, then, that the producers of architecture do not just 'follow' markets, but are able to attract users to sites where it can be produced relatively cheaply, but only once a large-enough territory has been appropriated, divided, and protected against unwanted external contingencies. It is only a short step from this market-driven condition to the closed boundaries of ancient Sumeria.

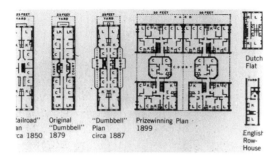

3.15   Comparative tenement plans, New York. Prohibitions against building on site boundaries increased as the century progressed and would eventually stimulate the invention of detached, modernist forms of construction.

The Methodological Inversion

Regard the universe often as one living being, having one substance and one soul; and observe how all things act with one movement; observe too the continuous spinning of the thread and the single texture of the web – Marcus Aurelius[2]

Those instances where the urban dialectic gives way to the self-interest described above are coming to dominate contemporary urban analysis. However, the instincts that seek to partition and appropriate urban territory often confront an entirely different kind of aspiration, which dissolves, if not the empirical manifestations of self-interest evident in boundary formation, then their expressive meanings. I should like to conclude this first part by referring to a particular type of complementarity, one of the more remarkable, if rather wayward, legacies covered in the ensuing chapters. The legacy begins with the idea of double meanings: that, as with the granaries of the Fali, the single edifice can be a cipher of the city; conversely, the single edifice is often symbolized by the whole city. Neither imagination nor practice is inevitably locked into an absolute division between architecture and urbanism but seeks to absorb the one with the other, then at times to ex-

change their expressive meanings. Here we encounter again the place of indeterminacy in the scheme of things where, as with the granaries of the Fali, constructed meanings are not literal and fixed, but binary. Here too we enter a liminal domain to experience the power of the in-between.

In 1919, in his project for a glass skyscraper on Berlin's Friedrichstrasse, Mies van der Rohe exchanged one set of boundaries for another. What seventy years later still looks like an attempt to plough history under by jettisoning every convention known to architecture turns out to be the spectacular reincarnation of an ancient dream. On a triangular site, surrounded by evidence of nineteenth-century bourgeois insularity, Mies located three translucent prisms, loosely connected at the centre to a single shaft of stairs and elevators (Fig. 3.16). Prisms and shaft are serrated in plan, their boundaries everywhere indented to atomize the structure into a thousand pieces; the whole perimeter and interior skeleton Mies reduces to a film, letting us see through his disaggregating act. But proliferation is only half the story; in kaleidoscopic

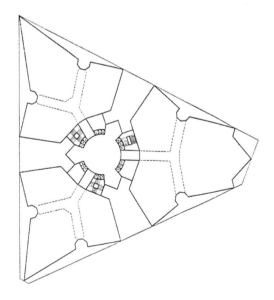

3.16   Mies van der Rohe, plan of a skyscraper on the Friedrichstrasse, 1919

3.17　Mies van der Rohe, model of a glass sky-scraper, 1919

3.18　Sunset Mountain Park, California, 1966. Model

fashion, the translucent splinters are just held together, their planes converging back to the fulcrum, which locks them into coherence. That finite autonomy we instinctively recognize in the idea of the monument is exchanged, on the Friedrichstrasse, for a manifold precariousness reminiscent of whole cities (Fig. 3.17).

Alongside all those social ills that have been read into contemporary architecture, what the best and sometimes the worst of it seem to represent frequently, the protean guise connecting it to history, is that of the *mythical city*, finite, integrated, and whole (Fig. 3.18). Whereas the Gothic cathedral was the city of God on Earth, and the Palladian villa a miniature symbol of *civitas*, the modern building is often a metaphor of a now impossible urban ideal. With modernism, all the elements of historical style that evoke timeless associations with the idea of a *building* – scale, ornament, decoration, pitched roofs, parapets, symmetry, entablatures, classical Orders, pediments, brick and stone – were excluded. The Modern Movement saw that architecture underwent the purging of any specific reference to those elements and conventions of the discrete, recognizable edifice. In its place we often discover the representation, not of the individual but, with the final realization that the empirical metropolis is the sure sign of disintegrating civic consciousness, the *idea* of sociocultural integration (Fig. 3.19).

It can also be said that urbanism, conversely, often carries a subtext which represents a single building. If architecture is often an act of proliferation, a small cipher stretching signification to the scale of the community at large, then does not urbanism sometimes reverse this act, striving to shrink an intractable metropolitan chaos to a symbolic unit, namely that icon of *communitas*, the cohesive architectural work (Figs 3.20 and 3.21)? If so, then between the poles of the single building and its aggregate, the metropolis, stands urbanism, caught up in the contradictions

3.19   Housing complex in Munich, 1975

that assail the confrontation of the part with the whole.

A glance at the fourteenth-century cycle of frescos by Ambrogio Lorenzetti known as *The Effects of Good Government in Town and Country*, from the Sala della Pace of Siena's Palazzo Comunale, will reveal a fascinating type of pictorial integration. He paints an image of Siena set within its subjugate *contado* and filled with detailed evidence of the well-being and industriousness of its inhabitants. Here is a theme so ancient it could be classed as a pictorial archetype. Lorenzetti's fresco, however, is an especially compelling version because it expresses the theme of unity at several levels. First, *nobili* and *popolo* are largely indistinguishable by dress, activity, and gesture. All are elegant, whether engaged in hunting, commerce, dancing, or conversation, and all are echoed by the architectural elegance of their city, a city that is not just a subordinate backdrop to their activities but an integrative construction, a confirmation of a non-hierarchical community (Fig. 3.22). It happens that Lorenzetti's painting was based not on only mythical truths. This was the time of the *mezzadria* – the 'gift economy' arranged between landlord and tenant, in which each would exchange 'acts of reverence, respect, love, protection, gifts and favours'.[3] Here too, for all its lapses, stood a centre of Christian virtue, recorded in acts of charity, the establishment of almshouses, and where, in this city of the Virgin, Simone Martini's picture of the Madonna speaks from the walls of the council chamber against 'the powerful who molest the weak.' Second (and my interpretation here contradicts that of

3.20 J.B. Bakema and J.H. van den Broek. Pampus plan for the extension of Amsterdam, 1964–5

3.21 Pedestrian plan of the new town of Hook, London County Council, 1960

3.22 Ambrogio Lorenzetti, *Good Government* ... (detail), fourteenth century. Palazzo Publico, Siena

3.23 'It is not unpleasant to see a town which looks like one house.' Le Barroux, Vaucluse, France

Denis Cosgrove, who in his keenness to put a material face on things seems to miss the larger point),[4] the city, while we may *think* that it subjugates the countryside, *appears* to be in a state of symbiosis with it. Siena is not represented as a closed-off precinct, but as a crenellated gate thrown open to the sustenance of orchards, pastures, and croplands. Town and countryside each becomes a different yet complementary type of haven, reminiscent of Virgil's complementarities in the *Aeneid* – the mythical birth of a city from the cornucopia of a voluptuous countryside. The nostalgic power springing from Lorenzetti's work also calls to mind John Ruskin's Arcadian dream: 'No scene is continually and untiringly loved but one rich by joyful human labour; smooth in field; fair in garden; full in orchard; trim, sweet and frequent in homestead; ringing with voices of vivid existence.'[5]

But most intriguing of all are the references in Lorenzetti's depiction to the city itself. He spreads an undulation of gables, defensive towers, gateway arches, and fenestration right across the fresco plane, yet these elements are rather difficult to distinguish as separate features, because the manner of their painting causes them to merge together. We are asked to see them not as an assembly of buildings but as a unit – as a kaleidoscopic villa set within a lush garden. One's mind switches accordingly from the idea of a city to that of a house, and back again. Streets and squares lead a double existence as halls and rooms, the foreground paving could be a carpet, the reticulated plane of the city walls for an instant becomes an interior screen or tapestry. We are being shown that Siena is accessible, penetrable, and inviting, a place where the secure harmonies of the household embrace the whole community and countryside. Here one is reminded of Plato's observation that 'it is not unpleasant to see a town which looks like one house'[6] (Fig. 3.23).

This kind of unitary theme, *domus pusilla urbs*, is repeated elsewhere, for instance, in a 1330 depiction attributed to Simone Martini, decorating the Sienese council chamber, showing the towns of Montemassi and Sassoforte. We are reminded that the Roman goddess Vesta 'ruled both the household fire ... and the civic hearth of the city.'[7] The civic hearth was *Mundus*, mysterious and feminine, located at the urban centre, just as the household fire burned as the pivot of domestic life. Pictorial representations of unitary cities go back at least to the fourth century A.D., to the mosaic of Alexandria in the church of St John the Baptist at Gerasa; the city is shown as compact, its forms overlapping so no streets are visible, and high in the centre, its silhouette suggesting a single gabled roof. With the breakdown of security and a unitary social life in the succeeding years, urban cohesiveness was limited to the nostalgic imagination, manifested in depictions of high, bounded cities that looked like houses; the mosaic on the triumphal arch of Santa Maria Maggiore shows Bethlehem and Jerusalem in this way (Fig. 3.24), while a host of paintings, from the fourth-century Consular Diptych of Stilicho to the Gospel Book of Augsburg produced seven centuries later, surround their painted scenes with a protective architectural frame of arches, columns, and pediments.

In antiquity, especially for the Etruscans and Romans, city and house were often symbolically matched part for part; gate was paired with threshold, defensive walls with domestic walls, hearth with hearth, each pair sharing the same protective god. Two-faced Janus, the deity of beginnings and ends, guarded the movement from one place to another, watchful of the passage over private thresholds as well as through city gates and triumphal arches. As for the city, it was accorded still larger, more comprehensive meanings; its founding and location were divinely sanctioned rather than matters of practical expediency. In structure and orientation the city often represented nothing less than the universe itself; but this will not concern us here except to demonstrate how, as Rykwert

tells, the *idea* of such things often transcended their practical purpose.[8] They were the anamnesis that banished the forgetting of origins and of divinely arranged unities.

Later, the Gothic cathedral became the *locus classicus* both of social memory and of the protean switch of building to city. From Florence to York one can witness the inversion of Lorenzetti's depiction of Siena as a dwelling in the form and symbolic content of the cathedral. The hierarchical accumulation of parts, each of which just retains a certain separateness, is what gives these structures their remarkable reference to the Celestial City[9] (Figs 3.25 and 3.26). Every half-detached Canterbury buttress, complete with tiny aedicule gable and spire, can be read as an address in a street of attenuated houses. The great Strasbourg edifice is a city within a city, its fabric penetrable and labyrinthine, its lost bell formation once a veritable carnival of public life. It takes a small imaginative leap to see the triple portico on the West Front at Amiens as three independent gates giving on to a layered cliff of monuments and dwellings. The niche arcades, the tier of aedicules above the portico, and the penetrable double arches in the right-hand tower form an accumulation of planes, lines, and openings whose intricacy rivals that of many a town.

But the cathedral is not a scaled-down city, a toy version of a larger and more intricate reality. The agglomeration of parts seems everywhere organized to express something better than reality, a revelation that illusion is necessary to experience. Victor Hugo gives Claude Frollo, the Archbishop of Notre Dame, the ability to 'read' his cathedral like a hieroglyphic scripture. To him, Notre Dame was a constructed *summa*, charged with meaning down to the last detail. At the same time, for Frollo, the city of God in the centre of Paris was an escape from a world that would remain forever riddled with conflict and imperfections. The appeal of Notre Dame rested on the axiom that mankind is perpetually flawed, so the cathedral was also a constant reminder of human failure, of the eternal abomination that is the secular city. Yet, Paris

3.24 Santa Maria Maggiore, Rome. Triumphal Arch (detail), fifth century

3.25   Bourges Cathedral, West Front, 1195–1265

itself, under Louis IX (1226–70) has been called 'the most perfect city of the Gothic period'[10] for reasons that show how the unitary principles expressed in painting often found their way into city building. The settlement on the Ile-de-la-Cité was itself compact and orderly, its cathedral facing a well-scaled open place – a medieval rarity – the compass of its wall short and embellished with gates and turrets. For a while, the whole city was formed like a house, an inversion of the urban metaphor of Frollo's cathedral at its centre.

In this sense, Paris and the Gothic cathedral herald the Renaissance utopia, although their purpose was not to transform the tangible world, but to demonstrate again that experience is not shackled by space and time. In an ambitious post-Enlightenment world, utopian thought, through a misreading of the purpose of these old symbols, would reach well beyond metaphor to a failed material realization, in an effort to change empirical life (Fig. 3.27). But neither the failures nor the half-successes of this continuing enterprise can dispense entirely with the single constant of aspirational representation.

An ability such as Frollo's has atrophied, no doubt, with the rise of the printed word. His stupendous memory was kept busy by reading at least two meanings from every bit of his constructed world. But the printed word, or the very intellectuality that it fostered, seems to have given a new if redirected impetus to the city-villa theme, lasting well into the Renais-

3.26 Florence Cathedral, West Front

sance and beyond. Wolfgang Braunfels, referring to the sixteenth- and seventeenth-century depictions of German Imperial cities, notes how 'each city wanted to present itself as complete, clearly defined architecturally, finished, secure, pious and serene'[11] (Fig. 3.28). Hans Wurm's 1520 drawing of Nuremberg is that of a festive house, its gate a welcoming threshold to the traveller, while Mattheus Merian drew Colmar as he drew so may other towns: as a jewel, its ramparts a faceted boundary between encompassing wilderness and the domestic haven of the city.

For Palladio and Alberti, society and architecture were not only coherent systems, but also, in a certain sense, interchangeable. It was not a matter of simple substitution, whereby

the wishful harmonies of social structure could be read directly from their architectural counterparts; or even that the principles around which society and architecture were then organized, being allegedly immutable and divine, were also isomorphic. Their interchangeability was more subtle and indirect, requiring the transformation of each into their common metaphor, namely, the city (Fig. 3.29).

The Renaissance was both blessed and plagued by the unity of the mythical and the empirical world, whereby imperfection was considered aberrant, a spoiling of the natural order of things. The ruins of Tivoli *were* the elegiac, Arcadian past, and the melancholy they evoked was at the fall from social grace,

3.27   Cumbernauld New Town, Scotland

as well as from architectural perfection. In fifteenth-century Florence, science and social organization were also works of art, capable of being placed before the mind's eye and judged for their mutual elegance, not by recourse to some assumed dialectic of culture and nature, but instinctively, from assurance of the ubiquitous presence of metaphors. *Domus pusilla urbs* – the house as city – meant, to Alberti, the identification of family and community, as well as the relational similarity of the isolated structure and the constructed town. The family, its *padrone*, the servants and retainers, guests and incumbents, were arranged hierarchically, and their various activities deployed accordingly. In like manner the community had its coherent structure, its parts differentiated and ranked, but coherent nevertheless. The household and society were each matchless and occupied equivalent forms. There were no shared essences, only striking resemblances.

'La città una casa grande, la casa una città piccola.' If the city was a big house, the house a little city, as Palladio imagined, it was the similar relationship of part to part that mattered, so that the one instantly conveyed the idea of the other. Family, society, house, city – all passed through the mind when contemplating any one of these protean images. So the architecture and unbuilt utopias of the Renaissance served as commentary and critique of a society that failed to aspire to

perfection. Sforzinda is the expression of a lost architectural and social ideal, not of some future utopian happiness, but of the recollection and possibility of a past one (Figs 3.30 and 3.31). Utopias were always urban, so More, Bacon, and Campanella were engaged in mythical recollection more than in prophecy. Merely exercises of the mind, not at all like the medieval bastides, which were pragmatic and had a political purpose, the Renaissance utopias reincarnated classical structures of the impeccable life that once was led. None was really meant to be built, the time in any case being inopportune for large projects, but cultural invention was propelled, as usual, quite independently of economic and demographic stagnation.

The purpose of all this illusion was therefore not to substitute for practical achievement. Art itself extended experience, if at times it diverted experience from its proper course. Consider the presence of the *Wunschtraum* in the architecture of the sixteenth-century Veneto villa. The decline of maritime Venice following the fall of Constantinople in 1453 and the discovery of the New World precipitated a shift to an agricultural economy over which the Venetian aristocracy presided. Between 1540 and 1600, some two thousand estates were developed in the Veneto by the old urban nobility, who used public money in a vast pioneering venture for canals, drainage, land reclamation, and road building. But the lands were settled and the villas constructed according to a nostalgic formula, whereby each estate was made into a utopia of the privileged. The *Wunschtraum* was historical immutability in the Veneto and elsewhere (Fig. 3.32): the eternal stability and dominance of the patriarchal family, separated in the countryside from a world of disappointment and conflict.

Architecture often had a social basis, society an architectural basis, although the architecture of the Veneto villa was not quite a metaphor of society but a confirmation of the preclassical principle that governs life; it predated the contemporary aberrations by reach-

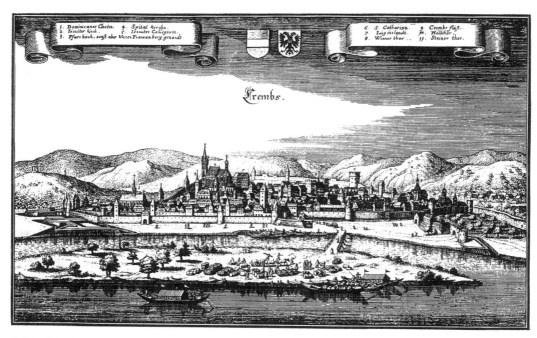

1. Dominicaner Closter. 4. Spital kirche.   6. S. Catharinæ. 9. Crembs fluß.
2. Iesuiter kirch.   5. Iesuiter Collegium.   7. Luginslande.   10. Mallthor.
3. Pfars kirch, sonst aber Vnser Frawen berg genandt 8. Wiener thor. 11. Steiner thor.

Crembs.

3.28   Mattheus Merian, View of Krems, 1649

3.29   Gentile da Fabriano, *Adoration of the Magi* (detail). Uffizi, Florence

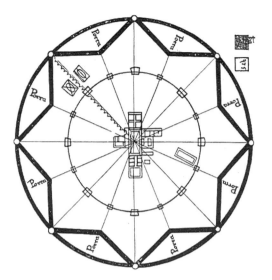

3.30   Plan of Sforzinda by Filarete, from the 1465 treatise

ing back through time, imposing and reimposing its mythical order on bestial reality. The hierarchy of the estate, therefore, represented both family and microcosmic state, while in the villa's architecture we can discern the classical city. During his Italian journey, Goethe was to sense the ubiquitous power of antiquity at the heart of these Veneto utopias: 'The wind drifting past the ancestral graves arrives full of a fragrance, as though passing over a hillside of roses.'[12] Nostalgia, classicism, tragedy, melancholy are close

cousins in the family of protean architectural symbolism, occupying a single indivisible stem whose roots are bedded in analogues.

Family Contradictions

In a sense, the interchange of city and household in depiction and urbanism is an embodiment through the ages of wishful thinking, although none the less valid for that. Lorenzetti, the Etruscans, the Modernists are players in a game reaching into many corners of reflective and everyday life. The pairing of antitheses, Hannah Arendt reminds us, has remained a powerful constant in philosophical history since Plato's analogy of life spent in a cave, which reversed the Homeric Hades to demonstrate how the security of a stone roof also shuts out man's view of the sky.[13]

Plato's analogy shows, by contrast, that the reversal game is often not harmless, and that while the juxtaposition of city and family may bring out a host of complementarities, the pair does have its antithetical side, creating a now familiar problem-strewn path through the history of urbanism. If, for the Etruscans, the familial order could be properly extended to the scale of the community, an entirely different position emerged in the Hellenic world, where *polis* and household were not only antagonists but, according to more than one Greek idealist, thoroughly irreconcilable. In his masterly treatise, written a century ago,

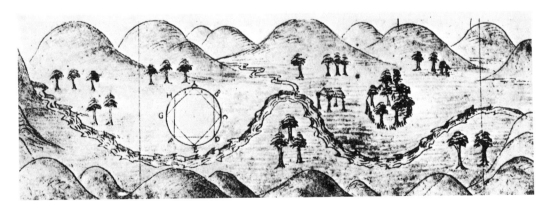

3.31   View of Sforzinda, from Filarete's treatise, 1465

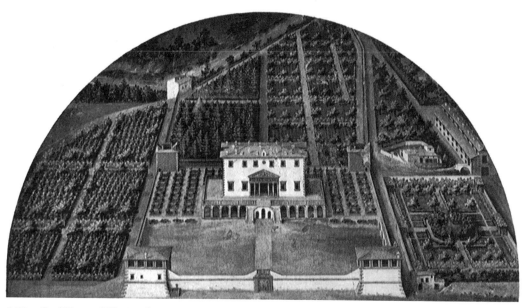

3.32   G. d'Utens, Villa Medici at Poggio a Caiano. Topographical Museum, Florence

Fustel de Coulanges's commentary on the ancient city turns out to be a prediction about the woes of the metropolis in the final years of the twentieth century: 'the same religion formed the ancient family organization and the ancient city state, but they were in reality two antagonistic forms of government ... Either the city could not last, or it must in course of time break up the family.'[14] The Greeks were able to stave off the disintegration of one or the other by proclaiming separate realms and never confusing that which belonged to the *polis* with the household realm, although in all matters the *polis* was considered superior to the family. The latter's purpose was to provide life's basic necessities, whereas the good life, which culminated in the politics of the agora, bred a fine contempt for material and family concerns alike. The good life, of course, was aspired to more than attained; we shall see in the next chapter that the everyday momentum required a mediating domain between household and city. Nevertheless, to a Greek, while the *paterfamilias* maintained his authority through tyranny, the affairs of the *polis* depended on persuasion. This belief,

watered down somewhat, passed along to Rome where, though the family was more esteemed than in Greece, both Augustus and Tiberius still refused the title of *dominus*.[15]

Nevertheless, the recurrence through history of a massive ambivalence regarding the respective merits of household and city seems to make few inroads into the frequency of reversed symbolic representation, with the possible exception of ancient Greece. There is no contradiction between Plato's observation that a city should *look* like a house and his assertion in the *Republic* that private property ought to be abolished as inimical to the human affairs of the *polis*. To him the house *qua* architecture, like that constructed by Hephaestus on Olympus, represented more than the family members contained therein, namely, the inhabitant as a political individual. In ancient Greek law (not followed everywhere), no two buildings were permitted to touch, which left each perimeter wall unadulterated and proclaimed the cipher of individuality;[16] the very word *polis*, like the Latin *urbs*, has its root in the term for *ring-wall*, so Plato's remark could have more to do with his penchant for unadulterated forms than any thought of imposing household references on the city. Alternatively, Greek public life simultaneously nurtured individuality and *phronesis* – the admired attributes of citizenship and civic virtue. The architecture of the house applied to the *polis* possibly displayed this rather more complex double meaning in the philosopher's mind. Even so, perhaps because the very existence of the *polis* severed ties of blood to foster what Aristotle called 'the sharing of words and deeds' through civic consciousness, there is little evidence that Plato's single reference actually found its way into construction, whether by intentional or unconscious symbolism. Given the Greek propensity, evident as late as the building of Pergamum, in the third century B.C., to structure cities in recognition of distant elements in the landscape around, whatever symbolic power an internal element like the house possessed does not reveal itself to us through Hellenic urbanism.

The medieval world presents an entirely different story, although one that often has been misapplied by three generations of modern urbanists caught up in the seductive nostalgia of community-based humanism as an antidote to metropolitanization. Our common error lies in regarding the constructed city, with its myriad forms and symbols, as completely derivative of observable social events and relationships. The interplay and limitations of technique, the dialectic set in motion by mechanical relationships operating through attributes of urban land and infrastructure, and finally the mysteries of artistic impulse, make a mockery of exclusively social analysis. In considering the medieval city, while it is as crucial to recall the destructive tendencies inherent in divided social loyalties manifested in the troublesome boundaries of medieval Genoa, Florence, and Siena as to admire what is often called a perfect model and container of *Gemeinschaft*, neither tells the whole story. There remains a large residue of medieval Christian imagination that 'modelled all relationships on the example of the

household,'[17] an imagination sometimes expressed and confirmed through thirteenth- and fourteenth-century urbanism. At the same time, it has to be recognized how this same confirmation depended as much on the coincidence – not always felicitous – of factors that were quite remote from city-household ideals, including the techniques of circumvallation and settlement intensity (Fig. 3.33). This complexity will be brought to the surface in chapter 6 by examining the remarkable case of Siena, not as depicted wishfully by Lorenzetti in 1340 but its actual structure in the Middle Ages.

This and other cases of reciprocal urban and household boundaries have expressive meanings that still invade the senses, even though their process and context require a kind of exegesis. Europe's Dark Ages produced countless cities of the mind, whereby a powerful urge for sanctity, refuge, and escape from a tumultuous world is apparent in the closed, familial patterns that dotted the landscape. The reality behind Lorenzetti's Sienese fresco will show how the will to stretch domesticity to an urban scale must eventually come to terms with self-interest. By the twentieth century, the city-household theme becomes wayward, scarred, as we shall see, by technical metaphors, the subversion of expressive meanings by an intellectualized urbanism, and the retreat into family life.

Boundary inversion, the reciprocity of city and household, nevertheless, remains urbanism's most powerful manifestation of the protean, of the universal wish to render visible those cherished transitional states that shape the passage through life. To enter such a state always brought a sacred moment, epiphanous, and a confirmation, too, of regeneration, of a *regressus ad uterum*. Everywhere the passage occurred in a particular place amid the symbols of transition, the protean icons, the threshold zones stamped with the initiand's own twofold plight, registering his or her state of metamorphosis (Fig. 3.34). Arnold van Gennep gave the name *liminal* to this state, recognizing how securely it was

3.33   View of Rothenburg-ob-der-Tauber

3.34   Monastery of St John, Patmos

anchored in history, its power to reorient life's passage, and the vital character of its in-between symbols.[18] His work has been taken up by the therapeutic professions, a sign that liminality's ancient healing powers no longer penetrate ways of life, and that the ritual landscape is finally in shreds.

Only the occasional protean shape remains of what once was a ubiquitous boundary condition, one that signalled the place of transition from one mode of being to another and took on 'the form of reversals, negations, disguises, inversions'[19] as a counterpoint to the fixed centres of orientation in the city (Figs 3.35 and 3.36). The expressive meanings that once saturated architecture and urbanism

through and through lie in fragments, but it takes a therapist, Robert L. Moore, to show us the magnitude of the loss: 'A *sign* is asked, to put an end to the tension and anxiety caused by relativity and dislocation ... The recognition of and respect for the boundary, then, is the most fundamental affirmation in praxis of the reality and importance of the heterogeneity of space in human life ... Without it, there would be no access to the powers of creativity and renewal, no access to the primordial patterns that are the source of all correct order, no access to a transhistorical centre which can give orientation and structure in a time of deterioration and impending chaos.'[20]

3.35   A liminal zone in Landshut, Bavaria

3.36   Osgoode Hall, Toronto

PART TWO

Urban Boundaries in Practice

CHAPTER FOUR

Cities in a God-Filled Landscape

Could it be that wisdom appears on earth as a raven, inspired by a little whiff of carrion – Friedrich Nietzsche[1]

The Crucible of Deconstruction

Literalness, applying single, unambiguous meanings to things, is a recent human trait. 'As emotions were the first motives that induced man to speak, his first utterances were tropes. Figurative language was the first to be born. At the beginning only poetry was spoken.'[2]

Before the first temple, gods were worshipped outdoors in the fields and sacred groves. For the Greeks, their deities lived *in* nature, in rocks and trees, the earth itself. Pliny tells us that trees were the first temples,[3] homage being paid to 'the oak of Zeus, the myrtle of Aphrodite, the laurel of Apollo.'[4] Each tree was not only sacred, but assumed to portray the god it represented. Later, Praxiteles' great lost statues of Aphrodite were thought of as sacred trees, thereby returning

what had been taken from nature to its source.[5]

George Hersey, echoing Joseph Rykwert's observation that 'in the ancient world everything means itself and something else as well,' reveals the brutal savagery which gave birth to architectural and decorative convention. An altar was the scene of sacrifice and bloodletting, its precincts a hoard of skulls, teeth, bones, and skins. All the paraphernalia of ritualized death – the garlands, votive tablets, masks, spears, knives, drums, and cymbals – were slung from branches and arranged before the sacred table.[6] The remains of victims were usually reassembled, cloaked in skins, fire-bleached and preserved, thereby reconstructing what had been dismembered by the sacrificial act. This bringing back to life, a returning to some previous whole state, saturated ritual through and through in the an-

4.1   Treasury of the Athenians, Delphi, ca 500–485 B.C.

cient world. The recycling of life and death was god-given, proof of time's reversibility and the staving-off of oblivion.[7]

Hersey shows how this blood-soaked landscape eventually became transformed into the conventions and refinements of classical architecture. By the use of tropes, a severed thighbone is a triglyph, a vertebra becomes an echinus, a skewer an obelisk, a spear shaft a column flute, a bone an apophysis[8] (Fig. 4.1). The human body, its vestments, and the movements of dance and revelry accompanying these events in the altared grove also became part of the architectural corpus: a foot was a column base, but also could be troped into a

stepping, rhythmic movement; and a head or headdress became a capital, from which the head garlands, hair, and horns of Ionic and Corinthian capitals were probably eventually derived.[9] From the first, fixed and stable things rooted to the spot by stone foundations could also, in the imagination, shift across the landscape (Fig. 4.2).

Consider the parallels between architecture and the characters in the famous archaic tales. Heroes and gods moved rapidly through space and time, alert to distant events and, above all, wily in their ways. Odysseus prevailed by craftiness, while the *Iliad* (Book XVIII) speaks of Apollo's nimble feet and the

4.2   Temple of Poseidon, Paestum, ca 560 B.C.

silver feet of Thetis. 'Wind-swift' Iris had 'whirlwind feet,' and Achilles was the Great Runner. But remember, too, the god Hephaestus, that master articifer and architect of Olympus who built houses for the pantheon on their mountaintop, forging his own dwelling from imperishable bronze so that it shone like a star. His name was Crooked Foot – lame, a deformed giant sweating over his bellows, rejected by his mother, Hera, wife of Zeus. Yet Homer's 'hairy beast' was more truly godlike than the rest, reaching beyond his immobility to fashion things that were 'brighter than blazing fire.' Hephaestus adorned his masterpiece, the shield executed for Achilles, with brilliant kinetic scenes: 'a dancing-floor like the one that Daedalus designed in the spacious town of Knossus,' wheeling constellations, a city filled with youths 'whirling in the dance,' and a second lovely town, defended by Ares and Pallas Athena, 'big and beautiful as gods should be' on their 'high-stepping horses.'

The savage meanings seem lost today in contemplating the sublimity of these once volatile, often murderous symbols. Indeed, if such meanings still clung to Greek architecture, it could hardly have been reincarnated again and again through millennia. What, then, appeals to us? Certainly our admiration for – indeed our continuing dependence upon – Hellenic civilization has something to do with it. Where else can we turn for such a cogent metaphor of the foundation of Western civilization – of what we prefer to call embodied rationality? But the *idea* of the Greek temple was fully developed long before Socrates and Plato came along. This idea was too fluid and restless to be termed classical, and does not sit well with our present understanding of reason.

On closer examination the rationality that supposedly changed these accoutrements of death into the apogee of harmonic grace is itself suspect. By the time of Pythagoras the old practical ways of Ionian science had been superseded by an abhorrence of manual labour, considered fit only for slaves and women. Rationality then often meant an effete and gentlemanly pursuit, tantamount to tracing abstract figures in the sand. The great technical progress of the sixth and fifth centuries had been displaced by sophistry; men like Solon, who 'invested the crafts with honour' and passed a law, according to Plutarch, 'that a son need not support his father in old age unless the father had taught him a trade,' were no longer revered. Nor were the old engineers, men like Anacharsis the Scythian, inventor of the bellows and the potter's wheel, or Theodorus of Samos, credited with all kinds of inventions, including the casting of bronze, the key, the lathe, the level, and the square.

This new indifference to practical things is epitomized in Plato, who denied that a human could originate anything; instead, the carpenter could make a bed only after contemplation of God's Idea of the bed (*Republic* x, 597), and so timeless Ideas, Truth and Beauty, established a new and problem-strewn path through religious and intellectual history. For the first time, those who *used* a thing were superior to whoever had *made* it, supposedly having true knowledge of its interior essence. Consumerism (and deconstructivism) had an early start.

Rationality, ever since, has been associated with those abilities so admired by Plato: the contemplation of perfection, of the abstractions that supposedly underlie the perceived chaos of life. Yet, however indispensable such abilities undoubtedly are, they seem alien to the half-mysterious and dynamic impulses that raise buildings and whole cities. By the time of Plato, architecture, we are told, had already succumbed to a decline in practical vigour, scarred by the repetitive nuances and niceties of intellectualism.

But, as with much urban history, we have tended to read what scholars wrote into construction, thereby denying much place for architectural ideas to take precedence over social ideas. True, the Hellenic world was collapsing by the fourth century. Aristophanes, in 392 B.C., would trash the corruption of the Athens congress in *Ecclesiazusae*. But the Oresteian Trilogy was still played and received with great passion, not because nostalgia brought on by the loss of the old ways

was setting in, but because Aeschylus had captured, in a way that Plato never could, the permanencies associated with life and death, which happened to be far more compelling than what we find in the *Laws*. Nevertheless the planned life of idleness the latter espouses, whereby the future is subject to deliberate choices, is one of Plato's more unfortunate legacies to us: 'We have now made excellent arrangements to free our citizens from the necessity of manual work; the business of the arts and crafts has been passed on to others; agriculture has been handed over to slaves on condition of their granting us a sufficient return to live in a fit and seemly fashion; how now shall we organize our lives?'[10]

Here, in a nutshell, the philosopher had already spelled out a formula for twentieth-century urbanism. The penchant for organization remains integral to the good life, and indeed becomes its unreflective surrogate. But wherever the king casts his net, or hews his *polis* out of stone, the boundaries of the city encounter human restlessness. Aeschylus's theme, like that of the *Iliad*, of epic conflict, tragedy, and final reconciliation, still occupied the centre of human experience and echoed the blood rites of the early temple groves. Everyday life, down through the Hellenistic period to Imperial Rome, was guided by the same aspiration: how to come to terms with fear and death. In the last scenes of the *Eumenides*, the final play of his great trilogy, Aeschylus fulfils this aspiration; the wisdom of Athena's ancient court, the Areopagus, solves the deepest moral problems by acquitting Orestes and embracing the ancient enemies of the *polis*.

Aeschylus's reconciliation is a theme so powerful in Greek life that it spreads out from the playwright's narrative to permeate the organization of the Hellenistic landscape itself. Indeed, the very construction of the Greek theatre, which was always set high, with an unobtrusive proscenium to permit vistas to the distant horizon, incorporated the landscape itself into the narrative enacted on stage (Fig. 4.3). Vincent Scully shows how this incorporation was especially a feature of the

4.3   Theatre at Delphi, fourth century B.C.

later Hellenistic theatres, at Megalopolis, Pergamum, and Ephesus. The theatre at Priene is tipped forward high over the Maeander valley, and oriented towards the sacred hills and tumuli set beyond the river; forming axes with the landscape in this way was done not to provide a pretty backdrop, but to rejoin the human drama to its sacred crucible in nature[11] (Fig. 4.4).

To the Greeks, the landscape had a narrative of its own, one eulogized in the old Homeric Hymns: 'well-founded Earth, mother of all, eldest of all beings.'[12] This narrative connected to the chthonian powers who ruled the fate of Agamemnon in Aeschylus's first Oresteian play. His spectacle, when performed in the high-set theatre, ricocheted between the spoken word and the symbolism of the encompassing frame of rock and water. As in the play, the gods are placated by embracing nature, and flourish side by side with the inhabitants of the *polis*:

Come, enter this dear earth, there to repel
Harm from our homes and borders,
And bring us wealth and glory.
Sons of the Rock of Athens, lead their way,
Welcome those Residents within your walls;
They come to bless our city;
Let our good-will reward them.[13]

Ancient architecture, the founding and layout of cities, had as much to do with such instincts as with what we choose to call reason. In the most profound sense, to disturb the landscape by the rude act of construction was to brutalize what one most feared. Reconciliation by articulating and dissolving the boundaries of the landscape became a primary *purpose* of architecture and city planning, the means of 'identification of the self and of reverence for that which is outside the self.'[14] The temple and the city could not be contemplated outside a context so saturated with meanings that they were the point of

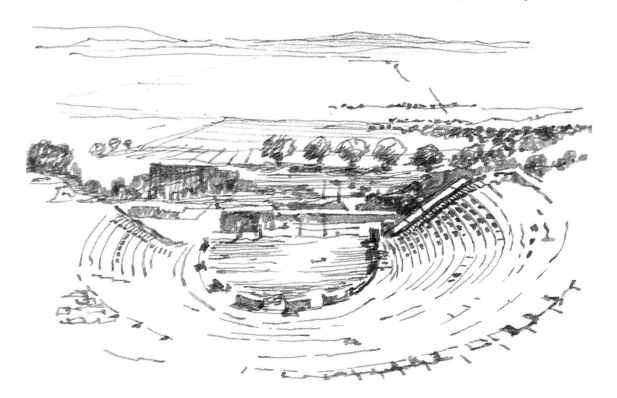

4.4   Theatre at Priene, fourth century B.C.

departure for the placing, orientation, and shaping of construction (Fig. 4.5). 'A profound repetition, at once the echo of ancient traditions and the syntax of a new art, informs the whole ... and which, by the classic period, produce an unmatched dialogue between oneness and separateness, men and nature, men and the facts of life, men and the gods.'[15]

Hellenistic Functionalism

But to trace city building to a single impetus does little justice to those who schemed, sweated, and marvelled at what they had done; even tyrants and whoever served them could be blessed and plagued with the usual human complications. In ancient Greece too, the primeval was more than touched by reflectiveness, but also by self-glorification and practical incompetence at times. The theme running through Roland Martin's great work on Greek planning stresses what he sees as a hard-nosed practicality that builders brought to bear in colonizing the Mediterranean.[16] His evidence is those early signs of regularity to be found even in certain primitive and archaic towns – in preclassical Miletus, Emporion, and Bayraki (Smyrna). As early as the seventh

4.5   The Tholos at Delphi, ca 390 B.C.

century B.C., agriculturally based colonies in the West display regular plans and are defined by axes and divided by rectangular boundaries. 'Theoretical and practical conditions ... determined the essential character of Greek planning – its functionalism.'[17]

The evidence for functionalism, particularly after the fifth century B.C., seems at first compelling. Ionian science was indeed based on the detached observation of nature, apparently pushing reverence aside in the pursuit of categorization, the subdivision of knowledge into analytical parts. Then there is the case of Miletus, home to Anaximander, a great archaic city spearheading the colonization of the Black Sea before its destruction by the Persians in 494 B.C. Its physical organization as well as the energy expended on re-establishment after the Athenian liberation of 479 B.C. is, without question, remarkable. Following the ruined axes of the old town, new Miletus seems modelled on some truly modern ideas of urban order and efficiency. Three residential quarters are divided orthogonally, aligned in unison and deployed around a central district of markets and public facilities occupying the low ground adjacent to the twin harbours of the peninsula (Fig. 4.6). A city for ten thousand, probably entirely preconceived and seemingly arranged according to principles that would now be called zoning, seems to embody the triumph of reason over instinct. Yet the modern analysis of old forms runs into trouble when original content remains half-perceived. Why should the subdivision of territory by orthogonal geometry and function be a rational conception, devoid of spiritual motivation or significance?

Such questions raise the spectre of an unlikely division between Greek reason and Greek practicality, because, just along the Anatolian shore, at Priene, the same Miletan principles must have presented all kinds of practical difficulties. This curious site, difficult to defend, rises through a thousand metres of altitude from Maeander plain to acropolis, causing Pierre Lavedan to remark on the gross incommodity of imposing a modular grid on steeply sloping terrain.[18]

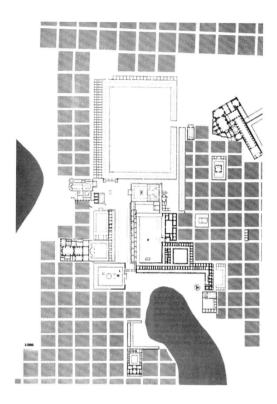

4.6   Plan of Miletus, fourth to second century B.C.

Every north-south street becomes a staircase, angled at forty-five degrees in places to peter out against the cliff dividing the walled site in half. The sanctuary of Demeter on the acropolis, isolated in a high northern corner, remains inaccessible, and the gridded incline below leaves little buildable room for housing (Fig. 4.7). Yet five thousand souls inhabited Priene when Alexander consecrated Athena's temple there in the middle of the fourth century B.C. Is it likely that the planners were simply maladroit, despite evidence that the site was probably occupied for more than a century? Priene had its problems, perhaps most evident in winter when the streets turned into cataracts, sluicing mud from the mountain slopes above. But the Hellenistic mind never equated the practical life just with technical things; function and geometry were admired even by Pythagoras as part of the character of nature, and imbued with mythic significance. The Prienean grid, like those of Rhodes, Paestum,

4.7   Model of Priene, fourth century B.C.

Ionian science, detached from all subjectivity and ritual. As a 'specialist in celestial phenomena' he probably called on the gods for inspiration and interpretation more than once, and from Aristotle (*Politics* 1267b) we learn of Hippodamus's dandified, eccentric ways. Would such a man 'invent' rational planning? Or have we wrongly identified, from a distance of more than two millennia, the possible culmination of myth-laden practice at Miletus as the first signs of modern planning reason?

Given the sustained passion with which the Greeks faced nature, it would be a mistake to conceive of Hippodamus's city grid at Miletus as evidence of a waxing empiricism in Hellenistic urbanism. Everywhere the grid boundaries confirmed the sense of being embraced by the landscape, carrying the eye beyond the confines of the street to the revered forests, outcrops, and hills shaped in the image of the deities. The landscape preceded the *polis*, and was still holier than the temple, which was often oriented towards the sunrise on the feast day of the god receiving the dedication. Elsewhere, as at Delphi, or Bassae, the shape of the terrain dictated placement, thereby resolving 'the tension between terrestrial and celestial mandates.'[20]

Permeable Boundaries

'Ancient history began with the foundation of the city, because everything prior to that was of no interest.'[21] Fustel de Coulanges recognized the equivalence once given to such founding acts and the Creation. The rites accompanying the birth of Etruscan towns were codified in *Libri Rituales*, fixing both ceremonial action and the shape of the settlement. Building, like all technology, was more an interference in the natural order than a scientific application, requiring ritual acts of atonement, purification, and divination.[22] Only a hero could found a city, the site being a gift of god, and, as in Rome, the hero-founder had to be buried in the very heart of the settlement which in turn, according to Dorieus of Sparta, must harmonize with the structure of the universe.[23]

Heraclea, and so many earlier towns, was oriented to the cardinal points, flexed *over* the terrain in the manner of the streets in Miletus itself, and aligned towards divine features of the mountain and river plain.

The shadowy figure of Hippodamus, alive in the fifth century B.C., has been called – but only by our contemporaries making much of a hint from Aristotle – the founder of the so-called orthogonal, functional school; but grid-like planning and the spatial adjacency of agora, market, and temple were a part of archaic practice centuries before new Miletus. Strabo (XIV, 654) informs us that Hippodamus first worked on the plan for Peraeus, although in what capacity we cannot tell, despite the agora named after him in that city. The same chronicler mentions Hippodamus in connection with the planning of Thurii and Rhodes, but while he probably worked on new Miletus, we cannot be certain.[19] Nor can we vouch for his alleged credentials as a man of

Laying out the Etruscan city itself was also an occasion governed by divine sanction, as Rykwert tells us. Boundaries were marked by the plough, care being taken to cast the earth inside the furrow. At the centre – the *mundus* – a hole was dug and filled with offerings. Vesta's sacred role was fitting and telling: she 'ruled both the household fire ... and the civic hearth of the city,'[24] revealing an early interchangeability of symbols between family and community which would become a dominant theme in city planning down to the present time.

These inaugural acts, setting up and dissolving boundaries, connecting the city to the cosmos, to the microcosmic household, and to its own history, were simultaneously accompanied by their opposite – by rites of destruction.[25] In Etruria, as in Greece, the passage of time always meant two things: transformation and the return to a prior state. The foundation of a city, while divinely sanctioned, was also the desecration of a pre-existing harmony, one requiring ceremonial apology and a showing of mortal acquiescence.

So, from the first, certain cities exhibit reticence, modulation, self-effacement, paying homage to the landscape by *mimesis*, camouflage, or shrinking from sight. Eleusis, the scene of the old mystery rites of Demeter and her daughter Persephone, Mother Earth and queen of the lower world respectively, was a hidden city, buried in a fold of the land. Thebes and Knossus were similarly cached, eschewing prominence in the landscape. Even the Mycenaeans, whose aggressions forced them to the heights above the Argos plain, fixed their megara to the site according to the direction of sanctified features around. In Crete, both Knossos and Phaistos are set within and oriented with respect to striking landforms once considered holy: horizon features resembling horns, cones, breasts, the female cleft. Scully notes too how the propylaia of Knossus faced the axis towards the horned mountain Jouctas, home of the shrine of the Cretan goddess[26] (Fig. 4.8).

As for the buildings themselves, architecture seems to originate in the same acts of atonement and self-effacement. Recent evidence of urbanization in the Early Helladic period at Tiryns and Aegina v reveals, not the primitive hut, but apsidal megara rounded to the shape of the Earth goddess.[27] Even earlier, the Egyptian temples were an interior landscape, representing nothing less than the whole sacred land of Egypt that lay outside their walls and colonnaded spaces. The columns were always vegetal: palm, lotus, papyrus; the ceiling, painted blue, crossed by stars and the solar disk, was the sky. The floor was inclined to a point symbolizing the primeval hill emerging from the 'chaotic mud of uncreation.'[28]

This reflexive, preconscious urge to mediate the raw consequences of building, to deflect attention from the rudimentary spoiling of places, was not limited to the Mediterranean. W.R. Lethaby spent half a lifetime documenting the pervasiveness of reverse symbolism in early building. If the ceiling of the Egyptian temple represented the sky, then the sky was also the ceiling of the universal dwelling. There were World Trees, World Houses, World Domes; floors were fields or, occasionally, the sea, and the domestic hearth could be the centre of the world.[29]

If the crucible of architecture lies in what Rykwert calls 'the irreducible, intentional core' of primitive construction,[30] this core can be discovered in the urge to disguise the latter's unacceptable materiality. Scully senses this in discussing the original purpose of the Greek peristyle. The columns in the first known peripteral temple on Samos had little or no structural purpose, being too closely spaced, and the roof could well have been supported on the cella walls. Nor did the columns provide much in the way of shelter or demarcate a processional route, which was probably located outside the peristyle. Their effect, says Scully, was almost certainly visual rather than empirical, mediating, in their shadowed tree-like forms, the impact of the solid walls enclosing the altar upon the land-

4.8   Knossus, 'The Horns of Consecration,' and Mt Jouctas

scape around.[31] The peristyle may well have echoed the forest grove where the deities dwelt; indeed, the fourth-century Corinthian and Ionic temples, taller, more expressly vegetal, strongly evoke arboreal canopies (Fig. 4.9). But these were later, when the tree-dwelling Zeus, Aphrodite, and Apollo were suffering from centuries of ambivalent reputations. The fear and reverence that had subordinated the archaic settlements and temples to the sacred structure of the landscape were more complicated than before, a mental shift that found its way into architecture and city formation.

Scientific and technical factors, the product of a more detached observation of climate and terrain, were also brought into play to work dialectically with those of the spirit in the fourth century B.C. In the *Laws*, Plato makes frequent reference to defensive considerations, urban resources, and the effects on health of site orientation. Hippocrates, too, in *Air, Water, and Location*, notes several times that health, morals, and human character depend on the aspect of towns: 'Cities exposed to the Levant are naturally more salubrious than those that turn to the north or south. The inhabitants have a better skin and are rosy-hued; their character is livelier, their sentiments and spirit are superior to those of people exposed to the north ... They have fewer illnesses.'[32]

In city building, it is true, the Hellenistic Greeks paid more attention to practical things than did the Etruscans, the Hittites, even the Romans, so no claim can be made that ritual and myth in their earliest forms continued to dominate construction everywhere. Nevertheless, it was the ghost of Homer who guided Alexander in founding the city that took the latter's name; Alexander's great teacher Aristotle, as far as we know, played no part. Archaic forms were still manifestations of a subconscious impulse that Hellenistic reason never completely erased. After the sixth century B.C., while feelings of reverence towards the landscape and the human community were rarely revealed in their earlier unadulterated fashion in architecture and urbanism, they remained in the foreground.

4.9 Temple of Zeus, Athens. Begun 174 B.C.

The Conquest of the Site

If Ionian science had made inroads into fourth-century city building, war and princely power brought about the 'progressive conquest of the site' less than two hundred years later to introduce a conscious monumentality into planning. In 201 B.C., Philip V of Macedonia laid siege to Pergamum, but was unsuccessful in scaling the ramparts. In a fit of rage he proceeded to ravage the suburbs, burning the sacred woods of Niképhorion and destroying the temples and Asclepieion situated outside the perimeter bulwark. The siege coincided with the beginning of the Attalid dynasty at Pergamum, a line of kings who would, over the next half-century, raise a citadel on the Ionian coast like no other in expressing the vast wealth and power of its makers. But even here, where conquest of the landscape was unmatched even by the Athenian acropolis, it is possible to recognize some of the old associations in the new monumentality that would inspire the Roman planners.

Attalus I had pieced together his Anatolian kingdom in the last decades of the third century B.C. through unremitting warfare; the situation of his capital at Pergamum matched the violence of his and his predecessors' campaigns. A convex incline, rising abruptly from the Aegean plain to the summit of a crag 335 metres above, had been occupied by the Pergamese for a least a century and a half before, and it was they who had partly enclosed the site with the bulwark that was to foil Philip the Macedonian. The origins of the capital remain obscure, but it seems that, prior to the Attalid period, the acropolis on the ridge had long been occupied; here an arsenal, a sacrificial terrace, and a Doric temple dedicated to Athena, probably from the fourth century B.C., had been built.[33] The violence of Pergamum's past, it seems, diverted royal attention away from matters of construction, although there is some evidence that Philetaerus earlier in the third century had devoted some effort to the site, including the arsenal and the Ionic sanctuary of Demeter, perched 300 metres to the south of the arsenal at the edge of a precipitous incline below the summit[34] (Fig. 4.10).

According to Strabo (XIII, 624), Attalus's son Eumenes II (197–159 B.C.) was responsible for much of the work at Pergamum during its period of greatest wealth and stability. He, more than anyone, must have commissioned the most radical and influential elements of the citadel: the great terraces, ramps, and staircases which knit half the mountain side into an urban assembly like no other. These gigantic planes, comprising a double series of horizontal and tilted platforms, fan out from the mountain in two giant complexes. The higher complex occupies the summit and is articulated southwards from Philetaerus's arsenal through three descending levels, via the Trajaneum and the old sacrificial terrace, to his sanctuary of Athena, then down to the agora of the summit assembly; the whole is bent into an arc oriented westwards to the Selinus River flowing some 300 metres below. In front of this arc and leaning into it sits the

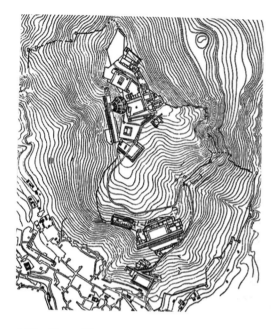

4.10   Plan of Pergamum

theatre and its 200-metre terrace, topped by a stoa and supported on a great rampart buttressed against the drop down to the river (Fig. 4.11). Access to the complex is afforded by an inclined street, in places as narrow as 3 metres, which negotiates the arc on its eastern flank, cutting through the agora, then descending the mountainside in a giant curve to the lower complex. There, 100 metres below the summit agora, but still almost twice that height above the plain, sits the sanctuary of Demeter and a gymnasium from where the street, flanked on its upper side by dwellings and stoas, bends into the lower agora, then drops to the main gate set in the bulwark above the modern town of Bergama.

Roland Martin has reason to believe that the Pergamum enterprise had been influenced by the giant scale of Persepolis, via the close if often belligerent contact which the Attalid dynasty experienced with the Persians.[35] Certainly no prior work of this kind existed in the West, and Pergamum, far more than Mycenae, was a monument to the power of

kings. Nevertheless, for all its grandeur and hubris, the citadel reveals other qualities echoing back to the spirit of reconciliation that so affected archaic and classical building practices.

While we have no chronicle giving the details of Pergamum's origins, the founding of a Greek city in the absence of rituals, however apocryphal, that paid homage to the site must have been exceptional. In many cases, as with the founding of Syracuse, Chalcis, and Myskellos, the Delphic oracle was consulted, and the chosen location deemed sacred. Herodotus laments the intransigence of the Lacedaemonians, who refused to consult the oracle when founding their colonies,[36] while Pausanius gives this account of the birth of Messina: 'When Epaminondas had examined the site ... he ordered his diviners to determine whether the gods approved of his enterprise; they replied that sacrificial ceremonies were necessary ... He then called together men who knew the art of planning roads, constructing houses and temples and raising ramparts. When all was ready the ceremonies began – the Arcadians provided the victims – sacrifices were made to Dionysus and Apollo, to Hera Argeia and to Zeus Nemeios ... and together the heroes were invited to take their place in the city. On the following days, the ramparts were laid out and work began inside on building the houses and temples.'[37] The first Pergamese probably went through rituals like these, after the gods had confirmed the divinity of their mountain, which was possibly first dedicated to Athena, then to Demeter.

An inspection of the Pergamum remains with a contour map shows that the elevation, orientation, size, and shape of the terraces have been determined perhaps less by functional considerations than by external factors having to do with the spiritual content of the terrain. The kind of judiciousness employed by Pergamum builders in seeking out relatively flat places in an otherwise precipitous topography cannot be explained by a desire to minimize the enormous work entailed in constructing platform substructures, a desire that

4.11   View of the upper complex at Pergamum

accounts for, say, much of the arrangement of medieval hillside towns in the Mediterranean. For instance, the gymnasium complex, Demeter's sanctuary, and the theatre terrace entailed massive buttressing and backfilling that would not have been necessary had they occupied the gentler shoulder slopes east and south of the acropolis. But to build on these latter sites would have violated a principle which had been followed throughout: all the terraces occupy positions at the top edge of a steep incline, just where the terrain abruptly moderates. Each terrace is also oriented, with formidable precision and consistency, towards the fall line of the slope. The tortuous character of the topography therefore creates a broken arc pattern whereby each platform is constructed as an entity, disengaged from the others and leaving the interstices to be taken up with a *poché* of ramps, staircases, embankments, and ancillary buildings (Fig. 4.12).

What could have been the purpose of such an arrangement? Are the vast scale and monumentality of the assembly only a conscious expression of royal power, as Roland Martin observes? If so, then we are left to explain why the king's residence, far from dominating the site, is rather prudently situated below the great upper terraces. The dominant positions, and the most monumental scale, are in fact reserved for temple precincts and other public places – the theatre and upper agora, the sacrificial temple, the sanctuaries of Athena and Demeter, and the Trajaneum (Fig. 4.13). It seems, given their function, that these constructions were designed and situated less to intimidate or impress the observer below than to structure the intercourse between the citizens of Pergamum and their surrounding landscape. The upper terraces in particular, sized to accommodate great crowds, poised at the edge of their mountaintop and reaching

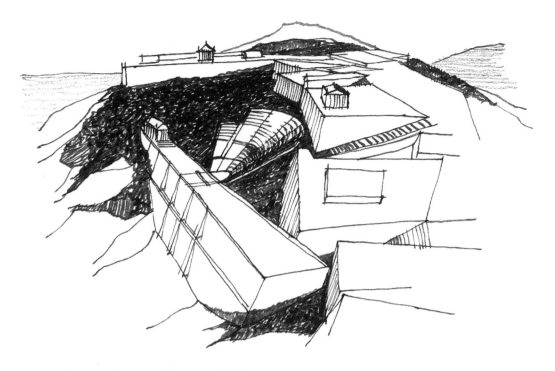

4.12   Schematic drawing of the upper platforms at Pergamum

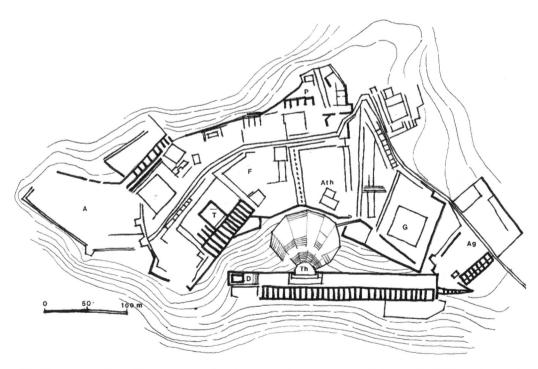

4.13   Pergamum, plan of the upper complex. A: arsenal; Ag: upper agora; Ath: temple of Athena; D: temple of Demeter; F: forecourt to Trajaneum; G: Great Altar; P: palace complex; T: Trajan's temple; Th: theatre

westwards across the coastal hills to the Aegean Sea, were formidable instruments of the spirit; the middle distance was masked by the silhouette of the theatre terrace, bringing the horizon features forward into apposition with the temple architecture and stoas, framing the spectator in the theatre and the celebrant on the platforms.

The Attalid dynasty might well have been aggressive in their dealings with other men, although the kingdom soon collapsed, to become the tame Roman province of Asia in 133 B.C.; nevertheless, the Pergamum builders seemed less intent on conquering their own landscape than on returning their mountain to itself in a spirit not unlike that which caused them and their ancestors to bring sacrificial victims back to life. True, the mountain had to be sacrificed to build Pergamum, but the process also involved acts of contrition embodied in the forms and symbols of construction: dressing the victim in its own skin, as it were, to breathe life into the carcass. The assembly of planes and their Doric simplicity become a literal *extension* of nature, enabling the celebration, not of mortal ascendancy, but of the continuity of human acquiescence driven by intuitions more ancient than kings.

Classical Absences

By the third century the old symbols of terror had long been troped into manageable conventions, and it was left to the sculpture decorating the classical tympana to express in literal terms images of murder, combat, and sacrifice. The brutality that can even today be read in the warrior-like columns of the sixth-century temples at Paestum had given way in the space of a hundred years to the grace of Periclean Doric. But what still remained, and indeed became more intricate, was the tension between the manifest encumbering of nature entailed in construction and the countervailing effort to return the landscape to the gods. This tension is a part of the essence of classical architecture, and separates it from the buildings of archaic Greece, Egypt, and

Mesopotamia. Whereas earlier architecture paid homage by mimetic reference and orientation to chthonian or celestial axes, by the fourth century the elements of the Doric and Ionic Orders had become so conventionalized as to have lost much of their bloody symbolic power. Now the whole system of refinement and nuance that we most admire in the fifth-century temples was to be directed to the architectural purpose of *dematerialization*.

Speculation about the motive that led the Hellenic architects to curve their columns, stylobate, and entablature into long arcs has tended to favour that of correcting for certain optical distortions and the illusion of sagging (Fig. 4.14). But as corrections they work only when viewed in elevation, a prospect rarely favoured by siting and orientation. When viewed from any vantage point closer than about seventy metres, the curves have the pronounced effect of leading the eye away from whatever element is being observed to the apprehension of the whole. The double curvature along the stylobate – an outward and upward swelling – suggests the existence of an expanding subterranean force, located, in fact, below the shrine within the cella. Similarly, the Doric entasis makes us read a cluster of lines – the arrises and shadows of the columnar fluting – as an upwardly moving force which would otherwise appear static (Fig. 4.15).

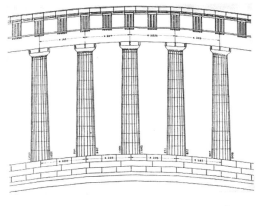

4.14   Curvature in the structure of the Parthenon

Finally, the sense of a permanently post-poned explosion is clinched by the roof-raising shape of the whole entablature. Could it be that we are being persuaded by such means to believe the impossible, namely, that an inert and permanent encumbrance – the whole temple – has not only taken on life, but is in the process of losing it in an instant? If so then the canonization of classical architecture presents a strange contradiction, because, in contemplating the fixed and timeless relationships between the parts, the ephemeral character of the whole escapes our attention. What was crucial to Greek consciousness – the playing out of inexorability; the folly of challenging the Fates; the inevitable cycles of death, re-birth, and reconciliation – was the basis of themes not limited to ritual and theatre; they also found expression in architecture through what has been called refinement, but one that is more reminiscent of the dynamic equilibrium with which the Fali peoples arranged their landscape.

That ever-present risk in the raising of buildings – the display of untempered hubris – was averted in classical structures, an accomplishment suggesting that other Greek forms of architectural modulation were not meant only to please the eye. Refinement itself is handmaiden to propriety, and the carving of wood and masonry has an effect cutting deeper than the ornamental: it also accomplishes a breaking down of mass and volume into something more fragile, a material loss that literally reduces the presence of construction (Fig. 4.16). The fourth-century Doric decline, associated with overelaborated carving, therefore signalled a regressive phase both aesthetically and in the reticences necessary to the dialectic with landscape. At Delphi, Epidaurus, and Olympia, a continuation of the trend towards slender columns in the hexastyle temples was neutered by the ornamented extravagance covering metopes, tympana, pediments, and friezes. By contrast, buildings of the Ionic renaissance in Asia Minor, characterized by their unprecedented size, mediated their presence in the landscape

4.15   Detail of the Parthenon, 438 B.C.

4.16   Ionic capital, north wall of Erechtheion, Athens

by increasingly spare proportions and a return to relatively modest carving. Colossal octastyles at Ephesus and Sardis, even an unroofed decastyle temple with 120 external columns at Didyma, were less assertive than the archaic Doric or later Ionic. Columnar slenderness and shallow architraves pushed the Greek's structural conservatism to its most radical limits, sometimes beyond the actual point of collapse (Fig. 4.17).

But literal architectural disembodiment achieved through the cutting, subdivision, penetration, or dismembering of solids required the structural virtuosity and cadences found in the Roman and especially the Gothic styles to realize its complete flowering. The Greeks had to rely more extensively on suggestion and metaphor to overcome constructional trespass into the landscape of the gods. In no single building was this more necessary than the Parthenon, at once dominating the heights of the Athenian Acropolis, symbol of mortal accomplishment as well as the gift of Athena. Not least among the admirable qualities of this building is the complex tempering of its undoubted hubris, first by the 'explosive' means referred to above, and second by the deployment of its sculpture, especially the great Panathenaic frieze attributed to Phidias, located on the temple's boundary wall. In this case, however, we depart from expressive meaning and enter the realm of aesthetics, in which perception is guided by contemplation and knowledge (Fig. 4.18).

The frieze contained more than 360 figures in a set of panels 160 metres long and 1 metre high along the exterior top of all four sides of the cella wall. Interrupted only by three small windows on the north and south walls, the frieze depicted in a continuous row the assembly, cavalcade, and procession of riders, chariots, elders, musicians, sacrificial victims, eponymous heroes and gods, beginning on the west wall and culminating over the main entrance door on the east.

Some doubts have been expressed recently as to whether the scene actually does depict the Panathenaic procession; such a subject, a

4.17   Ionic Orders from the old and new temple of Artemis, Ephesus

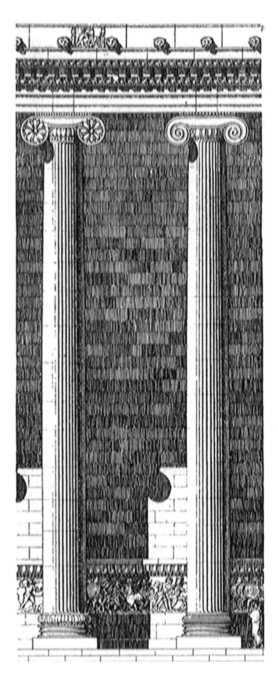

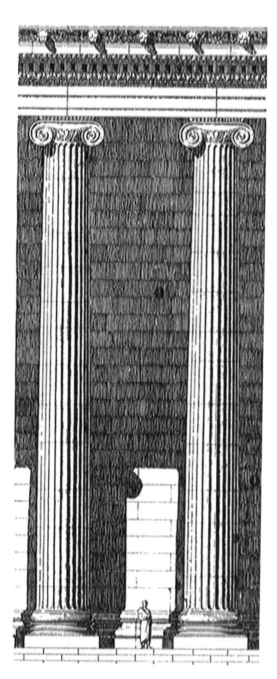

contemporary event enacted by Athenian citizens, was hardly fitting for a sacred building.[38] Even more suspicious is the inclusion in the frieze of heroes and gods as participants, and other doubts such as whether the ceremony on the east wall actually does show the presentation of the *peplos* – a woven cloak – to the Royal Archon, as it occurred in the actual procession (Fig. 4.19). Whatever the event depicted, the enormous scale, processional unity, and brilliance of execution surely point to a deliberate choice of subject-matter. Perhaps the frieze represents a figural equivalent of the architecture itself, namely, a celebration of the reconciliation of mortal and divine interests.

But the actual narrative content does not concern us here, beyond the accepted fact that the subject is processional and shown sequentially. The marshalling activities of the adolescent riders on the west frieze, as they control and mount their horses, is the place of preparation for the cavalcade, which then proceeds eastward along the north and south walls. Ten overlapping ranks of sixty horsemen, preceded by ten chariots and accompanying warriors, occupy roughly three-quarters the length of each wall. The pace of the equestrian drama then changes abruptly, as, for the length of two panels, again to north and south, a row of elders on foot is led by four lyre-playing musicians and a group of water carriers. From this point to the east corners, men on foot conduct sheep and cattle to the sacrifice. On the east frieze the spectacle continues from each corner to terminate in the centre, where the Archon Basileus receives the *peplos* from a young girl. To each side, Attic heroes, women, marshals, and seated gods are arrayed in order and sequence along the frieze (Fig. 4.20).

Phidias's masterpiece has many remarkable qualities, but let us consider just one, having to do with one purpose that is integral to the architecture of the Parthenon. Apart from a few minor departures (three sacrificial sheep are depicted near the eastern corner of the north wall, whereas none exists on the south),

4.18   Panathenaic frieze, south wall, Parthenon

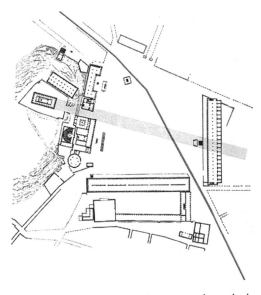

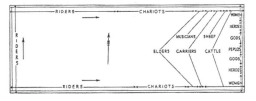

4.19   Panathenaic procession, route through the Hellenistic Agora of Athens

4.20   Panathenaic frieze, plan showing the location of the figures

4.21   Panathenaic frieze

the whole procession is in almost perfect bilat-
eral symmetry along the north and south
walls, and towards the centre along the east
frieze. Nearly every horseman, chariot, elder,
carrier, victim, eponymous hero, and god is
matched by its equivalent figure on the opposing side (Fig. 4.21). Why, of the conceivable
ways that Phidias could have displayed the
occasion, was this particular one chosen? It
seems obvious that the symmetry to left and
right of the east frieze, not unlike the disposition of figures on the tympanum, provided the
most appropriate frame to the culminating
ceremony above the central doorway. If this
were indeed Phidias's initial decision, then the
disposition of the rest falls logically into place,
because the procession would then have to
occur as it does, in reverse sequence from each
corner along the north and south walls, to the

scenes of preparation at the rear. But none of
this explains the consistency with which each
figure is matched on its opposing side, unless
Phidias is persuading us to read both sides
simultaneously as a unity; that is, to examine
the whole length of the frieze and then perceive not two overlapping ranks of horsemen
but four, not a single row of chariots but two,
and so on. In the process, the observer becomes a spectator to the actual procession,
and the intervening cella walls become etherealized, as it were, into a wafer of transparent
space.

We now have a clue as to why this unparalleled work occupied such an unlikely niche,
the least conspicuous one of all the Parthenon
sculptures. If a task of Greek architecture was
to dematerialize, by one means or another, an
intransigent mass of construction, then the

cella must have presented the most difficult problem. On the one hand, the internal shrine required protecting by a solid enclosure; on the other, the enclosing walls, while partly obscured from outside by the peristyle, remained the sole feature of undisguised solidity, tempered only by fine joints and the smooth finish to which its surface was rubbed. A ploy such as that used by Phidias, to be crudely theorized three millennia later as a 'decorated shed,' was a significant expansion of the architectural repertoire, although not one that lends itself to urbanism. As we shall see, the ploy was to be taken up again, most notably in the age of Augustus.

One of the noblest of Roman monuments once occupied a corner of the Campus Martius, not far from the Tiber, but has since been moved to a location nearby. The Ara Pacis Augustae is a sturdy piece of architecture with a four-square demeanour clinched by the flat Corinthian pilasters that occupy each corner (Fig. 4.22). But whatever real distinction this building has is decorative rather than architectural, namely, the sculptural double frieze of Luna marble enveloping the outside of the north and south walls, an accomplishment that is probably the work of Greeks from Pergamum. These carvings are a masterpiece, expressing all that was considered best in the newly ordered life of the Augustan Republic. This order had its moments of serenity and moderation, a rare interlude of peace when time was spared for children and the delights of nature, and when humour and informality threaded the deep, normally unconnected layers of social life (Fig. 4.23).

This blessed existence is captured for our eyes in the double frieze; it blends contemporary events with legend, with founding myths and images of nature's harmonies. The lower reliefs show a field of acanthus, vine, and ivy, of swirling leaves and floral motifs, their shoots and stems displaying the cornucopian harvest. But the distinction of the upper frieze holds most of our attention. It contains, on each opposing wall, a row of figures engaged in the actual procession of 4 July 13 B.C., to celebrate Augustus's return to Rome following his reordering of Spain and Gaul. This was the day of the altar's foundation when Augustus, accompanied by members of his family and by various priests, magistrates, attendant children and other personages, came to the site to witness the thanksgiving sacrifice commemorating his homecoming. No pomp or misplaced flattery is depicted in this scene; it is merely the portrayal of a great and dignified occasion; if a hierarchy exists between the participants, the signs of it are muted, hidden in a gesture, a detail of dress, a few centimetres of stature (Fig. 4.24). The theme is *pax*, and two barbarian children, one on each opposing wall, are the *pacati*. They represent the communities of east and west, the distant boundaries of the *oikoumene*, but their gestures, and those of the flanking Romans, have not a trace of subjugation or dominance. Instead, the children are being offered, and are delighted to grasp, the hand of affectionate protection. Such were the official advertisements put out by a territorially ambitious regime.

But, as if all this artistic distinction were not enough, the upper frieze is remarkable in yet another way. On both the north and south walls the sculptured figures walk in the same direction, that is towards the east, as though they are about to enter the altar precinct through the door in the eastern wall. What is being depicted, however, are not *two* rows of figures but virtually two sides of a single row, so that as we view the building from north or south we see the same participants, just as would be possible by standing on either side of a street. The reliefs are effectively two-sided, divided down the middle by the precinctual walls of the building. Whole groups of figures occupy equivalent spots on opposing friezes: Augustus himself appears in the same position twice, as do his relatives and household retainers; Ligure is reflected on the other side by Ligure, Augure by Augure. At symmetrical and opposing points, precisely where we pass the front of the holy altar hidden from view within, two *silentiarii*, each a veiled woman with a finger to her lips, seek the quiet respect of the onlooking crowd to right and left.

4.22   Ara Pacis Augustae, Rome, 13 B.C.

As with the Parthenon we are being invited, as it were, to finesse the building itself from our perceptions, to imagine the whole sturdy structure as a kind of diaphanous wafer. It is not just that the architecture seems relegated to the status of a backdrop against which the reliefs are displayed, because the building becomes nothing less than metaphorically etherealized. Nor are we confronted by some *trompe d'oeil* illusion, for the Ara Pacis Augustae contains no such sleight of hand or similar theatricality; indeed, to perceive what is intended demands an act of close attention as well as a deliberate suspension of belief on the part of the observer.

Is there a forgotten purpose behind this kind of sophistication, or does the two-sidedness of the reliefs have no deeper significance than artistic whim? Or are we being asked to regard the building as inconsequen-

tial, in order to force all our attention towards what are certainly artefacts of the highest artistic and symbolic order? None of these explanations seems likely, particularly when considering the similar case of the Parthenon. Everything we know about this apotheosis of Greek accomplishment confirms, down to the last detail, the uncompromising purposeful-ness with which every curve, plane, and line is brought into the uttermost synthesis. The Panathenaic procession, to be sure, is a display whose narrative purpose can be appreciated quite independently of the structure that it graces, which for just a moment lends a kind of autonomous significance to its double-sidedness. But the temple always has the final word, because the frieze is integral to *it*. The reliefs were located within the outer colon-nade, around the upper cella wall and above the two hexastyle porticoes; they adorned, in other words, the solid planes that make up the hecatompedon naos. Here, they adopt an architectural role; in the manner of the Ara Pacis Augustae we are invited to *see through* the masonry of the cella that intercepts our view of the great Panathenaic procession. The large and difficult element of the sanctuary wall metaphorically sheds its weight, and is thereby accorded the modulated character of every other element in the temple. So this double-sidedness, if seen in this way, seems to have a purpose identical to that of all those other refinements for which the Parthenon is renowned – the evolved entasis, the inclined column axes, the double curvature of stylobate and entablature, and the rest. The frieze as an *architectural* device calls on the imaginative powers more than our immediate sense of things, but its effect is the same: to make us forget the uncompromising facts of construction, to sway the mind's eye away from whatever rude evidence of a violated harmony that the gross act of building represents, and then to monopolize our attention with the restorative powers of architecture. As Pericles would have wished, the boundaries of the city dissolve, permitting his people and their gods to share an indivisible realm.

4.23   Ara Pacis Augustae, double frieze

4.24   Ara Pacis Augustae, detail of upper frieze

Hestia and the Black Hunter

So far our attention has focused on the dialectic between people and their gods. But our theme is even more ambitious than this. We wish to discover the links between forms of imaginative thought, social forms, and constructed forms. Did Greek urbanism also take account of social conduct? If the Parthenon calls on aesthetic knowledge to perceive the indivisibility of religious life, the temple was but a graceful embodiment of the same consciousness Greeks brought to everyday life, to their dealings with each other and to the expressive meanings that ordered the boundaries of their urban domains. Thucydides may have heaped scorn on whatever was mythical (1.22.4), but his opinions were not widely shared. That 'the Greek city knows no separation between the sacred and profane'[39] is more apparent when admiring the temple than in reading the old chronicler. The spirit of oneness pervaded much of the daily momentum too, and was epitomized in the *koinon* – the collective sphere. The *koinon* represented nothing we would regard as political, but referred to whatever Greek citizens experienced in common, in their minds, their recollections and activities, and this closely woven fabric of life became the very reason for the existence of the *polis*.

Here is what Xenophon makes Kleokritus say during the Athenian civil war: 'Fellow-citizens, why are you driving us out of the city? We have never done you any harm. We have shared with you in the most holy religious services, in sacrifices, and in splendid festivals; we have joined in dances with you, gone to school with you, and fought in the army with you, braving together with you the dangers of land and sea in defence of our common safety and freedom. In the name of the gods of our fathers and mothers, of the bonds of kinship and marriage and friendship, which are shared by so many of us on both sides, I beg you to feel some shame.'[40]

This appeal to the *koinon* brings out its twofold character, its demand for obligation as well as its offer of security and collective pleasure. Elswhere Xenophon joins Plato in sneering at manual labour, but does so because it leaves no time for things that are shared: 'the workers at these trades simply have not got the time for friendship and citizenship. Consequently they are looked on as bad friends and bad patriots.'[41]

As we have seen, the sense of indivisibility between humans and their gods was displayed in the dialectic of the *polis* and landscape, and in the ubiquitous refinement of sacred architecture. The *koinon*, too, found its way into urbanism, in a reciprocity with the conduct of life, because religion and civic conduct were one. But the Greek city was also, we would now say, inegalitarian, a fact creating a rather different boundary dialectic from the kinesis that joined men to their gods and heroes.

In the archaic settlements only the *aristoi* mattered, and the city belonged to them. The scenes of revelry, banqueting, and convivial rituals; the collective celebration of blood sacrifice, of hunting, choruses, and athletic contests – all were public events that took place in the agora, sanctuaries, and gymnasia, in the countryside itself. They were conducted for the sake of pleasure, but also for *paideia* – 'the development of the moral virtues, of the sense of civic responsibility, of mature identification with the community, its traditions and values.'[42] *Paideia,* with its collective events, endured to classical times and beyond, to become the foundation of political theory after Cleisthenes, while comprising, despite the insistence of Aristotle, a large slice of everyday life quite independent from politics. Athens had its administrative assemblies and its law courts, but also its gatherings to celebrate cults of every description and especially its *philoi* – groups of friends and companions 'eating and drinking together under the eyes of the gods' in the streets and other public spaces.[43]

If the *koinon, paideia,* and the *philoi* are evidence of a deep layer of cohesiveness that is not reducible to politics, this does not mean that the *polis* enjoyed a boundaryless domain.

Private life, as we have seen, had its own spaces, although even here the boundary dialectic left room for in-between states, despite the philosophers' assertions that *polis* and *oikos* were thoroughly irreconcilable. Since the early orthogonal settlements, the spatial organization of the house and its relationship to other houses and to the city at large varied little from place to place down through the Hellenistic period.[44] The archaic section of Olynthos contains no identifiable organizational idea; its houses, each containing a central courtyard, are jammed into the site, leaving a residue of interstices to act as streets. But the larger section dates from the fifth or sixth century, is axially planned, and contains no residual spaces betweeen the public domain and the contiguous housing lining each street (Fig. 4.25). Here, and in the later cities, each house usually occupied a rectangular plot some fifteen to eighteen metres a side, with little variation in size. 'From ... the division of private space we see that agricultural and residential land both partake of the concept of equal or comparable shares in the resources of the community'[45] (Fig. 4.26).

So, with respect to the boundaries of the space occupied by each household, the city imposed itself on the activities of the *oikoi*. It was mostly within these boundaries that the inegalitarian qualities of the city were manifested, although even here the walls between public and private were rarely absolute. The household, of course, contained the domain of women, children, and, money permitting, the non-citizen slaves and retainers. None played any part in political life, although, as Aristophanes tells us in *Ecclesiazusae*, the thought of women running the Athenian congress better than the men, then celebrating over a gargantuan meal in public, was far from inconceivable. The example shows, in fact, that whatever official strictures happened to be in place, the position of marginalized groups was more complex than one of outright servility. Paradox and ambiguity colour the legends about women, adolescents, even slaves. They were excluded

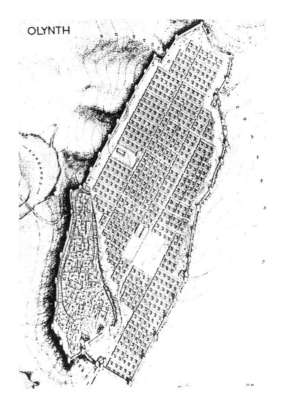

4.25 Plan of Olynthus. The archaic settlement covers the southwest section. The remainder dates from the fifth century B.C.

from warfare certainly (with the exception of conscripted slaves in Sparta), and as Jean-Paul Vernant has shown, the rules of war were also those of the *polis*.[46] The enfranchised male, having fought in a hoplite phalanx, wielded authority on both sides of his domestic threshold, but not exclusively so, as Vernant's colleague Pierre Vidal-Naquet has well demonstrated.[47]

Here, as in much of the subsequent history of city building, we encounter the place of paradox and inversion. Greek legend is filled with the double-natured measure of things – the simultaneous presence of human and animal, man and woman, servile and free in the same entity, which perhaps explains the philosophers' obsession with finding absolute categories. Urban space, not excluding the sacred precincts, possesses a similar ambiguity, and only within the innermost recesses of the Greek house does total exclusion prevail. Women, if not slaves, were permitted everywhere – in the streets, the agora, the sanctuaries, the theatre – even though their participation in formal ritual was restricted.

Young men, however, suffered periodic expulsion from the spaces of the city – during the Spartan *kryptos*, for example.[48] Here we recognize some early signs of a chilling constant in boundary formation and the occupancy of urban space. Two words were used to describe groups of young men in Greece: *agela*, meaning 'pack,' and *ila*, 'a platoon.' The adolescent male was assumed to be – and taught to remain – a wild beast; Xenophon describes how, like the *kryptoi*, boys are instructed to develop guile, to steal, and to indulge in night activities, but also to participate in the adult community at the common feasts (*Lacedaemonian Politics* 2.5–8, 5.5). This complicated practice, whereby the 'savage' character deemed to be intrinsic to youths was promoted in one kind of space (the countryside, the night-time streets) and purged in another (the 'civilizing' domain of the sanctuaries and the agora), had, of course, the purpose of schooling for warfare, but was not limited to Sparta.

In Athens, a supreme metaphor connoted the dual nature of pre-hoplite youth, namely, *Melanthos* – the Black Hunter. His legend originated in the ancient animosities between Attica and Boeotia and was sustained in works by Aristophanes and Aelius Aristides.[49] According to the legend, this hunter, bizarre in cloak and mysterious in origin, kills the Boeotian king by trickery, and claims the Athenian crown as his reward. This protector, but one who could never be trusted, has appeared out of nowhere, from the *terra incognita* along the frontier zone, and there the fight takes place. Vidal-Naquet, in an outstanding exegesis of the story, shows the extent to which ambivalence surrounds the Greek perception of the Black Hunter, and how its symbols are those of the insecure

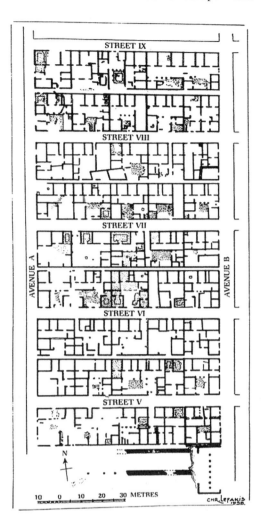

4.26   Olynthus, plan of a part of the fifth-century settlement

boundaries dividing forms of behaviour (initiation, the criminal saviour) and space (the frontier between safety and danger): 'But the ephebe's [youth's] relation to the world of the frontier is complex. As young soldiers, they occupy the frontier zone of the city, which is expressed physically in the ring of fortlets, ... When they take the oath that makes them full hoplites, they mention the boundary-stones that separate Athens' territory from her neighbours'. With these stones are associated wheat, barley, vines, olives and fig-trees – in a word, the world of cultivation.'[50]

Melanthos's story has many variants – notably that of Orion, who hunts by night – but nearly all of them deal in paradox and uncertainty, polarity and reversal, and their subject is the protean oscillation between trepidation and dependence that marks the Greek regard for young men. In the stories, boundaries always figure prominently, and their transgression by savage youth is a constant source of fear that would echo beyond the world of antiquity.

At this point we return to the alleged opposition between the *polis* and the *oikos*, to perceive why the boundaries between the two are far from simple. On the one hand, in *Oeconomicus*, Xenophon voices the perennial belief – clearly connected to the theme outlined above – that the gods made man to live outdoors, whereas woman was made to remain under one roof (7.30). But, on the other, Vernant shows that this belief was not fully expressed in social life: 'In marriage (but only in marriage) it is the woman who is the mobile social element, whose movement creates the link among different family groups, whereas the man remains tied to his own hearth and home.'[51] The goddess Hestia (Vesta), protector of the family hearth and metaphor of the female essence, also ventures abroad, linking one *oikos* with the other; her task, like that assumed by the woman in everyday life, is to ensure that the boundaries of the house are never absolute: 'The centre symbolized by Hestia defines, therefore, not only a closed and isolated world: it presupposes, as a corollary, other defined centres. By exchange of goods, movement of people – women, heralds, ambassadors, guests, and table companions – a network of alliances is built up among domestic groups.'[52]

Yet if the woman is endowed with a venturesome spirit, it has a benign character not present in that of the man, and its place does not extend outside the city. Here the expressive meanings of Greek boundaries are startling in their contrasts, and are incised, too, into the architecture and interior organization of the house itself. Consider again the power that dazzling sunlight, shade, and darkness hold over the Greek mind. It extends into male-female symbolism and the latter's corresponding territories. Outdoors is where man belongs, in the unlimited landscape under the sun's heat – but also with the terrors of absolute night. The woman's place, too, is associated with darkness, but of a different kind; she is white-skinned, living in the protective shade of the house and nurturing the young in turn, as the Homeric 'Hymn to Demeter' has it, within the shade cast by her body. Inside the house she has her own domain, in the secret innermost spaces forbidden to man – intimate, safe, shrouded in darkness, and close to the chthonian powers.

Nevertheless, the expressive meanings that characterize gender and territory are not straightforward; if the house is a sanctuary, its boundaries, we have seen, remain porous, and men and women too share certain qualities. In *Electra* (416), Sophocles brings out the analogy of the male as a shade-giving tree, and in *Agamemnon* (965) Aeschylus extends the same metaphor to the house, in a beautiful passage in which Clytemnestra fakes her joy at the king's return: 'For if the root still lives, leafage comes again to the house and spreads its over-reaching shade against the scorching dog-star; so, now that thou hast come to hearth and home, thou showest that warmth hath come in winter-time; aye, and when Zeus maketh wine from the bitter grape, then forthwith there is coolness.'[53]

We can confirm the measure of this evident complexity in thought and social life by returning to the constructed evidence. In a recent (and controversial) claim, Hoepfner and Schwander see the existence of *Typenhäuser* in Olynthos, Priene, and Kassope as a confirmation of democratic politics in the Greek city-state.[54] Each household was allotted its parcel of land, we have seen, in a manner that constrained individual variation and guaranteed a particular consistency in the relationship of each to the adjacent houses, to the street, and at a larger scale to the city as a whole. The 'type,' therefore, was imposed from above, presumably, one would now say, to maintain a certain efficiency of spatial organization and a cohesive public character. But, on closer inspection, the simplicity of this imposition becomes deceptive. Each house comprises a series of rooms, most of which open to a central courtyard from which they normally gain their daylight; only a very few windows face outward to the street. The immediate picture is one of absolute withdrawal from the public realm, of domestic life oriented inwards to the courtyard behind a closed boundary protected by the figure of the threshold god Hermes (Fig. 4.27).

4.27   Remains of Camiros, Rhodes, third to second century B.C.

This arrangement would, in the first place, support the textual evidence referred to above of the hazards perpetrated in the streets after dark by rootless adolescents. But domestic insularity was never complete, because the interior of the house was usually zoned in such a way that large sections – the courtyard, and certainly the room referred to as *andron* or *andronitis* – could be accessed by those outside the family. Guests, friends and neighbours, those brought within the orbit of the household by the woman's network as well as the man's, occupied this interior threshold space.[55] The women of the family had access to the whole house, including the *andron*, but the men, it seems, did not habitually enter the inner reaches, which were reserved for women. Otherwise, the family came together around the hearth, which, while always symbolized by the female Hestia, usually had no special room of its own. (Most houses probably used a portable terracotta brazier.)[56]

In two important senses then, urban space penetrated domestic space. At one level, the *oikos* was a sanctuary of the family, symbolized by its threshold guardian Hermes and the hearth goddess Hestia, but its behaviour and architectural partitions also made it a place of contact with the city at large. At another, the boundaries between domestic spaces were invariably contiguous, and each house occupied a plot of land no bigger than the others. Add to this a universal absence of external decoration or architectural pretension, then the prospect from outside brings the public realm with its continuous articulation, graceful sacred architecture, and the collective events of the stoa, the agora, and the theatre, into prominence.

Such is only a part of the interplay between house and city in classical Greece. Their forms and symbols, like the dialectic between the city and the divine landscape, were anchored in the archaic past to remain stubbornly mythladen. Here again certain scholars, entranced by the doubtful equivalence of regular geometry and a rational, stable order, are inclined to regard the Greek city as the product of a theoretical idea. But imaginative thought and everyday life are not easily reconciled to abstractions, particularly where city building is concerned.

CHAPTER FIVE

Dividing the Urban Realm

The Intransigence of Nero

Perennial beauty (but bound inexorably to perishing, to images, to earthly vicissitudes, to history, and thus *illusively* perennial, as Palinurus will say) assumed in my mind the aspect of Aeneas. Aeneas is beauty, youth, ingenuousness ever in search of a promised land, where, in the contemplated, fleeting beauty, his own beauty smiles and enchants. But it is not the myth of Narcissus: it is the animating union of the life of the memory, of fantasy, of speculation, of the life of the mind; and it is, too, the fecund union of the carnal life in the long succession of the generations – Giuseppe Ungaretti[1]

It was in first-century Rome that an early desecration of a human landscape – as opposed to that of divine nature – occurred by the actions of one man, who assaulted the boundaries of the Republican city. Ironically enough, nostalgia for the old, Greek ways precipitated the event more than anything. 'Times have changed, and our god is not the same,' says Corydon in Calpurnius Siculus's fourth eclogue. While the Greeks had confronted their gods at home among the trees, rivers, and rocks, well before the advent of the Christian era men had distanced themselves

from unadulterated nature in the confining warrens of Rome. Whereas Hippodamus of Miletus felt compelled to devise his plans according to cosmological dictates in order to shape his *polis* as an adjunct to nature, Rome had become a panorama monopolized by man's works, ever since the Servian wall shut off four hundred hectares from the surrounding hills in pre-Republican times. Hellenic and Hellenistic Greece had their own fortified boundaries, certainly, and city walls were widespread by the fifth century B.C.[2] But they were invariably partial, and some managed to temper their intrusiveness by a modest decorative tradition that spread westwards from Ionian cities like Smyrna. The wall around fourth-century Eleusis had fine joints and coloured string-courses, its surface handrubbed to a smooth plane.[3] But the gigantic scale of Rome's Servian wall remains a puzzle, given the stunted siege technology of the day. Seventeen metres across the top, here stood the ultimate divide between the old Hellenic complementarities and the near anthropocentrism of Roman urbanism.

Meanwhile, outside the Servian wall, nature herself suffered relegation at the hands of estate builders intent on converting late-Republican Latium into a pretty resource, although not without the protests of those who advocated the good, simple life. The loss of small country farms outside third-century Rome caused Cicero to mourn the contrast between the luxury of his father's house and the thatched homestead of his grandfather (*De Legibus* ii, I, 3). Hellenistic-style villas, with their porticoes, paintings, marble peristyles, and atria, epitomized the new display of wealth, consumption, and nostalgia in the countryside, although not without criticism.[4] Pliny, like Cicero, preferred to recall the vigorous simplicity of Hellenic life, rather than its classical symbols; he objected strenuously to 'great columns of costly marble' that were being raised in the city and environs (*Naturalis Historia*, XXXVI, 6). Horace, who hated what he called 'Persian elegance,' had no doubt that nature would wreak her own kind of vengeance: 'Amid your varied columns you are nursing trees, and you praise the mansion which looks out on distant fields. You may drive out Nature with a pitchfork, yet she will ever hurry back, and ere you know it, will burst through your foolish contempt in triumph.'[5] Wisdom such as this would be repeated, to deaf ears, down through the centuries to our own times; with the advent of urbanization, man began to deal nearly exclusively with other men, forgetting that gods had been born among the rocks and the trees, and that the boundaries of their domain were not to be violated.

On the first day of the year in A.D. 42, the Senate and People of Rome voted to recognize Julius Caesar as god, and marked the occasion by erecting the Temple of the Divine Julius. This enabled Caesar Octavian (Augustus), his adoptive son, to be called 'son of god.' The divinities were now more visible and manageable than the old incalcitrant ones, just as their works could be, and were, subject to human intervention. In *De Rerum Natura*, Lucretius would write (5.1370–7): 'And day by day they forced the woods to recede up the mountains and give up the land below to cultivation, so that on hillsides and plains they might have meadows, ponds, streams, crops and glad

vineyards and let a belt of olive trees run between to make a clear division, stretching over mounds and hollows and level ground, even as now you see the whole patterned with the charm of variety.'[6]

Charm and variety had never been central to the Hellenic world; but part of the 'sovereign classical principle of propriety' embedded in the Greek attitude to nature had passed over during the Roman Republican period into urban rules governing man's dealings with other men. These rules grew spontaneously from practical reason, into the complementarities of *res publica*. In Latin, the adjective *civilis* (*demotikos* in Greek) refers to the kind of modesty displayed by kings during the first years of their reign in refusing the title *pater patriae*, an honour normally offered on accession. This refusal displayed virtue, whereby the recipient insisted on remaining no more than a first among equals, and shunning autocratic behaviour. The noun *civilitas*, applied to the young Nero by his tutor Seneca, meant the path to universal approval, to be followed by congenial behaviour and close attention paid to the welfare of all citizens. Accessibility was also crucial to *civilitas*, causing Pliny to write approvingly of Trajan, who would rather mingle with the crowd at the games than be shut away in a box, as was Domitian's bad habit. So the fall from *civilitas*, heralding Nero's ultimate fate, was marked by fear, insecurity, and the self-glorification usually associated with paranoia.

To be *civilis princeps* was thus to offer oneself as a model of *res publica*, of decency in dealing with one's fellow citizens; but with the spread of corruption and uncertainty through the later Republican and Imperial hierarchies, *civilitas* became an idea more linked to aspirations than to reality. A residue of such aspirations took on multiple forms of nostalgia, fed by memories anchored in a pre-urban past, which sustained a recurring philhellenism. Virgil (100–19 B.C.) more than anyone epitomized both elements of Roman aspiration. He spent most of his life as a member of the Epicurean colony near the Greek city of

Neapolis, and the widespread appeal of his great epic poetry reveals the extent to which the psyche of Rome still depended on recollection of a life spent in nature's realm to cope with everyday reality.

One wonders, in contemplating Roman poetry and Imperial architecture, whether much of Rome's urban reality was but a veneer covering a core of frustrated yearning for what was no longer recoverable; the civil wars, power intrigues, and pathological daily spectacles seem the stuff of fantasy compared with the sanity of memory. Recognizing the place of iconic power in Roman life, at the beginning of his *De Re Rustica*, Varro rejects the twelve urban gods whose statues decorated the Forum in favour of the twelve patrons of husbandmen. In the prologue to Virgil's first poem of the *Georgics*, the gods are Olympians in company with the old spirits of the forest groves: Pan, Aristaeus, the Greek satyrs and dryads. The fourth book contains his story of the commonwealth of bees as a didactic analogue of *res publica*, a reminder of the connections between animate and inanimate nature, and of the divine recycling of all life: 'Some have affirmed that bees possess a share of the divine mind and drink ethereal draughts; for God, they say, pervades the whole of creation, lands and the sea's expanse and the depths of sky. Thence flocks and herds and men and all the beasts of the wild derive, each in his hour of birth, the subtle breath of life; and surely thither all things at last return, dissolved, restored. There is no room for death: alive they fly to join the stars and mount aloft to Heaven' (4.219–227).[7]

Faced with the awful gap between imagination and reality, the tyrant Nero made philhellenism corrupt by propagating only its shallow, fashionable side. He never understood the deeper Hellenic meanings, lodged in the reverential dialectic of man and nature, embodied in Virgil's lines and in the old reciprocity of city and landscape. There stood a wisdom ready-made for shaping Rome according to the idea of *civilitas*, for what was civility if not a reaching back to the kind of active respect that ordered Greek boundaries? But Nero wasted his chance, and perhaps our own, ushering in what became a two-thousand-year tradition of urban renewal that turned Greek urbanism on its head. The lyre-playing, verse-singing tyrant was guilty of aestheticism, cut away from any understanding of existence outside the self, and of turning urbanism, despite its ornaments, into the raw construction that devastates the finely tuned boundaries of places.

Nero's chance was, of course, the great fire of A.D. 64. Lasting for nine days, it left untouched only four of the fourteen regions into which Augustus had divided Rome. Three regions in the centre were completely levelled, along with whole streets of shops, tenements, temples, and private villas ranging across the Palatine, Esquiline, and Capitoline hills. It appears that Nero did devise a plan of reconstruction, which met with the mild approval of Tacitus on certain social and aesthetic grounds.[8] Until the fire, according to Livy, Rome was 'a city filled up rather than laid out.'[9] 'Laid out,' by this time, had as much to do with empirical matters, like traffic circulation, water supply, and fire prevention, as anything else; the irritations of overcrowding in a large city had long been intolerable for the plebs, many of whom existed in the vilest of tenement quarters.

It turned out, nevertheless, that the reconstruction plans were nothing more than a prelude to the appropriation of the centre of Rome for Nero's private use. He had long complained of never having lived anywhere fit for a man, considering his luxurious country villa at Subiaco, completed in A.D. 60, and the Domus Transitoria, a palace built for him on the Palatine but ruined in the great fire, to be unworthy of the Princeps. Nothing less than a new palace extending over one hundred hectares of central Rome, with all the scale and accoutrements of a magnificent country villa, would do. This project, the Domus Aurea, rendered visible all the character of Nero's tyranny, and, it seems, raised enough ire to contribute to his assassination a few years

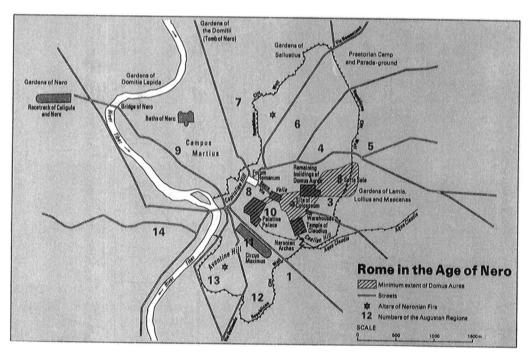

5.1   Plan of Rome in the age of Nero, showing the extent of the Domus Aurea

later. The Golden House was never finished (and is still being excavated), but it rivalled Hadrian's villa at Tivoli in size, stretching from the summit of the Velian Hill, filling almost all the Colosseum valley, and invading the slopes of the Caelian and the Oppian hills. From there it reached outside the Republican wall, encompassing the area around Trajan's Sette Sale, reaching to the southeast of the Palatine over the site of the ruined Domus Transitoria, and almost filling the valley between the Caelian and the Esquiline. Nero planned nothing less than to countrify Rome's centre for his personal use – to fill it with 'fish basins, groves, flocks of caged birds within colonnades' (Fig. 5.1).

In determining the extent of the Domus Aurea, Van Essen concludes that the palace grounds must have encompassed the natural basin of the Colosseum valley, with a lake – Nero's Pond – at the centre, and included buildings occupying the summits of the surrounding hills.[10] As such, the whole complex must have been an enormous private precinct,

replacing the former network of commercial streets, traffic arteries, and residential quarters that made up *Roma veta*. In a matter of months, Nero tore up the old urban palimpsest and cordoned it off for himself. Griffin notes the anonymous epigram circulating through what was left of the city: 'Rome will become one house; move to Veli, citizens, if that house does not take over Veli too.'[11]

At this time, we know less about the character of the Golden House than its extent, but enough to appreciate that the ensuing storm of protest was not just directed at its size. Pliny no doubt exaggerates in claiming that the estate enclosed the whole town (XXXIII, 54), but we can side with Suetonius in complaining that the centre of Rome should not have been turned over to pastures and wild animals. If Nero possessed a modicum of reticence in the earlier years of his reign, the Domus Aurea attests to the evaporation of all reason by A.D. 60. The main axis of the Forum, the Sacra Via, was transformed into a monumental avenue leading to the Imperial palace; Nero had the

ancient axis widened and straightened to provide a vista of a bronze colossus of himself on
the summit of the Velian, forty metres tall and
visible from most parts of Rome. This colossus faced the Forum, and was flanked by the
great arcades and pillars of the covered spaces
lining either side of the transformed Sacra Via.
Behind Nero's statue rose 'the hated entrance
hall of the cruel king.' Three colonnades enveloped the front, which was encrusted with
gold and precious stones. As if this self-glori-
fying edifice were not enough, to the south,
across the Colosseum valley and beyond the
private lake which now occupied much of it,
Nero converted the unfinished temple dedicated to his predecessor, Claudius, into a
nymphaeum. This conversion effectively
closed off any view of the great public aqueduct Claudius had built, and from which
water now cascaded into Nero's pond.[12] Nor
was the self-proclaimed philhellene reluctant
when it came to rearranging nature. The park
and gardens of the Domus Aurea attest to the
heavy use of the shovel, as did his estate at
Subiaco.[13] The Velian Hill was lopped away
to accommodate the entrance hall, and the
Oppian levelled off as a platform for the
northern and western parts of the palace.

All opulence and megalomania aside, the
real perversity of the Golden House lay in
Nero's contempt for the life and work of his
fellow citizens, embodied in the very place
they had been piecing together over generations. Prior to him, the Republican and Imperial leaders had been expected to commission
works that were both publicly useful and
displayed the propriety necessary to the position of Princeps. So Augustus had preferred to
narrow the confines of his planned forum
rather than resort to confiscating the surrounding houses, whereas Tacitus informs us
that the hated Nero 'used the whole city as his
house.' Clearly, the outcry against the Domus
Aurea is evidence not only of the precariousness of Imperial leadership, but of the continuation among the populace of that Greek
aversion to territorial desecration. But whereas the Greeks built to appease only the gods,

Rome now added mortal politics to the architecture of reconciliation.

Through a Machiavellian lesson that even
today seems peculiarly hard to grasp, those
who hold power wisely do not extend its
abuse into the arena of urbanism. In the
construction of Rome men had to come to
terms with each other by the judicious use of
boundaries, so the Domus Aurea was regarded as an aberration that inevitably had to
give way to the corrective work of Nero's
successors: It was Vespasian who altered the
hated colossus, rededicating it to the sun god,
and Hadrian who had it moved to build the
temple of Venus and Rome at the end of the
Sacra Via. Before long, the palace succumbed
to more civic policies. Martial's poem *Liber de
Spectaculis 2*, written later in the reign of
Titus, celebrates the events whereby 'Rome is
returned to herself' from the abominations of
the Golden Palace:

Here where the heavenly colossus has a close
    view of the stars
And high structures rise on the lofty road,
There once shone the hated hall of the cruel king
And one house took up the whole of Rome.
Here where rises the huge mass of the awesome
    amphitheatre
In sight of all was Nero's pool
Here where we admire the baths built so quickly
    for our benefit
A proud park deprived the poor of their houses.
Where the Claudian temple spreads its wide
    shade
Stood the last part of the palace.
Rome is returned to herself and under your rule,
    Caesar,
The delights of their master have become those
    of the people.[14]

Illumination and Disaggregation

It was only on Italian soil that the Greeks and
Romans between them ... succeeded in producing a building type which, though conceived
within the framework of the traditional orders
and of traditional materials, managed to look

inward as well as outward ... suddenly, it seems, architects became aware that interior space might be something more than the void defined by four walls and a roof, and that it could itself be treated as the *raison d'être* for the envelope which enclosed it ... Roman architects found themselves confronted by the almost totally unexplored possibilities of an architecture in which the traditional structural verities yielded pride of place to purely visual, and often elusive, effects of space, light, and colour.'[15]

If the Greek reverence for the world as given caused them to bring the temple to life as a reminder of its ultimate demise, and, through the spectators' imagination, to deconstruct in an instant their most precious building, the Romans deployed both literalness and illusion to the same ends. The Hellenic ability to explore tropes, metaphors, and subtle layers of meaning gave way to picturesque disaggregation and the dematerializing effects of light in Rome, when it came to reconciling the crudities of building, first with the sanctity of nature, then with the imperatives of urban boundaries.

Since Republican times the Roman house had been a kind of pierced, half-open shell, comprising for the most part a series of roofless, porticoed courtyards and open atria. At first, as was true of the Hellenic dwelling, ostentation was rare, and luxury houses were severely criticized in the Senate. But ironically, as far as we know, the first dematerializing use of light, already referred to in our discussion of St Denis, occurred in the notorious Domus Aurea, which launched a disembodying technique durable enough to find its apotheosis in the extreme transparencies of twentieth-century modernism. Why the hyper-assertive Nero, of all people, would initiate such a technique we cannot tell, although there may well have been precursors to the Domus Aurea in other private villas destroyed during the Great Fire of A.D. 64, and the Princeps happened to be an enthusiast for novel and dramatic ideas. In the Domus Aurea, we find traces of this technique in only a single room,

the octagonal focus and probably the symmetrical heart of a complex placed between two major trapezoidal courts on the Oppian Hill.

The room was domed, projecting up through a second storey and surrounded by five radiating chambers roofed over by cross vaults and barrel vaults. An oculus occupied the centre of the dome, but the chambers received their light from a series of upper windows arranged around an ingenious well located between the extrados of the dome and its supporting piers (Fig. 5.2). The room is usually identified with the circular dining-room described by Seutonius, which contained large elements that rotated like the world, as well as cascading waterfalls and devices for showering perfumes over guests. All this opulence, provided for a cause that scarcely evokes sympathy, was in fact used in a highly original way. Nero's idea was certainly to transform this brick and concrete facility into a magic garden, as an extension of the vista through the porticoed south wall of the rotunda to the landscape beyond. This transformation was accomplished in part by the more obvious theatrical means of waterfalls and rotating screens; it was the light, however, shining directly through the oculus and indirectly via the well around the dome through the upper windows into the chambers, that provided the greater effect. We can

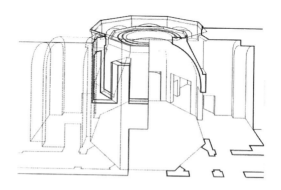

5.2   Domus Aurea, Rome. Sectional perspective, ca A.D. 65

5.3 Interior of the Domus Aurea

assume that all interior surfaces were lavishly decorated, probably in vegetal motifs; the curve of the vaults, ribs, and dome guided and gradated the incoming light over these painted surfaces such that the whole edifice boundary seemingly evaporated into a luminous mirage of trees, flowers, and sky (Fig. 5.3).

As will be seen, this particular use of light works best upon curved surfaces and is least effective on four-square, trabeated forms. The technique, therefore, had to await the vaulted and domed innovations found in the Domus Aurea, and applied thereafter to the monuments of Imperial Rome, most significantly in the Pantheon.

The evaporating power of light relied usually – but not exclusively – upon the controlled setting of interior spaces, so much of Roman architecture at its best has a dual effect: a kind of external presence and internal absence. Ward-Perkins calls attention to this feature in describing the Aula Regia, the great hall of Domitian's Domus Augustana, completed in A.D. 92.[16] In this instance, however, a quite different dematerializing technique was employed, again probably for the first time. The hall, designed by Rabirius, had a span of almost thirty metres, pushing the then-current concrete barrel-vault technology to its limits. To carry the substantial roof load, Rabirius

5.4   Pantheon, Rome, section, A.D. 120–4. From Andrea Palladio, *Four Books of Architecture*, Book 4, ch. xx, 1570

had to incorporate massive piers into the flanking walls. He then proceeded to alleviate their massiveness, not by excision, but by subdividing the entire circuit of the walls into a series of alternately curved and rectangular bays. Between each bay, on the pier face, he attached an order of fluted marble columns; half the bays contained doorways and an apse, while the remainder held projecting columnar and pedimented aedicules to receive statuary. Through this deliberate accumulation of forms – the rhythm of receding and re-entrant planes, the suggested domesticity of the 'little house' aedicule, the mask of vertical lines framing the bays – Rabirius succeeded in neutralizing the unwelcome presence of cumbersome stone. The 'breaking down' procedure initiated in a controlled manner in the Aula Regia, and later manifested quite differently in the picturesque Markets of Trajan, would characterize both internal and external organization throughout much of the subsequent history of city building. Together with the dematerializing properties of light, it revealed the essential place of illusion when dealing with ubiquitous construction (Fig. 5.4).

Imperial Rome: The Porous City

When Dionysius of Halicarnassis visited the Augustan capital his impression was of 'a city stretching to infinity' (*Antiquitates Romanae*, 4.13.3–4). Certainly a view from the Esquiline Hill would have offered but a few glimpses of Latium's fields and orchards in the distance well beyond the Servian walls. We cannot be sure if a million people inhabited Rome at the close of the Republic, but the Neronian projects were no alleviation of the dense crowding to which the average citizen was subjected. Privacy was hard to find, so Martial hardly slept; he occupied a third-floor apartment on the Quirinale, constantly bothered by noise from the streets, courtyards, and rowdy neighbours (12.57, 3–17).

Our estimates of population density become more respectable with the building of the Aurelian walls in the third century (Fig. 5.5). They enclosed about one million people within 1,373 hectares, which gives a gross density of 730 per hectare. But, as John Stambaugh points out, about 40 per cent of the city was reserved for villas, gardens, and public buildings, so Rome in the days of the Principate must have contained whole quarters whose population density rivalled that of present-day Calcutta or Bombay.[17] Most Romans lived in the lower districts threading between the hills, while the senators and equestrians – those rich enough to keep a horse – occupied the villas located atop the Oppian, Esquiline, and Avenine, enjoying the cooling breeze and views of the mob below. Apart from the squatter slums across the Tiber, home to the poorest migrants, the low-lying urban quarters probably housed a mixture of social types: small merchants, tradesmen, labourers, and slaves shared the streets and apartments between them, and were divided, according to Juvenal, by neighbourhood more than by class.

The writings of poets and chroniclers confirm what the structure of Imperial Rome itself suggests – that there were two ways of coping with ubiquitous humanity apart from building a hilltop villa. One could embrace the city with its flaws and often repellant aspects in the conduct of everyday life, or reject it by retreating into nostalgia. The educated and moneyed classes were so steeped in nostalgia that at times it served political interests. Augustus was pleased to be called 'the restorer of the old ways' as well as a bringer of peace. He lived on the Palatine, but, like Cicero, occupied an unpretentious house with a modesty lesser men chose not to emulate. Nevertheless, the official encouragement of *mos maiorum* – the ancestral ways – permeated the city's architecture, the decoration of public places and its poetry. In the *Odes*, Horace identifies Augustus with Aeneas, the pre-urban hero who personified the antithesis of Rome, that city which the poet detested. Epic poetry, to Horace, constituted an offence against the quiet simplicity that one might

5.5   The Aurelian Wall, Rome, third century A.D.

recall but never experience in the city again. In the *Satires* he describes how the crooks and lechers had taken over the streets and how the mobs distracted his mind from dwelling properly on those peaceful things to be found far away in the countryside.

But, perhaps like most of us, Horace was often of two minds, depending on his mood. Elsewhere in the *Satires* (1.9) can be found his well-known reminiscence of walking to the Forum. Now he relishes the crowded streets, swinging along the raised sidewalks with an eye for the girls, and the merchandise being loaded into shops; his other senses too enjoy the splendid assault of vendors and orators, the smell of olives and vegetables cascading in his path, feeling the sweat and muscular pull of traversing the city on foot. There are many such descriptions of Roman streets and street life. Martial spent much of each day on foot, noticing every detail of the city. Seneca, Ovid, and Lucretius were often given to nostalgia, but that did not keep them at home when colour and animation filled everyday life outdoors; their tales about 'whores, pimps, vagabonds, hustlers, peddlars, cooked beans, sausages, dancing and begging priests'[18] show them as prepared to indulge in Rome's urbanity as the next man. Carnivals and festivals were not occasions for mere attendance: showing up meant joining in. The great December *Saturnalia* was a time for street dancing and merrymaking; on Mother's Day – the *Matronalia* – women dressed in their finest and paraded through the streets, while the *Caristra*, an annual celebration of family life, always took place outside the home, revealing again the transcendant power of *res publica*.

This dialectic between quotidian existence and the reassertion of tradition found its expression in city building, which provided a resolution of sorts to the binary spirit of the capital. If propinquity and civic dignity produced their own forms, their boundaries and symbols were usually complementary, and moulded into the connective patterns necessary for access and display. Each neighbourhood (*vicus*) had its central street, embellished

with squares, monuments, and remnants of the feature from which the neighbourhood derived its name and identity: The *Vicus Aesculeti* grew up around a grove of oak trees, while the Palatine Temple of Apollo gave its name to the *Vicus Apollinus*, to which it formed the central anchor. Axel Boethius remarks on the openness of these neighbourhood streets, especially where they were lined with arcades, colonnades, and *taburnae*[19] (Fig. 5.6). Doors, windows, and shutters at ground-floor level were thrown open, so that the interior became part of a permeable boundary threshold between the public and private domains. The neighbourhood streets in turn were stitched into larger assemblies; some formed links into arteries that traversed the city, while others, like the Vicus Tuscus and the Vicus Jugarius, gave directly onto the Forum Romanum (Fig. 5.7). The Forum itself, which Cicero called 'the shrine of holiness and majesty, wisdom and statesmanship, the very centre of the city's life,' never completely shed the informality of its attachment to the adjacent neighbourhoods, although the markets on its northern flank were eventually displaced by the Imperial fora in the first and second centuries. Wedged astride the confluence of streets funnelling along the low ground between the Palatine, Capitoline, and Oppian hills, this most illustrious symbol of Roman consciousness was shaped, for five hundred years, around the contingencies of a plebeian setting. Even the largest structure in the Forum – the first-century Julian Basilica – was sized no wider than the distance between two neighbourhood streets entering from the south, to maintain access routes that probably predated the Republic.

Despite her power hierarchies and the hilltop villas where the rich detached themselves from community affairs, Imperial Rome was allowed to come to terms with congestion and squalor by turning itself into a vast, fluid spectacle which alternated spatially between the dignities accorded the past and a tumultuous present. The one permeated the other in a dense kinetic web of streets, squares, ramps,

5.6   Via dell'Abbondanza, Pompeii, first century A.D.

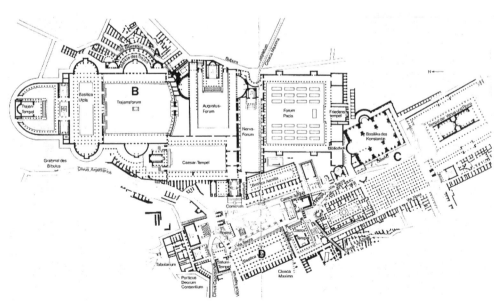

5.7   Plan of Rome during the second century A.D. A: Trajan's markets; B: Trajan's Forum; C: Sacra Via; D: Julian Basilica

stairs, and precincts; for the most part, they were not thrown together haphazardly, as historians once thought. On the contrary, their arrangement was often subject to the idea of *res publica*, whose origins were more ancient than Rome itself, and which we can recognize in the protean forms of preclassical Greece.

Crafted Towns

In city building, the organic and the picturesque have close affinities, although they seem to emerge from very different conceptions of good urbanism. To the late-nineteenth-century theorist Camillo Sitte, organicism was a process whereby cities grow out of the natural instinctiveness embedded in a cohesive culture. Ironically, the processual basis of organicism, as described by Bruno Zevi, for instance, makes it akin to modern comprehensive planning, but only in this sense: process is all. The picturesque, by contrast, is concerned exclusively with visual consequences, so the point of departure is always the evocative power attributed to certain forms, a power deemed to override all processes of formation.

Yet one wonders if each is a different rationalization of a deeper common source. Those who favour organicism often do so selectively, not so much from any serious understanding of the processes involved, but from an *a priori* preference for a universal connectedness, working back from selected expressive meanings. Conversely, what is generally considered picturesque are those forms evoking the very absence of rational formalism, held together by seemingly unconscious shared values. At their source, the organic and the picturesque are united by suppression of the extremes of individual wilfulness, of inviolable boundaries, and of institutionalization in all its forms. As such, they are constituents of the historical current of practical reason we observe in Hellenic urbanism, to be dashed to temporary oblivion under Nero. The wisdom of Aeschylus again, as expressed in *The Eumenides*, is apt:

Seek neither licence, where no laws compel,
Nor slavery beneath a tyrant's rod;
Where liberty and rule are balanced well
Success will follow as the gift of God,
Though how he will direct it none can tell.[20]

The durable appeal of the organic and the picturesque in urbanism lies in the practical way of life they express – associations dependent on unspoken agreements, rules voluntarily adhered to, the respect and tolerance that are the dues of inventiveness. By the time Rome had been 'returned to herself' under Vespasian, she could again aspire to, if not actually achieve such a life. Whereas the Imperial Forum, by the time of Trajan, rendered visible through its monumental symmetry the more rule-governed traditions of the old Republic, it was the neighbouring Markets of Trajan that best expressed the everyday associations of Roman society culled from that unteachable Greek skill: *kairos* – knowing when and how to speak. Here, for the first time stood the deliberate representation in construction of the *idea* of the picturesque.

Such an idea, in this case, depended on the revered presence of the Forum itself. This ultimate symbol of Roman unity, founded as a market-place to celebrate the first tribal union had, long before Trajan, evolved into an historical agglomeration of temples, shrines, and halls of justice, all set within their colonnaded precincts. Since the first days of Rome, the Forum was the supreme place of ritual and collective memory, the urban equivalent of the divine Hellenic landscape, although, as we have seen, even its boundaries were judiciously pierced to receive the kinetic life thronging the streets around.

Trajan's markets were the work of Apollodorus, whose mandate was to build a new commercial quarter into the remains of a saddle of land linking the Esquiline and

Capitoline hills. The project required a lot of ingenuity because the saddle had been cut away to provide a level space for Trajan's Forum, which lay immediately to the west. What remained was a steep incline into which a series of terraces, staircases, and ramps had to be incised to take the market complex. The spine of the new complex comprised a winding street of shops following the contours halfway up the slope, and which today survives as the Via Biberatica (Fig. 5.8). Below, a second street occupied the foot of the slope, curving into a re-entrant semicircle tracing a projecting exedra in the east perimeter of Trajan's Forum. A two-storey façade faced the perimeter wall and backed onto shops served by the Via Biberatica above. Along the eastern side of this upper spine, Apollodorus dug a bewildering array of shops and apartments, some of which were accessed from intermediate terraces farther up the slope. At the northern end stood a three-storeyed market hall, while to the south the Via Biberatica turned and ramped upwards into the third and highest street, in turn lined by market facilities and housing (Fig. 5.9).

In execution, the complex was spare and virtually unadorned; brickwork, modest vaults, arches, and simple fenestration monopolize its decorative characteristics. Otherwise, the markets depend entirely upon a single ancient principle for their success: judicious subordination to the boundaries of the Forum. Apollodorus begins with the semicircular re-entrant at the foot of the slope as an echo of the shape and symmetry of the Forum perimeter. This he decorates modestly but in the classical manner, applying a continuous moulding, shallow brick pilasters, and triangular pediments over the arched windows to form a row of aedicules along the second storey. The curving re-entrant, re-echoed in the horizontal mouldings of its façade and in two smaller hemicyclical halls to right and left, matches at a more intimate scale the grandiose sweep of the Forum. This intimacy

is enhanced by foreshortening all views of the re-entrant from its narrow facing street, thereby muting its façadal symmetry. In sum, those elements of the market nearest the Forum comprise a domesticated version of the latter: a mediating skin between the formal expanse below and the kaleidoscopic pile above (Fig. 5.10).

The terraces and buildings occupying the upper slopes of the saddle overlook the Forum from behind the perimeter wall, in a reticulated arc following the curve of the exedra and the façadal salient. Viewed from below, no single mass predominates because each element is fitted into its site according to the exigencies of the terrain rather than some superimposed compositional idea. But what lifts the whole complex above the merely natural is Apollodorus's insight in permitting the fan-shaped hillside to act as a kind of architectural theatre: the Forum itself is the spectacle, and the variegated audience occupies the commercial quarter above, with a respect whose expressive meaning depends on an assembly being literally *broken down* into its constituent parts and echoing the forms of the Forum boundary.

Here, in brick and stone, stood the representation of an aspiration grounded more firmly in the mythic past than in aestheticism, theoretical knowledge, or the sentiment normally attributed to the picturesque. The possibility that actual social events in Imperial Rome may have been not unlike the foul scene depicted by Lewis Mumford in *The City in History* is irrelevant: urbanism is no more required to placard the commonplace than to cater to the manipulations of the élite. What the Markets of Trajan, in their particular association with the Imperial Forum reveal, is a life that might have been, or better, a life that could be, in which the complementarities that *should* guide urban existence are made visible. Neither the markets nor the Forum, in their different modes of publicness, is subjugated to the other, yet what represents the new, the

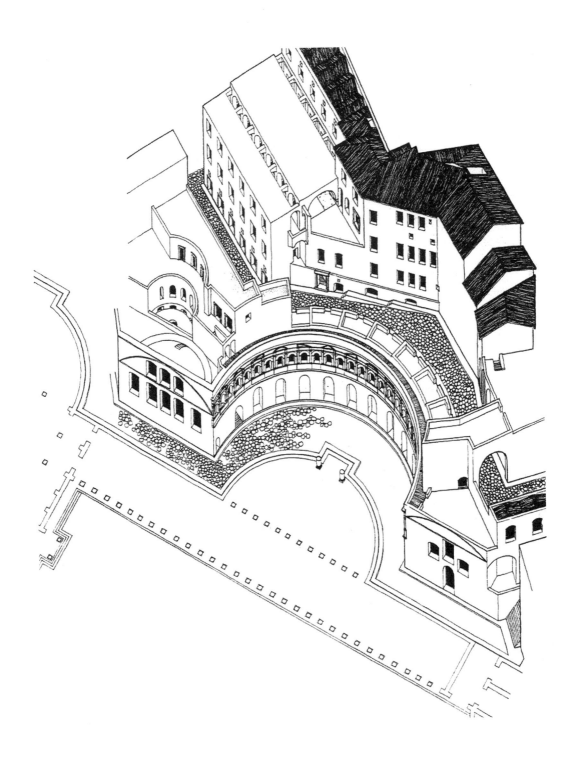

5.8   Markets of Trajan, Rome, second century A.D., axonometric

5.9   Markets of Trajan. View of the Via Biberatica

5.10   Markets of Trajan. View from the Forum

material, the brash, is made to signal the transcendence of those more lasting verities embodied in the Forum.

Yet it would be misleading to imagine this assemblage in the capital, whose principles were soon to shape urbanism across the Roman Empire from Britain to Syria, as the product of theoretical cogitation. On the contrary, the Markets of Trajan were derived from something akin to the prerationality that had governed Hellenic complementarities. In this case, however, we witness a reflexiveness, not to revered features in nature, but to the contingencies of an urban landscape. Vitruvius, the conservative theorist of the first century, chose to ignore these contingencies in order to validate his rules governing architecture and urban features. Yet while Imperial building is unmistakably Vitruvian in detail, its vernacular stamp follows few rules of any sort.

Anti-Theoretical Townscapes

'Roman design was shaped largely in response to urban needs and civic ambitions,' writes William L. MacDonald at the beginning of his recent appraisal of Imperial architecture.[21] If a city like Timgad began as a Hippodamean grid, with two main streets, the *cardo* and *decumanus*, crossing the town from gate to gate, its evolution scarcely depended upon a preordained geometry. MacDonald coins the term 'armature' to describe a particular system of boundary articulation – the unfolding chain of 'main streets, squares and essential

5.11   Ephesus, view down the lower Embolos to the Celsian library, A.D. 115

public buildings ... with junctions and inter-sections prominently articulated'[22] as the characteristic unifying feature of Imperial cit-ies. This feature was apparently never precon-ceived as an entity, but was a consequence of accretion, elaboration, and boundary adjust-ment over time. Few important urban ele-ments were located independently of the ar-mature, so fora and other squares, and public buildings such as amphitheatres, temples, ba-silicas, shops, markets, and baths, were usu-ally linked to it as local needs and urban contingencies demanded. Whether these ele-ments straddled the armature, as did the fora at Trier, Paris, and Ostia, or stood beside it, as at Lepcis Magna, Palestrina, and elsewhere, the armature was essentially a connective de-vice, so movement through it was always fluid

and unimpeded (Figs 5.11 and 5.12).

Infinitely variable from one city to the next, armatures were fitted into and around topo-graphic shapes and existing development, channels of movement articulating their way through prior forms via platforms, staircases, and 'passage architecture' – points of transi-tion marked by significant monumental events such as arches, quadrifons, *tetrakoinia* and statuary. From one end of the armature to the other, the city could be instantly sensed as fluid, accessible, and cohesive, a veritable analogue of *civitas*. These multiple forms, with their joints and connections to each other, then to the precincts which occupied their interstices, were never derived from the few contemporaneous texts written about ar-chitecture or urbanism. Neither Flavenius nor

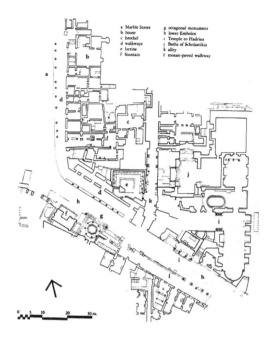

a Marble Street   g octagonal monument
b house   h lower Embolos
c brothel   i Temple to Hadrian
d walkways   j Baths of Scholastikia
e latrine   k alley
f fountain   l mosaic-paved walkway

5.12   Ephesus, plan of the lower Embolos and Marble Street

Palladius was inclined, as MacDonald points out, to abandon his pale aestheticism to deal with what was essentially an artisan undertaking. Vitruvius in any case preferred Greece to Rome as the source of architectural verities, and made no reference to any work that required pragmatism and a social imagination. As we shall see, from the time of Vitruvius down to the present, architectural, even urban theory flourished and was put into practice usually when urban contingencies were absent, or could be wished away. Such theories were made, for the most part, for an empty landscape, whereas Rome, then the Imperial settlements of Ephesus, the Antiochs, Palestrina, Baalbek, and so many others, were densely packed agglomerations by the third or fourth century. Abstract planning had literally no place in the middle of close propinquity, where opportunity, a modicum of flair, and a native feel for propriety guided urbanism.

It has become common to draw a distinction between town planning and the mental processes that make untheoretical elements like the urban armature.[23] But these processes could also be described as planning, although of a special sort: nothing as porous as the armature boundaries traversing, say, the remote and minor African city of Djemila from gate to gate could have been assembled without some rational foresight, although one that first rejects complete predetermination, then allows echoes from the pre-urban past to work on the imagination (Figs 5.13 and 5.14). No line between planning and the absence thereof could be drawn between regular and irregular layouts without ignoring the contamination of both sides. City building happens to be a procedure that properly works back upon itself, demanding that kind of reflexiveness towards shifting boundaries with which the Fali peoples are gifted. The same restlessness so characteristic of the Fali village, whereby inert features convey the sense of shifting across space, also suffused the Imperial Roman cities. The podium temples, with their forward-projecting arms and robust mouldings, possess, in MacDonald's nice phrase, the poised energy of stationary locomotives on their tracks: 'Podium arms help join sacred architecture with open spaces for worship and assembly ... The force of this connection, of the visual and axial functions of the arms, is suggested by the disengaged condition of temples that have lost them, for example those in Rome to Mars Ultor, to "Fortuna Virilis" ... or the Antonine temple at Sabratha.'[24]

Consider, too, how kinesis of this sort could animate whole urban armatures, as in Ostia or Djemila, from end to end. In the small town of Djemila, by the third century, the principal street had been extended southwards from a complex of temples, baths, and forum, through the original gate into a new square flanked by basilicas, a market, fountains, past another fountain marking a place where the street narrowed, then climbing to a grand system of baths, apsidal buildings, and what later housed the Christian quarter. Within the old southern gate this street was colonnaded on both sides and perhaps lined with *tabernae*;

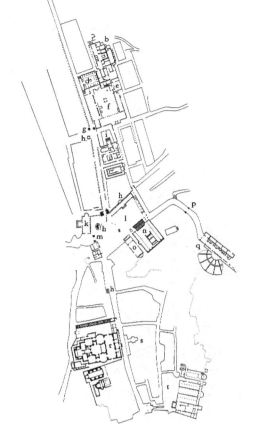

5.13   Djemila, aerial photogragh

5.14   Djemila, plan

here, at the centre, where the road shifted direction to follow a slight ridge, stood a simple arch and fountain, planted there to signal an inflection in forward movement and the presence of the Forum, Capitolium, and Senate House beyond, which were accessed to one side via staircases to their higher platforms (Fig. 5.15).

To walk such a street, less than a kilometre in length, whether as stranger or lifetime inhabitant, meant being absorbed step by step into the uniquely structured town life of Djemila, formed around and symbolized by its armature. As the population grew and spread southwards over a 200-year period along the same ridge followed by the principal street, we can imagine its communal structure

taking shape around the exigencies of prior relationships and hierarchies which adjusted and were adjusted in response to newer social forms. The judgments and procedures of town building probably possessed a concomitant history, the community extending, then embellishing its boundaries according to constructed legacies so that its continuities were both spatial and temporal. To properly articulate a connection between adjacent forms in Djemila required a proficiency that many a modern designer should envy: ingenuity in handling joints, points of transition, boundaries, and changes in level displays a keen sense of the interplay of vision and bodily movement like that experienced by Horace while walking across Rome. In the old centre, a

5.15   Djemila, view of armature towards the arch and south gate

market hall addresses the colonnaded street and is entered directly from it, while the forum and adjacent temple, dignified by being set beside and elevated above the arched point of inflection, must be reached after first passing through a small precinct, then by turning to make a staircase ascent. From here the street, always half contained within its rhythm of columns and shops, inclines upwards slightly for a hundred metres to the southern gate, later transformed into another arch announcing entry to a trapezoidal square. Through the arch the square opens sharply to the left, where the Severan temple axis is echoed across the square by a shaded podium and fountain set against the old town wall (Fig. 5.16). Resting in the shadow cast by the gate, a second-century traveller could have taken in at a glance, and no doubt relished, the whole animated length of the armature.

Must we assume the existence of some kind of locally based egalitarian democracy to explain townscapes such as this? Djemila had its share of political classes, some of which were empowered from Rome, and their presence can be discerned in grand houses off the Forum, in the Capitolium and Senate House, in statuary and an Arch of Caracalla in the new square. But the town stood in a distant province, founded during the *immensa pacis romanae maiestas* of the first and second centuries, and overseen by a hierarchy more accessible and relaxed than the capital's. Public life, sanctioned by custom and endorsed by the local state, needed its facilities and symbols, a townscape apparatus designed for the pleasures of walking, assembly, and transactions in the open air. Decisions about this apparatus were neither anticipated in long-term plans nor made piecemeal; instead, what Aristotle had once called *forensis dignitas* – the dignity of public places – seems to have become a principle of practical reasoning held and put to use by other actors on the scene besides politicians and plutocrats. While local culture – expressed in public life and the townscape which catalysed it – and politics may not have been entirely extricable, the

Roman jurists' definition of natural law, inherited from the Stoics, offers a clue to the source of the mutualist urge that shaped places such as Djemila: 'the aggregate of general relationships established by nature among all animate beings for their mutual preservation.'[25]

The Fall of Roman Urbanism

If the shape of certain Imperial Roman towns can be traced to a commonly held belief, upheld through law, and expressed by the porous character of armature boundaries, in mutual dependence, empirical social unity itself was far from complete. Like Latium, Timgad and Lepcis Magna had their share of suburban villas, of private wealth used in bad imitations of Hellenic reconciliation; if they did not exactly maul the countryside, they aestheticized it. In town, families with money turned their nostalgia inwards, seeking predictability in domesticity, their interior peristyles made exquisite, like the House of Europa in Cuical, by the addition of plants, fountains, and pools. The occupant of the House of the Fisherman in Bulla Regia had his peristyle walls painted to resemble nature reflected in the water that covered the floor.[26] Such houses began to copy the porticoes and vestibules used to give temples and fora their dignified distance from the street but, as with the second-century entrance to the House of Hercules in Volubilis, their lavishness hardened the street boundary as well as signalled the presence of money on the inside. Behind these vestibules, private space expanded into *triclinia* for fine dining, *exedra* for conversation, and *cubicula* where outsiders were never admitted.

Both townhouse and villa represented different kinds of escape from the noise and disorderliness of the urban armature, but were also early signs of a subversion of its interdependent spirit, heralding an eventual collapse of *res publica* in the fifth century. Meanwhile, the dialectic of privacy and mutualism continued to be played out partly

5.16   Djemila, Severan Temple, view across the new plaza, third century A.D.

along class lines in Rome and the Imperial colonies, setting up divergent patterns of land occupancy and constructed form. But if the wealthy needed privacy and lavishness, other influential men advocated the opposite. In second-century Rome a new brick-faced concrete architecture made its appearance in public buildings and *insulae* – multipurpose tenements lining the streets – to the approval of Cicero who, in an early espousal of functionalism, declared that the fulfilment of practical requirements was enough to produce charm *suavitas quaedam et lepos.*[27] His voice did not go unaccompanied: since the late Republican years we hear time and again the indignation expressed by assorted literati and statesmen alike against ostentatious display in dress, manners, or architecture. Whether or not these objections had any effect, by the time of Aurelian and Diocletian in the third century, Rome was of necessity a utilitarian city. *Urbs vetus* – the old city that Suetonius claimed had been filled in rather than laid out – had disappeared under the great fire and Nero's schemes. However, a marble fragment from a plan of Rome made about A.D. 200, the so-called *Forma Urbis*, shows a compact, orthogonally conceived quarter that in one important aspect, at least, reminds one of a nineteenth-century industrial city: the 'sweating' of frontage along public thoroughfares by endless ranks of *tabernae* and *insulae* (Fig. 5.17). Here is decisive evidence of a force that would play havoc with ancient and modern boundaries alike regarding urbanism, namely, self-interest, working on the urban landscape to divide territory and harden boundaries.

The enclosure and continuity of principal streets, the formation of connective urban corridors such as we have admired in Djemila, does not, of course, occur solely as a consequence of some cultural-aesthetic consensus. Instead, the evolution of such towns is an ancient version of the perennial working out along urban boundaries of a resource-allocation process in which the symbols and empirical desires of privacy confront those belonging to the community. The resultant synthesis, embodied in myriad allocations of construction to urban land, carves the city along the seams where public life stops and private life begins.

In Imperial times, especially in the third-century tenemented cities of Rome, Constantinople, Tyre, Ostia, and Antioch, except where families had enough money to build their self-sufficient domain behind an impervious screen of vestibules, porches, and peristyles, the seam between public and private life appears to have been highly porous. Most of the insulae dwellings were small, a clue that much of what is now conducted privately was then public activity. Bathing, eating, recreation, and other forms of social life took place outside the dwelling, and the *Forma Urbis* fragments suggest that the animation of the streets infiltrated flanking rows of *tabernae* with their open stalls and workshops. The peripatetic Martial describes (in *Epigrammaton libri*, Book 7, 61) scenes in which wine flagons were chained to portico columns and how the paraphernalia of bakers, smiths, and moneylenders tended to spread out from vestibules over the thoroughfares of the city. Gregarious habits, low incomes, and high densities squeezed the crowds into and along the public armatures so that Rome's architecture became a utilitarian channel to movement on foot (Fig. 5.18).

Vitruvius claimed that the high tenement house was a form unique to Rome (*De architectura*, Book 2, 8, 17), but he could not have known that it was less a locally derived type than the consequence of intensive mechanical relations that not only produced multi-storey buildings wherever urban land was in short supply, but pushed their perimeters to the lot boundaries and the frontage of scarce public territory along the thoroughfares. The pressures of these demands were for a time resisted along the armature's length in the name of civic dignity, and resolved by the intercession of small and large public spaces – a flanking colonnade or sheltered sidewalk here, a forum or temple forecourt there.

But by the close of the Western Empire, the old civic consensus that had built the Markets

5.17　A *Forma Urbis* fragment, ca A.D. 200

5.18　Pompeii, street of the theatres

of Trajan and Djemila was in tatters. Justinian promulgated his famous sixth-century code as a last vain assertion that the city must not succumb to a hoard of little Neros intent on partitioning urban territory into an exclusive club. For seven hundred years this code, and the remnant spirit of *civilitus* that gave birth to it, were consigned to oblivion; it took the flowering of twelfth-century Bologna to bring them back to life and embody them in the statutes that governed building in the communes of northern Italy.[28]

CHAPTER SIX

Intensity, Insularity, and Communitas

Cities of the Mind

As we have seen, the Imperial Roman settlements were far from being perfect models of harmony and communal solidarity. Propagandists in the capital made sure that official culture permeated the farthest reaches of the Empire by maintaining a sometimes oppressive colonial magistery with its supporting armies. Officialdom also rendered itself visible in the prominent positioning of its monuments and facilities along the armatures of such cities as Ostia, Lepcis Magna, and Timgad. Materialism, working through the competitive instincts of urban landlords, petty retailers, and status-seekers, patterned the spatial organization of Djemila, Constantinople, and the Antiochs, squeezing *insulae* and other profitable development into gaps along the boundaries of main streets and back alleys. But among this constructed evidence of state imposition and private greed we can find remains of a different sort, which bring to mind what Hans-Georg Gadamer has called the 'dialectic of mutual recognition.'[1] When Martial or Horace describes the outdoor life of Rome, one notices only scant traces of an imposed authority; instead, the scenes and events manifest an apparent common con-sciousness rendered visible in the city's porosity and its human motility. Whole stretches of Rome were arranged to cultivate friendships, greetings, and mutual respect, even though intermeshed with a rather different record of street brawls and institutional corruption.

The enterprise of city building, even in its most recent phase, somehow still manages here and there to transcend the material facts of economic and social life. If we dismiss those examples from urban history that fail the test of uncontaminated high art, then we are left with virtually nothing at all, because the traces of communal solidarity and constructed artistry must usually come to terms, in their fashion, with the rule-governed search for status and profit that drives urbanization forward. Indeed, that is the hallmark of urbanism's art. So the evidence of mutual recognition, that impetus which oriented whole Ionian cities towards a god-filled landscape, then caused the Romans to embellish their articulated civic domain, must often be sifted from more dominant traces of self-interest.

We have become used to the idea that mutual recognition no longer encompasses the whole city, but is at best selective, retreating before the incidence of self-interest and public animosity into inwardness, which sets up its own constructed boundaries. With the contemporary metropolis, this recognition shrinks finally to the scale of the household, and can retreat no more. But there has existed, since antiquity, a middle ground which subdivides the landscape selectively, forming precincts of communal protection that are often intertwined with symbols of idyllic recollection. So, while Virgil's bees did better than the modern household, creating an analogue of communal solidarity, the poet reminds us that their constructions were also insular, and set within a hostile world. As the Roman world fell to pieces, Virgil's analogue began to take shape across Europe.

As early as A.D. 276, Frankish platoons forded the Rhine, and soon, along with the invading Alamanni, had established themselves across a region of the Empire that stretched westwards to Autun. In the ensuing bloodshed, seventy towns were annihilated, causing the remaining few, which had previously been unwalled, to throw up their first fortifications. Within a matter of years, much of Gaul, once a relatively cohesive, secure territory, was divided into autonomous strongholds, their suburbs having been laid waste and turned into vast cemeteries. But even inside these newly built bulwarks both public order and predictable life collapsed, while the countryside, much of it reverting to wilderness, was carved up into fiefdoms, each one ruled over by an aristocrat ensconced in his fortified estate.[2]

With civic culture in ruins, the post-Imperial age began to be obsessed, like our own, with the acquisition and protection of private property, which was fought over and argued about in the few primitive courts to the virtual exclusion of everything else. The Frankish, Merovingian, and Carolingian legal systems were monopolized by the German invention of private law: 'Boundary disputes, contested wills, complaints by buyers against sellers, and disputes among heirs all but overwhelmed the judges.'[3] The idea of the *res publica* withered as the often violent appro-

priation of municipal and other state property by private warrior-kings increased; the whole of Merovingia, for instance, became little more than a stretch of real estate run for the exclusive benefit of its owners. Even within what was left of the towns a law had to be passed, as Alaric's Breviary records, in a vain attempt to prohibit the building of houses against the city walls.[4]

Throughout this darkest period in the West, Byzantium continued to flourish, as did the old colonies of Anatolia and the Levant. Even in Gaul itself, not everywhere suffered the fate inflicted upon its northern regions. Poitou and Aquitaine grew wealthy, and maintained a semblance of urban order in cities like Cahors, where the Bishop Desiderius 'girdled the town with defensive walls and built aqueducts ... He saw to it that his cathedral city was given new houses, a monastery and several churches.'[5] Aquitaine flourished in the sixth century, exporting marble carvings, capitals, and sarcophagi to other parts of Gaul. But even here, culture and technical competence regressed into near-archaism, and settlements neglected the old crafts of ornamentation, civility, and urbanism (Fig. 6.1). An awakening taste for sorcery went hand in hand with public insecurity, as the Gallo-Frankish Hypogeum at Poitiers, a tomb chamber dating from the seventh century, exemplifies; the structure retreats half-underground and is afforded the protection of magic from cabalistic rune carvings (Fig. 6.2). There a Latin inscription heralded the sacking of Poitiers at the hands of the Moors: 'All things go from bad to worse and the end is near.'

For half a millennium, urbanism served the cause of fear as the porosity of the old Imperial cities gave way to boundaries selectively designed to protect and exclude. If barbarian art tells us anything, it seems that the invaders themselves brought no architectural concepts with them that could be assimilated into post-Imperial building. The Lindisfarne and Echternach Gospels and the Irish *Book of Dimma* may be splendid achievements of illumination, but they contain no sign that their

6.1   Baptistery of St Jean, Poitiers. Detail of south wall, seventh century

6.2   Entrance to the Hypogeum, Poitiers, seventh century

cultures were at all interested in architecture or possessed a culture dependent on boundaries. Where the occasional Gallic manuscript does depict buildings, as in the *Lex Romana Visigothorum*, or the so-called *Quaestiones in Heptateuchon*, probably from Laon, they tend to be primitive, incidental structures, obviously not having been worth the expenditure of much imagination (Fig. 6.3). But the painting of this period is telling in a quite different respect. The murals of San Lorenzo, dating probably from as early as the fifth century, reveal how the imagination of artists was already turning away from material reality. Painted space becomes flattened to a two-dimensional plane upon which the figures of saints, emptied of all emotion, are transfixed. In Early Christian art, the depiction of architecture and towns takes on a particular character, reinforcing the sense of retreat to the

predictability of a static, inner world. On the triumphal arch of Santa Maria Maggiore in Rome, the human scenes take place outside the walls of a city, but the latter, depicted as a high, bounded artefact, together with the fragile arches traversing the picture, frame and protect the icons. This theme, whereby buildings embrace a sacrosanct and static domain, sheltering it from adversity, is detectable as early as the second century, in the Consular Diptych of Stilicho. In the sixth-century Italian *Gospel Book of Augustine* and in the Tours Pentateuch, painted a century later, the saints and acolytes are housed in decorated towns whose perimeters trace a clear line dividing sanctity from profanity. The beautiful *Codex Egino*, written at the end of the eighth century and presented to the cathedral in Verona, repeats what had by then become a common theme, showing St

6.3 'Lex Romana Visigothorum.' Stiftsbibliothek, St Gall

565 the poet Fortunatus describes the estate of his friend Nicetus, bishop of Trier:

A defensive wall flanked by thirty towers surrounds the mountain on which stands a building occupying the site formerly covered by a forest; prolonged on either side, the wall runs down to the bottom of a valley, all the way to the Moselle, whose waters bound the estate on this side. At the summit of the rock is built a magnificent palace, like a second mountain placed on top of the first. Its walls enclose a vast area, and the house itself forms a kind of fortress ... It has three storeys and when one has reached the highest, one gets the impression that the edifice covers up all the fields below ... On these once barren hills Nicetus has planted vines bursting with sap, and the rock which once was covered with brambles is now carpeted with green vines. Orchards of fruit-bearing trees grow here and there, filling the air with the fragrance of their blossoms.[6]

Withdrawal from a disintegrating, unpredictable world proceeded in concert with the consolations of the imagination and the spirit, to inspire insular cities of the mind. The Psalter of Utrecht, painted between 816 and 835, depicts God as a fortified city under siege. Outside the walls the ground is strewn with contorted bodies of the vanquished, trampled upon by an invading army. The city itself is compact, circular in plan, and secure, its walls drenched in sunlight and set within a dark and treacherous landscape. Here we see the human unconscious at work, projecting an archetypal image of psychic wholeness on to the outer world. Nicetus's walled estate by the Moselle answered to practical requirements, but in Fortunatus's recollection it took on all the character of the archetype, like an enlarged version of the mythical enclosed garden of Mary and Venus recorded in the Song of Solomon: trellised and bowered, filled with the scent of lily and rose, vibrant from the intimacies of the picnic; here was a recollection that would outlast the Middle Ages (Fig. 6.5). The line between heaven and hell was

Gregory and St Augustine seated within their protective frame of arches and ornamented columns (Fig. 6.4).

This subject of the artistic imagination echoed beyond the mosaics, paintings, and manuscripts into ways of life and their constructed forms. Hermitry was everywhere revered, as demonstrated, for instance, in seventh-century dedications to the reclusive Paul at Jouarre. Walled gardens became metaphors of paradise, where 'crimson-coloured brings forth the green grass and the air is redolent with the heavenly fragrance of roses.' In about

6.4 Verona, *Codex Egino*: St Gregory, eighth century. Deutsche Staatsbibliothek, Berlin

strongly drawn as different kinds of enclosures representing the gap between refuge and incarceration (Fig. 6.6). One version of Hades, often depicted as the city of Dis, brings to mind the incubus of Ur; at Dis the souls of the damned were locked forever within the city's buttressed perimeter, which denied them a glimpse of the smallest ray of light.

At first the quest for sanctity began, not by a retreat into fortified cities, which were mostly lawless places up to the ninth century and beyond. On the contrary, the boundless deserts of Africa and the Near East became the original refuge of the *monachoi* – the lonely ones – who were to give new shape to symbols of refuge and the return of psychic wholeness. 'By the end of the fourth century the role of the Christian church in the cities had been overshadowed by a radical new model of human nature and human society created by the "men of the desert."'[7] If public spaces along the armatures of Roman cities had once provided the setting for companionship, this role was now challenged by monasticism. Amid the devastation of northern Gaul, the abbey of Jouarre was founded in the Marne valley by the year 630, the focus of an awakening that raised two hundred monasteries across the region between the sixth and eighth centuries at such places as Nivelles, Moutier-Grandval, and Fleury. About this time, along the remote shores of County Kerry, a few young men began piling stones into crude boundary walls around huts that would become the monasteries of Kildrenagh and West Feaghmaan. For the first time, the architecture of urbanism would take the form of small cloistered cities, each populated by an extended household of companions.

The Cloister

In A.D. 676, St Cuthbert of Lindisfarne, who loved his neighbours, detached himself from his sect, choosing to spend his remaining years alone on remote Farne Island. There he built a hermitage, but found the wilderness of coast and cliff too distracting. He therefore shut himself off behind 'a wall higher than a man standing upright.' When even this did not provide the insularity he required, Cuthbert added to the wall's height 'by cutting away the living rock so that the pious inhabitant could see nothing except the sky from his dwelling, thus restraining both the lust of the eyes and the thoughts and lifting the whole bent of his mind to higher things.'[8]

Paradisus Claustralis: If Cuthbert's enclosure seems more like a self-affliction than a paradise garden, his is only an extreme case of the liminal wish to remove oneself periodically from the here and now. His escape was a return to the world of the soul, and proof that experience is not limited to the senses. If *community* is a theme spanning the history of urbanism, then so is *liminality*, which is not the former's logical opposite but the completion of a dialectical pair, cutting much deeper

6.5   Detail of the Hardwick tapestries, fifteenth century. Victoria and Albert Museum, London

than association and privacy, and developed to their culminating state in a few urban variations on the monastic cloister.

To an anthropologist, liminality represents a threshold condition, one accompanied by *rites de passage* during transformation from one status to the next. The words *threshold*, and *passage* are reminders again of how ways of life have their equivalents in constructed boundaries and how too these forms are endowed with significance, in this case again by two-faced Janus, that mythic guardian of thresholds and gates. Victor W. Turner writes that liminality is itself an act of remembering, of the rootedness of human life in a society whose institutions are no more than instruments to serve this end.[9] Like Cuthbert's withdrawal, the liminal condition requires a profound humility accompanied by silence, obedience, simplicity, even foolishness to remind the initiand of his prehuman state. 'Nowhere has this institutionalization of liminality been more clearly marked and defined than in the monastic and mendicant states in the great world religions.'[10]

But liminality cannot be sustained for a lifetime without revealing its subversive underside, which brings disillusionment.[11] As with the abstemious vigil of the medieval knight, liminality is a springboard to action,

ICI EST ENFERS ELIANGELS KI ENFERME LES PORTES

6.6   'Here is Hell and the angel who locks the door.' Detail of the Winchester Psalter, ca 1150. Trustees of the British Museum

presaging a return to social life, while recognizing anew society's dependence on the human bond to the world around. This recognition, in turn, throws into sharp relief the essential place of *communitas* in breaking down the boundaries which rigid social and urban structures place between individuals.

Such things would not concern us here were it not for the fact that, through its constructed patterns, urbanism was once the means whereby *communitas* confronted institutional structures in a dialectical play which now rarely occurs. Now, the patterns favour only structure, and the metropolitan landscape becomes an analogue of 'that incredible hard-heartedness which collective man displays towards his fellow men.'[12] That the expression of *communitas* was not limited to ceremony, art, and myriad forms of human intercourse, but also found its way into city building should come as no surprise; *communitas* is the product, not only of 'instinctual forces, but also rationality and memory,'[13] and all were brought to bear in the construction of countless places, including Priene, Djemila, even Pergamum.

The architects of early Christianity reveal the constructed face of *communitas* most clearly, however, as an intensifying response to the collapse of imperial social structures and institutions. At first, a prolonged liminal phase undergone by Cuthbert's predecessors the *monachoi* – the lonely ones – by its very nature rejected the significances and conceits of urbanism. In the fourth century, Pachomius, who established a string of monastic retreats in the deserts of Egypt, built an oratory in one of them. Finding it too beautiful, he ordered ropes attached to the columns to set them askew.[14] The solitary life of liminality meant a return to the fold of God's nature, which could be neither matched nor hemmed in by the pretences of architecture. In A.D. 313 the ageing ascetic Antony, 'fleeing from fame,' travelled three days into the wilderness, settling at the foot of a mountain where, for years, he gazed from his cave upon a pristine landscape.

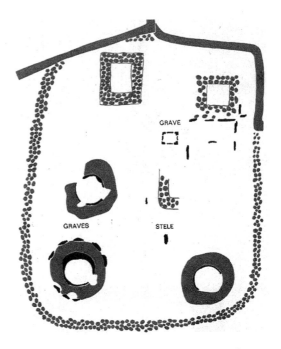

6.7   Kildrenagh monastery. Ireland, seventh century

As hermitry began to give way to desert-dwelling clusters of men, then women, the first experiment with *communitas* produced no particular constructed models, austerity being the only common theme (Fig. 6.7). A fourth-century anchorite settlement at Chariton, near Bethlehem, began as a group of caves, then evolved into a characteristic *larra* – a street with shops like an eastern souk. At Canopus, around the same time, the monks inhabited an abandoned pagan temple. The Syrian ascetic Julian Saba founded the first monastery on Sinai in the middle of the fourth century; he built a cluster of cells around the mountaintop, with a little church and a cave at the peak. In 556–7, a 'castrum' was built there by Justinian, who also commissioned the church with its great apse mosaic of the Transfiguration.[15]

Then, St Benedict, at Monte Cassino, wishing to plant oases of a predictable life here and there, envisioned the ideal claustral complex, which was to contain 'all necessary things …

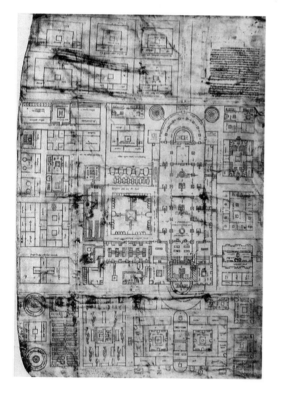

6.8   Plan of St Gall, ca 820. Stiftsbibliothek, St Gall

water, mill, garden, various crafts … so that the monks may not be compelled to wander outside it.' There, 'let the novice brother prostrate himself at each one's feet, that they may pray for him. And from that day forward let him be counted as one of the community.'[16] We see his vision given shape in the mysterious Plan of St Gall, drawn on parchment during the Carolingian Renaissance (Fig. 6.8). The monastery had fallen on hard times when, in 816, Gozbert was made abbot of St Gall and took it upon himself to instil spiritual vigour into the place once again. Gozbert managed to reappropriate the monastery's lost lands and sought a strategy to restore and extend the fabric. His unknown senior provided the Plan of St Gall, prefaced by a letter worth comparing to the tedious covering letter of today's commissioned report: 'For thee, my sweetest son Gozbertus, have I drawn out this briefly

annotated copy of the layout of the monastic buildings, with which you may exercise your ingenuity and recognize my devotion, whereby I trust you do not find me slow to satisfy your wishes. Do not imagine that I have undertaken this task supposing you to stand in need of our instructions, but rather believe that out of love of God and in the friendly zeal of brotherhood I have depicted this for you alone to scrutinize. Farewell in Christ, always mindful of us, Amen.'[17]

The drawing accompanying this letter is the first known specification for laying out the elements of a monastery, and its precepts were to be followed throughout the subsequent era of monastic foundation. What is more, several important ideas embedded in the plan may be recognized in sundry urban-development schemes down to the present time. They all have to do with the meticulous interplay that occurs between the paired ideas of community and seclusion.

The plan assumes a *tabula rasa*, and its main elements are disposed according to an orthogonal modular grid based upon divisions and multiples of forty Carolingian feet. The number forty has the highest value in the *Numeri Sacri*, the series considered sacred in Christian liturgy and scripture. The church, for instance, is symmetrically aligned along an east-west axis 160 feet from the northern boundary; ten columns flank each side of the nave to form bays measuring 20 feet by 40 feet; the aisles are 20 feet wide, as are ancillary rooms along the north and south walls; the crossing and transepts are 40 feet square; and so on.

The claustral complex, in which the refectory, vestiary, larder, kitchen, bake house, laundry, and dormitory are located around the cloister, abuts the south wall of the church. Church and claustral complex together form a precinct that is literally, functionally, and symbolically detached from the remainder (Fig. 6.9). The points of contact with the outside world are limited to three reception porches for pilgrims, paupers, and distinguished guests. Only the abbot passes freely

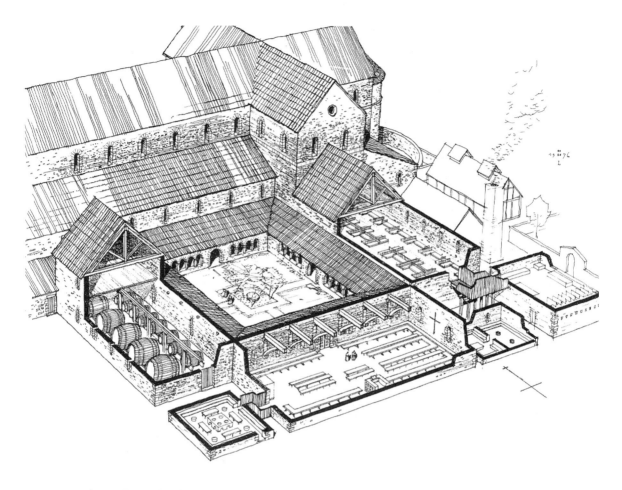

6.9   Claustral complex, based on the Plan of St Gall

between the sanctuary precinct and the secular world, an exception reflected in the location of his house, linked to the north transept between the outer school and the hospital.

The remainder of the monastery is made up of buildings devoted to the education of the public and novices; care of the sick; the housing of pilgrims, paupers, and nobles; the agricultural pursuits of poniology, horticulture, and husbandry; and various crafts. All are sited orthogonally along the north-south and east-west axes, but none is subjected to the discipline of the modular grid, and all are delineated, for the most part, more abstractly than the inner precinct.

The plan of St Gall has been admired for its rationality and paradigmatic status; the unprecedented precision, dimensional coordination, and efficiency characterizing the zonal distribution of activities are all merits that appeal to modern thinking. Nevertheless, the most decisive element, in terms of future influence, is the existence and arrangement of the cloister. While galleried courtyards and atria were a feature of antiquity, St Gall's square arcaded garden, overlooked by protective buildings and only indirectly accessible from outside, has no significant precursor. In size, the cloister is one hundred feet square (2 1/2 modules, this number being the smallest subdivision of 40), conforming to a ninth-century interpretation of the Rule of St Benedict. Its shape suggests a place of arrival and contemplation, and the perambulatory arcades – an integral, essential feature – foil the bulk and scale of the enclosing structures. As a type, it renders visible the idea of companionship, of fraternal self-containment in both a material and a psychological sense.

Up to the various monastic reforms of the sixteenth century, the St Gall cloister, whether attached to the north wall of the church, as in the Mediterranean, or to the south wall, typical north of the Alps, remained virtually unaltered from first to last. It spread from the great Benedictine establishment at Cluny to the Cistercian and Augustinian orders. By the fourteenth century, only a library and a chapter house for assembly had been added to the original concept.

What concerns us here particularly is the expressive character of the cloister boundary, because its dialectic is of a special order, and a ubiquitous hallmark of those intermediate urban structures that are neither public nor completely private. The dialectic in this case is fully worked out, and fastened to a simple system of architectural rules that match the stringent ordering of monastic life. 'Without a Rule no monastery can endure' echoes through all the edicts of the monastic founders, first through the Rule of St Augustine, then those of Benedict, Francis, Basil the Great, and the Jesuit Constitutions. But the longevity of their Christian utopias also depended on the slow, imperceptible turning of monastic architecture around a handful of ideas having to do with the manner in which the community defines the boundaries around its existence (Fig. 6.10). The *stabilitas loci* required by Benedict was soon given a shape spelled out in the earliest description of a monastery, that of Jumièges, the eighth-century *Vita S. Filiberti*: 'Arcades accompany the laboriously stone-built cloister.' Then the Fontenelle chronicles (822–33) record 'three buildings of equal height round the cloister – dorter, refectory and study hall.'

Once constructed, the cloister was rarely enlarged when the monastery expanded. Instead, more cloisters were added; Santa Maria Novella in Florence has a group of seven, and while they vary in shape and size, their expressive meaning, like those across Europe, is everywhere the same: an enfolding architecture of tranquillity, where arcaded rhythms frame the birdsong and foliage of the seasons (Fig. 6.11). Monastery life, its essence austere, serene, and complete, kept a careful watch over this powerful expression, wary of any decorative digression. 'What are those laughable monstrosities doing in the presence of the brethren reading in the cloister, such perverted beauty and such accomplished ugliness? If one is not ashamed of such improprieties, why not at least rue the expense?' Here St Bernard complains in *Apologia ad Guillelmum* about the decorated capitals commissioned by Abbot Suger at Cluny.

Embellished or not – and after Bernard, a certain plasticity of detail was not uncommon – consider how the cloister boundary holds its special expressive meaning in place. The perimeter walls beneath the arcade are invariably pierced by entrances only at the corners, and occasionally, as at Clairvaux and the 'Green Cloister' of Santa Maria Novella, by a single entrance near the centre of opposing walls. Cloister access is like that to a hidden sanctuary: discreet and incidental. One cannot step directly from the entrance to the central garden, for the latter intersects with its threshold, the arcaded perimeter, in a certain way; one must tread the length of this perimeter, seeking an opening in the knee- to waist-high parapet from which the columns rise (Fig. 6.12). In so doing, the walker senses the domestic scale and rhythm of the arcade in the low, dark vault above, and the close columnar interval with its shadows cast underfoot (Fig. 6.13). Across the garden, in a veil of light, the identical scale of the opposing arcades gives precise clues to the width and length of the intervening space, which is further stabilized by a modest fountain and one or two cypress trees or, in the north, a single sycamore, beech

6.10   The ideal convent portraying, in the lower half, a procession through the cloister. From *La Sainte Abbaye* (Fr.), ca 1300. Trustees of the British Museum

6.11   Salisbury Cathedral, the cloister, thirteenth century

6.12   The cloister of Mont-St-Michel, Manche. Completed 1228

6.13   The upper cloister of Santa Maria della Pace, Rome, by Bramante, 1504

6.14   The Cistercian cloister of Heiligenkreuz. Austria, fourteenth century

or oak (Fig. 6.14). Very occasionally, there were departures from this ubiquitous boundary expression; in the Great Cloister at Santa Maria Novella the scale of the perimeter is increased to match the seventy metre–by–fifty metre space in the middle, so domesticity gives way to a civic quality, carried through by the presence of monumental statuary and Brunelleschi's Pazzi Chapel, which interrupts the arcaded perimeter. Elsewhere we may find a diversity of detail – double columns and a two-level hierarchy in arcadal spacing, as at Fontenay and Saint-Trophîme in Arles, for instance – but such things rarely subvert the idea of the cloister (Fig. 6.15).

In urbanism, wherever the idea of the cloister has been taken up, its purpose was neither for hermitry – think of Cuthbert's private yard – nor for licentious congregation. Instead, it depends upon those rules of conduct essential to the formation of that special kind of community in which reflection and conversation fill much of one's life. The cloister recognizes a particular level of association spanning a large and subtle stratum between complete withdrawal and licentious interdependence: an assertion that there is more to life than indiscriminate association and privacy (Fig. 6.16). Thus, while we may admire the shape of the inner court carved out of the *poché* of the seventeenth-century Parisian *hôtel*, it represents an idea quite different from that of the cloister. The *Grande Cour* of Antoine Le Pautre's Hôtel de Beauvais (1652–5) does not seclude so much as exclude, and is the starting-point for a whole class of private spaces that eventually became far more pervasive than their claustral prototype. Place Louis-le-Grand (now Place Vendôme), begun in 1699 by Jules Hardouin-Mansart, denies room, in its proclamation of publicness, for the essential dialectic of community and sanctuary. Only slightly better are the patrician squares of London, in which the park at the centre was accessible only to those occupying the surrounding houses. From Inigo Jones's Covent Garden (1631) to St James Square (1755), urbanism served the interests of exclusion

6.15   The cloister arcade of Heiligenkreuz

6.16   Arcades of Piazza San Carlo. Turin, eighteenth century

while borrowing the forms and boundaries of seclusion.

It is true that all of these – the cloister, the *cour*, the *place* – have this in common: they tend to take precedent over the surrounding architecture, which falls into place around them, subjected to their shape and purpose[18] (Fig. 6.17). But this is only a technical thing, having little to do with larger meanings captured, for instance, in a letter written by one Haimo, recorded in the *Annales Ordinis Sancti Benedicti*. In 1145, Haimo had witnessed the provisioning of an abbey church by the Norman community of St Pierre-sur-Dives. The townspeople had spent the day dragging supplies and construction materials across the coastal inlets. 'And when at last they had reached the church, the wagons were placed in a circle around it like a spiritual encampment, and all that night the whole army kept watch with hymns and canticles. – And there while the priests preach peace,

enmities fall asleep, disagreements are driven away, debts are lightened, and unity of spirit is restored.'[19] Here, a boundary made up of wagons – surely a catalyst of the ensuing events – sufficed to give expressive meaning to the communal and the liminal idea.

One turns then, to the colleges of Oxford and Cambridge to detect the vast but poorly provisioned middle ground of the mind embodied in the cloister (Fig. 6.18); we see more than a trace of it, democratized, enlarged, restructured, in the campus of Thomas Jefferson's University of Virginia at Charlottesville (1817–26). Is one forced to the conclusion that the cloister is but an artefact of institutional order requiring membership and behavioural stricture? Not at all; the *idea* of the cloister precedes institutions, being modelled on a return to the Paradise Garden, where one may be accompanied but never distracted, a place from which contemplation and co-existence have not been purged (Figs 6.19 and 6.20). Such places, or their traces, exist outside of institutions, but have become an endangered species since their banishment under the cumulative rigours of European neoclassicism and modernism. One searches in vain for some remnant in the utopias and planted towns of the last hundred years to find only a highly polarized vision of the ideal life: either public or private, of which the small urban park, as an underdeveloped metamorphosis of the claustral idea, belongs to the latter.

Competing Boundaries

The cycle of building that raised the towns of northern and central Italy in the thirteenth century depended on a kind of urbanism crucial to the rapid, intensive occupancy of scarce urban land. By the end of the fourteenth century, this rationality was being replaced by another, namely, that of the Renaissance, one more in tune with economic decline, offering plenty of time to cogitate about abstract ideas and the yielding urban boundaries to put them into effect.

6.17 Courtyard of the Ducal Palace, Urbino, 1464–8

6.18 Aerial view of Oxford

6.19 Piazza San Pellegrini, Viterbo. Drawing by Imre J.J. Koroknay

In 1164, Pisa had no more than 11,000 inhabitants living within their new defensive walls at a density of fewer than 100 persons per hectare. Like Florence, Milan, and Bologna, at the beginning of the twelfth century Pisa had spread its wings, recognizing political opportunities in the surrounding *contado*, benefits in warfare and maritime commerce, and an incipient exhaustion of their distant rulers in Germany and Rome. This new-found assertiveness was turned inwards too, towards the physical structure of the town, which for centuries had been a half-empty shell, rubble picked over and discarded, the streets but an extension of the swamps that rendered much of the region uninhabitable. But then, the Pisans won a small victory over the Saracens and in 1063 were able to take over Palermo. In celebration, they drained a piece of land at the edge of town and there laid the foundation of a new cathedral, although half a century passed before any serious progress could be made on the fabric. Then, about the year 1100, the city burst into activ-

6.20   Giardino Giusti, Verona

ity. One Benjamino da Tudela visited Pisa in 1159, doubtless carried away by his imagination but nevertheless astounded by a skyline bristling with 'ten thousand towers.' A baptistery was started in 1152, aligned on the cathedral axis, and the famous campanile, whose foundations in the former swampland were too hastily constructed, began to rise behind the south transept. So began a century and a half of brilliance.The city's golden age occurred in the mid thirteenth century under Federigo Visconti, who completed the Camposanto and the cathedral baptistery; by 1293, the population of Pisa had increased to about 38,000 and the urban density had more than doubled, turning the city into a blossoming, decorated precinct. Only thirty years later Pisa was in ruins, its population decimated by war and malaria, foreshadowing what would happen elsewhere under the Black Death. In

1550, only 8,600 souls were left in what again was a semi-rural backwater.[20]

Like Syracuse, Pisa had once been a Greek colony, and each presents the unusual case for this period of having constructed its cathedral complex in precinctual fashion as a series of free-standing structures, not unlike the arrangement on the Acropolis itself (Fig. 6.21). Elsewhere, even in the smallest of towns, if sizeable open areas were still present inside the walls by the twelfth century, within a matter of years they usually suffered encroachment from interstitial development, as happened in Ferrara, Pistoia, and Siena. In 1200 no Tuscan city contained more than 20,000 people, but, by the end of the century, Florence, which easily outstripped the rest, housed 96,000 persons on the 630 hectares enclosed by the new walls.[21] Here, too, within thirty years, the Florentine population began its decline, not to

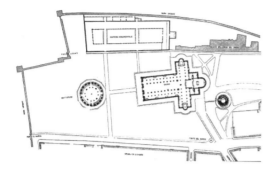

6.21   Plan of the Piazza del Duomo, Pisa

recover until the nineteenth century. Its only near-rival was Venice, containing about 100,000 persons in 1338, at a density of more than 300 persons per hectare. In 1424 the Venetian population had been reduced, but only to 84,000, a relatively small decline held within limits by Italy's strongest economy.[22]

So everywhere across northern Italy the building surge was cyclical, plateauing through the second half of the thirteenth century, and coinciding, more or less, with the rise and fall of a much-vaunted communal system of government that brought a quasi-republicanism to the cities for the first time. Throughout this period, municipal politics shaped the character of medieval urbanism, but so too did the pressure of intensifying mechanical relations and their subsequent reversal, revealing again how the fashioning of architecture is tied to boundary formation.

By the close of the twelfth century, partly as a consequence of the quarrels between Papacy and Emperor, a number of city constitutions and largely independent cities, the communes, were already in place. The old judges – *buoni homines* – who represented the supramunicipal interests of bishops and counts – had been replaced by the *consoli*, locally elected to act as chief executive officers.[23] Their rights were those of the communes, including the right to levy taxes, adjudication, self-defence, the construction of public works, and the regulation of private building. In addition, the *consoli* needed their own quarters, so in cities

like Reggio, Perugia, Pistoia, and Todi, small parcels of land were cleared at the civic nucleus, usually on the ecclesiastical square, to build a *palazzo del comune* (Fig. 6.22).

But the consulates from their inception were themselves marked by political intrigues and manoeuverings, and were superseded by or paralleled by another institution, that of the *podesta*. A report by the Genoese chronicler for the year 1190 describes what happened: 'civic discords and hateful conspiracies and divisions had arisen in the city on account of the mutual envy of the many men who greatly wished to hold office as consuls of the commune. So the *sapientes* and councillors of the city met and decided that from the following year the consulate of the commune should come to an end and almost all agreed that they should have a podesta.'[24] Not least among these intrigues was the widespread incidence of graft in matters of urban land and territoriality. So, to ensure his absolute integrity, the *podesta* was appointed from another city for a period of six months or a year. Usually a nobleman schooled in law, he performed the tasks of chief executive officer, judge, and army commander, although his power was usually shared with an assembly of citizens, the *consiglio generale*. They met in their own facility in the Lombard cities, where a special *palazzo del podesta* was constructed on the central square. These buildings had a characteristic form, often with an open portico on the main floor below the assembly hall; from the hall a loggia would open to the square for purposes of public address. Often a campanile was attached to double as a watch tower, and a wooden staircase, which could be destroyed whenever danger threatened, accessed the street below. Overhead bridges sometimes led to adjacent buildings, connecting at the second-floor level.[25]

Prior to the building of these civic palaces, the councils assembled in the cathedral or a suitably large church, an arrangement that would sometimes induce the authorities to locate their facilities on the ecclesiastical square. This was the case in Volterra, where

6.22 View of the Palazzo del Comune in the Piazza del Duomo, Todi. Drawing by Imre J.J. Koroknay

the Palazzo dei Priori was not completed until 1257. Siena's council met in the San Cristoforo church until 1280, and in Viterbo civic sessions were held in Sant'Angelo before the Palazzo del Comune opened in 1264.[26] The Florentine *parlamento*, the council of one hundred, often met outdoors before construction of the civic palaces.

By the third decade of the thirteenth century, the *podesti* had been installed in towns throughout northern and central Italy. But then a rival institution began to appear, namely, the *capitano del popolo*, a special leader elected by dissatisfied popular factions in Ascoli Piceno, Orvieto, Perugia, Genoa, and elsewhere. The *capitani* tended to express their popular roots by establishing seats close to the market-place, so the spatial arrangement of many towns, by the mid thirteenth century, symbolized a dichotomy in local politics. This polarization could not be resolved by democratic means, so inevitably the communal system of government began to give way to the establishment of landed power with the advent of the *signoria*. At first, hybrid arrangements make it hard to distinguish the

aristocratic *signoria* from the communal institutions, but by the close of the thirteenth century Italian republicanism was virtually finished, and the *signori* were soon to build their own palaces.

So the cycle of economic growth, construction, and decline was closely matched – although one cannot assume causality – by an equivalent political cycle. Each was woven into local culture and ways of life, and placed its stamp on architecture and the urban pattern. Particularly striking are the similarities between the town-building practices of the imperial Roman colonies and those of thirteenth-century Italy, although the differences are large enough to dispel any notion of outright continuity; nevertheless, some circumstances do present interesting parallels between the two contexts.

In the first place, the competition for a limited supply of urban space produced intensive, contiguous forms. Axel Boethius correctly notes the close identity between the narrow-fronted insulae of ancient Rome, pierced at the ground floor by tabernae and flanked by staircases accessing the tenements above, and their thirteenth-century counterparts.[27] But he attributes this similarity to the recurrence of an Italian legacy, an archetypal idea, whereas it was more likely affected by the recurring dialectic of mechanical relations working upon a condition of land scarcity. Whatever the source of the similarity between ancient and medieval building practice, the configurations depicted on the *Forma Urbis* fragments, for instance, do resemble the arrangements lining the streets and back alleys of Florence and Bologna: sweated frontage, party-wall architecture, barrel-vaulted ground floor shops, staircases behind doors leading directly from the street (Figs 6.23 and 6.24). True, the streets of Imperial Rome were often 'laid out,' as Livy informs us, whereas the private interests of medieval Florence, for instance, usurped that city's ancient grid boundaries by undertaking a series of incremental distortions and adjustments. Orthogonal planning hardly fitted the needs of a

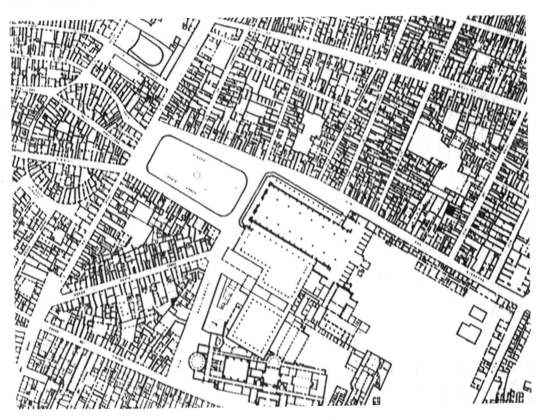

6.23   Medieval development in the Santa Croce district of Florence. The trisected oval block on the left is the former site of a Roman amphitheatre

society that clung tenaciously to its territorial legacy and paid scant heed to the boundaries of public space.[28] But recall, too, that Rome had its own labyrinthine quarters, straight streets being reserved for the subdivision of open land, or for a few arterials in the capital. In thirteenth-century Italy, while the urban streets were officially perceived as an instrument of subdivision and rational order, self-interests everywhere distorted official strategy, which had to await the extension of Ferrara almost three hundred years later. Instead, as with the connecting alleys of the Doria quarter in Genoa, and their contorted relationship to the larger hierarchy, urbanism served a contradictory order that operated at least at two levels of loyalty: neighbourhood and city.

This double connection, first and foremost to the boundaries enclosing oneself and one's friends, acquaintances, and blood ties, and only then to the larger urban territory, harks back to antiquity as the second link between Roman and medieval city building. (Indeed, this double link would be taken up as an organizing logic in twentieth-century suburban planning, with questionable success.) By the time the communes had been established, even in places that had once been Roman castrum towns with their characteristic grid patterns – Bologna, Faenza, Florence, Lucca, Pavia, Reggio, and Verona – their internal boundaries were being transformed in response to the thirteenth-century version of divided loyalty. In Siena and Genoa, the bonds to one's own quarter were extreme, precipitating fierce internecine vendettas as well as generating a marked enclaval pattern of city

6.24   Territorial competition shapes medieval urbanism. Drawing by Imre J.J. Koroknay

building. Here again we see that the actions of unmanageable young men are not insignificant in the process of boundary formation.

The Genoese system of neighbourhood territoriality, the *compagna communis*, transcended all other socio-economic and ethnic ties. There were dozens of quarters like this in fourteenth-century Genoa, each one oriented inwards to a complex of shared facilities and spaces. Some were appropriated by great extended families, like the della Volte settlement around the Mercato San Giorgio, with its nucleus of shops and church on a small piazza, its own communal baths and shared warehouses. The Doria family, with its distant cousins, friends, and retainers, settled in the district of San Matteo, reorganizing the streets and buildings to their taste, occupying adjacent houses on the tiny square that fronted their private church of San Matteo.[29] In 1365 the Sant'Ambrogia neighbourhood persuaded the visiting Pope Urban v to donate some church houses, which were then demolished to provide space for the Piazza Nuova. The new square became a regular meeting-place in the neighbourhood centre. A piazza, suitably embellished with a loggia, fountain, and other shared facilities, accessed directly on foot via a street network threading a well-bounded quarter, became essential for any territorially based clan with ambitions. Given the resources necessary, such ambitions required both solidarity and durability, characteristics that were often guaranteed through the establishment of formal neighbourhood associations led by elected residents.[30]

With judgments and decisions about urban development so balkanized, urbanism at a supraneighbourhood level found little fertile ground, having to cope with a Dark Age legacy of the appropriation of whole quarters by rival clans, a legacy lasting well into the fifteenth century. As late as 1425, Martin v complained in a papal bull of the 'abuse and sacrilege' to which public property was being subjected through illegal street closings and the conduct of private business in *piazze* and ecclesiastical precincts.[31] It was not at all uncommon to find rights of way completely blocked by houses, nor did neighbourhood entrepreneurial spirit stop short of turning the streets and squares into private workshops or warehouses, or cordoning off whole districts for the exclusive use of their inhabitants[32] (Fig. 6.25).

Nevertheless, a sufficient residue of loyalty to the city – which perhaps survived out of practical necessity – gradually neutralized some of the neighbourhood-based monopolies on territorial organization, although the so-called organic quality of medieval towns owed more than a little to local intransigence when it came to devising plans of urban-wide significance. In Siena, a statute of 1309–10 stipulated that at least a third of the main street leading from the Porta Camollia to the cathedral must remain 'open to the skies,' placing limits on the number and extent of private bridges, overhangs and other impedimenta. As we shall see, this statute exemplifies many promulgated on behalf of the civic interest against private and neighbourhood tenacity in the latter half of the thirteenth and throughout the fourteenth century.

The character of medieval towns in Italy is therefore derived from these highly competitive circumstances: divided territorial loyalties, manoeuvring for space along boundaries, specious bargaining, demands for compensation, then finally, with the advent of the more autocratic *signori*, statutory imposition and official edicts. What to us may seem like picturesque charm was to the communal officials a life of hard-won compromise, usually falling well short of their ideals. Wolfgang Braunfels cites, for instance, a 1262 statute of Parma, calling for the demolition of houses adjoining the baptistery 'so that the edifice can be seen ... and walked around on all sides.'[33] But both cathedral and baptistery ended up with a mere sliver of space a few metres wide (Fig. 6.26). Public monuments were meant to be free-standing, capable of being viewed from a distance along treeless, ornamented streets, and situated in a spacious context of regular geometry; these principles first attrib-

6.25   Territorial competition. View of Genoa by Cristoforo Girassi, 1480. Museo della Marina, Pegli

uted to Renaissance theorists like Alberti were vainly pursued long before the quattrocento, falling victim, in most cases, to the contingencies of rampant territoriality.

The Armature of Florence

In his great account of the building of Santa Maria del Fiore, Cesare Guasti writes of the difficulties confronting the Florentine authorities in their century-long battle to wrest a cordon of space around the cathedral from the abutting owners. Florence did not have a Maurice de Sully, bishop of Paris from 1160 to 1196, who had enough authority to clear away the labyrinth of houses in front of Notre Dame to form a well-proportioned square. Nor did the Florentine buildings enjoy the location of the cathedral complex of Pisa, situated by the ramparts and protected as much by its early start and near-suburban location as by municipal injunctions against encroachment. By the time the foundations of Santa Maria del Fiore were laid in 1296 two blocks from the Mercato Vecchio, the environs were already congested in the heyday of the city's most active period of building[34] (Fig. 6.27). Liturgy required that the new edifice be positioned on the axis of the existing baptistery, in a space that had accommodated the

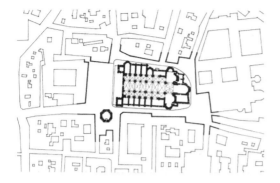

6.26   Plan of the Piazza del Duomo, Parma

previous church but was now, from what we can gather of subsequent clearing activities, far too small for the intended bulk of the cathedral. Arnolfo di Cambio, the illustrious *capomaestro* of Florence and restorer of the baptistery, ordered the clearing of the old cemetery and the demolition of the hospice between San Giovanni and Santa Reparata,

an action supported by Dante himself in the communal assembly.[35] Arnolfo, however, who began work on the western façade, was dead by 1302, and nothing more was accomplished until the ageing Giotto took over as *capomaestro* in 1334, to spend the last three years of his life building the lowest storey of the campanile (Fig. 6.28). The record leaves no doubt that extricating the giant edifice from the encroaching fabric was a tedious and, finally, half-accomplished process. Only in 1367 could a building next to the campanile be demolished to permit a reasonable view of Giotto's work, then it took another twenty years to disentangle the north transept and apse from the adjoining houses by expropriating land for the Via delle Fondamenta[36] (Fig. 6.29).

For years, private intransigence, embodied in extensions of all kinds spilling out over the hard-won boundary around the cathedral, frustrated Florence's officials. Only in the

6.27   Aerial view of Florence

6.28   View of the campanile and dome, Santa Maria del Fiore, Florence

second half of the fourteenth century, when declining fortunes and a slackening demographic growth eased the pressures on urban space, did statutory prohibitions begin to take effect.[37] But, even today, signs of compromise mark the structure of medieval Florence, for instance, in the narrowness of the arc of the Via delle Fondamenta, around the transepts and apse, and the unfinished state of the Via Calzaiuoli, intended as a splendid link between the cathedral and the Piazza della Signoria (Fig. 6.30). There, too, what have been assumed to be Renaissance ideas on town design – the *vedute*, a unified setting for important monuments, even street façadal symmetry – were applied as early as the fourteenth century, but frustrated in the end by private tenacity. The high front of Orsanmichele and the almost-completed

façade of San Carlo dei Lombardi faced each other along the Via Calzaiuoli two blocks north of the Piazza della Signoria, and the authorities were able to acquire a few houses around and south of Orsanmichele, opening up a small square and widening the street to the municipal piazza (Fig. 6.31). The owners received compensation and the building stone was sold to the cathedral.[38] By a municipal order dated 29 March 1390, the houses along this stretch of the Via Calzaiuoli were rebuilt, their new façades and materials made identical to those of a stipulated house in the street, acting as a model.[39] But north of Orsanmichele nothing was accomplished, so for most of its length what was intended as a great civic axis remained an unimposing alley. A similar fate overtook the Via Cimatori a century before; a municipal edict of 1297 ordered

6.29   Aerial view of the district around Santa Maria del Fiore, Florence

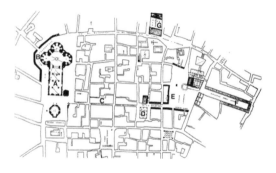

6.30 Plan of Florence between the cathedral and the Arno. A: Santa Maria del Fiore; B: Via delle Fondamenta; C: Via Calzaiuoli; D: Orsanmichele; E: Piazza della Signoria; F: Uffizi; G: Bargello

'a completely beautiful street between the Or San Michele piazza and the Bargello for the honour, beauty and accomplishment of the city.'[40] But in this case the old Benedictine cloister stood in the way, so only a fragment of the link could be completed.

So far as we know, no single comprehensive scheme held these false starts together in Florence, but an organizing structure not unlike a great Roman armature half-emerges in the tangle of streets, squares, and monuments lying between Santa Maria del Fiore and the Arno. Its least compromised element is post-medieval, tying the Palazzo Vecchio to the river; but the Uffizi had to await not only the power of Cosimo Medici and Vasari's talents, but the relative doldrums of the sixteenth century when urban boundary conflict had, for the time being, passed into history.

Siena: Urbanism versus the Feuding Household

The Florentine chronicle is a story of illustrious individuals, whether of commercial or artistic persuasion. Urbanism in that city benefited from, but also had to come to terms with such men, so its cohesive spirit met the resistance of self-interests in a conflict that could never be resolved. In the rival city-state of Siena, in contrast, communality rose to the surface, fostered by tradition and a municipal politics that rewarded fraternal actions more than individuality. There, more than anywhere, the aspirations and structures of the civic household shaped urbanism; but even here the outcome is flavoured by loyalty to the quarter, ultimately frustrating, in urbanism's characteristic fashion, the pursuit of the single idea.

Neither a Roman nor an Etruscan foundation, Siena had been a tripartite settlement – called the *terzi* – since the sixth century, each part shaped at first more by difficult topography and the narrowness of the valley lands than by any wish for cohesiveness with the other two; in fact throughout most of the Middle Ages their relationships with one another remained largely antagonistic. By the

6.31 View of Orsanmichele from Via Calzaiuoli

6.32   Plan of Siena in the fourteenth century. A: di Camollia; B: di Città; C: di San Martino; 1: Cathedral; 2: Palazzo Pubblico on the Campo; 3: Croce di Travaglio; 4: Porta San Martino; 5: Porta Camollia; 6: Porta San Agostino

eleventh century, the trio, having merged physically at the valley confluence, began to develop in linear fashion away from the centre (Fig. 6.32). To the north lay the district *di Camollia*, a ribbon of buildings strung out along the road to Florence but eventually contained within the Porta Camollia gate. The southwest district – *di Città* – was home to the original cathedral and bishop's seat, located on a hilltop overlooking the confluence below; *di San Martino* stretched southeastward along its valley road to the Porta Romana.

By the end of the thirteenth century, Siena's partial circumvallation enclosed roughly 35,000 persons, within what Bortolotti estimates as a 50-hectare enclave, at a remarkably high gross density of 700 persons per hectare. As in Imperial Rome, the wealthy tended to inhabit the hilltops, leaving the intervening

valley lands to the shacks and animal pens of the poor.[41] These were violent times, exacerbated by territorial loyalties to the *terzi* and, at a more immediate scale, to the sort of family settlement patterns with which Genoa and Florence were afflicted at this time. In the Camollia district, the powerful Tolomei clan clustered around the Piazza di San Cristoforo, while the San Domenico parish was home to the Malavolti. The San Martino hill housed the Ugurgieri family and the Piccolomini, whose descendant Pope Pius II commissioned that famous piazza named after him in Pienza. Città also had its share of rival families, like the Squarcialupa, who for years monopolized a palatial enclave near the cathedral.[42]

Death-dealing and conspiracy against rival territories co-existed strangely with city-wide celebrations and charity in Siena's streets. What began as boisterous games in the Campo often turned into brawls and worse; a riot by the *popoli* in 1318 threatened to bring down the communal government, while armed units of the fifty or so *contrade* usually settled their vendettas in the streets. The civic chaos following the Black Death of 1348, for instance, turned into a city-wide siege against the boundaries of rival clans.[43]

So, from the beginning, Siena suffered internal political division and lacked the compact shape and short perimeter necessary for secure defence, a flaw that would eventually prove fatal in the trecento wars against Florence. But, more pertinently, the absence of a 'ring-wall' enclosing a dense, closely bounded cluster of buildings abruptly separated from the surrounding *contado* posed a serious challenge to the image the city wished to have of itself as a unified community. In spite of the destructive loyalties of its people, no Italian city, and few anywhere before or since, was so ferociously committed to the unification of its architecture and urban structure – in a word, to presenting itself to the world as a fully integrated, harmonious household[44] (Fig. 6.33).

Two things are brought sharply into focus when one studies the events of Sienese

6.33 The Virgin Mary, protectress of Siena, presents Christ to the City. Detail of a fresco by Simone Martini, 1315. Palazzo Pubblico, Siena

this context of official power and determination, artistic genius and technical proficiency, a gulf still separated intention and consequence. The tragic side is the eventual failure to transform Siena into a reality whose archetype we see depicted in the pristine house-cities painted on the Utrecht Psalter and the Egbert codex. The saving grace, however, derives precisely from this same failure: Siena ends up being its own kind of masterpiece because, like a half-hewn sculpture of Proteus, the city reveals its *telos*, in which end-state and formative process are bound up together in a dialectic apparent neither in the psalter nor in the codex, nor for that matter in so many planted settlements and new towns of more recent vintage.

The Hearth and the Seam

By the time the formidable Giovanni Pisano began work on the cathedral façade in 1284, Siena had reached a zenith of accomplishment given to few cities anywhere; while internally fractured and constantly under threat from Florence, the city possessed great wealth, and the energy of the commune was being poured into building a denial of these unsavoury political facts. The very terms of Giovanni's appointment are salutary, for they show just how much importance the Sienese *consoli* and *popoli* placed upon urbanism as an instrument of propaganda, but also perhaps, for its own sake. Never before had an artist or craftsman been officially accorded the status of immunity from taxation and military service *tutto il tempo di sua vita*, a privilege first recorded in a municipal statute of 8 May 1287, and an early sign of the impending Renaissance attitude towards artists in general.[46]

Giovanni's status also coincided with the first election of the 'Nine' in 1287, a council of merchants which dominated Sienese politics until 1355. The Nove Buoni Mercanti di Parte Guelfa turned municipal government into an exclusively middle-class affair, confronting the private interests of the urban aristocracy

urbanism occurring in the thirteenth and fourteenth centuries. First, all the constitua of the city-household inversion reveal themselves forcefully in the statutes, proclamations, and public works of the civic authorities, with respect both to the placement, form, materials, and relatedness of its boundaries, and to the doctrine whereby every citizen was assumed responsible *come homini obedienti* for the 'beauty and honour of our magnificent city.'[45] Second, the working out of these events tells a story about the tragedy and saving grace of urbanism in that, even within

and district factionalism alike in a series of actions designed against all odds to house and represent internal unity. Their strategy in governing the commune looks like an analogue of household politics, with the Nine donning the cloak of paternal or fraternal wisdom, and invoking the maternal presence of the Virgin Mary; in fact, membership of the Nine drew heavily from the Fraternita della Vergine Maria e di Sancto Francesco de' Servi, Siena's leading confraternity since the Mother of God had been deemed protectress of the city in 1260.[47] Armed with all the symbolism of *paterfamilias*, the Nine dispensed justice and imposed sanctions on a fractious citizenship with remarkable impunity in the name of 'our good and pacific city of Siena.' If this now seems outrageous, it should be pointed out that the Nine apparently never abused their position for personal gain, a sign, perhaps, of their own serious belief in parental politics. As with any well-run family, the celebration of shared achievement was as essential as strict impartiality in governing the commune; festivals, processions, the games that sometimes got out of hand – all mirrored and confirmed the sense of relatedness which the Nine embedded in their building programs.[48]

The most well-known of these programs, and the only one to reach anything like completion, was the development of the Piazza del Campo (Fig. 6.34). Here, where the armatures of Siena's three districts converged on a low saddle of land, stood the most compelling place to fuse them together by building a communal hearth. A central market-place sloping steeply towards the open countryside to the south had stood here since the eleventh century, but when the first public building, a customs house, was built next to the market in 1250 the Sienese council still had to make do with renting private residences for their meetings. Only in 1281 would the council agree 'to find a location [for a communal palace] with all possible speed and to identify a method of building and a design ... that would cost the least.'[49] This peremptory edict by no means anticipated a course of events that paralleled

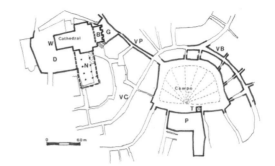

6.34   Plan of central Siena. B: Baptistery below the cathedral choir; D: Piazza del Duomo; G: Piazza San Giovanni; N: Uncompleted south extension of the cathedral nave; P: Palazzo Pubblico; T: Torre del Mangia; VB: Via (Strada) di Banchi; VC: Via di Città; VP: Via dei Pellegrini

the expense and protracted confrontations then being experienced by the Florentine officials in building their cathedral. It took seven years to settle on a suitable site, and not until a decisive session of the Nine that took place on 10 May 1297 was an annual sum of 2000 lire allocated *pro honore Communis Senensis pulcritudine civitatis*.[50]

Although the plans for the palace were not approved until two months later, they must have been presented during the May session, when the Nine passed its first major control over the aristocracy, many of whom, like the Tomolei and the Piccolomini, owned property adjacent to the new site. The residences of these families, like that of the Bishop, had been finished in travertine marble, whereas the communal palace, with the exception of its loggia and the cap to the tower, was to be built of red brick like the houses of the *popoli*. Moreover, the Nine legislated in a famous statute approved that day that all private buildings located on the Campo should have windows identical to those of the proposed communal palace with their double-columned pointed arches[51] (Fig. 6.35).

Considerable scholarly attention has been paid to this statute as a first step in the legislation of urban aesthetics, but other and

6.35 North wall of the Campo, Siena

earlier laws passed by the Sienese council probably had a larger effect on unifying the character of the Piazza del Campo and, indeed, that of the whole city. Beginning with a statute of 1262, then repeated through the remainder of the duocento and the early trecento, are references to the beneficial role that dense contiguous architecture must be allowed to play upon urban character.[52] The consequent expressive meaning embedded in much of the public face of Siena, and reinforced by injunctions against any private building activity that interrupted the visual flow of streets and squares, is of a place shared by its citizens, built according to common consent, and blessed with familial intimacy. Nowhere is this sense more striking than in the Piazza del Campo where the idea of the family hearth is given shape, not through some happy coincidence of 'organic' development, but by

a century-long commitment to a plan based exclusively on *ordine e regola* (Fig. 6.36).

What is often referred to as the shell form of the Campo denotes only the contours and pattern of its paving; if considered in relation to the whole city, the scale of the Campo, the almost unbroken run of the five-storey wall addressing the communal palace from three opposing sides, the modulated corners, and discreet entry ways, all synthesize into an effect more like the inside core of a Russian doll, an intimate version of the perimeter fortifications Siena had so much trouble finishing. Within this miniature city within a city one's sense of being ensconced at the centre is complete, the citizen instantly recognizing that this place, where the boundaries of the *terzi* join, ringed by double-columned fenestration and the ubiquitous red brickwork, expresses the spirit of communal integration.

6.36   View of the Campo and Palazzo Pubblico, Siena

But most compelling of all in such a setting is the face of the Palazzo Comunale itself, underpinned by a giant substructure to facilitate its being angled around the lower south perimeter; in scale and height the façade only just exceeds those of its neighbours through the additional fourth storey of the middle section, but the Torre del Mangia (1338–44) then cuts a hundred-metre shaft vertically through all the horizontal tiers of brickwork and windows. In front of the tower stands a single intrusion into the square's perimeter, the travertine entrance loggia; here lies the civic hearth, behind which stands – of all things – the civic chimney (Fig. 6.37).

To call the Campo a living-room and to reduce its symbolism to a purely political landscape does little justice to the six or seven generations of Sienese who built it, however. The Ufficio del'Ornato, a municipal commis-sion charged with regulating urban develop-ment, properly referred to *vostra piaza del Campo che è la piu bela che si truovi*; this declaration that the city possessed the most beautiful square to be found anywhere was made in 1398, when Siena had lost half her population to war and to the pestilence which had killed Ambrogio Lorenzetti in 1348. By the end of the trecento, if the original meanings had been political, they were now compounded by recollections of a less transient significance. The rule of the civic household now turned towards keeping the house in good order, which meant assigning things to their place in the urban structure, a task first exemplified by the purpose of the Ufficio's reference to the Campo, which was to introduce a contentious form of zoning to Siena.

The declaration of 27 November 1398 continues: 'You [the citizens] have this jewel the

6.37   View from the cathedral to the Campo, Siena

Strada dei Banchi, which begins at the Piazza Tolomei and runs to the Porta Solaria, and no city in this land, neither Venice nor Florence, has one finer. Now it is spoiled because shoemakers and tailors live there. We declare, through our mayor, that a committee of four citizens be chosen. They shall be responsible for the beauty of this street by ensuring that the bankers are drawn together from one place to another, the drapers from this place to the next, the goldsmiths, furriers and weapon makers from place to place when necessary, so that location by location no trade but one may be allowed to settle.'[53]

Let us concede, given the composition of the authorizing commissions, that this decision may have been motivated in part by the kind of class territoriality that underlies exclusionary zoning today; class interests, however, hardly complete the story of the Strada dei Banchi, whose development must be understood against the wider logic governing the whole community. The Sienese statutes, both before and after this occasion, rarely distinguished between classes in pursuing prohibitions and injunctions. For that matter, to have done so would have sabotaged the fraternal doctrine which furnished both means and ends to the cycle of communal projects. The Strada forms a giant loop around the Piazza del Campo, to which it affords access via seven short connecting streets. This particular arrangement, as opposed to the alternative of permitting a main thoroughfare to penetrate the piazza directly, was chosen with the obvious plan in mind to preserve the continuity and integrity of the latter's perimeter wall. Yet despite this detachment of one from the other, Campo and Strada perform roles that are complementary: if the Campo was conceived as the civic hearth, the Strada was the civic corridor, the centuries-old armature forming the boundary between the *terzi* since the Sienese foundation. This explains why the street had received close attention from the Ufficio del'Ornato and their predecessors dating back to 1262, including the regulation of its set backs, house façades, and materials.[54] All this early attention probably had but a single purpose, namely, to establish a seam along what otherwise would have been a continuous closed boundary. But by the quattrocento, as Wolfgang Braunfels has pointed out, the concept of order was central to medieval ideas about beauty, just as order governed the workings of the harmonious family.[55] In both instances, order imposes predictability, as a 1357 Sienese protocol proclaimed: *Senza ordine non si fa alcuna cosa buona* (Nothing good can come without order).[56] So the activities along the Strada dei Banchi were reallocated not as a gratuitous imposition, nor even primarily to secure an exclusive territory for the privileged, but to bring a measure of predictability to a disintegrating world.

Transforming the Thresholds

If the Campo and the Strada dei Banchi seam, whose ring-wall shape along its inner circuit matched and reconfirmed the shape of the Campo, could be endowed with expressive meanings reminiscent of the household, the same could not be said for those two other protean elements – the cathedral and the urban perimeter. In each case, circumstances beyond the control of the commune finally intervened to foil 'the obedient men' in their ambitious dream.

As far as the perimeter is concerned, repeated exhortations from the Ufficio del'Ornato about the merits of dense, contiguous architecture had little effect on the private activities that pushed development outwards along the three district armatures. For all the powers at their disposal, it seems the officials were largely impotent when it came to impos-

ing an absolute prohibition on building outside the boundary gates and then directing it towards the steep-sided interstices left undeveloped within. Private intransigence and perhaps the will of the districts took over, creating a problem compounded by the new monastic orders who decided to locate their facilities beyond the developed perimeter. In consequence, the frustrating effort of building and rebuilding the defensive walls and gates to encompass both ribbon growth and large stretches of empty terrain continued unabated from 1141 until the end of the fourteenth century (Fig. 6.38). During this period the gates, with their partly built defensive flanks and towers, had to be demolished or sold off, then replaced farther out in an endless round of adjustments that never succeeded in containing all the peripheral development.[57] Lorenzetti's fresco, painted when Siena's physical extent had reached its maximum just prior to the Black Death, represents more of an aspiration than reality; he painted a continuous boundary wall and gate through the middle of 'Good Government,' to the left of which lies a completely contained city, while the contado outside shows no trace of the suburban appendages surrounding Siena at the time.

If topography and the mechanical relations that stretched urban development along the frontage of main thoroughfares undermined the containment of Siena's communal household, they also subverted the extraordinary plans initiated by the Nine to enlarge and reorient the cathedral precinct. If the 1348 epidemic dealt a final blow to this project, designed to give the world's largest church to a city half the size of Florence, then impassable slopes and the intensity of the intervening urban fabric had frustrated the project long before. What to Camillo Sitte and a more modern eye seems to be a picturesque, 'organic' juxtaposition of Siena's hilltop cathedral and the Campo below, to a trecento Sienese was a large flaw in that special order through which communal integration was manifested. Whereas the Church had main-

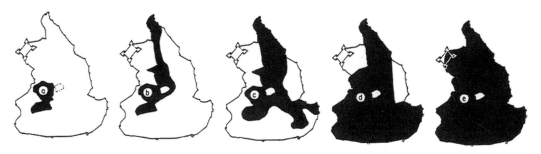

6.38   Stages of development of medieval Siena. Drawings by Shoukry Roweis. a: in the tenth century; b: at the beginning of the twelfth century; c: by the mid thirteenth century; d: by the early fourteenth century; e: a century later

tained its autonomy from civic affairs up to the middle of the thirteenth century, a separateness revealed in the independent nature of decisions affecting the planning of the cathedral and the location of the Campo, the subsequent ascendancy of communal intervention in ecclesiastical matters ushered in the necessity for a rather different symbolic order.

Since the city's foundation – indeed up to the momentous session of the Nine on 10 May 1297, when the subvention was made to build the Palazzo Comunale on the Campo – the centre of Sienese life had been located on the Piazza del Duomo. Here stood the baptistery and bishop's palace, flanking the lovely Romanesque edifice, whose west façade was in the process of being embellished by Giovanni; but this important façade happened to face away from the city, across a narrow square to the great church hospital of Santa Maria della Scala (Fig. 6.39). By this unfortunate legacy, the attractive power of the ensemble was therefore compromised as an element of Sienese urbanism. Consider William Bowsky's description of the local nature of religiosity and the Church, which long had a particular influence on Sienese life: 'That church was traditional, structured, and family-run in an almost pre-Gregorian sense. Local families exercised control and patronage over urban and suburban parishes and, indeed, the bishopric itself, to an extent unknown in Florence.'[58] The cathedral, then,

represented a source of authority and privilege in Siena which by no means was limited to spiritual matters; so the family name Malavolti, for instance, figured largely in the ecclesiastical hierarchy along with those of many other influential clans through much of the thirteenth and fourteenth centuries.

Relations between the communal and church leaders were therefore complicated and ambivalent, given the extent to which ecclesiastical authority washed over into safeguarding private interests, a situation that, with the advent of the Nine, became inimical to the politics of serving the common good. At the same time, Sienese public life depended on a special combination of civic and religious virtue, a symbiosis which the communal leaders could neither break nor ignore in their dealings with the Church, and which would powerfully influence the convoluted history of cathedral construction throughout the trecento. So although the fiscal and political fortunes of the municipal realm rose steadily up to the 1340s, causing an increasing laicization of the Church economy, the balance of urban and architectural symbolism tilted more towards seeking a reconciliation between these two centres than a complete transfer of dominance from cathedral to Campo. Again, we have to be wary of explaining these events solely in political terms; if the restructuring of Siena happened to be subject to official sanction, the hierarchies involved

6.39   Siena Cathedral, West Front, 1284–1380

could manoeuvre only within restrictions set by various physical legacies and overriding patterns embodied in a city-household urbanism whose roots, as we have seen, reach deeper than politics.

The century-long program of transforming the cathedral assembly had been set in motion by a dawning realization in the 1260s that the all-but-completed twelfth-century cathedral, with its hexagonal cupola, campanile, and baptistery, was already too small to house Siena's growing population. But in the first of a series of questionable judgments, some of which have yet to be explained, Nicola Pisano was permitted to complete his exquisite pulpit as planned, in 1268. Matters concerning the financing of church construction were already, at the time, in the hands of the civic government; they then, in 1285, effectively closed off the option to lengthen the cathedral nave by commissioning Nicola's son Giovanni to complete the west façade.

The situation around the cathedral at this time is in one sense reminiscent of the difficulties then facing the builders of Santa Maria del Fiore in Florence, namely, those of extricating an adequate amount of space for extension purposes from an already tightly packed site. The hospital, an eleventh-century foundation of the cathedral canons, occupied the western

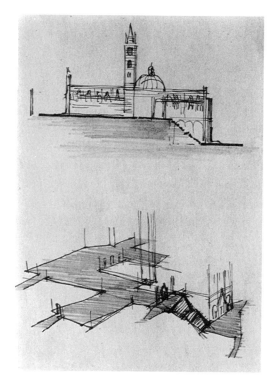

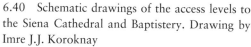

6.40 Schematic drawings of the access levels to the Siena Cathedral and Baptistery. Drawing by Imre J.J. Koroknay

6.41 Staircase connecting the Piazza San Giovanni to the Piazza del Duomo, Siena

flank, while the House of the Canons and the Bishop's Palace stood to north and south of the cathedral, respectively.[59] To the east, the terrain dropped precipitously towards the Croce al Travaglio, whose nodal location at the intersection of the *terzi* armatures had been intensively developed since the beginning of the duocento (Figs 6.40 and 6.41). In fact only the southwest flank, on which stood the Palazzo del Capitano, presented a relatively flat terrain. On the narrow L-shaped piazza itself, between the Bishop's Palace and the hospital, stood the circular eleventh-century baptistery whose condition, according to a 1296 report, was *in molti luoghi sia crepato et fesso* (an edifice on the point of collapse.)[60]

Some evidence suggests that the commune did consider extending the cathedral westwards despite the façadal work begun by

Giovanni; the old baptistery had been demolished in the first decade of the trecento, and in 1306 some gravestones were removed from between the hospital and the west front.[61] One could also speculate, with no proof, that here lies the reason why Giovanni abandoned his work and left the city in 1297, having completed only the bottom storey. In any event nothing happened for twenty years, a period during which the commune's attention and resources were monopolized by the Campo and new Palazzo Comunale.

Harald Keller has recorded three different fourteenth-century proposals to enlarge the cathedral, and they are worth considering here because of the light they shed on the trajectory of Sienese urbanism.[62] The first suggested the complete demolition of the Romanesque edifice to build a new, larger one, using additional space to the west of the old cathedral; Lorenzo Maitani, a Sienese and builder of the Orvieto cathedral, was the chief proponent. Second, the masters of the cathedral works pursued the idea of enlarging the choir over the eastern slope towards the Campo. Finally, the most original scheme envisioned converting the existing fabric into a pair of transepts to which an enormous southern extension would be added to act as a new nave.

So far as the record shows, the Siena council never gave serious consideration to Maitini's advice to demolish the old cathedral, an action that the Florentine commune decided to take in constructing Santa Maria del Fiore. Instead, on 21 April 1316, work began on one of the most daring projects of the Middle Ages. It had been decided to locate a new baptistery near the foot of the slope east of and immediately below the choir, with the intention of extending the choir over the baptistery roof (Fig. 6.42). The technical uncertainty involved in this enterprise was phenomenal, and led to serious misgivings on the part of the building commissioners as early as 1321. Then, as this unlikely fabric rose before their eyes, on a hillside whose stability had been in doubt from the beginning, in 1333 the commission sought the advice of twelve master masons on whether it would be at all feasible to construct the new double-storeyed east façade without the additional stiffness provided by marble cladding. The masons' committee raised doubts about the whole unprecedented experiment, but building was allowed to proceed for another six years.[63]

Meanwhile, the commune had been acquiring properties to the south of the cathedral, on what is now the Piazza Jacopa della Quercia, since 1331, and possibly before. In 1339, the Sienese council, with a sizeable minority voting against, decided to enlarge the cathedral to the south and literally turn the edifice ninety degrees so that the existing choir and nave would form transepts to a new nave whose dimensions would exceed those of any cathedral in existence. The author of this most

6.42 View from the Siena Baptistery (right) towards the uncompleted nave (Piazza Jacopo della Quercia)

extraordinary project is believed to be Lando di Pietro, although, in typical Sienese fashion, so unlike that of Florence, the role of individuals was rarely emphasized in communal enterprises such as this. In any event the proposal appears to have been based on what is the oldest plan still in existence from the Italian Middle Ages. It shows an aisled nave projecting six bays south from the old cathedral on the axis of its cupola; an eight-sided apse with an interior ambulatory lengthens this axis as a projection through the north wall. The existing choir and nave are lightly indicated as flanking transepts.[64] Apart from this document and the record of the council's vote, we remain virtually uninformed about the background to this remarkable undertaking, which even under felicitous circumstances would have proven too ambitious for this most ambitious of city-states. Nevertheless, work began immediately on the walls and arcades of the new nave only to suffer the devastations of the Black Death shortly thereafter; in 1355, the last year of the rule of the Nine, the project was abandoned, never to be resumed (Fig. 6.43).

Despite the calamities of mid-century, attention at once returned to the unfinished choir and baptistery on the eastern slope; within three years, the roof vaults were in place, and Duccio's great circular window, originally installed in the old fabric, was relocated to decorate the new eastern gable. The latter terminated the clerestory covering the choir and rising above a continuation of the thirteenth century nave roofline. Either the Sienese preferred the higher Gothic proportions of their choir to those of the nave, or were unhappy with the external and internal

disparity between the two, because in 1369 they began adding a matching clerestory to increase the height of the original nave. A few years later, almost a century after Giovanni's appointment, final work on the west façade gave Siena a cathedral that was more or less complete.

What could have brought the Sienese to subject themselves to this remarkable architectural Odyssey? In a city renowned for its daring and far-sighted decisiveness, such vacillation seems out of character. Why, at the close of the thirteenth century, did the council sacrifice an opportunity to extend the cathedral westwards, then after a twenty-year period of inactivity, during which the communal population in all likelihood reached its maximum, opt for a technically questionable eastern extension? Then, in 1339, when the number of inhabitants had probably stabi-

6.43 View of the uncompleted nave from the Facciatone (intended south front) towards the cathedral

lized or even begun to decline, what brought the council to embark on their fantastic reorientation to the south? We know that the 1348 epidemic and perhaps the demise of the Nine put paid to this latter scheme, but why then opt for completion of the problematic eastern extension, with a much-reduced population weathering the worst kind of economic and political circumstances?

If the shift from one project to another were simply a matter of resolving architectural and accommodation deficiencies, these events would not concern us here. In fact, it could be claimed that the eventual enlargement of the Romanesque basilica introduced certain architectural flaws that must have been apparent to the Sienese, such as the unfortunate plane where the added clerestory collides with the drum supporting the thirteenth-century cupola. Factors that were deemed to override this flaw must have intervened, although we can only speculate about their nature.

Here I am inclined to agree with the thesis put forward by Wolfgang Braunfels, although I shall extend his thesis somewhat.[65] The higher cause of the whole trecento program in Siena was urbanism. The Sienese were concerned primarily with the manner in which their cathedral addressed its external context, and what seems like indecision from an architectural point of view turns out to be not only a sign of remarkable determination and reason, but a style of judgment consistent with the integrating spirit of Sienese urbanism.

Let us recall the date when the commune first committed itself to setting up an alternative focus to the Piazza del Duomo on the Campo: could the fact that Giovanni, honoured above all other artists, his masterpiece unfinished, departed Siena in the same year – 1297 – that the council allocated two thousand lire annually for the Palazzo Pubblico, be entirely coincidental? Here, perhaps, is an early indication that a radical idea already circulated in Siena: in basilicas throughout Europe the west front had long been considered the threshold of God's house, the first

symbol of his presence and the processional point of entry; the city around was often arranged subordinately, and the façade itself decorated like a jewel. Such was almost certainly the aspiration of Siena in 1284, for why else would an artist as esteemed as Giovanni have been brought there? But the armatures of the *terzi* had their own attractive power, and they connect at the Croce al Travaglio on the low saddle east of the cathedral. The location of their confluence was so compelling that the commune inevitably chose an area in the immediate vicinity for its civic hearth. So as things stood in 1297 the communal nucleus was about to take shape in a position that seriously diminished the symbolic and liturgical significance of Giovanni's façade. By the same token, extending the cathedral to the west – towards a vista containing only the canons' hospital and open countryside – would merely have made matters worse.

In ecclesiastical tradition great liturgical importance is attached to the position and symbolism of the baptistery. Its close association with the west façade was the normal condition throughout Tuscany, as it was in Siena's original Romanesque complex, because ritual ablutions took place immediately before processional entry to the church; the culmination of many religious processions through the streets was also patterned upon this sequence. We know that Giovanni was asked in 1296 to design a baptistery to be located near the decrepit one soon to be demolished,[66] an order that was rescinded a few years later when the foundations of the new eastern baptistery were laid at the foot of the Valle Piatta. A position such as the latter, relative to the body of a church, was unprecedented, especially as in this case the route from baptistery to west front then entailed negotiating a tangle of streets occupying the slope below the cathedral, then crossing the full length of the Piazza del Duomo. Here, apart from the technical doubts expressed in 1331 and 1333, lay what could have been a fundamental liturgical problem with the new baptistery. But this follows only if the eastern and southern extensions are regarded as alternatives to each other, as Keller and Braunfels have suggested, although the documentation has yet to reveal that they were considered as such by the Sienese builders. The remains of the great southern projection (although not its extant plan) are sufficient to show that the southern wall was conceived as a monumental entrance façade aligned on the north-south axis. The plan also shows how the three bays of the *future* choir would act as an east transept in this vast enterprise. Does this not suggest that the choir-baptistery project and the southern extension, far from being mutually exclusive alternatives, were parts of a single concept, the latter part of which had to be sacrificed because of the troubles following in the wake of the plague?

If so, then shifting attention from the half-finished eastern wing in 1339 in order to start work on the new nave cannot mean that the Sienese intended to abandon the choir and baptistery for good; as with the west façade, which stood incomplete for a hundred years, here was an occasion when an alteration in phasing priorities is no sign of having given up the cause.

If we take into account the temper and direction of Sienese urbanism as manifested through innumerable statutes, projects, and declarations, in the determination to counter private intransigence with patterns that spoke of municipal unity, then the chronicle of cathedral building turns out to have a beautiful logic. From their early years of rule, the Nine directed their urbanist programs towards the goal of bringing *ecclesia* into the communal family; so while a westward extension of the cathedral would have been a straightforward-enough task, it must have been rejected as severing a key urban axis that intervening boundaries already rendered tenuous. That this deficiency so troubled the Sienese they were prepared to face the herculean travail entailed in putting it right it is a source of wonder.

Opening the Boundaries

The new baptistery under the choir gave the cathedral a foot, as it were, planted at the lower level no more than a hundred metres from the Campo, making it accessible along the Via dei Pellegrini; and the double-height east façade designed by Domenico di Agostino, capped by Duccio's great choir window, in effect replaced a rump with a face turned obliquely towards the communal hearth. Similarly, the proposed south front, although elevated on the hilltop, would have entailed little more than a hundred-metre walk from the Chiasso del Bargello which reaches into the Campo, then along an extension of the Via delle Campane. The combined flank of the nave and east transept would then have embraced the civic core below, as indeed its remnant does to this day.

The modern visitor, charmed by the picturesque, might be tempted to believe that the cascade of houses and streets on the slope separating the cathedral and the Campo are proof of the 'organic' character of medieval planning, and certainly the documents have nothing to tell us about what was intended for this intervening stretch. Nevertheless, what we do know about Tuscan urbanism suggests that the reorientation described above by no means tells the whole story of what the Sienese probably had in mind. Is it likely, in a culture which prized order, spaciousness, and the *vedute* as ideals of beauty, that the splendid baptistery and Domenico's east façade were meant to be seen from such a dark triangle of space as the Piazza San Giovanni, or that the procession from baptistery to south front should follow a tortuous alley along the Via del Poggio? Here, in all probability, is a case where the energy and resources of the commune finally succumbed to the sort of private tenacity that frustrated the Florentine officials.

It may be a conceit to speculate about which pattern the commune might have imposed on this intervening slope, had circumstances been more congenial. We can be certain neverthe-less that the accumulation of dwellings now attached to the eastern and southern remnant of the nave would not have been permitted; nor for that matter would the commune have hesitated to acquire the block bounded by the Via Monna Agnese and the Via dei Pellegrini, thereby extending the Piazza San Giovanni to the southeast. These measures alone would have opened up an inclined middle link, suit-ably stepped and ramped, in a chain of three great *piazze* connecting the elevated Piazza del Duomo with the Campo below, the whole lying perpendicular to, and intersected by, the armature of the Via di Città.

To suggest more than this means resorting to fantasy; medieval city building in Italy is everywhere a litany of unfinished projects, of municipal enterprise curtailed in boundary struggles, not excluding the examples of Flor-ence, Milan, or Venice. Siena, it could be claimed, achieved more than these other great centres, when one considers her size and inter-nal difficulties. Unlike the others, which sus-tained some city-building activities through the Renaissance with the aid of despots and declining pressures on urban boundaries, and were often able to complete what had been abandoned, Siena is a product of the duocento and the trecento. Another aspect has been noted by William Bowsky: where are the Sienese equivalents of the glittering private edifices that grace the landscapes of Florence, with its chapels built for the Bardi and Peruzzi families? Or great individuals like Dante and Boccaccio and guilds like the Arte della Seta and Orsanmichele?[67] Whatever happened to flourish in Siena seems to have been driven and rewarded by the *bonum comune* – the common good – which, while it could not be pursued without opposition, was pervasive enough to ensure that only truly communal work earned prestige.

Such is the constructed manifestation, if not the perfect realization imagined by Lorenzetti, of the city as household. It has been remarked that Siena had the most *pagan* of Italian cultures,[68] and given the ancient roots of reversed symbolism, the concept of Sienese urbanism as being the most dramatic embodi-ment of this paganism is a compelling thought.

CHAPTER SEVEN

The Subversion of Everyday Life

Up to the close of the Middle Ages in the West – and, indeed, well beyond it in most places – those who were involved in city building did so at close quarters to their task. They were mostly ordinary men, concerned with materials and their weekly money, engaged in the vicissitudes and poetry of everyday life, from which they took their cues. If a distant authority intervened in the boundary dialectic, then it usually had to come to terms with local ways of doing things, and with a discourse limited by wrangling and a suspicion of single ideas, but patterned, too, by respect for certain kinds of artistry. Yet the dialectic could keep this shape only as long as practical reason prevailed over the work of city building, suppressing imported species of reason seeking to transcend the local motley. So wherever the confluence of events empowers some distant voice intent on presiding over urbanism's discourse, then the diversity of everyday life gets undermined.

Distance, as we have noticed, plays an unsettling part in the boundary dialectic, which often labours under some tyrant's far-flung authority, the urge to escape from shared quotidian space, or the detachment of theoretical reason. In this chapter, we shall see, these things are enjoined in the production of schemes to stretch the boundaries of the city into a colossal household, and practical reason suffers the onslaught of the distant, single idea.

The Land Question in Renaissance and Baroque Architecture

In an essay replete with unconscious ironies written in 1753, an obscure French abbot played his part in altering the course of urbanism by insisting that architecture be stripped down to what he thought should be a few bare facts. He invoked the myth-laden practices of antiquity in order to cleanse architecture of those self-same practices, asserting that the artist 'needs choices.' Since then, the eyes and minds of so many urbanists have been fixed on probing the city's abstract principles, believing them to be the fruit and object of reason.

The archetypal primitive hut, according to Abbé Marc-Antoine Laugier's frontispiece to the 1755 *Essai sur l'Architecture*, sits in an Arcadian, empty landscape (Fig. 7.1). While similar objects have been observed in the crowded *barrios* of Latin America, they are usually unfinished; walls are eventually added for various practical reasons, including for the

7.1 Frontispiece to *Essai sur l'Architecture*, Marc-Antoine Laugier, Paris, 1755

is intrinsic to Laugier's treatment of this principle because his hut, like the classical temple whose fragments litter his drawing, is meant to be seen in the round, a natural object with an existence as independent as the trees that conveniently stand four-square to serve as columns (an unintended double meaning about natural subjugation and reverence). Nor is Laugier's choice of landscape an incidental thing: classicism by definition expresses its immutable superiority primarily by its separateness from whatever is fleeting and mundane. Laugier's gaff, however, lay in not knowing that superiority is also expressed by recognition of whatever is permanent and revered in the landscape itself, as we have seen. So the hut, an unritualized work of *homo faber*, never transcends the primitive to become architecture.

The chance for a building to occupy centre field, to enjoy a proclamatory position, presents difficulties in a landscape to which architecture does not respond. Laugier, like the neoclassicists who followed him, may have borrowed ancient forms but he purged them of expressive meaning. Palladio's Villa Capra-Rotunda (ca 1550), in contrast, not only takes from its landscape but adds considerably to it (Fig. 7.2), just as the Bramantesque Santa Maria della Consolazione (1508) is a metaphorical echo-chamber of the Virgilian character in the Umbrian countryside around Todi (Fig. 7.3). These buildings, each representing a different phase of the Renaissance, share the same ancient capacity for camouflage; round-topped hills, crisp foliage, the play of light and shadow through the wooded slopes – all are absorbed into their architecture so the serenity of the countryside can be returned to it in equal measure. This sort of reflexivity seems to work best in a field of space saturated with its own character, and to which the architecture, no matter how prosaic, can respond (Fig. 7.4); we immediately recognize a building as distinctive, privileged, when separated out from other construction, but only where critical features of the space around are taken up in the architecture

obvious sake of privacy from encroaching neighbours. Laugier's unwalled hut, however, is in a finished state; the question of privacy (assuming that the Arcadian climate is perpetually balmy) not being so compelling in such an isolated spot, the structure might well be a little less ridiculous than it seems. Everyday utility in any case is not the purpose of Laugier's engraving; it is an expression of theory, an abstraction from which the superfluities of practicality, such as walls, are stripped away, permitting certain matters of supposed principle to appear in their unadulterated form. But the surrounding emptiness

7.2   Andrea Palladio, Villa Capra-Rotunda, ca 1550

7.3   Santa Maria della Consolazione, Todi, 1508

7.4　Robin's Hood Bay, Yorkshire, England

through mimesis and other means of acknowledging the contingency of adjacent symbols or forms.

This condition applies in the city as well as the countryside, except, in the former case, detachment from an otherwise contiguous urban fabric brings its own challenges of camouflage and mimesis that we call *contextualism* nowadays. However, the incidence of separation in a field of urban space depends not only on the special status accorded to public buildings, but on the dynamics of mechanical relations.

It happened that the flowering of the Italian Renaissance coincided more or less with a dormant phase in the history of urban expansion. Giovanni Villani, in his 1336–8 chronicle ten years before the Black Death, could write: 'Florence within the walls was well built, with many beautiful houses and ... people kept building with improved techniques by importing designs of every kind of improvement ... And besides this, there was no citizen, whether commoner or magnate, who had not built or was not building in the country a large and rich estate.'[1] But, by 1427, at the time of the tax survey (the *catasto*), the Florentine government was desperate for funds. The nobles who effectively ran the city had accumulated enormous wealth, imposing a flagrantly regressive fiscal order whereby personal property remained untaxed. Most Florentine households were struggling, and the rural districts and other Tuscan towns were destitute. In Florence, the richest 1 per cent owned a quarter of the wealth, while 15 per cent had nothing.'[2] In much less than a hundred years, the competing boundaries of medieval urbanism in Florence yielded to new economic disparities, which gave the edge to a very few. So sizeable parts of the old town could be bought, if not for a song, then without encountering the resistance formerly experienced by the municipal officials in trying to extricate Santa Maria del Fiore from encroaching boundaries.

Although conditions varied across Europe, by the fifteenth century the Mediterranean textile economies, commercial transactions, and merchant banks were already in decline, and the unprecedented population growth of the previous hundred and fifty years was long over. There were no longer many great building enterprises to match the scale and verve of thirteenth-century civic and private construction, that surge out of the Dark Ages which raised churches, palaces, city halls, and defensive walls across the European continent.

Prior to the Renaissance, while most of Europe remained decidedly agrarian, some of its thirteenth-century cities began for the first time to exceed their population levels of the Roman era; but the Florentine population peaked at about 100,000 before the plague of 1347–8, and no enlargements were made to the Piazza della Signoria after 1385–6. Thereafter, certainly by the time Filippo Brunelleschi watched his proto-Renaissance dome rise over Santa Maria del Fiore in the 1420s, the pressure on what available space existed within the third city wall had abated as economic restructuring and stagnation set in. So the newly emergent style was restricted to fragments: the portico of the Ospedale degli Innocenti, the proto-Renaissance façades of a few urban palazzi, and the Pazzi Chapel, significantly located in the cloistered oasis of Santa Croce away from what remained of urban volatility. Similarly, work commissiond by Pope Pius II for the edge of his partly structured village of Pienza gave rise, in the mid-fifteenth century, to what has been mistakenly called the 'cradle of Renaissance urban design.' With an axial symmetry, spaciousness and splayed arrangement heralding Michaelangelo's Campidoglio, the Piazza Pia

7.5   Plan of Pienza, showing the development commissioned by Pius II in 1462

represents, perhaps, the first fully realized application of principles espoused since the thirteenth century, but frustrated by territorial competition in the cities. Pienza gave birth to Pius, but remained a backwater, which made his task of assembling enough land for the complex a relatively simple matter (Figs 1.12 and 7.5).

The second half of the quattrocento witnessed a flowering of theory, with Filarete, Alberti, Francesco di Giorgio, and Leonardo insisting that architecture must obey mathematical principles. But, in the case of these four, the opportunities for practice were either few and far between, or non-existent. It was a rare building indeed that measured up to espoused principles, as Alberti admitted in his famous letter to Matteo de' Pasti. Only in 1503 did the early Renaissance style belatedly find its purest urban expression, awaiting not only Bramante, but just sufficient urban space to permit what was no longer such a luxury: a small cordon of unbuilt space around the Tempietto in Rome's San Pietro in Montorio (Fig. 7.6).

Self-interest, meanwhile, continued to work against theory in every city where despotism insisted on appropriating its own territories. The *condottieri* preferred to reinforce their boundaries at the street line, as did the Florentine aristocracy; Michelozzo's Palazzo Medici (begun in 1444) and the Palazzo Strozzi (completed by Cronaca in 1507), like

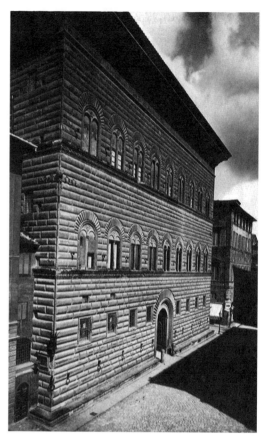

7.6   Tempietto of San Pietro in Montorio, Rome, by Bramante, 1503

7.7   Palazzo Strozzi, Florence, completed in 1507 by Cronaca

many another fifteenth-century urban fortress, face inwards to a graceful courtyard, yet turn an impregnable rusticated wall to the world outside (Fig. 7.7). The character of absolutism looms in the bulwark dividing the citadel of the Dukes of Milan from their hapless subjects; Jacob Burckhardt describes the 'passion of fear' spread by these dukes, the Visconti and the Sforzi, the profound brutality of Galeazzo and Lodovico il Moro, whose metaphor was the urban citadel: 'Whoever entered the citadel was watched by a hundred eyes; it was forbidden even to stand at the window, lest signs should be given to those without'[3] (Fig. 7.8).

An absence of boundaries in the countryside, meanwhile, provided a location for putting some of the new ideas into practice on occasion. Their abstract character ushered in the method of preconceiving the complete edifice, and as far as we know, the first architectural models date from this period. Giorgio da Sangallo put his training as a joiner to use by producing wooden models of his designs for country villas, and his Medici Villa at Poggio a Caiano, with its symmetrical façade and Ionic portico, is an early example which depended more on preconception than on surrounding contingencies (Fig. 7.9). Near the end of the century, Baldassare Peruzzi would make fuller use of this technique in his design for the Poggio Reale (1490) outside Naples. His villa became an influential type, which attests to its level of abstraction: four identical

7.8   Castello Sforzesco, Milan

7.9   Giorgio da Sangallo, Villa Medici at Poggio a Caiano, 1480–5

porticoed façades and a *cortile* hollowed out from the core mark the building as having been designed in the round and suitable for transfer to any open territory (Fig 7.10).

We should not read too fixed and simple a principle into the detailed architectural effects of mechanical relations; rural sites had been occupied by monasteries, castles, and even palaces long before the fourteenth century with little noticeable effect upon architecture, and certainly a hallmark of Imperial Rome was the manner in which classical buildings were squeezed between flanking ones with little apparent concern for a self-contained symbolic organization. Nevertheless, is it entirely coincidental that the dome; the colonnaded drum; the symmetrical, circular plans; the Greek Cross plan; and indeed most of the theoretical apparatus of quattrocento architecture were elements of a *static* composition set within and conditioned by an urban formation that had lost momentum?

Both Florence and Rome, in the first half of the fifteenth century, contained whole districts that were like unfinished suburbs (Fig. 7.11). The countryside invaded and passed through the defensive walls, so each city took on a semi-bucolic aspect, its outer reaches laced with orchards, market gardens, and farms. New buildings were scarce, but in such a loosely structured setting the contingencies of urban propinquity no longer dominated architectural invention. Spatial self-containment still required a skilful eye for the features of what lay around, but to this end it was now possible to invoke the abstractions of theory, geometry, and proportion. The intellectual detachment from an unfortunate material world which Brunelleschi, Donatello, Ghiberti, Michelozzo, and later Alberti and Bramante brought to architecture was probably conditioned by an equivalent spatial detachment from a formerly intrusive city.

This distancing from urban events neces-

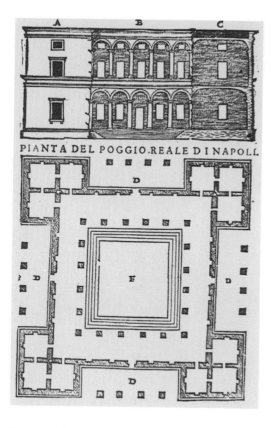

7.10 Baldassare Peruzzi, Poggio Reale, 1490. From Serlio's Treatise, Venice, 1619

Florentine buildings attest to the varying force of urban conditioning upon architectural invention, especially when comparing his plan for the sacristy of San Lorenzo (1419) with that of San Spirito (1428). Like his project for the Ospedale degli Innocenti, whose public expression is limited to a loggia of nine arches facing the Piazza San'Annunziata, the layout of the sacristy had to conform to the shape of existing surrounding buildings (the Ospedale being positioned by the further necessity to complete the regularity of the piazza fronting the church of San'Annunziata). The architect was therefore unable to carry his theory of proportional relationships through to fruition in these earlier works. At San Lorenzo, as Leonardo Benevolo has noted, the ground plan of the sacristy chapel was based on an awkward double module of $5^{3}/_{4}$ and 8 Florentine *braccia*, while the vertical module was determined independently with ratios of $1:7^{1}/_{2}$ (Figs 7.13 and 7.14). Neither one could be applied consistently throughout the extension, which depends for its success on the intricacy the architect employed in fitting his new motifs around the contingencies presented by the intensive built-up context (Fig. 7.15).

San Spirito, in contrast, was built south of the Arno River, among a loose conglomeration of structures interspersed with gardens and empty lots. It seems certain, given the shape and detail of the outside wall which Brunelleschi designed, and from a fifteenth-century depiction of Florence now in the Bier Collection, that the original structure was largely free-standing, although it is now attached along part of the west wall and transept (Figs 7.16 and 7.17). In such a location, the geometry could be fully derived from whatever coordinating schema happened to take Brunelleschi's fancy. The church plan takes the form of a Latin cross whose dimensions are multiples of exactly eleven *braccia*, this being the side of a square bay which forms a continuous ambulatory against the perimeter wall. The two main axes of the cross are four bays wide, and the crossing beneath the

sary to the Renaissance style is dramatically evidenced by the predominance of the centrally planned church in quattrocento drawing and painting over those actually constructed. Before Leonardo gave a pure fantasy landscape as background to his *Virgin of the Rocks*, figures were usually depicted against an architectural setting, which often, as Kenneth Clark has observed, was a more fully evolved version of the Renaissance style than could be found in a solid state. Perugino and Raphael painted closely similar scenes of the 'Marriage of the Virgin' in which a centrally planned church, elegantly construed, dominates an otherwise empty middle ground (Fig. 7.12).

The sequence and location of Brunelleschi's

7.11   Capitoline Hill, Rome, late fifteenth century. Anonymous drawing. École italienne, Louvre, Paris

7.12   Perugino, *The Remission of the Keys to St. Peter*, 1481. Vatican, Sistine Chapel

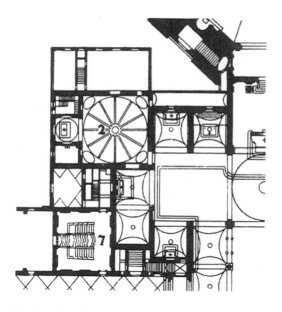

7.13 Plan of the sacristy, San Lorenzo, Florence. Brunelleschi, 1419

7.14 Interior of the sacristy, San Lorenzo

dome superimposed on its drum is two modules square. It seems that the architect gauged the size of his module very carefully from the resolution of problems occurring at the re-entrant corners, where the nave intersects the transepts. He decided to form the perimeter wall into a series of semicircular niches, each containing a window; at the re-entrants, therefore, two niches would collide unless they could be joined by a single window, an event made possible by making the niches $5\frac{1}{2}$ *braccia* in depth. In elevation the combined height of the order and arches along the nave equals 22 *braccia*, and this dimension is repeated from the level of the archivolt to the roof of the nave. The relationships between all these elements, moreover, conform to constant ratios of 2:3:4:5.

The internal coherence of San Spirito was expressed on the exterior – in fact, one could say that it originated externally, given that the source of the crucial modular dimension happened to be at the re-entrant corner – by the rhythm and proportion of the niches, an undulating wall that originally enveloped the whole church (and which the executors subsequently covered with a flat surface). Nevertheless, without a free-standing location, the opportunity to carry the internal aggregations through to the exterior with such consistency could not have occurred. But the dynamism of the pre-Renaissance city had ground to a virtual halt, leaving architecture to the serenity of ideas that were first fully embodied in San Spirito, then taken up in the treatises of Vasari, Giorgio, Alberti, and Palladio.

By the mid sixteenth century, many cities were again experiencing growth and consequent pressure on their boundaries. This time, unlike during the duocento, new development tended to be accommodated by suburbanization or wholesale expropriation rather than in the interstices of the urban fabric. In Rome, for instance, laws were introduced in 1480 to enforce the compulsory sale of abandoned or derelict property (provided it was not owner-occupied) to those contemplating building afresh; and from 1565 to 1571 even the occupancy-status restriction was lifted.[4] This was

7.15   Plan of Florence, showing development around San Lorenzo (SL) and San Spirito (SS) in the fifteenth century

turous interpretation of Brunelleschi's, Alberti's, and Masaccio's early work on the subject, medieval practice suggests that this cannot be the full explanation. Piero della Francesca almost certainly painted *The Flagellation* in Urbino prior to 1451, to give the world a dynamic model of urban perspective which was taken up enthusiastically in Tuscan painting through the second half of the quattrocento (Fig. 7.18). For the first time, foreground figures were silhouetted against actual street scenes, as in Ghirlandaio's mural of St Francis in Santa Trinita in Florence. It can only be concluded that very few opportunities existed in the dormant cities of the time to conceive a project large enough to incorporate Piero's innovations. So Pienza, founded in 1459 by Rossellino, stands virtually alone as a fifteenth-century new town, its cathedral setting notable for its *vedute* – the optimum serene viewpoint so admired in the murals and frescos of the period.

Apart from a few short-lived, isolated bursts of economic energy, the capital and fiscal resources essential to a revitalized urbanism were not forthcoming until well into the sixteenth century. Then, as though the true potential of perspective were accidentally discovered, the directional vista began to appear as an element of the civic pattern. An early example was the Strada Nuova in Genoa, conceived in 1550 as a 75-metre long axis on what was probably open terrain (Fig. 7.19). The street was beautifully paved, and flanked on both sides by continuous rows of urban palaces. Architecture was here deployed to the periphery, its purpose being to form a decorated channel to guide movement, but also, perhaps, to reassert some territorial boundaries in a city long known for its divided internal loyalties; as the city flourished anew it provided a taste of an impending paradigmatic change in urbanism (Figs 7.20 and 7.21). Vasari greatly admired the Strada Nuova, and incorporated the idea in his design of the Florentine Uffizi (1560–80), celebrated for its partial termination by the Palazzo Vecchio at the edge of the Piazza della

the period of the great Baroque plans. Mark Girouard claims, contrary to the evident popularity of the *vedute* in medieval towns, that prior to the mid sixteenth century a conscious *aesthetic* of straight streets did not exist, even though perspective had been developed in Florence in the fifteenth century.[5] Certainly, perspective came late to urbanism, although the great projects in Rome were preceded by the single significant case of Ferrara, whose perspective-based plan was devised before the end of the fifteenth century, as we shall see. In Florence, nevertheless, the new pictorial science had been limited in application to the demonstration of spatial relationships between objects, a limitation that is apparent in the static and highly formal juxtaposition of architectural objects. Even in painting, the second half of the quattrocento seems to have suffered from a kind of hybrid perception of space which often mixed planar and perspective representation together; Leonardo's famous diatribe against this 'absolutely stupid' practice exempted no one but himself. While this static application of perspective might be attributed to the unadven-

7.16   Florence in the fifteenth century. From an anonymous drawing in the H. Bier Collection, London. a: San Lorenzo; b: San Spirito

7.17   Exterior, San Spirito, Florence. Brunelleschi, 1428

7.18   Piero della Francesca, *The Flagellation* (detail), Ducal Palace, Urbino

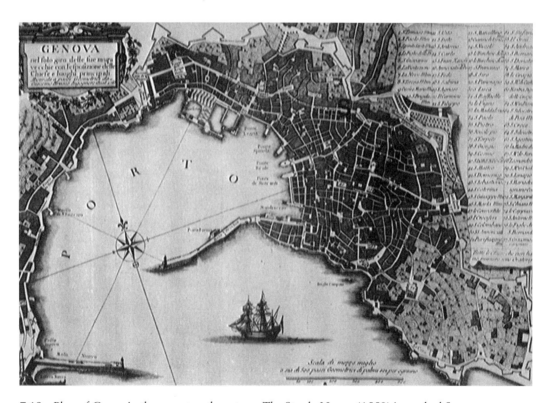

7.19   Plan of Genoa in the seventeenth century. The Strada Nuova (1550) is marked S.

7.20 Nineteenth-century view of the Strada Nuova (Via Garibaldi)

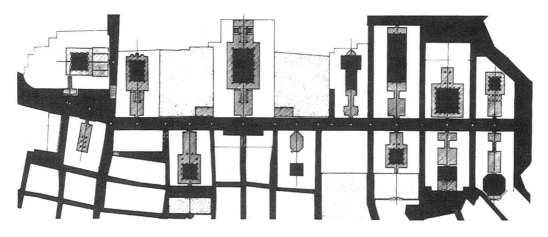

7.21 Plan of the Strada Nuova, showing the dialectic involved in reviving street boundary architecture

7.22   View of the Uffizi (1560–80) towards the Piazza della Signoria, eighteenth-century drawing by Giuseppe Zochi, engraved by Giuseppe Vasi

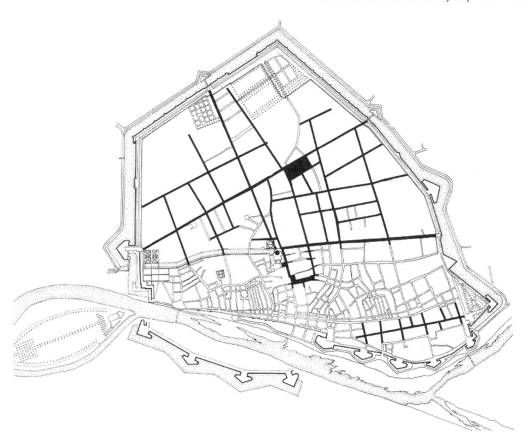

7.23   Plan of Ferrara in the sixteenth century. In black are the extension roads of Borso and Ercolo, shown in a plan of 1498 by Pellegrino Prisciani

Signoria (Figs 6.30 and 7.22). At last a final piece was added to the city's great flawed armature, begun around Santa Maria del Fiore over two and a half centuries before.

But the experiments at Genoa and Florence were really evolved versions of an urban extension plan that had been conceived for Ferrara half a century earlier (Fig. 7.23). Here, Leonardo Benevolo informs us with some truth, occurred the first split between architectural practice and town planning. He attributes the split to events that enabled the layout of urban territory to proceed quite independently of subsequent building construction; but, as we have seen, the example of San Spirito paved the way for an internally derived architecture that had dominated the Renaissance style since 1428. Moreover, because the new employment of urban perspective at Ferrara could be realized only by incorporating continuous façadal alignments, the architect's freedom was once again constrained by urban-boundary contingencies. A complete split in practice on a large scale had in fact to await the eighteenth-century suburbanization of Paris, using neoclassical abstractions well suited to the mechanical relations of the urban hinterland.

Nevertheless, the case of Ferrara remains paradigmatic; no prior plan had been conceived in which the symbols of social cohesiveness depended upon subordinating architecture to the idea of urban perspective as conceived by Piero. In 1492 Biagio Rossetti was appointed supervisor of an ambitious project to double the area of Ferrara. The originator, Ercole I, fearing a renewal of the war of 1482 with Venice, decided to construct a new defensive wall north of the city at a time when a strengthening industrial economy brought in a flood of migrants and wealthy exiles. The ensuing housing shortage convinced Ercole to enclose as large an area within the new bulwark as was fiscally possible, and he instructed Rossetti to lay down a series of streets extending between the old city and the defensive ring to the north. This project, called the *addizione ercolea*, was carried out by almost entirely disregarding the existing pattern of ownerships in the extension area. As much as any other feature of the plan, the superimposition of orthogonal boundaries upon an

evolved landscape separated it from what had gone before.

As far as we know, most of the street grid and the *piazza nuova* which served as the new civic centre of the extension were completed under Rossetti's supervision. He must have designed at least twenty buildings and approved many others, regulating their siting and other details to conform to the demands of urban perspective (Fig. 7.24). But circumstances were to thwart the plan's full implementation. By 1516 Rossetti was dead, and the economic fortunes of Ferrara once again had fallen into decline. As a result, construction proceeded through the sixteenth century and thereafter only in a piecemeal fashion, giving the city the semi-rural character it has today. Much of the street frontage was lined, not with the continuous façades of villas and apartments, but the walls of gardens and

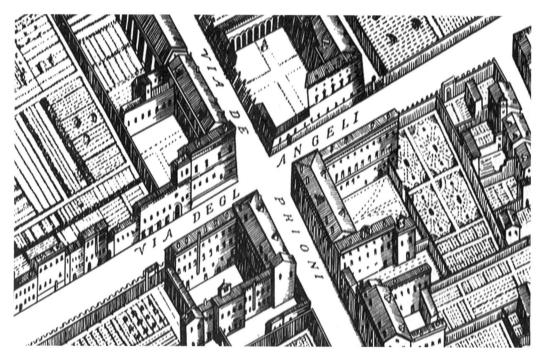

7.24   Ferrara. The intersections of Via degli Angeli and Via dei Priori. From the drawing by Andrea Bolzoni, 1747

7.25   View of Via degli Angeli with the Palazzo dei Diamanti, Ferrara

7.26   View from the centre of Ferrara to the *addizione erculea*

orchards, interrupting vistas meant to be contained by buildings twenty metres tall (Figs 7.25 and 7.26).

The New Suburban Boundary Architecture

The experiments in Ferrara, Florence, and Genoa were, without exception, partial or incomplete. Another much-admired use of perspective was Vincenzo Scamozzi's stage-set Teatro Olympico at Vicenza, designed by Palladio in 1580. The perspective is false and painterly however, rather than architectural, giving the illusion of three radiating city streets on stage. It was in Rome, therefore, that the Baroque urban paradigm was clearly embodied for the first time.

This paradigm, often attributed to that papal assertiveness underlying the Counter-Reformation campaign, owed as much to the material facts of suburbanization, but also to the urge to vivify once more the revered boundaries of Christian and classical antiquity. As late as the fifteenth century, Rome was still a city in ruins, as much a quarry for scholarly thieves as an elegiac landscape. Three centuries before, the Abbot Suger, no less, thought of plundering the Baths of Diocletian in search of granite columns for rebuilding St Denis, while Dante writes in *Convivio* that the very stones of the city deserve reverence and how her ground is more worthy than men can know.[6] This desiccated panorama had its own expressive meaning, one whose power inspired the melancholia of so many, from Petrarch to Boccaccio; for a time, whole quarters of Rome, strewn with great arches, pediments, broken entablatures, and countless ancient inscriptions, seemed to belong to no one but the ghost of a glorious past, inviting poets and antiquarians to wander freely where they chose among the cypresses. But this rare boundaryless state, while inspiring nostalgia in some, was a source of action to others.

In 1447 Blondus of Forli dedicated his *Roma Instaurata* to the dying Eugenius IV, an early sign of the impending crusade to embody in restorative construction memories of the Imperial city. Two decades thereafter, Pius II, stricken by gout but intent on pursuing a lifelong interest in the classical past, had himself carried through the ruins, surveying the boundaries of the city's founding tribes, then tracing the old military roads and aqueducts through the suburbs.[7] That the recovery of history depended not just on protecting the monuments but also on re-establishing ancient territorial lines is apparent in Raphael's celebrated letter (1518 or 1519) to Leo X, in which he campaigns ambitiously for restoring the urban landscape in its entirety.

However, by the time of Raphael the slumbering local economy that at least had saved large sections of the ancient city from clearance activities was on its feet; if the painter's appeal to Leo advocated an epiphany in stone, the pressures of urban growth soon put paid to all ideas of a serene and sparsely peopled landscape. Despite the sack by papal forces in 1527, the city had grown fivefold between 1450 and 1592 to almost 100,000 residents; moreover, only eight years later, Rome received 500,000 visitors and pilgrims, whose intent was to join the processional movements in confraternities from shrine to shrine,

mostly across open countryside and through the Imperial ruins[8] (Fig. 7.27). The famous partially completed plan by Sixtus V for the northeast suburbs, beginning in 1585, to construct a network of processional avenues to link these important religious monuments and obelisks was not the first important incursion onto open land in Rome, however. Such an incursion had been accomplished in 1561–2 by Pius IV, to a magnificent design by Michelangelo for a street called, naturally enough, the Via Pia. Extension planning like this, relying as it did on boundaries that give a sense of connection between one place and another, required its own urbanism, to which the static classicism of the fifteenth century

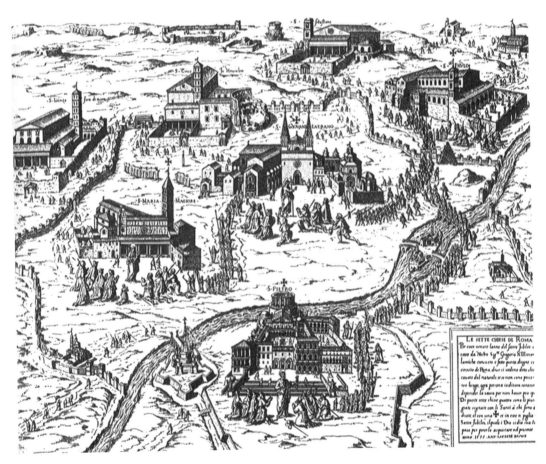

7.27   Antoine Lafréfy, *Vedute delle Sette Chiesi di Roma*, 1575

was unsuited; the moment had arrived a century after its invention for the culmination of perspective application. The channel boundaries of urban organization, the way in which additions were distributed, but particularly the demand by Pius IV, Sixtus IV, and Gregory XIII, as well as by Sixtus V, for urban and suburban land were crucial to this cycle of work. One could claim that if the new forms were derived partly from the awakened state of the Counter-Reformation economy in Rome, their dissemination depended entirely upon opening up the hilly tracts inside the Aurelian wall, abandoned in the fifth century because of the failure of the water supply (Fig. 7.28).

Suburban streets and new water systems, such as the 1583 aqueduct from the Pantano de Griffi, were certainly the technical instruments that made possible such a sweeping increase in land supply, but it would not be true to say that planning here was entirely divorced from architectural conception. If Sixtus V wished to consolidate the loose structure of Rome by offering privileges, for instance, to anyone building near the unfinished Quirinal Palace and elsewhere in the northeast suburbs, his plans were not only administrative and infrastructural. The network of streets from the beginning was meant to have great symbolic content. How else could it appropriately serve the procession of pilgrims between the glorious monuments of Santa Maria Maggiore, Trinità dei Monti, Santa Croce in Gerusalemme, San Giovanni in Laterano, and San Lorenzo Fuori le Mura? The streets that met on the Piazza del Popolo were already in place and the two churches at the intersections came later, despite their being attributed to Sixtus V; but it was he who was responsible for the obelisk in the piazza, located pivotally to catch the eye from a distance along the converging roads (Fig. 7.29).

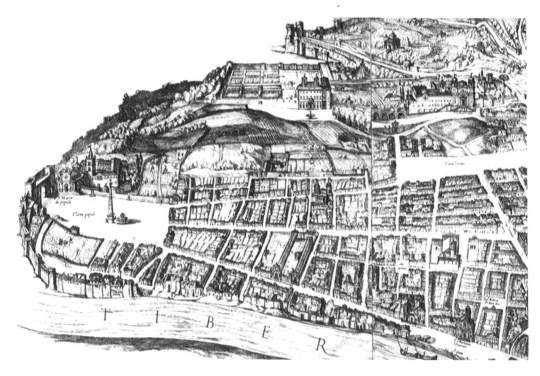

7.28   Detail of a 1593 map of Rome by Antoine Tempesta, showing the Piazza del Popolo (left). Magnus Gabriel de la Gardie Collection, Royal Library of Stockholm

7.29   Culmination of the renewed boundary dialectic. Piazza del Popolo, showing Santa Maria dei Miracoli (right), Santa Maria di Monte Santo (left). Architects Rainaldi, Bernini, and Fontana. Collection of Plino Nardecchia, Rome

The Franciscan pope also commissioned Domenico Fontana who, using Santa Maria Maggiore as the hub, built an axis almost three kilometres long to Santa Croce in Gerusalemme in the southeast. The Via del Quirinale intersected its northerly extension, the Via di Quattro Fontane, which eventually connected through the Via Sistina and the Via del Babuino to the Piazza del Popolo in front of the northern gate. Still cutting through largely underdeveloped terrain, the new Via Merulana joined Santa Maria Maggiore to San Giovanni in Laterano, located just inside the Aurelian wall to the south. These basilicas, and the squares containing them, formed the monumental punctuation of this great network; the latter's symbolic power was secured in turn by reviving the Constitutio Gregoriana, enabling the expropriation of small properties for architecture at a more monu-mental public scale. So population growth, infrastructure, and law combined to introduce Baroque urbanism, which took its forms from the *tabula rasa* of open countryside, setting up its boundaries to channel the eye from one fulcrum to the next (Fig. 7.30).

We should not be misled, then, into thinking that architecture finally split from planning in fifteenth-century Ferrara. It would be more accurate to describe what happened in the sixteenth century as the invention of a *dual* urbanism, one that was to prevail up to the twentieth century. The Renaissance habit of arranging space subordinately around an architectural object was still alive, but reserved for the display of important public landmarks: basilicas, city halls, obelisks, fountains, and statuary had pride of place, but in an urban organization that was quickly be-

7.30   Engraving of the Strada Felice intersection with Strada Pia (Four Fountains), showing Santa Maria Maggiore in the distance. Borromini's San Carlino alle Quattro Fontane on the left. M.G. Rossi, *Vedute della Chiesa e Convento di S. Carlino alle Quattro Fontane*

coming symbolically hierarchical. Previously, little or no civic significance had been assigned to construction other than to public monuments; residential and commercial quarters, even the great urban palaces of the Middle Ages and the Renaissance, were usually elements in a symbolically undifferentiated mass. What organized suburbanization in the sixteenth century then permitted, however, was an opportunity for the architectural display of non-civic buildings, but not to the extent that adjacent space was subordinated to them. Quite the opposite, in fact: public unbuilt space moved to the centre, in the form of axial streets and symmetrical squares, while private buildings were shifted to the rim to form boundaries. Public works – not just in the sense of civic architectural space, but also scarce and expensive planned services – became the organizing system of a new hierar-

chical symbolism in the baroque city. Visual prominence within the system denoted prestige. It required wealth and power to buy more street and piazza frontage than was empirically necessary in a city of escalating land prices, and only the most powerful – a very few civic and church institutions – could appropriate enough to maintain an unbuilt cordon around their buildings. In a sense then, sixteenth-century Rome witnessed the resuscitation of boundary architecture, one that had been dormant through the Renaissance but was reawakened by a shift in the mechanical relations of urban land.

As the burgeoning population and economy of sixteenth-century Rome showed no signs of slackening, the emphasis in architectural display continued to shift to a single boundary façade and the interior, even in the case of important buildings. The baroque city

7.31   Covent Garden, London, by Inigo Jones, 1631. From the engraving by Hollar

was a return to visual competitiveness, a circumstance quite different from the more modest serenity of the Renaissance. In the quattrocento it had not been at all unusual for the whole building to be exposed to public view, whereas now only a single wall could be seen from the street.

In this respect most cities in Europe were not like Rome; they continued to muddle through or to stagnate for the next couple of hundred years. If they took up the Baroque style at all it was because Rome, the centre of Catholic Europe and of architectural fashion, had done so. But the differences between Palladio and Borromini are worth considering here. The Palladian villa is a *contado* version of the early Baroque, an attribute that made it attractive to the circumstances of an unwalled and still-bucolic London. Inigo Jones did not have to cope with competitive boundaries, like those around Innocent x's Piazza Navona, when building on Whitehall or in Covent Garden, and could replicate Palladio's rural style quite well (Fig. 7.31). Borromini,

however, had to make do with only a few metres of frontage to say what was publically necessary in his 1635 design for Sant'Agnese in Agone. The churches of San Carlo alle Quattro Fontane and Bernini's Sant' Andrea Quirinale are even less privileged. In Rome, newly structured boundaries had finally overtaken the detached theories of Alberti, whereas Palladio, away from the centre, could continue to indulge in the abstractions of harmonic proportion; his message could be spread thinly over four walls, and composition still included a concern for the structure that was isolated in nature. Borromini's famous sinusoidal profiles, meanwhile, best exemplified on San Carlino's façade, are certainly plastic art at its most brilliant, but do they not also *extend* in their folds a pitifully short street frontage (Fig. 7.32)?

The changing circumstances around St Peter's in Rome should also not go unnoticed. Even this most privileged of structures did not escape the effects of urban encroachment from round about, and the consequent effort to respond. What has been called the 'Third Style' of the early sixteenth century included the final lapse of the centralized church plan, exemplified in the supersession of Bramante's proposal for St Peter's (Fig. 7.33). The eastern addition to the nave caused several well-known problems, including obscuring the view towards Michelangelo's dome from the square by Maderno's unfortunate façade. Another is the circumstance whereby the overriding impression from the piazza, especially given the great power of Bernini's colonnade, is of the basilica addressing the square almost in a subordinate manner, as opposed to a more symbolically appropriate solution in which the church predominates over an arrangement of subordinated public elements. Only from a position outside the square does the bulk of the drum and cupola begin to play such a role, and even then the flanks of the nave and its truncated transepts are almost entirely neutral in an architectural sense.

Because, by the sixteenth century, expressive meanings in Rome again depended on boundary architecture, exposed flanks were often an embarrassment to the High Baroque style, concentrated on entrance façades, interiors, and whatever happened to protrude above the line of pediment and cornice, so the flanks were usually architecturally redundant, an awkward interval of foot-shuffling that only rarely turned out to be an opportunity to be exploited (Fig. 7.34). Longhena's Santa Maria della Salute in Venice (1631–85) does not have this problem: standing quite separate, it is Renaissance in its urban relationships and plan, but Baroque in style (Fig. 7.35). However, the long and problematic development period of St Peter's (1506–1626) spanned the transition from the abstract rigour of Bramante, which required that encroaching buildings be cleared away at the beginning of the sixteenth century, to Baroque axiality, which drew the encroaching urban fabric within its orbit. St Peter's church, like so many other big enterprises since, fell victim to volatile mechanical relations, causing

7.32   Façade of San Carlo alle Quattro Fontane, Rome, Borromini, 1667

7.33   St Peter's, Rome, prior to Maderna's addition to the nave. Drawing by de Cavalleris, 1575. Trustees of the British Museum

7.34   View of St Peter's from the northwest. Victim of a shift to new boundary architecture

7.35   Santa Maria della Salute, Venice. Longhena, 1631–85

urbanism to switch back from free-standing to continuous boundary architecture (Fig. 7.36).

Borromini's 'Corrosive Light'

If baroque urbanism, working through newly intensive mechanical relations, superimposed continuous boundaries on the Roman suburbs, architecture served to reinforce this competitiveness in one direction, and neutralized it in another. The return to classical forms a hundred years earlier in Florence – in Brunelleschi's Ospedale and his Pazzi Chapel – had brought with it a reincarnation of the tempered boundaries of antiquity. The Florentine Renaissance allowed urban space to flow around and into structures, forming wide thresholds, porticoes, and arcades lined with slender columns; perimeter walls were patterned, modelled, and incised to evoke expressive meanings of porosity and a shedding of weight (Fig. 7.37).

Then, when architectural contiguity returned to sixteenth-century Rome, single façades and silhouettes monopolized expression. Architecture no longer retreated from

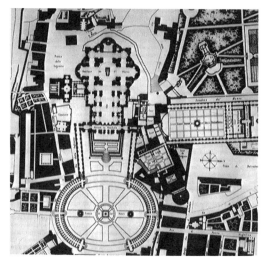

7.36   Plan of the area cleared around St Peter's, drawn by Letarouilly

boundaries but was thrust forward with an insistence signalling the self-interest of individuality. Yet this sign of an unremitting presence yields, in many instances, to its opposite, recalling the architect's fascination with the power of light we have already observed in Nero's Domus Aurea, a fascination felt and put to use by Borromini and several of his contemporaries.

As we might suspect, from our discussion of the Abbé Suger's accomplishment at St Denis, there is more to the effect of light on architecture than the sun's powers of disclosure. As far as we know, Vitruvius was the first to remark on the reason that led the Greeks to thicken the angle columns on their peripteral temples. This refinement, like all the others, obviously had more of a visual basis than a structural one, but the task of giving optical stability to the temple corners was already accomplished

by reducing the intercolumnar spacing at the peristyle angle. Vitruvius deduced that the thickening, therefore, could only have been to compensate for the tendency of sunlight, when shining from behind the temple, to 'consume' the silhouette.

Now, at first reading, the architecture of Borromini in seventeenth-century Rome gives an impression of unparalleled assertiveness. The sinusoidal sweep of his façades and interiors, after all, is surely meant to envelop our attention; consider again how the alternating convex and concave planes of the façade literally *extend* the presence of San Carlino at the Quattro Fontane. However, as Paolo Portoghesi has remarked, Borromini's assertiveness often went hand in hand with its antithesis, especially where he put the corrosive effects of intense luminosity to work[9] (Fig. 7.38). Unlike the Greeks, who Vitruvius says tended to

7.37   Ospedale degli Innocenti, Florence. Begun by Brunelleschi in 1421

7.38   Chapel of Re Magi, College of the Propaganda Fide, Rome, by Borromini. Completed in 1664

7.40   *Sfumato* illumination of a cornice at San Carlo alle Quattro Fontane

counteract these effects, Borromini deliber-
ately set out to increase them, by carving out
whatever might have impeded the consumption of his silhouettes by the sun's rays. In the
Collegio of the Propaganda Fide, the Fal-
conieri chapel altar of San Giovanni dei
Fiorentini, the chapel of Re Magi, and several
other churches and villas, his cornices, pediments, aedicules, and windows are cut and
shaped to expose silhouette after silhouette to
corrosive sunlight. From the start Borromini's
stones appear to be at the point of disintegration: the knife-edged horizontals are eaten
away, their hubris reduced by an augury of
final dilapidation (Fig. 7.39).

If his cornices are on the point of being
consumed by focused sunlight, any latent
brusqueness occurring at the lines of transition from plane to plane is softened by delib-
erately calling upon the *sfumato* effects of
diffused light. All the Borrominian profiles are
remarkable at the level of detail for their
robustness: mouldings are deeply incised, and
cyma curves swell into a fully shaped S, to end
abruptly in a backward-turning edge. But, so
often, their forcefulness is subdued by gradu-
ated shifts in tone induced by light spilling into
all but the deepest cleft. At San Giovanni, as in
the octagonal room of Nero's Domus Aurea,
chambers are let into the roof to shed indirect
light horizontally over the vaults, soffits, and
pilasters of the intermediary nave, while at the
Oratory of the Filippini lateral lighting is
permitted to neutralize what would otherwise
be a system of uncompromising shadows
where vault meets pier.

It is not easy to characterize the incredible
range of the Borrominian dialectic wherever
he confronts an assertive construction with its
countervailing artifice; nor can we always tell
what is intended and what is accidental. We
do know that the result is invariably an indivisible whole, so that while these tensions
might be immediately apparent to the senses,
their source can be discovered only after the
most careful scrutiny. It follows that
Borromini was dealing, through these effects
of light, with the expressive meaning of his

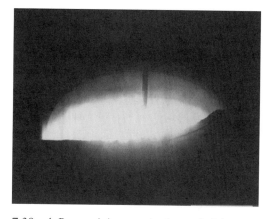

7.39   A Borrominian cornice 'corroded' by sunlight. College of the Propaganda Fide. Completed
1664

work; after close attention the impression of
material erosion evaporates as we recognize
the game being played, but only then does
aesthetic admiration take over from awe (Fig.
7.40).

The boundaries of Baroque Rome were not
everywhere modulated in this fashion; but
enough examples exist to save the city's
urbanism from sinking into the uncompromising geometry soon to invade France.
There, the lessons of the Renaissance and of
Borromini went unheard, as the landscape of
France was turned into an object of conquest
and division. With unprecedented hubris,
kings began to cast their nets to the horizon
and beyond.

Lorenzetti Reborn

Of the many things that irritated Le
Corbusier, few were more insidious to him
than the *organicism* of the metropolis. *Les
villes pêle-mêle* – Paris, New York, Buenos
Aires – were all natural catastrophes, gigantic
landscapes that had reverted to wasteland
through the geometry of organic accretion.
But his demands for a rational city also
masked a belief that the metropolis as it existed was a symbol of an intransigent household; the term 'to straighten things out' was to
take on a chilling literalness.

By 1930, his frustrations had been worked over on paper several times, but a reputation as a young crank did little to endear him to the authorities. Poetic vision, he had realized long before, was a worthless gift if unaccompanied by executive power. 'For many years, I have been haunted by the ghost of Colbert,'[10] he wrote in 1930, referring to Louis XIV's great controller general. Jean Baptiste Colbert (1619–83) was a visionary above politics and political systems, who single-handedly pulled France from the brink of economic collapse wrought by the follies of Richelieu and Mazarin. Colbert was the Cartesian organizer *par excellence*, one whose doctrine of centralized administration has affected France ever since. But consider the extent to which his crusade for efficiency was driven by symbols of household perfection. Colbert's reach extended well beyond economic matters to the implementation of a nation whose future would be an integrated whole, down to the last detail. Artistic and architectural production were subject to his personal approval, Colbert considering them vital to the interests of the state. Even the aged Bernini, summoned to work on the early plans for the Louvre in 1665, would be summarily dismissed for not living up to Colbert's expectations.

The controller general was an avid builder, taking personal charge of a hand-picked committee responsible for the control of construction from one end of the country to the other. The royal roads were reclassified, widened, and extended; canals, lighthouses, harbours, and other infrastructural schemes brought decrepit regions to life; and France, for the first time and ever since, fell totally within the controlling orbit of Paris, 'where all businesses have their beginnings.' The whole country, in effect, had been reworked according to Colbert's vision of the ideal household, guided from the centre, cohesive, and elegantly housed.

It was to Colbert, the first great executive, that Sebastien Le Prestre de Vauban, the first modern engineer, owed his appointment in 1665. For nearly forty years Vauban, the siege and explosives expert, took on the city-planning work of the nation, designing a string of fortified towns along France's eastern border, including Neufbrisach – his masterpiece – in 1698. Both Lille and Brest owed their extensions to Vauban, who also devised plans for Strasbourg, Besançon, Montdauphin, and Rochefort. It was Vauban who first transformed the myth-laden boundaries of the ideal city-household into utilitarian geometry, but the metaphors of integration at a grand scale are just recognizable. For a man with such a background, his scientifically rigorous work was well tempered by a sympathetic eye to symbols of domestic life. His treatise *Maximes bonnes a observer par tous ceux qui font bastir* is full of observations like 'consider in so far as is possible the fireplaces and the bed, so that a person lying on his side may see the fire.'[11] Even the siege expert could instil the precincts of Neufbrisach and Montdauphin with images of domestic harmony (Fig. 7.41).

It would be unkind to suggest that we might have been better off had Le Corbusier paid more heed to Vauban's ghost than to the spirit of Colbert because the work of all three did better than impose scientific efficiency on the landscape. But what seems to have escaped general attention is the unacknowledged debt that Le Corbusier owes to Colbert's chief antagonist, Cardinal Richelieu. It was Richelieu who built the walled town named after himself on the family estate, beginning in 1633 (Fig. 7.42). He commissioned Jacques Lemercier, architect of the *cour carée* at the Louvre, to draw up the town plan and design the château. Lemercier more than anyone had been responsible for finally purging French architecture of its Gothic vestiges, and the Richelieu project was an exercise in displaying his fascination with the subdividing powers of Cartesian geometry. This entailed the superimposition of a large diagonal grid (although still tentative) upon a more closely spaced orthogonal one: what had begun as a charming setting of landscaped paths and *parterres* around the château at St-Germain-en-Laye a

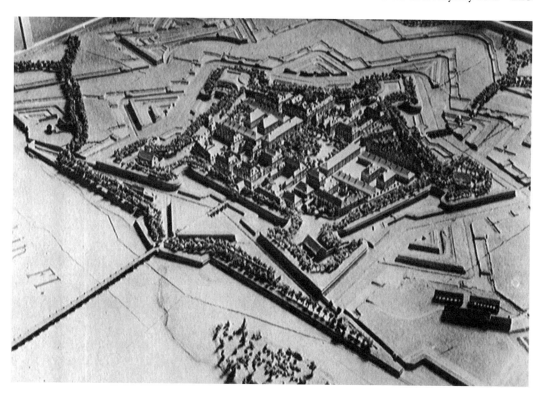

7.41   Vauban, model of Montdauphin, 1692. Musée des Invalides, Paris

7.42   Jacques Lemercier, town of Richelieu, begun 1663. From an engraving by Perelle

7.43   Aerial view of the main street and twin squares at Richelieu

few years earlier now emerged as a system that stretched to the horizon. Whereas Palladio had followed the ancient practice of paying homage to the Veneto landscape, allowing it to permeate the mythical shape of his architecture, Lemercier reversed the old dialectic when he spread a proprietor's geometry across the terrain.

At Richelieu, Lemercier was faced with the problem of subordinating the new town to the château, so he related them in such a way that the town was just an event on the axis connecting the château to its park. In its passage through the town, this axis became a *grande rue* between two treed squares symmetrically placed behind the two town entrances (Fig. 7.43). Here was the development of a durable urban theme that began with the ninth-century cloister of St Gall whose form, but not its

purpose, was taken up in Henri IV's Place Royale in Paris in 1604: a more-or-less continuous boundary wall of dwellings, arcaded on the ground floor and enclosing a formal square. At the point of access to the square, the wall is cranked away at ninety degrees to contain the entering streets and establish an alternating boundary system of compression and release (Fig. 7.44).

This binary form stuck to France, and especially to Paris: not only in what became known as the Place Vendôme (Fig. 7.45), which is enclosed by an abrupt wall dividing the *poché* of the surrounding private hotels from its public space, but in several later mutations. In 1903, Eugène Hénard published his *Études sur les transformations à Paris* in which he formulated his ideas concerning the *alignements brisés*. The broken

7.44   Place Royale (Place des Vosges), Paris, 1604. Musée Carnavalet, Paris

alignment consisted of two alternatives, a *boulevard à redans triangulaires* and a *boulevard à redans*. The first aligned the buildings at forty-five degrees to the street axis, leaving an open triangular space as an extension of the street between each projecting building corner. The second employed alternating long and short setbacks, to form semi-enclosed rectangular street extensions between projecting fronts. In each case the extensions were landscaped, and served the mundane purpose of lengthening the effective street frontage (Fig. 7.46).

The corridor-room-corridor metaphor, when judiciously employed, cuts much deeper than economic expediency, however, as is particularly evident in the famous complex at Nancy (Fig 7.47) designed by Emmanuel Héré de Corny, beginning in 1752, to connect the medieval town to its *ville neuve* extension. Héré de Corny located the Place Royale at the intersection of the old town moat and a transverse artery cutting through the new town. Like the Place Vendôme, this square had cut-off corners and gave onto a single *grande rue*, in this case reaching across the moat to an elongated square, the Place de la Carrière. At the far end, de Corny placed the Fer de Cheval, a square with semi-circular porticoes, as the entrance court to the palace of the royal intendant, thereby terminating the axis. The fluidity of this alternating system depends less on its connective purpose than on the *reticence* with which this purpose has been achieved. The underlying Cartesian geometry of the complex is only just evident, being filtered through a layer of arcades and open porticoes to form an ephemeral boundary that

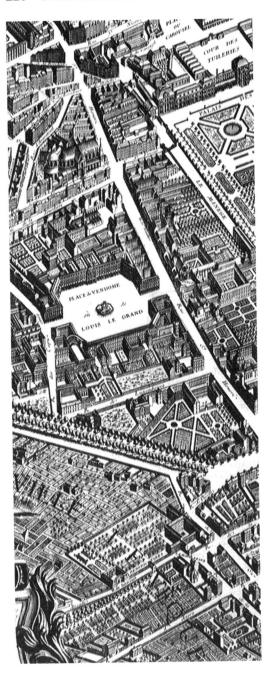

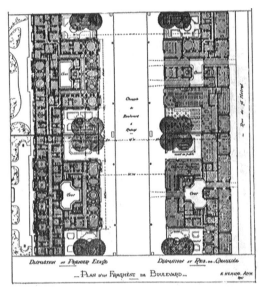

7.46   Eugène Hénard, *Boulevard à redans*. From *Études sur les transformations de Paris*, 1903

absorbs the surrounding tissue of Nancy into its composition.

In 1922 Le Corbusier took up this theme and inflated it to a gigantic scale in *La Ville Contemporaine*. It was the basis here, in the Plan Voisin (1925) and in the 1935 Radiant City, of his own giant *redans* – the highly articulated apartment blocks for the élite (Fig. 7.48). Le Corbusier widened the axis of Lemercier's *grande rue* device so that what had been a passage from outdoor room to outdoor corridor at Richelieu became a progression between alternating squares, but the fundamental theme is still recognizable in raw geometric form. The arcades of the Place Royale, both in Paris and in Nancy, apart from their practical value as shelter, mediated the boundary threshold between the publicness of the square and the privacy of the dwellings above. In the Radiant City and the *Unités d'Habitation*, the arcades are just recognizable as the famous *pilotis*, which mediate the same kind of transition by means of overlapping the zone between public and private territory, but without a trace of the liminal expression of the Place Royale.

7.45   Place Louis-le-Grand (Place Vendôme), Paris. Jules Hardouin-Mansart, begun 1699. Detail from the Turgot plan of Paris, 1734–9

7.47   Place Royale and Place de la Carrière, Nancy, by Emmanuel Héré de Corny, begun 1752

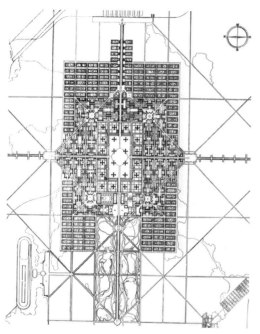

7.48   Le Corbusier, plan of *Ville contemporaine*, 1922. From *Oeuvre Complète, 1910–1929*

Constructing the Proprietary Boundaries

If the alternating boundaries of Richelieu and Nancy were appropriated by Le Corbusier, their domestic expressive meaning was not. The real extent of Le Corbusier's reincarnation of the seventeenth century becomes rather more apparent when we turn to Vaux-le-Vicomte (Fig. 7.49). Only three weeks after the opening of Vaux, on 17 August 1661, Colbert arrested its owner, Fouquet, the wealthy superintendent of state finances, and confiscated his château. This prize was the work of Le Vau and Lebrun, but it is Le Nôtre's arrangement of the landscape into which the château was set that is of most interest to us.

In Italy at this time, the gardens adjoining a country villa were of the same manageable scale as the architecture itself. Leonardo Benevolo remarks that these villas were often placed on a hilltop, to afford distant views *over* the gardens, which were designed to contain and complement the territory devoted to construction.[12] We recall Palladio's description of such a landscape, around whose features the Villa Rotunda was articulated. By contrast, it has often been said of the style of landscaping devised by Le Nôtre, the French preference was to overpower nature with the symbols of deritualized geometry. Fans of interminable vistas radiate from each château,

the ensemble a vast microcosmos with the seigneur occupying the hub of an appropriated landscape. According to this view of things, Le Nôtre's aim was: 'to attempt the physical representation of the infinite, rather than the [Italian] figurative representation: in other words, to control a whole portion of the countryside, from foreground to background, according to the criteria of regularity and symmetry. He used avenues, flowerbeds, terraces, pools and fountains to this end, but

7.49   Gardens at Vaux-le-Vicomte, Le Nôtre, 1656–60

organized them in a calculated system which interpreted the geographical situation of a place, and aimed at the total rationalization of the landscape, including the background at infinity.'[13]

What had begun as the realization that when the connective indoor elements of the house were threaded through the landscape, the latter would be imbued with the virtues of the household, was now corrupted by the symbols of self-interest. The protean double meanings once evident in the city-house utopias were recoverable only at Nancy. Elsewhere in France, the double idea of integrating house and city had given way to the imposition on the landscape of a subjugating will. When it comes to what Le Nôtre did on behalf of Louis XIV at Versailles, any visitor there will learn more than enough about the Sun King's inflated notion of *grandeur* at a glance (Fig. 7.50). But the difference between Vaux-le-Viscomte and Versailles is more than one of size. J.F. Blondel, who represented very well the self-doubt and aversion to extremes which were intrinsic to the new *bon sens*, hated Versailles, recognizing immediately its bombastic oppressiveness.[14] The garden at Vaux does contain vistas that place the 'background at infinity'; in fact the park measures three kilometres in length, and its two main axes, including the transversal canal, are over a kilometre long. But at Versailles these dimensions are inflated beyond reason: the main axis originating at the château ends three kilometres away, at which point a fan of ten avenues radiates to the horizon (Fig. 7.51). In 1671 the triangular panels between these avenues were sold off to court retainers and other officials, creating a whole set of districts, which in turn were laid out in blocks and served by the same infrastructures, ancillaries, and public buildings as would be found in a small modern city. But the whole assembly retained its strict subordinances; nothing intruded upon the supreme authority of the king, who commandeered the whole environment to the point of having the fountains turned on and off at precisely stipulated times during his procession through the gardens.

By the 1680s, when Hardouin-Mansart was commissioned to undertake his great architectural expansion at Versailles, Louis XIV's obsession with the place as an extension of himself reached new heights. He had the façade of the palace extended in two wings to a length of 600 metres, now matching the scale of Le Nôtre's gardens and embracing its vistas from end to end. A separate residence was built some distance away, at Marly, and connected by a tree-lined avenue to Versailles; here the king caused an enormous contraption to be assembled to carry the waters of the Seine 160 metres uphill.

It would be a mistake to imagine that this sort of thing somehow heralded what we often deem to be new confidences inspired by the growth in the *grand siècle* of rational thought and action. Even as the palace at Marly was being constructed, Vauban had enough nerve to write to Louis XIV that 'kings are indeed masters of their subjects' lives and goods, but never of their opinions, because men's inmost feelings are beyond their power.'[15]

While the moderns – men like Claude Perrault, Fontenelle, Furetière, and even the contemplative writer La Bruyère – were fond of pointing out that the exact sciences had a kind of beauty that could be extended into the arts, their radicalism in this respect was never absolute. Fontenelle's belief that the 'order,

7.50   View of Versailles from the Bassin de Latone

7.51   Langlois, view of Versailles, 1688

clarity, precision and exactitude' of geometry might well spread to politics and ethics as well as poetry never became dogma. To a man, the moderns were cautious about transforming the arts based on single ideas. The Enlightenment concept of reason itself was built upon principles of human dignity, the didactic etiquette surrounding the whole debate, and an antipathy to intellectual absolutism of any sort. Indeed these were the very weapons deployed against both the humanistic tradition and, as we see in the case of Vauban, political authority. So even in the minds of the moderns, the displacement of the older dialectical forms by Cartesian precision had its limits, because they were committed to a special rigour that also encompassed what remained scientifically intractable, namely, the proprieties of civility.

The enormous and continuing influence of Versailles in city planning – its pathological insistence on undialectical boundaries and hierarchies, its fascination with carrying these boundaries to the horizon – cannot, then, be traced directly to the emergence of the Enlightenment. The leaders of the Enlightenment enjoyed Vaux, Chantilly, the parks of St-Germain and Fontainebleu, but not Versailles. In 1741 Voltaire wrote: 'If Louis XIV had spent on Paris a fifth of what he lavished on Versailles to violate nature, Paris would be as beautiful throughout as it is between the Tuileries and Palais Royal, and would have become the most magnificent city in the world.'[16] He was referring to method as much as to money but not to form; aristocratic authority was bad enough, but how bad still depended on the form it took. The boundaries around the Place Vendôme and the Tuileries were expressions of a tempered civility, admirable because contained, not by a metalogic that encumbered the spread of a single idea

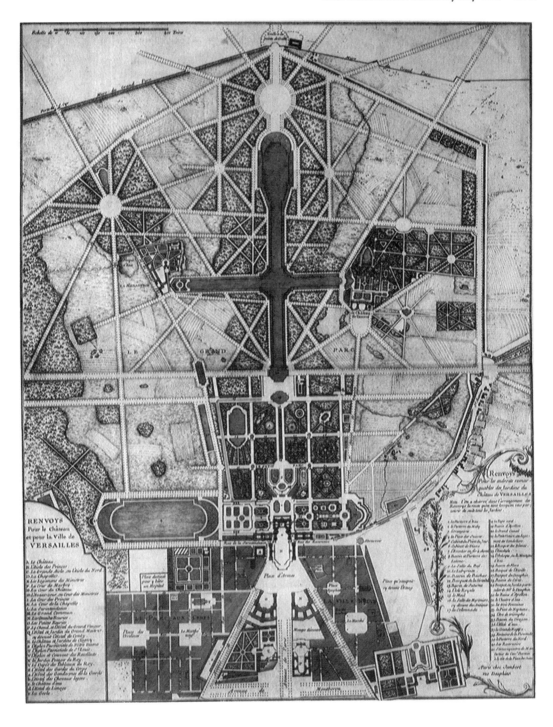

7.52   Blondel's engraving of the plan of Versailles. From *Architecture Française*, Paris, 1752

7.53   Karlsruhe, plans for the town and ducal palace, 1715. From an engraving of 1739

but, fortuitously, by royal neglect. Unfortunately, what ensued across continental Europe was the expression of large authority, and its single model was Versailles. During this period, remarks Fernand Braudel, kings preferred to govern their cities from a distance. But this hardly impeded many of them from carving up the intervening countryside, giving a new meaning to the ancient analogy of the king casting his net (Fig. 7.52). At Aranjuez, Caserta, Turin, and Munich, axes radiating from the royal palaces to infinity changed the environment of those lower down the social scale, penetrating whole urban precincts. Even Fischer von Erlach at Schönbrunn, seduced by *le grand goût*, spread a vast complex of *parterres* and avenues in front of his hilltop palace, although here, as happened frequently, a lack of finances placed limits on what was finally carried out. In 1715, the Versailles fans were applied for the first time to the organization of a complete city: Karlsruhe, the new capital of Baden and Hochberg, built by the margrave Karl Wilhelm of Durlach, was based on a star of thirty-two roads converging on the palace tower from a great distance (Fig. 7.53). But here, as at St Petersburg, where royal dominance over development seemed absolute, various urban contingencies intruded upon the final realization of the plan. Local geography, market forces, administrative difficulties, the waywardness of opposing boundaries shattered the *a priori* geometry into fragments. Even Colbert, left largely by Louis XIV to his own devices, never accomplished – nor was he able to attempt – an absolutist plan for Paris.

Prior to metropolitanization, European urbanism took its character from the fact that the most powerful authorities were almost always met at least half-way by resistance of one sort or another, and it seems that the best minds in France and elsewhere at the time were quick to notice that the progress of Enlightenment depended upon putting a stop to interminable ideas (Fig. 7.54). But too much of this admirable scepticism was to fall

7.54   Gardens of the Belvedere, Vienna, begun 1693. Upper Belvedere Palace by Hildebrandt, 1721–3

by the wayside by the time of industrialization and was nearly submerged by the later demands of automobility. They created empirical grounds once again for forging sharply bounded hierarchies, connections, and continuities in the metropolis, which, at the level of geometry at least, are strikingly similar to those that began at Richelieu in a small way and were exploded beyond all reason to the scale of Versailles. We correctly read this geometry as anti-dialectical, the pursuit of connections not in order to bring distant opposites into respectful association, but to subjugate the urban landscape and its inhabitants to a single, uncompromising idea.

So if Lorenzetti's vision of Siena displayed the virtues of the household – secure and internally cohesive, Versailles and its twentieth-century mutants unwittingly reveal the oppressive side of household life through metaphors of incarceration. What was once a haven becomes a trap as its structures, no longer porous and finite, shut off all chance of access and of escape. The unitary theme in urbanism has not been dashed to pieces, but appropriated by insistent minds who fail to notice the fine line separating the benign from the malignant.

From Poché to Pavilion: French Urban and Suburban Space

The Italian boundary transformation from Tempietto to Strada Nuova was subsequently reversed in Paris by the neoclassical suburbanization of Paris. The second version of Place Louis-le-Grand (now Place Vendôme), begun in 1699 by Jules Hardouin-Mansart, was located on the then advancing edge of the St Honoré district, just inside the Nouvelle Enceinte separating the fields of the Montmartre *faubourg* from a warren of streets north of the Tuileries (Fig. 7.55). Commissioned by Louis XIV, like Hardouin-Mansart's first version of 1685, this one began as an articulated free-standing façade, an orderly public front to the lots which lay behind, divided for sale to private bidders. An engraving by Perelle shows this façade, two grand

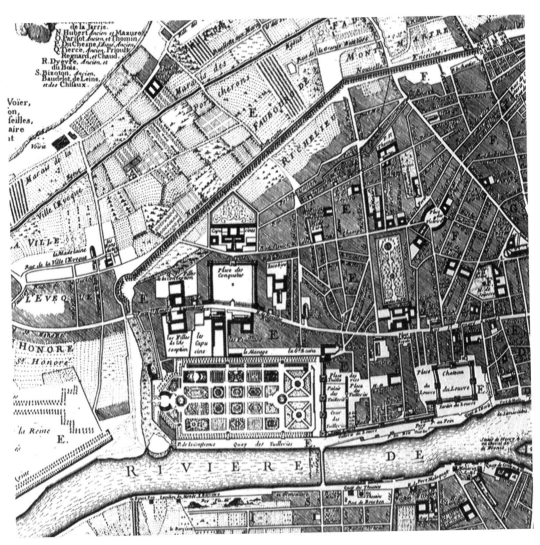

7.55   Location of Place Louis-le-Grand, first version (Place des Conquêtes), Paris. From the 1697 plan by Nicolas de Fer in *Atlas des anciens plans de Paris*

pincers enclosing a square measuring 124 by 140 metres, open to north and south, awaiting the attachment of residences at the back (Fig. 7.56).

This was a period when burgeoning trade and commerce placed the ascendant bourgeoisie in the financial position of a Parisian aristocrat. New wealth generated substantial building activity which was still largely contained, nevertheless, inside the old ring of defensive boulevards and had been since Louis XIV, by an ordinance of 1672, opposed further expansion. So interstitial development in a context of intensive mechanical relations governed urbanism and architecture (Fig. 7.45). Michael Dennis has elegantly described the hierarchical use of *poché* in accommodating the interior shapes of residential design to the constraints imposed by irregular lot patterns and the abrupt boundary of the façade

surrounding the Place Vendôme[17] (Fig. 7.57). Two adjacent residences occupying the northwest corner, the Hôtels Crozat and d'Evreux, designed by Pierre Bullet in 1702 and 1707, do not suffer from these contextual impositions; indeed, each is arranged around its own *grandecour* with considerable flair, the main rooms filling in, as *poché*, the space left between façade, party walls, and courtyard. These rooms are backed by an interstitial *poché* of corridors and vestibules, which in turn subordinate a third *poché* level comprising the service and storage areas (Fig 7.58). As in medieval Florence and Baroque Rome, where development intensity was high, buildings were designed from the outside in, as it were, with little apparent loss of convenience or elegance, while preserving the prize of a unitary public presence upon street and square.

7.56   Place Louis-le-Grand (Place Vendôme), Paris. Second version by J. Hardouin-Mansart, from the engraving by Perelle. Bibliothèque Nationale, Paris

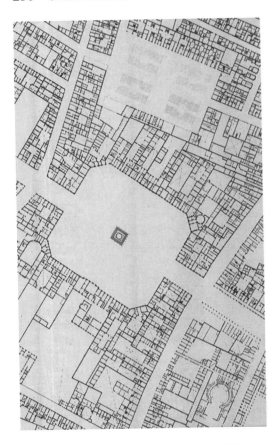

7.57   Place Vendôme, plan of the ground floor in the nineteenth century. Reconstruction after the Vasserot plan by Bruno Fortier et al

With the falling away of spatial restrictions, can it be entirely coincidental that a new kind of architectural rationalism, one that gave primacy to function and classification, began to surface? Certainly at least two treatises dealing with the question of *convenient* spatial arrangements in the residence just precede the onset of this period. In 1737 Jacques François Blondel published *De la distribution des maisons de plaisance et la décoration des édifices en général*, followed in 1743 by Charles-Etienne Briseux's *L'Art de bâtir des maisons de campagne*. Each was a compendium of practical ideas on the distribution and servicing of seigneurial houses in the countryside, where functional allocation, the distribution of fenestration, and the shape of the whole edifice were unhampered by small sites and the presence of adjoining structures. There were readers aplenty; beyond the reach of Louis XIV's decree, on the plateau around Brie, for instance, nobles and bourgeois from Paris had been acquiring large estates since the 1670s, amalgamated from small agricultural plots, orchards, and pastures.[20] Just as in sixteenth-century Veneto, to own a country estate near Paris, preferably worked by someone else, was a sign of having arrived. Some knowledge of the rural economy, and of the architecture appropriate to such a setting, came with the privileges of proprietorship. *L'Agriculture et la maison rustique*, published by Charles and Jean Liébaut, went into 103 editions by 1702. In a way, the early work of Blondel and Briseux heralded the reversal of architectural procedure soon to take over the environs of Paris under the name of neoclassicism: the process of working outwards from a set of relatively abstract principles, a process impossible to follow around the Place Vendôme, demands an empty landscape, or at least the loose facsimile of one then offered by the nascent suburbanization of the Paris region (Fig. 7.60).

Without the kind of external template induced by intensive mechanical relations that had governed development around the Place Vendôme, the suburban villa could become a

But once the fabric of Paris was allowed to extend beyond the *grands boulevards* into the Faubourg St-Germain and the Faubourg St Honoré following the end of the Seven Years War (1763), the subordination of private architecture to the expense and public initiative evident in the Place Vendôme came to an end. By 1751, records Charles Oulmont in *La Maison*, a house in the Place Vendôme cost 104,000 livres.[18] But twenty years later land that had been forbidden to development was available in large measure, at a price considerably less than were locations inside the old cordon, unleashing a wave of speculation in the Faubourg St-Germain[19] (Fig. 7.59).

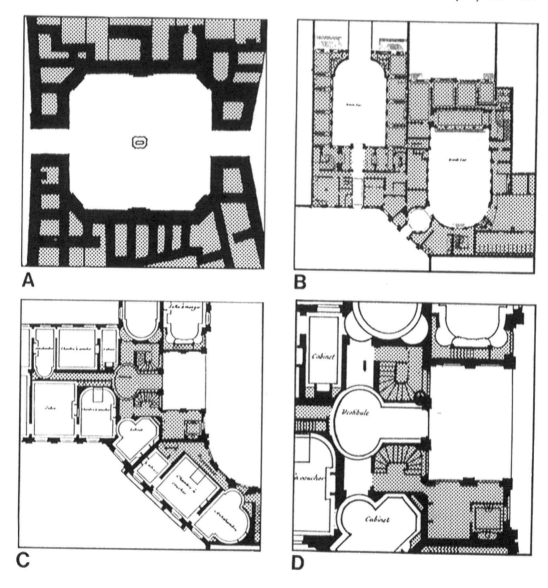

7.58   Boundary hierarchy around the Place Vendôme, by Michael Dennis. A: Urban *poché*; B: Primary *poché*, Hôtels Crozat and d'Evreux; C: Secondary *poché* within the hôtels; D: Tertiary *poché* within the hôtels

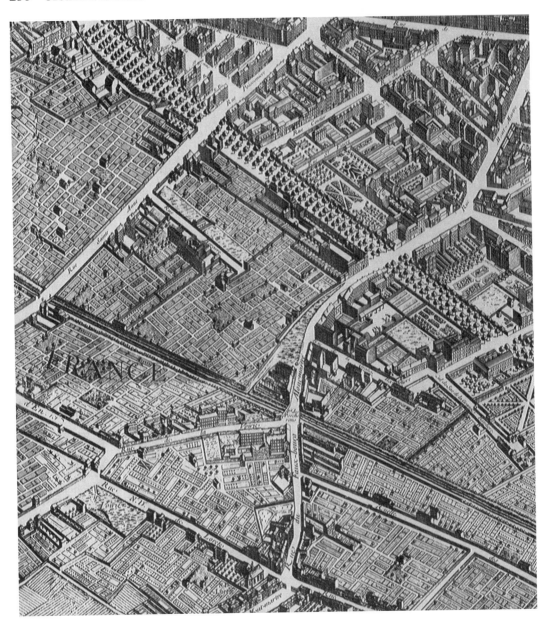

7.59   Part of the Faubourg Montmartre, showing the undeveloped terrain beyond the Paris boulevards. From the Turgot plan of 1734–9

7.60   Croissy, The Villa of Light. Drawn by J.M. Duc

retreat in the fullest sense, impelled as much, perhaps, by the insalubrity of the capital as by the philosophical individualism of the Enlightenment. If the rich were leaving Paris, the poor were flooding in: 'The scum of the countryside becomes the scum of the cities,' wrote Sébastien Mercier of the 150,000-strong army of domestic servants in Paris.[21] Simply disposing of the dead in Paris – some 20,000 per year – was well beyond the resources of the authorities, and traffic congestion in the tangle of streets in Le Marais, the Quartier St Antoine, and around Les Halles brought peril to pedestrian and rider alike.[22] So the urge and opportunity for the wealthy to escape the warrens of Paris proceeded hand in hand, at mid-century, with the scholar's will to shake loose from the intellectual strictures of history. This weird alliance of nostalgia for a rural past and the advocacy of scientific reason was about to be played out in the neoclassical landscape.

Positivism and the Neoclassical Paradigm

We have seen how the boundaries of the city are often the subject of practical reason applied to the working of materials to fashion the raw symbols of human relatedness. The efficacy of these symbols depends, in turn, on expressive meaning, which invades the crevices of the imagination, is charged with values, and is inimical to theoretical reason. We have seen, too, that the canonical texts of the Renaissance, like that of Vitruvius, were *techne*, rule books suffused by the myth-laden values on which expressive meaning depends. But the Enlightenment and the growth of scientific positivism called this legacy to order; their adherents, uncomfortable with practices they mistakenly associated with the *ancien régime*, tried to overturn the legacy with texts and a system of architectural education purged of archaic messages. Inevitably, in the attempt to bring new certainties to practice, the insistent residue of expressive meaning could not be assimilated without doing violence to the very principles upon which their system of thought was based. Ironically, a new equivocation began to pervade the salons, one that marks architectural and urbanist discourse to this day, because the symbols of boundary formation can neither be purged from actual practice nor sealed from the unfolding pattern of urbanization. But with the advent of professionalism, what had once been a craft, fed by imagination and guided by the *techne*, gave way to the categories necessary to theoretical reason; theory and practice began to part company just when the boundaries of the city started to engulf the countryside.

The birth of an architecture of rationalized categories was already apparent in the contributions made to the *Encyclopédie* by Jacques-François Blondel; Louis, Chevalier de Jaucourt; and even by Diderot himself, between 1750 and 1776. These tentative, even ambivalent beginnings were gradually to build, over the course of a century, to the epic advocacy of categories in Eugène Viollet-le-Duc's *Dictionnaire raisonnée de l'architecture française du XIᵉ au XVIᵉ siècle*, a seven-year project completed in 1861; and his *Entretiens sur l'architecture*, published in 1863 and 1872. Throughout this period, we can also observe the growth of what was until recently a commanding presence in architecture, namely, the extent to which reasoned design is guided by the social, political, and national role of architecture. Social change and progress are much in evidence in Blondel's later contributions, in contrast to the entry by Jean le Rond d'Alembert's discussion of architecture in the very first 1751 volume of the *Encyclopédie*. There, architecture had been classified in the *Système figuré des connoissances humaines* under 'imagination,' along with the fine arts of sculpture, painting, poetry, and music (in Diderot's *Prospectus* of the previous November architecture had been classified under 'reason'). Here is what d'Alembert wrote:

Architecture, that art which is born of necessity and perfected by luxury, can be added to [sculpture and painting]. Having developed by degrees from cottages to palaces, in the eye of the philosopher it is simply the embellished mask, so to speak, of one of our greatest needs. The imitation of beautiful nature in Architecture is less striking and more restricted than in Painting and Sculpture. The latter expresses all the parts of beautiful nature indifferently and without restriction, portraying it as it is, uniform or varied; while Architecture, combining and uniting the different bodies it uses, is confined to imitating the symmetrical arrangement that nature observes more or less obviously in each individual thing, and that contrasts so well with the beautiful variety of all taken together.[23]

It is apparent from this and other entries, as Kevin Harrington has noted, that the author clearly was not at all comfortable with his own explanation. The *encyclopédistes* were nothing if not reasonable men, so their zeal in the pursuit of classification was tempered by a certain scepticism when it came to the finality of knowledge categories. This was certainly the case with architecture; its 'practical' components (stereotomy, statics, materials) happened to be listed elsewhere, under 'memory,' and d'Alembert's equivocal explanation concludes by leaving open the question of architecture's inclusion in the category of 'imagination.' (Human knowledge in the *Système* was regarded as progressing from memory through imagination to its highest form, reason.)

Now the whole question of beauty was of considerable interest both to Diderot the philosopher, and to d'Alembert, the mathematician, although in such matters they would normally have deferred to the opinion of the expert contributor, who in this case was Blondel. He, however, seemed to take little interest in architecture's relationship to knowledge, and offered no guidance in this regard. Kevin Harrington surmises that the original placing in the *Prospectus* under 'reason' was attributable to d'Alembert's own discipline, and his temporary conclusion that architectural principles were derived from mathematics.[24]

In any case, it is clear that no one was sure, around 1750, about the nature and purpose of architecture as a reasoned activity. Even Blondel, who campaigned vigorously against the excesses of the rococo style, seeking to replace its superficial attractiveness by principles that were *sage et consequent*, was among those who believed in the transitory nature of all such principles. Certainly, although a skilled mathematician himself who taught calculus to his students, he refused to *equate* mathematics and architecture. For him, it was neither possible nor desirable to subject architecture to any form of abstract generalization, nor had it occurred to him that architecture might well be one of the few bridges across many categories of human understanding. His frequent references to *conveyance* are made in the context, not of mathematics, which was all very well in its place – building technique – but of taste and genius. For instance, under *chambre* (vol. 3), while Blondel admits that architectural and public spaces should be made to fit the needs of the occupant, such a fit could emerge only from the application of experience, intelligence, resourcefulness and genius. Here is Harrington's description of his concerns in designing a *chambre à coucher*:

It should be deeper than it is wide. The windows should be opposite the bed. The fireplace should be opposite the door, centred along its wall. The door should terminate an enfilade in the house, but it should also be a deep doorway, so that one could not stumble into the room. To illustrate that even these four simple prescriptions can lead to complications and variations, Blondel notes that if the fireplace is placed in the wall opposite the door, the enfilade is terminated, rather than visually continued, as it would be if a window were opposite the door. He even mentions a failure of this sort in the Hôtel de Soubise. Obviously, in weighing the claims of visual continuation of the enfilade against the sense of arrival, welcome and warmth symbolised by the

fireplace opposite the entrance, Blondel is advancing an argument which is clearly a matter of taste and which must, to be persuasive, be supported by cogent reasons. Thus, in addition to familiarizing the reader with the completion of designing even a single room, he has also introduced the idea that decisions are made not by recourse to unvarying standards, but by identifying and analyzing a problem with care and diligence.[25]

In his later contributions, Blondel is even more definite in his opposition to rule-governed architecture. An extreme relativism, indeed, begins to creep in over the question of the appreciation of form. In the article *Balustrade* (vol. 2), he falls back on virtues akin to craftsmanship, emphasizing long training, a skilled eye, and an intuitive understanding of proportion. He senses that even the classical Orders are not absolute, but arbitrarily chosen. They, like all forms, acquired meaning from the use made of them.

If Blondel's ambivalence originated in his sense that focused, abstract reasoning could neither explain architectural history nor preside over its future, his was a forlorn, last attempt by an eighteenth-century theorist to prevent an ensuing crisis in which privacy, self-interest, and scientific classification began to monopolize consciously held ideas about the articulation of urban boundaries. Cogitation about the division of the terrain succumbed to the slow death of magic, and of the ritualized orientation to nature and humanity. Theory, however, became separated from practice, which still, for the most part, depended on the old instincts. So life and knowledge, thought and action were being compartmentalized, and not only to the detriment of a theorized unity. 'Before the seventeenth century, the primary place of perception as the ultimate evidence of knowledge was never questioned. *Mathesis* explicitly maintained its symbolic connotations, and the hierarchical structure of the cosmos established by Aristotle remained valid. It was a world of predominantly mythical character, qualitatively different from our present universe of precision.'[26] Alberto Pérez-Gòmez indicts the mode of thought required to accumulate scientific knowledge in his cogent analysis of the impoverishment of architectural thought. He traces the fall back to Galileo, then to the systematic displacement of Aristotelian myths by scientific knowledge in the seventeenth and eighteenth centuries: 'The fundamental axiom of the sciences since 1800, as well as of the humanities, has been "invariance," which rejects, or at least is unable to cope with, the richness and ambiguity of symbolic thought.'[27] The disintegration of symbolic thought was far from being an overnight event. Two centuries were required to change not merely the architectural imagination but our orientation to the world. What had been instinctive became procedural, and a complex, poetic reality was ordered according to scientific models; whatever happened not to fit the methods of science was deemed to be without epistemological validity.

This 'inversion of priorities' can be attributed, according to Pérez-Gòmez, to two great transformations. The first, occurring towards the end of the seventeenth century, was the destruction, in traditional cosmology, of the link comprising number and geometry between the human and the divine. 'At the same time, technique and the crafts were freed from their traditional magical associations. In architecture, this laid the basis for a new approach. Architects began to consider their discipline a technical challenge, whose problems could be solved with the aid of two conceptual tools, number and geometry.'[28] Nevertheless, the belief in Divine Nature, as intrinsic to scientific understanding, persisted. Plato's cosmology remained a central part of Newtonian physics for the time being, in which number and geometry retained a crucial vestige of transcendental power. But then, 'around 1800 a second great transformation took place. Faith and reason were truly divorced. Scientific thought came to be seen as the only serious and legitimate interpretation of reality, denying any need for

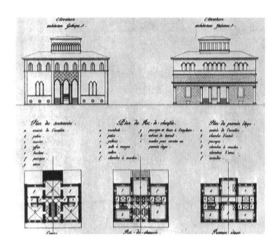

7.61   L.A. Dubut, alternative styles for a house, 1803

metaphysics. Euclidean geometry was functionalized. Infinitesimal calculus was purged of its residual symbolic content. Geometry and mathematics were now purely formal disciplines, devoid of meaning, value and power except as instruments, as tools of technological intentionality.'[29]

To the rationalists nature became objectified, no longer regarded as the representation of a hierarchically ordered divine cosmos, the symbol of immutability in an eminently mutable quotidian life. Architecture was assumed to have lost its rituality, whereby the act of building had been the symbolic joining of humanity and nature. Practice, equated with positivist science, was deemed incapable of imitating a nature now rendered meaningless. 'Deprived of a legitimate poetic content, architecture was reduced to either a prosaic technological process or mere decoration.'[30] As Laugier would have wished, architecture was finally a matter of making choices (Fig. 7.61).

Accordingly, what was no longer ideal could not be imitated. In the place of imitation stood rationalism and, eventually, following Durand's 1802 *Précis des Leçons d'Architecture*, functionalism. Transcendental meaning had given way, finally, to the principles of love of well-being and aversion to pain, the well-spring of a materialism that was to underlie the conceptual inheritance of the nineteenth century. Comfort and economy were finally established as the objectives of building, so that even Laugier's theory of the primitive hut seemed ridiculous. Architecture, according to Durand, was not like the other arts, and could not turn to nature as its source of imitation. 'He could only understand it in a *literal* sense, as two terms of an equation, not as a metaphorical relation.'[31] Durand's mistake, therefore, lay in making the 'obvious' assumption that the purpose of architecture was to please the eye. 'For Durand was unable to realize that the mythical dimension was actually the realm where the transcendental justification of architecture had to be found. By now, architecture had ceased to be a metaphorical image of the cosmic order. True, the new self-contained and necessarily prosaic architecture seemed to be ruled by similar categories; but the categories were now totally autonomous, and their structure was logical, not symbolic'[32] (Fig. 7.62).

The structures of rational thought had their limits, nevertheless, when it came to application; strong spiritual legacies refused to give way entirely before intellectual discourse. The discourse itself, moreover, unwittingly reincarnated old themes in a different guise, as Carl Becker has shown. The *philosophes* 'demolished the Heavenly City of St. Augustine only to rebuild it with more up-to-date materials ... They denied that miracles ever happened, but believed in the perfectability of the human race.'[33] If they upheld nature and her laws, it was as a surrogate for the authority of God, and in the end, a sufficient confirmation of the old virtues to sustain the archetypal narrative through the ensuing Romantic movement. The effects of material life on practice, however, were quite another matter; the economies of great cities, as well as their political events, gave a new impetus to centrifugal migration which began to alter the patterns of settlement in the hinterlands. Urban intensity, human relatedness, and bound-

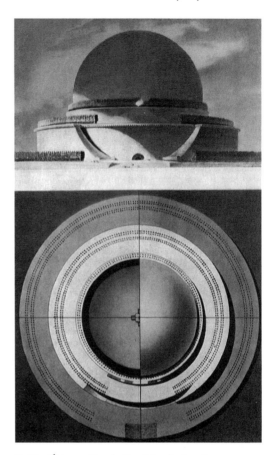

7.62   Étienne-Louis Boullée, design for a monument to Newton, 1784

ary architecture were all caught up in the process.

As we shall see, the death of architectural symbolism was not quite so universal or final as Pérez-Gomez believes, because practice had to come to terms with the expressive meanings that continued to be manifested in the boundary dialectic. Nevertheless, he is essentially correct in identifying a cause of the theory paradigm that took hold at the close of the eighteenth century and burdens us to this day. The advent of intellectual materialism, moreover, served and was in turn fostered by the cult of privacy, soon to be spread across the Paris hinterland.

'Privacy was an eighteenth century phenomenon,' writes Fernand Braudel.[34] But this
was so only for those wealthy enough to
afford it, and it went hand in hand with
convenience in a new architectural dialectic
that combined geography and metaphor in
the flight from urbanity. While function and
the ideals of neoclassicism cannot be completely attributed to extensive mechanical relations, they cannot be disentangled from the
outward spread of urbanization that made
low-density development possible at the time.

While Claude-Nicolas Ledoux may be remembered for the theories that he recorded in
the *Dictionnaire* late in life, his built work is a
more cogent expression of this material underside of neoclassicism, a reverberation back
to the dormant land market of the Renaissance and forward to the edge of the twentieth-century metropolis. In 1783 Ledoux completed the Hôtel Thélusson, located on
extensive grounds on the Rue de Provence just
north of Paris. His own engraving shows a
perimeter walled off from what lies around,
and entered via a rusticated triumphal arch
placed at the roadside. Behind, the house of
Mme Thélusson, set between two smaller
pavilions for each of her sons, withdraws into
its own archaic landscape of rocks and trees
(Fig. 7.63). Despite its formal symmetry, the
plan reveals an inversion of the Place
Vendôme: Here it is the landscape that acts as
a kind of *poché* to absorb the complex perimeter of the house, the consequence of an internally derived program that placed most ancillary functions at the periphery. The section,
however, is far more ambiguous; if the landscape absorbs the house, the reverse is equally
true, because the lines between exterior and
interior are blurred by semi-enclosures, open
colonnades, a half-round Corinthian portico,
external staircases which mediate the passage
from garden to house, and rocks piled against
the stonework of the main entrance. The
theme again is integration, evidence of the
nostalgic side to neoclassicism and of the
reincarnation of that ancient dictum whereby
nature's sanctity must remain unsullied by
man's work (Fig. 7.64).

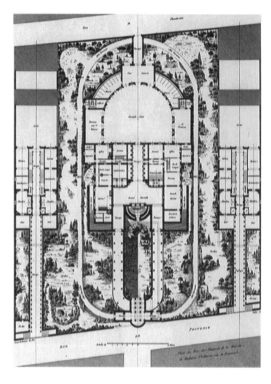

7.63 Claude-Nicolas Ledoux, Hôtel de
Thélusson, Paris. Ground-floor plan, 1783

Such instances were not rare in France. If
scientism coupled to Enlightenment rationality could not ascend above the level of a
panlogism that excised old meanings in the
pursuit of functionality, practice went its own
way; but if baroque urbanism was defeated in
the Paris hinterland in the eighteenth century,
extensive mechanical relations were as culpa-
ble as novel ideas that placed individuality at
the centre of things. As with so many theoretical projects, Ledoux's own architectural theo-
rizing contained none of the dialectics most
evident in the Hôtel Thélusson, and present
also in his earlier Hôtel Guimard (1770–2) in
the Chausée d'Antin. We turn to his proclamatory engravings, however beautifully
executed, for sombre evidence of the limits of
the undialectical single idea. *The House of the
Agricultural Guard* is only the most alien of
his surreal paper fantasies, portraying a world
encumbered by pure geometry (Fig. 7.65).

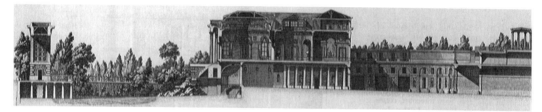

7.64   Hôtel de Thélusson, section

More prophetic even than that is Ledoux's engraving *Village of Maupertius*; an austere temple sits astride a crossroads at the centre of a landscape parcelled out into private lots, each surrounded by walls and fences. The lots are occupied by small houses of similar size but diverse *physiognomy* – a word more apt than *style*, because the houses possess a cartoon anthropomorphism. In this parody of mid-twentieth century suburbia, nothing but the temple in the intersection – surely a traffic hazard – signifies the presence of anything transcending the monad of the individual household, attached solely, irrevocably to its little parcel of land (Fig. 7.66).

7.65   Claude-Nicolas Ledoux, House of the Agricultural Guard

7.66   Claude-Nicolas Ledoux, Village of Maupertius

CHAPTER EIGHT

Urban Boundaries in Turmoil

Proust was right: life is better represented by bad music than by a Missa solemnis ... History is closer to what Sue narrates than to what Hegel projects. Shakespeare, Melville, Balzac, Dostoevsky all wrote sensational fiction. What has taken place in the real world was predicted in penny dreadfuls. – Umberto Eco, *Foucault's Pendulum* (1988)

Berlin: The Courtyard and the Street

Whoever conquers the streets conquers the State. – Joseph Goebbels, *Kampf von Berlin* (1931)

The neoclassical spirit, in so far as it touched a corner of European urbanism, offered a seductive compound of nostalgia and scientific rationalism to those who theorized about cities. The theorists' dream of Cartesian order reincarnating a stable past persisted and gathered strength as the early years of the nineteenth century witnessed a growing unruliness in urban formation, but practice tended, as usual, to follow its own course.

London, more than Paris, was beset by an accelerating transformation of old places, although one tempered by practices, cultivated over centuries past, of architectural reticence. Much intellectual heat may have been generated in the salons of the English capital about which appropriated style best represented a society whose trajectory no one could fathom, but the consequences of this exchange paled in comparison with the persistence, not of old styles, but of ancient expressive meanings. Sir John Soane (1753–1837), arguably the most original enemy of the rococo in Europe, produced more than an aesthetic feast for the discerning in his design for the Dulwich Gallery (1811–14) and his 1812 house in Lincoln's Inn Fields. The façade to this house – a triple-bayed screen of pilasters and arches – takes its cues from the simple Georgian terrace of which it is a part, forming an elegant exclamation mark in an archaic message (Fig. 8.1).

This message – that self-interest should still give way to the boundary dialectic – was taken up elsewhere in London, to penetrate through the fancy architectural detail imported from history. The façades of Regent's Park and Regent Street, designed by John Nash between 1811 and 1825, are pierced and screened by modest fenestration and colonnades, the pilasters barely project an inch, and the boundary lines are atomized into clusters of receding and re-entrant planes (Fig. 8.2).

8.1   Sir John Soane, Architect's House, Lincoln's Inn Fields, London, 1812–13

flood of events as massive urbanization dominated practice and subdued theories with its banal, material facts. Nowhere was this more apparent than in nineteenth-century Berlin, which switched from a largely inertial backwater to a dynamic, malstructured field during the period of its genesis as a great industrial metropolis. There we will find all the ingredients of a catastrophic transformation in mechanical relations displayed in full. The story is an intricate one, because the clash of political wills that brought Bismarck to power and spawned the German nation, then gave birth to the Social Democratic movement, is also enmeshed with the kinetic street mobs mobilizing in the wake of rampant industrial expansion in the latter part of the last century. We shall see how these facts are connected, in turn, to the anarchy of Berlin's land markets, and from there to the confrontations between the social reformers who foreshadowed the planning profession and those who sought profit and a secure life. This constellation of events coalesced and was half resolved around the question of urbanism, because Berlin more than anywhere else was the stage where the schism that ushered in what has been called architectural modernism, as the eventual constituent of the boundaries located between the antagonisms of urbanization, took place. Here, with extraordinary consequences, wily Proteus began his push against the incubus of the nineteenth-century city.

The Formative Years

For a short time, during the first decades of the nineteenth century, Berlin was as well decorated as any capital in Europe. Much of this, as elsewhere, was attributable to the presence of famous men, although, like London and Amsterdam, Berlin was not burdened at first by anyone who happened to pursue self-aggrandizement through construction.[1]   In 1800, Alexander and Wilhelm von Humboldt commissioned a modest connection, to be named the Chausseestrasse, between the family estate in Tegel and the Oranienburg gate,

These reticences were not limited to the classical or Italianate; the Gothic Revival – whether rationalized as the epitome of socialism by Viollet-le-Duc or of Catholicism by Pugin – offered its translucent voids and pared-away screens to urbanism, and their expressive meanings prevail long after the Battle of the Styles had occupied the minds of so many intelligent men.

But if more than a trace of the archetypal narrative endured despite the alleged victory of scientific reason in the field of urbanism, neither one would withstand the ensuing

8.2   John Nash, Cumberland Terrace, Regent's Park, 1826

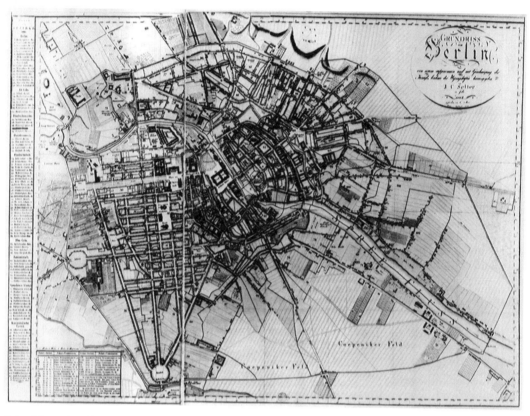

8.3   Map of Berlin, 1804, by J.C Selter. Updated by Charles Maré, 1811. Staatsbibliothek Preussischer Kulturbesitz, Kart. 14631

which at the time, according to a plan drawn by Jean Chrétian Selter in 1804, overlooked a pastoral vista of woods and meadows (Fig. 8.3). On the Gendarmenmarkt, the Royal Theatre, a classical work by Carl Gotthard Langhans, was flanked by the near-identical French and German cathedrals, whose slender and elongated cupolas graced the skyline. To the west and southwest, just outside the old fortification line, lay the rectangulated street pattern of the Dorotheenstadt and the Friedrichstadt, the former traversed by the tree-lined axis of Unter den Linden. Elsewhere the city had until then kept the signs of slow, incremental growth, where winding or sharply articulated streets were lined with single-storey rowhousing, or more typically with three-storey buildings, elevated half a

level to permit a windowed cellar, their front steps directly accessing the street (Fig. 8.4).

In those days the city was blessed with the presence of some notable architectural talents who were well versed in the rather stringent classical style of Brandenburg. The largely unsung Friedrich Gilly (1772–1800) died in his twenties, but left some remarkable drawings of two projects, for a Doric monument to Frederick the Great intended for the octagonal Leipziger Platz, and for a National Theatre; his most telling legacy, however, were two pupils, one of whom was Leo von Klenze (1784–1864), who fashioned the face of Munich so well. The other was Karl Friedrich Schinkel (1781–1841), the son of a Brandenburg pastor.

Unter den Linden at this time connected the

8.4 Berlin, 1786. Klosterstrasse with Parochialkirche. Etching by Johann Georg Rosenberg. Berlin-Museum

Royal Palace and its associated Lustgarten and old cathedral via the so-called Hundebrücke, a narrow bridge over the fortification moat, to the Brandenburg Gate, which had been built by Langhans in 1791, then its axis continued west as a tree-lined carriageway through the Tiergarten. The 'Linden,' linked to the Gendarmenmarkt and embellished piece by piece over the previous century, had already developed into a graceful civic armature by the time Schinkel contributed his masterpieces to it (Fig. 8.5). Just across the Hundebrücke from the Royal Palace stood the Zeughaus, pilastered and porticoed in the classical manner, to the west of which, almost facing the Opera House and flanked by the University, the small chestnut park called Kastanienwäldchen opened from the north side of the boulevard. In 1816 Schinkel built his Neue Wache, square in plan and fronted by a Doric portico, in this park (Fig. 8.6). Then just to the east he replaced the Hundebrücke with the graceful sweep of his Schlossbrücke, simultaneously readjusting the axis of the bridge to align it with Unter den Linden and bring the Lustgarten, the Old Cathedral, and the Royal Palace within the boundaries of his extended armature. Between 1817 and 1822 Schinkel worked on the Old Cathedral itself, adding an Ionic portico and two ancillary cupolas flanking the central dome; then, in 1829, his design for the Old Museum completed the Lustgarten ensemble, occupying the latter's northern edge and

8.5   Berlin, Schlossbrücke with Old Cathedral. Painting by Wilhelm Brücke, 1870. Berlin, Verwaltung der Staatlichen Schlösser und Gärten, GK 11480

linked to the Old Cathedral along the River Spree by a double stand of trees. The stand continued southward to the Palace, thereby terminating the Linden armature at the river in a square with a beautifully modulated perimeter (Fig. 8.7).

Schinkel added other jewels to the Berlin landscape, including the Allgemeine Bauschule across the River Spree and, in the Gothic style nearby, the Friedrich–Werdersche church; they belonged, without exception, to the great urban monuments of the Romantic movement, giving to the city, for all their austere demeanour, a serenity destined to last but a few years.

The prosperity that had enabled all this embellishment to occur was also attracting newcomers by the thousand to a city whose culture and politics had been nurtured for two centuries on a stable, conservative hierarchy.

Between 1800 and 1830, the population doubled, to 328,000, most of the influx having settled in the northern suburbs. Then, just before the onset of industrialization in 1829, a municipal boundary law was passed in Berlin – and reconfirmed in 1841 – fixing the city limits along the line of the old defensive moat. Any street that happened to be built beyond this line fell into disrepair, because the ancient *Gemeinde* outside the moat refused to accept responsibility for providing even the most rudimentary services. Extension of these streets, already home to an undisciplined crowd of inmigrants from Brandenburg and Silesia, was unthinkable, and rightly regarded by the King and government of Prussia as the root cause of political instability, a contamination of their long-standing support in the surrounding rural communities.[2] But Canute-like gestures could do little to stop the effects

8.6   *Die Neue Wache in Berlin,* by Wilhelm Brücke, 1842. Niedersächsisches Landesmuseum

of Berlin's locational and other advantages when it came to attracting industry and people.

In 1837 the locomotive firm of Borsig occupied a jumble of buildings along the Chausseestrasse just outside the Oranienburg gate at the northern edge of the hemmed-in city (Fig. 8.8). There an iron foundry, machine shop, smelter, drying room, boilerhouse, and press had been put together on an irregularly shaped plot, fronted by an old house (Fig. 8.9). By the following year, when the firm contemplated expansion, it was already clear that even reasonably efficient growth was becoming difficult without relocating onto prohibited open land farther out. The problem was not simply a matter of finding enough space; industrial architecture was already concerned in a rudimentary way with the same functional questions that the English had encountered long before. These questions related to material flows, labour divisions,

and the latent efficiencies of spatial organization designed around specific industrial procedures. The new capital goods for the making of Borsig's locomotives were, in any case, large and heavy, precluding assembly in anything other than single-storey sheds, so that the more intensive use of developed urban space – the time-honoured consequence of rising land prices – was seriously limited here, and the firm's immediate plans were thwarted.[3]

Fifteen years later, in 1852, the Maschinenfabrik Schwartzkopff, which later became the Berliner Maschinenbau-AG, opened a factory on the Chausseestrasse in a location that was also quickly becoming cramped by competitive bidding for space. In 1869 this firm resorted to building an affiliated works nearby on the Ackerstrasse, with a special telegraph and railway link to the first site, rather than acquiring what had by then become congested adjacent land on the

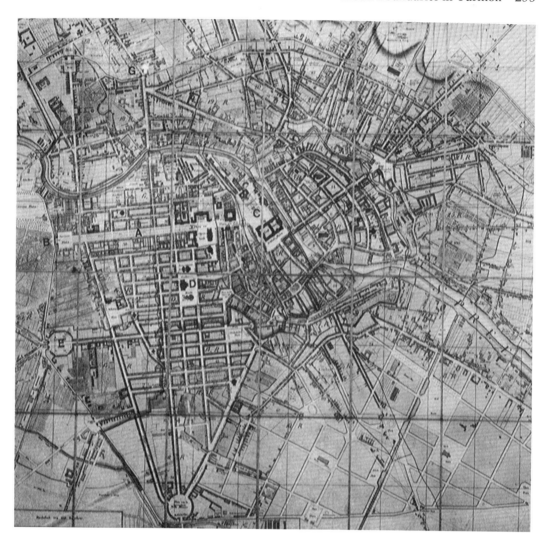

8.7 Berlin about 1850. An updated map of 1826 by the Klg. Akademie der Wissenschaften. Landesbildstelle, Berlin. A: Unter den Linden; B: Brandenburg Gate; C: Lustgarten with Old Cathedral; D: Gendarmenmarkt; E: Leipzigerplatz; F: Leipzigerstrasse; G: Oranienburg gate

Chausseestrasse.[4] The new plant was laid out in an entirely functional manner, permitting production in fewer and larger buildings than had been the case elsewhere. Their architects, Ende and Bockmann, had designed a fifty-metre-long single-storey ironworks with a high central clerestory, a steam-powered crane in the centre, and ancillary functions to both sides. The hall was flooded with light, and well aired through vents in the roof.[5]

Opportunities like this, where enough space could be found for industrial efficiency to work, were now rare, and rapidly intensifying mechanical relations filled the northern districts with a characteristic landscape. The novelist and engineer Heinrich Seidel, builder of the great Anhalter Bahnhof, had a keen eye for the ensuing clash of boundaries: 'From the Oranienburg gate stretched one giant machine factory after the other in an almost

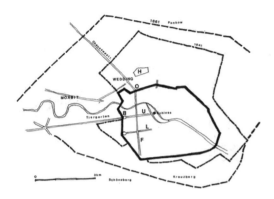

8.8   Berlin after the boundary changes of 1841 and 1861. B: Brandenburg Gate; F: Friedrichstrasse; L: Leipzigerstrasse; H: Humboldthain; O: Oranienburg Gate; U: Unter den Linden

unbroken row. Borsig's world famous locomotive works started the chain with great colonnades built by [Heinrich] Strack; then followed Egells, Pflug, Schwarzkopff, Wöhlert and many others of lesser renown. Everywhere above the street noise a terrible pandemonium sounded, and the dull pounding of mighty steamhammers shook the ground so that in the adjoining tenements the floors trembled, the glass rattled and the lamps vibrated. At certain hours the streets turned into a mighty riverbed of blackened workers, disgorged from all the factory gates.'[6]

At mid-century, and during the following decades, no one had grasped the inexorable logic of mechanical relations, nor their power to overwhelm the processes of architectural formation and urban growth. The connection between development profitability, construction intensity, and boundary articulation was not understood, let alone deemed to be linked to the public interest. In Berlin at this time, the official position associated the control of urban growth first and foremost with the question of public security; accordingly it was the police president who wielded authority over construction control. Police planning – what a century later would evolve into strategies of

deintensification by prohibiting construction on site boundaries, combined with programs to increase the supply of serviced land – in pursuing public stability, innocently served to usher in the opposite.

In 1853, a year after the new Schwarzkopff factory on the Ackerstrasse provided an experiment in urbanism that officialdom failed to notice, the Police President of Berlin introduced his new construction statutes. Wherever streets were more than 15 metres wide – almost everywhere – a building height of 22 metres was now permitted. If frontages were at least 20 metres wide, then a building depth exceeding 50 metres became legal. The statutes contained no prohibitions on built form, other than the necessity for linked interior courtyards as a firefighting measure whose dimensions could be as small as 5.30 by 5.30 metres. As far as light, air, ventilation, and restrictions on density were concerned, nothing was mandated[7] (Fig. 8.10).

If the statutes, in conjunction with mechanical relations, were to determine the character of the city's street boundaries, their distribution depended upon the police president's 1862 street plan, called the *Hobrecht-Plan* after its chief designer, the sanitation engineer James Friedrich Ludolf Hobrecht (1825–1902). As it turned out, the whole scheme became little more than a convenience for tenement builders. Hobrecht had merely traced in a hierarchy of street alignments, occasionally punctuating them with rectangular and star-shaped intersections. Gone were the series of linked green spaces, proposed by Peter Joseph Lenné (1789–1866) in 1840 for the northern and eastern districts; only the Tiergarten – a piece of royal property – remained as a park.[8] No land-use restrictions, monument-protection provisions, community facilities, or trace of civic decoration was contained in the plan[9] (Fig. 8.11).

In Moabit at this time, just across the River Spree from Berlin's central district, growth was particularly anarchic and made up exclusively of two building types – the factory and the tenement. Here more than anywhere the

8.9   Borsig Ironworks, Berlin, ca 1845. Berlin-Museum

Hausmannesque plan devised by James Hobrecht was to have a devastating effect. Hobrecht had determined that long diagonal streets, such as Perleberger Strasse and the westward extension of the Huttenstrasse, would give new internal boundaries to this rapidly developing industrial suburb. But here, as elsewhere covered by his plan, the proposed streets were so widely spaced that the intervening parcels of land were excessively deep (up to four hundred metres in places). Whereas this depth was fine for large factories, it meant that the four- to six-storey tenements that had started to spread across Moabit had to be organized around a relay courtyard system in order to access the full depth of each lot. This arrangement has been regarded by everyone since as completely exploitative. Certainly it meant that direct access to the street was compromised by the necessity to pass through intervening court-

yards, which made an already congested and noisy environment even worse (Figs 8.12 and 8.13). But compared with the notorious railroad tenements or even the dumbbell tenements of New York's Lower East Side during this same period, which generated far higher residential congestion (averaging 1,000 inhabitants per hectare in some precincts), those constructed after the demise of the 1853 Building Code in 1887 were marginally better. Building heights and courtyard sizes were governed by more restrictive construction statutes and, by including a connecting room in the deeper buildings – the *Berliner Zimmer* – access to a minimal amount of daylight and ventilation was finally assured.

Moreover, it has to be said that even the meanest *Mietskaserne* (tenement) occasionally had some architectural pretensions, unlike most of the Lower East Side tenements, which were pared down to hovels of the

8.10   Berlin, tenement courtyard, ca 1870

grimmest sort. Pediments, cornices, pilasters, and decorative brickwork were façadal accoutrements here and there in the working quarters of Berlin, while entrance lobbies and staircases were trimmed out in plaster mouldings, terrazzo, marble, and faience. Floor-to-ceiling heights occasionally exceeded 3.5 metres, even in the poor districts of Moabit, Kreuzberg, and Wedding. The *Hobrecht-Plan* had at least insured that streets were generally wide, a minimum of 22.6 metres, often over 33 metres, and were sometimes boulevarded and lined with linden trees. The courtyards, even when used by small manufacturing, artisan, and servicing concerns of various kinds, were the everyday gathering-place for women's social intercourse and children's play.

Men and youths preferred the streets (Fig. 8.14).

But, as usual, comparative data of everyday life do not mean a great deal to those who lead it. The Berlin tenant knew nothing of New York; his assessment of his own well-being and the formation of his political consciousness depended upon what was seen and heard on the spot. Seen in this light, both the street riots and the intense reformist urge that were to revolutionize housing and planning in Berlin become more understandable, because what fuelled the ensuing reforms was not the evidence of absolute standards but the enormous gap between rich and poor living conditions, most clearly manifested in the differences in street boundaries and therefore in access to unbuilt, uncontrolled space The first Berlin census was taken in 1861, and revealed some appalling figures. Half of all the city's dwelling units had but a single room, in which lived an average of 4.3 persons. Every tenth inhabitant lived in a cellar, and more than 10,000 people lived nine to a room.[10] By 1871, when the city's population had almost reached a million, two-thirds occupied dwellings with one or two rooms, and 162,000 lived in a single room accommodating an average of seven persons.[11] Figures like this prevailed for another forty years or more, during which time Berlin was built to every site edge in the industrial quarters, and spatial segregation of the classes was complete (Fig. 8.15).

As early as 1870 the Berlin statistician Ernst Bruch had visualized what was to be a principle of superblock planning fifty years later, namely, an absence of hard boundaries: 'The unification of a street quarter into an organic whole, with large central parks and courtyards so that light, air and sun may reach each dwelling.' He also proposed, in his hefty critique of the *Hobrecht-Plan*, the reintroduction of row housing, which had been a part of the city's medieval past, as in the old Marienkirche area, an idea that was taken up again in the Social Democratic *Siedlungen* of the 1920s.[12] But he was to die in Breslau in the

8.11   J.F.L. Hobrecht's Plan for Berlin, 1862

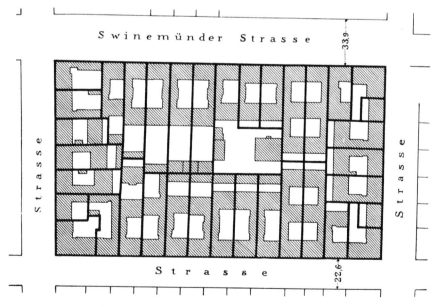

8.12   Berlin tenement block, later nineteenth century. From R. Eberstadt, *Handbuch des Wohnungswesens*, 1909

8.13   Relay tenement courtyards, Meyers Hof. Wedding, Berlin

8.14   Tenement street, Berlin. From the 1927 documentary *Berlin: die Symphonie einer Grossstadt*

year his critique was published, at the age of thirty-six.

The theme of sociospatial integration as an antidote to class warfare, poverty, and territorial insularity seduced the Berlin reformers more than their counterparts elsewhere. As for James Hobrecht, the sanitary engineer–cum–planner, after a trip to England he wrote this apologia of his own plan, denying the inevitable effects the plan would have on reinforcing the boundaries between classes:

As is well known, our way of living is the opposite of that in England. In a so-called Mietskaserne are a 500 taler apartment on the first floor, on the ground floor and second floor each two 200 taler apartments, two 150 taler apartments on the third floor, three 100 taler apartments on the fourth floor, and in the basement, rear courtyards of similar space, apartments for 50 talers. In an English town we find, in the West End, for example, the villas and detached houses of the well-to-do; in other parts of town are the homes of the poor, always bunched together, whole quarters only for the working-class population ... In the Mietskaserne the children from the basement go to the Free School via the same hallway used by the merchants' or consultants' children on their way to private school. Wilhelm from the garret and old bedridden Frau Schulz in the back are well known characters on the first floor. Here a bowl of soup if you are sick, there a piece of clothing, the consequence of close ties between people who live together, even though their circumstances differ ... An English working class quarter is visited only by the police and sensation writers. When the young lady has read the spicy novel, she might ask to be driven quickly through the quarter, never to return there. She is scared of poverty; she is scared of the horror and the crime, saving her soul only by a contribution to the poor commission.[13]

Others saw the English situation differently, including the influential Berlin reformist Rudolf Eberstadt, who regarded

8.15 Berlin tenement landscape

Hobrecht's apologia as a cover-up for doing nothing, especially as segregation by location was in fact quite common in nineteenth-century Germany and, as his fellow liberal Julius Faucher pointed out, the Berlin Westend was far better than Kreuzberg.[14] Nevertheless, with respect to Berlin's social geography in the 1860s, even after taking account of Hobrecht's biases we are left with at least a temporary grain of truth, although one that suggests more than a single interpretation. In the first place the earlier European tenement (for the type extended throughout the northern mainland) did lend itself to the differentiated rent structure that Hobrecht describes. Add to this the supporting circumstance of a complex urban geography of micro-segregation in the distribution of workplaces and amenities and a pattern resembling spatial integration often emerges in parts of the city.

However, even in the 1860s, more than a few districts at the extreme ends of the social scale – those accommodating the paupers and the very wealthy – were 'pure,' in the sense of catering exclusively to a single class. Such areas were rarely tenemented; Berlin around the Alexanderplatz, for instance, had its equivalent of the *îlots insalubres* of Paris, which were little more than medieval hovels or peripheral shacks, while the wealthy everywhere tended to occupy suburban villas, as in Grünewald, or fashionable town houses, as in the Tiergarten. But tenement life was bad enough, and one wonders whether the new alleged attractions of the Berlin tenement are little more than nostalgia, a sign of the current popularity of pre-modernist ideology. No amount of *Schmuck* – façadal frills, fake marble, and mirrors could hide the litany of social misery that was industrial Berlin, nor could it

8.16   Lübbenerstrasse, Kreuzberg, Berlin, 1926

fail to be overwhelmed by the impending dominant expressive meaning of Berlin urbanism – incarceration within a bricked-up landscape (Fig. 8.16).

Mobilizing the City: Mobs and Reformers

The strands of reformist influence upon Berlin housing were initially stronger and more varied than upon the conditions of work, which took their own course with the later advent of Taylorism and its various German precedents. As early as 1901 it was realized in Germany that a reduction from a fourteen-hour day to even nine hours actually increased daily productivity, although a number of die-hard industrialists refused to believe that their own interests could somehow coincide with those of the workers.[15] Wages and other financial benefits were another matter, and each small

gain had to be earned through insurrection and street violence.

In Germany, as in Britain, housing reform was tied closely to land reform and the fight against landlordism long before the beginning of the Garden City movement. But, as with the latter, these efforts were guided by a vision of social integration and access to light, air, and nature, which implied a complete overhaul of urban boundaries; life encumbered by unyielding structures must give way to spaces whose horizons, while not exactly limitless, could be seen from afar. But the emphasis of more enlightened officialdom was upon pragmatic reformism rather than spatial revolution; that is, the future depended upon incremental change. The belief was common among reformers that only the structure of land ownership needed a thoroughgoing overhaul, a task they assumed could be accomplished within the relatively liberal

Bismarckian tradition without recourse to wholesale political upheaval. However, they had not reckoned with the real fragility of their urbanism, nor with the mobs who were quick to apply pressure outside the industrial ghettos. Massive street boundaries and proletarian motility were becoming the antagonistic, unforeseen themes of Berlin urbanism. Against this setting, the reform groups' efforts fade into the background.

As early as 1847 the conservative Victor Aimé Hubor formed, with his friend the architect C.W. Hoffmann, the Berlin Cooperative Building Society. Theirs was a private effort to carry through the idea of subsidized self-help communities, not unlike Louis Bonaparte's famous experiment just then undertaken in Mulhouse. Hubor's idea was to build a string of new settlements around Berlin, each to be connected by train to the industrial areas closer in. These settlements were to be cooperatively created and organized with gifts of seed money from the upper ranks of society. But even the presence of Prince Wilhelm (later Wilhelm I) as the society's chairman was not enough to enable the organization to raise the required capital of one million taler. They settled for a quarter of that figure, so only 209 houses were finally built, an insufficient number to prove anything one way or the other.[16] Hoffmann went on to write *Die Wohnungen der Arbeiter* in 1852, a treatise that was more critical of the bureaucratic apparatus than of the political climate of the times; political systems were seen to be less of a problem than the absence of money and ideas. Hoffmann tried again in his plan for a Prussian Model Homes Union for industrial workers, but failed to gain the crucial support of the Berlin Architects' Union, because the scheme 'had too little architectonic interest.' Architecture, in Prussia as elsewhere at this time, had nothing to do with social justice.[17]

The times were clearly not ripe for Huber and Hoffmann. In fact, their proposal was taken up much later, in 1880, by the Berlin Social Democrats, only to suffer the same fate. Nevertheless, the fantastic urban growth rate

8.17 Berlin, building activity in the 1870s. Painting by F. Kaiser, ca 1875

of the entire period from 1845 onwards (a 5 per cent annual rate was not uncommon) and the ensuing congestion and land speculation could no longer be ignored (Fig. 8.17). Thousands of unemployed men began living on the streets, prowling the districts of Moabit and Wedding. By 1870, just before the onset of aggressive commercial redevelopment in the city centre, the available urban space per inhabitant was just 24 to 31 square metres. Around the gate districts of Oranienburger and Kottbusser Tor to the north and northeast, this figure was 8.5, or well over 100,000 inhabitants per square kilometre.[18] In 1871 alone, when the population was 800,000, 133,700 persons migrated to Berlin (although another 78,000 left, presumably fleeing the squalor, or realizing too late that the news about opportunity gets inflated along the way). Nevertheless, the pace of building actually declined as population growth accelerated, so rents were increasing much faster than industrial wages.[19]

Business optimism reigned, nevertheless, among landlords and speculators, who fed off a seemingly endless need for cheap accommodation. One of the effects of the Hobrecht boundaries was to create the illusion of long-term certainty in the land market. What little agricultural land remained within the city was designated in the plan as urban, and could now be sold at development prices, thereby inflating rents to eight to ten times their original level.[20] These investments were made secure by politics: Rudolf Eberstadt shows the extent to which, throughout the second half of the century, landlords dominated municipal affairs in the three-tier electoral system. Their strategy was simple: to carve up the Berlin landscape into money-making fiefdoms. Even Bismarck could do nothing about them, although he was never one to keep his opinions to himself: 'This electoral system is nothing more than the representation of money capital, camouflaged as the voice of the people. It is the hegemony of a new monied aristocracy by which the dignity and honour of ordinary people are ground into the dust of low materialism'.[21]

Who the 'ordinary people' were is not clear; the Iron Chancellor did not exactly build a reputation for throwing in his lot with common folk, so his opinion should not be interpreted as quasi-Marxist, despite the language. Nor was he averse to helping money capital when it suited him. In 1868 his friend, the Berlin merchant J.A.W. von Carstenn, an operator if ever there was one, bought up parts of Lichterfelde and Giesendorf, which lay outside the jurisdiction of the *Hobrecht-Plan*. Using money he had won from speculating in the Wandsbek area of Hamburg, Carstenn intended to build a vast English-style suburb for the bourgeoisie and to connect it to Berlin by extending the Kurfürstendamm through the Grünewald to Potsdam. Bismarck supported him, but for once the obstinacy of the Prussian bureaucracy against expansion of any sort beyond the city put a stop to villainy.[22]

Meanwhile, the police were losing control every week over the rampage spreading outwards from the industrial quarters. Strikes, lockouts, demonstrations, mass evictions, and pitched battles against police and army alike became commonplace. As early as July 1872, a gang of 4,000 to 5,000 men stormed the area around Blumenstrasse, rioting against the eviction of a shoemaker from his room. A thousand police failed to breach the barricades thrown together with paving stones torn up from the streets, until two dragoon squadrons were called in to help.[23]

The Berlin boundary crisis forged some strange, if temporary alliances. By the 1870s, when, following a brief depression, the tempo of industrial growth reached a phenomenal level – the Siemens-Halske factories, for instance, turned out a sevenfold increase in production over three years – serviced open land in the city was practically non-existent. Everything seemed to work against the expansion of Berlin's boundaries. The Prussian government provided virtually nothing in the way of servicing infrastructure, and the Brandenburg municipalities around Berlin were, for the most part, terrified of losing the bucolic character so prized by the *arrivées* occupants of country homes. Their campaign against urbanization was to last beyond the First World War; in 1911 a few trade unions managed to scrape together some money through a worker's bank to propose the *Tuschkastensiedlung Falkenberg* in Alt-Glienicke, but the reaction from the local villa owners was predictable: 'Social democrats, communists, anarchists and chickenthieves jeopardize the public order and must not be allowed to settle in the municipality.'[24] The architecture of the workers' colony bothered them as well. Bruno Taut had devised a rather unsettling colour scheme for the houses: lemon yellow, olive green, black, blue, rust, and ochre. Finally, only 130 units were constructed during the war, when the old order was finally on the point of collapse. The plaintive cause of socio-economic integration succumbed here, as it did everywhere else, against the campaign for territorial exclusiveness.

For decades, industrialists and workers alike were hemmed in by this campaign, so for the first and last time they joined forces at the century's end to contest the anti-development stranglehold of the suburban landowners. Industrial decentralization therefore came late to Berlin, not beginning until the Borsig and Ludwig Loewe works finally wrested some approvals in Tegel in the last decade of the century.[25] Prior to this, peripheral land kept changing hands, proposals were made, but little was built that was not exclusively for the wealthy. Fortunes were made and lost in amateur speculation, with farmers, peasants, and other small-timers coming off best in the long run, perhaps because their greed was tempered by caution.[26] As early as 1861 the market-gardeners Matthes and Beussel sold a small part of their plot in Moabit to some builders, covering most of the rest themselves with tenements. Beussel soon retired, able to live quite comfortably from his investment upon the family property until at least the mid 1880s.[27]

Because Berlin's three-tiered electoral system gave a decisive political edge to property owners, peasants and monied upstarts soon began to dominate local politics as well as the land market. Seen in this light, we can begin to comprehend Bismarck's remark about 'ordinary people.' The new political élite possessed only guile and money; they had neither aristocratic titles, nor good manners. Those who were pushed aside were the old élite – people like Bismarck's friends – along with frustrated industrialists and the proletariat. They had a common enemy, so the workers' friends, for the time being, were not limited to a watchdog core of middle-class intellectuals.

Certainly the most unlikely and remarkable ally of the workers – for Prince William's short-lived chairmanship of Huber and Hollman's cooperative society came to nothing – was the Countess Adeleid Dohna-Poninski. At the age of seventy, under the *nom de plume* 'Arminius,' she wrote *Die Grossstadt in ihrer Wohnungsnot und die Grundlagen einer Durchgreifenden Abhilfe* (The Metropolitan Housing Crisis and the Basis for its Thorough Resolution) in 1874. The style and imagination of this sophisti-

cated woman have been largely unsung in planning history, despite Werner Hegemann's accolade in *Das steinerne Berlin* (1930). She may have been inspired by Saint-Simonism and the British industrial philanthropists Robert Owen and Titus Salt, but her ideas were far more practical than those of her precursors. Most of all, these ideas heralded many of the principles that became the foundation of twentieth-century extension planning, in terms of both urban design and institutional organization.

In general, the countess believed that the problems of the metropolis could not be solved by half measures; only concerted action by agencies of government, trade unions, and other powerful units would work against those she considered the enemies of humanity – the speculator and the land monopolist. Her approach at first glance seems to have been derived just from the conditions and latent alliances peculiar to Berlin at the time, but this was not so, for her theoretical scope ranged over the whole European experience: 'If a metropolis is expanding, nothing is more important than to provide for small dwellings – their number, purpose, and relationship to other development. The Mietskaserne, like those of Vienna, or the "military plan" of Paris to "clean it all up" are an expression of the fear of the propertied classes that the workers will unite and rise against them. The occasional concession is made only to keep them in regimental good order.'[28]

Her most original concept included the provision of a green belt around Berlin, eighteen years before the similar semi-official proposal for Vienna, and twenty-four years before the publication of Ebenezer Howard's *Tomorrow*. The belt was to be publicly owned, with new lower-density settlements planted beyond it: 'The need to live as humans in the broad sense does not simply mean good housing; the edge of the city should consist of recreation areas set amidst fields and woods. Urban expansion can be so designed that the right of everyone to live within half an hour of open country can be secure. This implies, if we consider that the old, the sick and children cannot travel further than two kilometres, that this distance should be used. Here a belt, about four kilometres wide, except for say a fifth of the area on which buildings would be permitted, would be devoted to farmland, pastures and the recreational needs of the whole population.'[29]

The buildings permitted in the green belt were to be solely for public purposes – churches, schools, hostelries for textile and factory workers. 'Trade unions and other special groups' were to be given development rights for their own use. Within the existing suburbs inside the green belt, parks were to be embellished with public restaurants and public promenades. The whole was intended to be knitted together by a system of railways and publicly operated tramways. The freedom to move – between classes, across all the city's boundaries – lay at the core of the countess's plans for the working family, as it did in the dreams of all her fellow reformers.

Nevertheless, no prior system of thought was so thorough or so fearless in attacking the injustices of the industrial metropolis. But her work was no more prophetic than influential: the Prussian state in 1892, when it was far too late, unsuccessfully tried to acquire 26,000 hectares around Berlin, based on a plan more or less as Dohna-Poninski prescribed, and shortly afterwards German planning theory (although not much practice) came under the sway of the Garden City movement. Here, too, a plaintive call for spatial integration succumbed to the absence of any boundary dialectic.

From this distance the kinetic history of nineteenth-century Berlin seems as much a result of fear, incompetence, and bureaucratic bungling as of outright indifference to the exploitation of the masses. Even before the ascendency of the Social Democrats prior to the 1880s, those who advocated reform were not a tiny minority, and however lapsed, given the difficulties facing the police in the streets, Bismarck and the Berlin municipal government were hardly blind to the continual decline in the plight of the poor. There is no easy

way to characterize the urban politics of the time, especially when placed alongside the New World indifference to those who were forced to live in squalor in North America's industrial cities. The consequences, however, were nearly everywhere the same: urban politics favoured the spread and entrenchment of insular territories, each contained within a characteristic architecture designed to discourage every potential intruder.

Inertia takes on multiple meanings when contemplating the official posture to the latent dynamism of street life. Things came to a head in June 1885 when striking construction workers were savagely attacked by police and strikebreakers, and the strike leader, Heinrich Fassel, was taken to a cellar and murdered. Rioting spread throughout the city and, for the first time, beyond the municipal boundaries, resulted in a declaration of martial law and the order to tear down the squatter settlements that had been spreading around Frankfurter Tor and the Landsberger Tor[30] (Fig. 8.18).

The Landscape of Officialdom

If the worker's life was grim, that of the official was stodgy. We can see it in his architecture, for while Prussian buildings were never the place to exercise frivolity, their aspect was turning decidedly unfriendly. The Reichstag itself, designed by Paul Wallot in 1881, was 'a first class hearse'[31] (Fig. 8.19). Elsewhere stood interminable walls twenty metres high and more, ground floors raised a man's height above street level, heavy double doors, windows barred and shuttered, superhuman entrances; such were the features greeting anyone outside (Fig. 8.20). The spare legacy of the Brandenburg style was borrowed and purged of all reticence, to stand guard at the sidewalk's edge along the Wilhelmstrasse, around Hallischen Tor, through the Luisenstadt, Charlottenburg, Tiergarten, and many of the axes planned by Hobrecht (Fig. 8.21). Even Karl Friedrich Schinkel, the Romantic master, had been an exponent of austerity: witness his lovely but undecorated

8.18 Berlin street riot. Bildarchiv Preussischer Kulturbesitz

8.19   Building the Reichstag. Archiv Klünner

1834 scheme for the country estate of Prince Wilhelm at Babelsberg, near Potsdam. Prussian architecture had long mirrored the discipline and stringency of the Junker social order. In Berlin this atmosphere had been muted here and there by royal influence ever since Frederick the Great, who preferred the French language to German, set up court: the Schloss Charlottenburg, and especially the Sanssouci pavilions in Potsdam, reveal a gaiety foreign to the history of Prussia. But now architecture too often erred on the wrong side of the fine line dividing dignity from stolidness. Bourgeois and official architecture in industrial Berlin, like manners and dress, were not noticeable for their spontaneous spirit, and a gloomy neoclassicism or heavy failed eclecticism was the hallmark of local style until well into the twentieth century, stamping the city's boundaries with its bulk and weight.[32]

What seems paradoxical at first sight is that this architectural tradition continued despite the virtual overturning of Berlin cultural life, in concert with giant population shifts, in the last decade of the nineteenth century. But here architecture served a purpose that was political rather than cultural, closing off one way of life from another. The city, like Chicago, had been a backwater less than a hundred years before. Those who migrated in were not from Brandenburg for the most part, and they seemed to have left their bucolic ways behind with some relief. They were mostly young – half were between sixteen and thirty – and looking for a good time as well as money. In a remarkably short space of time they had established the now-famous tradition of Berlin street humour, a wiseacre repartee turned against oneself and used to dispel the quotidian grimness. The cartoonist Heinrich Zille was the chief comedian of the rear courtyards, which the 1853 statute had stipulated should be a minimum of 28 square metres, not for light and ventilation, but for firefighting convenience. Zille's cartoons of the *Hinterhof* say it all: The landlord displays the courtyard to prospective tenants: 'Not too wide, but nice and high.' Or, shouting above the racket of intransigent children: 'At least the acoustics are first class.' But comical satire still had its object, which was the burden of everyday existence, including that of a fully employed

8.20   Berlin, Stadthaus am Molkenmarkt, by Ludwig Hoffman, 1902–11

8.21   Turmstrasse, Moabit, Berlin, 1907. Archiv
Klünner

craftsman at Borsig's firm: 'The metalworker
Kieckhofer earned 35 pfennigs an hour in
1900, for a ten hour day without a break. He
paid 20 marks [monthly] for a small room and
kitchen. A loaf cost 45 to 48 pf. Because butter
cost 72 pf. per pound he, like his fellow
workers, never ate it; the best they could
manage was "barrel fat." A pound of sausage,
being 80 pf., was never bought by the pound,
but by the pennyworth. There were no holi-
days, and no one managed to save a week's
wages. There were no Christmas bonuses, no
employee health or food benefits. Whoever
was sick got his walking papers after a couple
of days. It was better to go to work with a
fever.'[33]

Such was life in the northern districts, in
Pankow, Wedding, and parts of Reinic-
kendorf; in Neukölln, Rixdorf, Kreuzberg,
and Moabit. Small wonder that these places
were seen to be threatening, insurgent; and
that boundary architecture in such places, in
the centre, and in the walled suburbs of the
southwest augmented the role of geography in
maintaining social order.

Then, all prices climbed dramatically in
1901, by which time the speculative interest in
building Mietskaserne had declined to almost

nothing. Capital now went to industry, which
was finally picking up land to left and right
outside the city since its boundaries had been
breached, and finally abandoning the inner
sites in Wedding and Moabit to the burgeoning, but still labour-intensive firms in the
electro-mechanical sector[34] (Fig. 8.22).
Money for housing now went mostly into
building more three or four-bedroom homes
for those families who were better off. For the
first time the bourgeoisie's habits of paying
the rent on time and disciplining the children
figured in investment security and maintenance costs.[35]

So, by the century's close, what Hobrecht
had claimed about social integration forty
years earlier no longer applied. The way in
which land was distributed for housing on a
per-capita basis was a solid statistical proxy
for the distribution of wealth. According to
the income tax data of 1900 fewer than
10,000 households, or 0.5 per cent of the total
Berlin population, had annual incomes
greater than 12,000 marks. This was enough
to place them among the upper and middle
classes. A further 16 per cent earned more
than 1,200 marks per year, a group that
included shopkeepers, small tradesmen, fore-
men, and highly skilled craftsmen. Of the
remaining 83 per cent a quarter of a million
officially earned nothing – that is, they paid no
taxes.[36] As might be expected, population
density varied inversely with income, and the
classes were now completely divided by geography. At the time, Rudolf Eberstadt esti-
mated Berlin to be the world's most densely
populated city.[37]

By the 1890s public insurrection by an ever-
increasing nomadic crowd was completely
beyond police control, and with the Social
Democrats in ascendency, labour was finally
getting itself organized. Class enmity became
more open and confrontational as industry,
now well into a phase of concentration, mar-
shalled its forces against the unions. Demonstrations and strikes made life intolerable for
the vestigial middle class left in the 'specula-
tion-ring,' who were soon initiating the urge

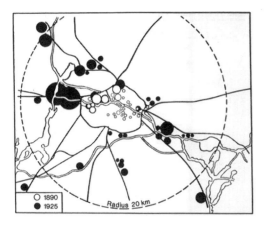

8.22   Location of industries in Berlin. White circles indicate abandoned sites

for spatial separation from the workers by fleeing 'ins Grüne' away from the industrial and working quarters.[38] Whole suburban areas that had remained only partly developed – the consequence of too much optimism in the 1880s – were filled in with villas and graceful apartments. Areas in Charlottenburg, Steglitz, and Schöneberg, which, for years, had been merely a couple of villas and a street sign set into fields, became exclusive suburbs within the space of ten years. The developers saw to it that such locations catered only to monied households. The Kurfürstendamm-Gesellschaft of the Deutsche Bank financed only large houses, built in the manner of a Parisian *hôtel*, usually contained within walled gardens, with salons, 'Herrenzimmer,' central heating, and electric light. Here the Gartenhof replaced the Hinterhof, and the Ku-damm became a street of luxury restaurants and expensive shops. The most sought-after commercial properties were the 'well-cut corners,' so those in charge of development made sure that the Ku-damm had plenty of transverse streets, including the Tauenzienstrasse, which soon rivalled the Ku-damm as the fashionable place to be.

Between 1900 and 1905 the 'top ten thousand' moved even farther west, to Zehlendorf, Mariendorf, and the Wannsee. Infant mortality, with an accelerating birthrate, took on a telling geographic pattern: up to 30 per cent in the industrial quarters of the north and east, 10 per cent in the Westend.[39]

Urban Space Turns Fluid

Meanwhile, as the wealthy outlying areas blossomed, Schinkel's old inner city was finally being put to the shovels of the demolition gangs. Civic and commercial boosterism were rampant, and the officially sought-after status of *Weltstadt* demanded a complete overhaul of the historic centre. Here the powers that be – Church, Prussian state, Berlin council, and building entrepreneurs – saw eye to eye, so nothing stood in the way of almost total reconstruction. Only in 1908, when the damage was nearly complete, was it suddenly realized that the city's history had also been demolished. That year was marked by the opening of the Märkisches Museum, which displayed pathetic remnants of the old life – simple domestic and craft artefacts. By then land in the centre cost a fortune – 500 marks per square metre – but this did nothing to deter the public authorities, whose projects were as extensive as they were architecturally awful. Nevertheless, the price of a lot on the 'Linden' was so high that, for many years, it served to *conserve* the old buildings, such as the famous Hiller restaurant or the fabulous Bristol Hotel. Eventually, even these disappeared, as did Schinkel's elegant Radernsche Palais. Its owner, Count Radern, owed a fortune in gambling debts to Edward VII of England, and had to sell. The buyer, the wealthy gastronome Adler, tore it down to build his hotel.[40]

Profitability and status seemed to govern all development decisions: 'The businessmen could not have cared less that Humboldt was born here, or that E.T.A. Hoffmann and Devrient lived there, or where Lessing, Kleist or Heine had worked. Most councillors were themselves businessmen or land speculators and kept an eagle eye on any attempt to curtail the "god-given" right of free use of land.'[41]

8.23 Generalstabsgebäude, Königsplatz, Berlin, 1876. Archiv Klünner

Their power, and whatever taste they possessed, were thrown into an architecture that was designed to intimidate and act as anchor points in an increasingly fluid urban structure. Frequent use was made of massive sandstone blocks and overscaled façades. Entrance steps were mighty, and foyers overpowering. The Ministry of War headquarters was an early, if unwitting, case of form following function (Fig. 8.23), while a huge new barracks – the Kasernopolis – was constructed in Tempelhof. In the old Royal Palace setting, considered by Wilhelm I as 'totally inadequate,' dozens of buildings were levelled to make room for a bombastic national monument to the Kaiser. The Palace itself was renovated at a cost of millions, while Schinkel's lovely old church in the Lustgarten disappeared to make room for the new cathedral, aptly named the 'gasometer of the soul' by the tenants of the courtyards[42] (Fig. 8.24).

The few Social Democrats on council lobbied for schools and hospitals, but hardly any were built; one exception was the Rudolf-Virchow Hospital in Wedding, designed by the new Stadtbaurat Ludwig Hoffmann. Much more common were works like the monster fountain (sculpted by Reinhold Begas, who also chiselled the National Monument) in the Schlossplatz, and the carving up of the Tiergarten by the regrettable Siegesallee axis (Fig. 8.25). A whole block of houses on Judenstrasse was pulled down to make way for the Neue Stadthaus. Huge squares, expansive boulevards, and monuments to the rich and powerful symbolized the new *Weltstadt* – the Herrenhaus, a massive palace on Leipzigerstrasse; a colossal courthouse on Littenstrasse (Fig. 8.26); and, the ugliest of the lot, the Abgeordne Fenhaus on Prinz-Albrecht Strasse.[43]

If civic architecture and design tried to kill public street life in large parts of the old centre, commercial architecture offered some compensation, even if its purpose was simple profit. Here, at least, things were no worse than anywhere else; who would have thought at this time of preserving the historic remnants of a city that was more like Chicago than London or Paris? Perhaps only the regulated maximum height of five storeys prevented the construction of a Chicago-like centre. The urbanist theories of the time, such as they were, could not cope with highly intensive redevelopment except by simple prohibition. Neither Theodor Frisch, in his 1896 book *Die Stadt der Zukunft*, nor Camillo Sitte's nostalgia for a lost art, had confronted the issue. Even the Countess Dohna-Poninski's attention had been monopolized by the hinterland.

8.24   Parade in front of the Berlin cathedral, 1914. Archiv Berliner Feuerwehr

In 1902, under Ebenezer Howard's influence, the *Deutsche Gartenstadtgesellschaft* began pushing for garden cities, but theoretical emphasis everywhere was upon how to bring a measure of stability to suburbanization. In the centre, it was every man for himself, and any development rationale quickly succumbed to the *laissez-faire* market-place.

In Berlin, even today, the street was always the place to be, and while the official tendency was to turn the centre into a petrified museum, the anarchy of the market-place at least produced the crowds that went with having a good time in public. The habits of the street were learned in the working quarters: 'on every corner stood the "flying merchants" – carts and wagons full of Johannisbrot, apples, plums, even oranges.' Their pushers were known as Gherkin Henry or Sausage Max. 'Hahains from the Schönhauserallee offered plaster figures. Ragmen with dogcarts went from house to house. Over 6,000 licences were granted annually, supplemented by hundreds more during the bad times.'[44] The street was friendlier than the *Hinterhof*, where notices forbidding children's play were now nailed. Most people were young and new to the city, so their urge was to discover it, and perhaps adventure, outdoors. Nor was public outdoor life limited to the poor. Even Berlin

had its fashionable classes prior to industrialization, and the Tiergarten and Unter den Linden were still the place for officers and accompanied ladies to parade on a summer's evening, either on foot or in carriages. But such parades were governed by manners and expectations of social reciprocity. For the poor newcomer, the social anarchy of the streets had its own rewards appropriate to the temporary release from a daily round of hard graft.

So, between 1890 and 1918, the transformation of the centre of Berlin became a tableau of two worlds. Officialdom had its own territory where it planted monuments to itself, while elsewhere it relinquished practically every hold, and boundary changes were swift. Public land was sold at the wrong time. Even the Royal Mills on the Mühlendamm were acquired by private developers for a pittance. Near the Halleschen Tor several municipal parcels were practically given away, while later, at the height of the boom, the city paid a fortune for the tiny Waldeckplatz park in Kreuzberg. The final pieces of the Zollmauer land, which had been planned as a Parisian-style boulevard, went to private interests. Meanwhile, whole tracts of central land in the poorest quarters were assembled by the large developers: in the Hansaviertel of Moabit by the Berlin-Hamburger Immobiliengesellschaft; elsewhere by the Aktienbauverein Friedrichhain and the Berliner Bauvereinsbank AG.[45] By the 1890s the aristocrats – more astute than the government – were selling off their mansions in the inner city at boom prices and spending the winter season in hotels. Whole streets of rococo and classical palaces were, in a few years, to be replaced by fancy restaurants and 'Bierlokale.' Historic Friedrichstrasse, between Leipzigerstrasse and the 'Linden,' became the fashionable place to eat and drink.

In the interstices between areas where the developers took over, there quickly grew districts that catered to the inevitable underside of city life. The *Studentenquartier* filled the gaps between the Charité district and the

8.25   Königsplatz (Platz der Republik) with Siegesallee and Victory column, pre-1914

University, while the side streets leading to the Stettiner railway station were lined with sleazy night cafés and street walkers. Around the Halleschen Tor, hotel rooms could be rented by the hour, and night clubs offered those Berlin-style cabarets that were soon to acquire fame and notoriety throughout the world. The Friedrichstrasse, meanwhile, had been turned into the city's commercial and tourist hub while still in the process of building, demolition, and rebuilding. Hotels, variety clubs, and theatres already lined the street in the 1890s, and the Wintergarten of the Zentralhotel was its international focus. Here, since 1895 the photographer Pankow Skladanowsky astonished the fashionable crowd with mighty showings of his Bioscop-Apparat. The *Passage* on Unter den Linden had its Panoptikum and wax museum, while the *Kranzlerecke* at Friedrichstrasse and the 'Linden' became the most famous corner in Germany. The streets were thronged twenty-four hours a day when, finally, on 'Golden

Sunday' before Christmas 1902, a policeman regulated traffic with a whistle, but with scant effect. The cacophony was such that, in the following year, he had to use a trumpet.[46]

By 1900, with land at 500 marks per square metre on the Friedrichstrasse, few could afford any longer to live in the inner city. The noise alone, in any case, was inescapable as automobile horns began to replace the sound of hoofs. Just outside the centre, however, between the River Spree and Alexanderplatz, there developed a vast industrial and commercial slum. It was still common practice, at least up to 1913, for manufacturers to farm out work to sweatshops and homes to avoid the high rent, overhead, and costs of control in operating central-area factories. Sordid streets of tenements around the 'Alex' were stuffed, from damp basements to garrets, with working families, materials, and cheap goods. The best of what was made went to a new kind of outlet, the department store.

The year 1900 saw the introduction of the

8.26   New criminal courthouse, Berlin, 1902 design

8.27   Berlin, Potsdamerplatz, with Leipzigerstrasse in the foreground, 1931

8.28 Hermann Tietz department store, Leipzigerstrasse, Berlin, by Bernhard, Sehring, and Lachmann, 1889–90

display window and the electric sign as the shops on Leipzigerstrasse all the way to Potsdamerplatz competed to attract a flood of passers-by (Fig. 8.27). Within two years the whole street had turned into a fabulous free theatre, with the Wertheim and Hermann Tietz stores being the star attractions. They led the way with their arcades and slender columns, to reveal windows piled high with exotic things made seductive in an electric glow (Figs 8.28 and 8.29). Finally, with the arrival of streets filled with glass and light, the protean society of Berlin had been given its metaphors[47] (Fig. 8.30).

Earlier than its American counterparts, the Leipzigerstrasse led the way in reincarnating that magic landscape first described by Homer, a landscape whose expressive meaning would become the most powerful hallmark of twentieth-century urbanism. Yet, unlike what was left of Unter den Linden, which parallels the Leipzigerstrasse a few blocks away, here were no rational plans, no memorable architecture, no motivations touched by civility. Instead, in a city where life had been encumbered by unyielding boundaries at every turn, the Leipzigerstrasse offered a first taste of escape. Vicarious, or not, this offering took root earlier, and more surely, than all the reformers' dreams of a new urban order.

Berlin was the unique European proof that the conditions creating Chicago and New York were not peculiar to the New World. The differences, however great, are less astonishing than the overwhelming similarities; in fact, nowhere else was American and European life so fused together, just at the onset of the great cultural contradiction of modernism. On both continents, industrialization and intensive mechanical relations suppressed the diversity of everyday life and simultaneously buried the kaleidoscopic range of boundary formation. Henri Lefebvre almost put his finger on the malaise in recognizing that the *purpose* of industry should have been to give meaning and direction to urbaniza-

8.30   The first electric lights on the Schlossbrücke, Berlin. Bildarchiv Preussischer Kulturbesitz

8.29   Wertheim department store, Leipzigerstrasse, Berlin, by Alfred Messel, 1896–7

tion, but the reverse occurred: 'Industry in itself is only a means, and when means are taken for ends rationality becomes absurdity.'[48]

On 16 July 1894, Otto von Bismarck, after a lifetime of official indifference towards Berlin, told a group of history students that, having lived in the city since the age of four, he had grown to know and love every inch. In truth, as child and codger he never understood the place he could have done so much for, as Lord Roseberry did for London.[49] Soon thereafter the city's boundaries were to be breached, to juxtapose squalor, the anarchy wrought by material self-interest, and a failing authoritarianism; these ingredients of the city's compound spirit constituted the force that toppled the old order. The old Brandenburg culture, fatally fractured, hung on for a few more years, supported by the conservative side of industrialism. But the newly resistant strains of radicalism, nurtured in the uncontrollable, kinetic spaces of the city, were soon to surge out and collide head on, in the suburbs, with that other unstoppable force – industry.

CHAPTER NINE

The Dissolving Boundaries
of Modernism*

Mirage effects have far-reaching consequences. Under the conditions of modernity, as absolute political space extends its sway, the impression of transparency becomes stronger and stronger, and the illusion of a new life is everywhere reinforced – Henri Lefebvre[1]

Industry, Boundaries, and Architectural Ideology

On most occasions, the urban landscape becomes a distillation of the more important forces around which society at large is organized, although not only because cities are a repository of contemporary aesthetic ideals, technology, and capital. As we have seen, since the building of the boundaries of Ur, this landscape has also been associated with the wielding of power, less as a giant political signifier than as an instrument used to sustain authority and control, whether on behalf of the state, in production and the market-place, or even in the family. We have seen, too, how architecture itself undergoes mutations in conjunction with large-scale alteration in mechanical relations, as integrative and self-interests work their dialectic along the boundary zones.

What follows is an examination of events that took place around the end of the first decade of this century. It is no coincidence that the crucible of what has been called modernist architecture and urbanism existed at a historical turning-point in the adjustment of mechanical relations connected to the tidal wave of movement from the centre to the urban hinterland. Then, certain local events in conjunction with those more durable circumstances we have been discussing were woven into a new boundary prototype: the Fagus-Werk, a small factory mainly designed by the Berlin firm of Walter Gropius and Adolf Meyer; the crucial first stage of this prototype was built in 1911 in the small Saxon town of Alfeld an der Leine.

Although the roots of architectural modernism are multifarious, the Fagus-Werk is still regarded by many as the building that finally propelled the urban landscape into the

* This chapter was drawn largely from an article written by the author, entitled 'The Fagus-Werk: Industry, Urban Land, and Architectural Ideology,' published in the *Journal of Architectural and Planning Research* 2/3 (1985), 201–25. Reprinted by permission of the publisher, Locke Science Publishing Company, Inc.

twentieth century, the exemplar upon which many subsequent oeuvres, both in Europe and the Americas, were based. Of immediate concern here, however, is the extent to which the ideas that inspired the Fagus-Werk were woven from new initiatives taken by industry to sustain its dominant position, and to understand the influence that widespread urban boundary change was destined to have upon ensuing architectural, as well as city-planning practice. Urbanism – an instrument of Kant's paradoxical 'antisocial sociability' – wings its way into the century in the protean guise of the suburban factory.

German Industry and Architecture

From 1910 to 1914, the firm of Adolf Meyer and Walter Gropius was engaged in designing several projects located in the small town of Alfeld an der Leine in Lower Saxony. Of these, the Fagus-Werk 'is frequently taken to be the first building of the Modern Movement.'[2] There are two qualities which make it so. The first is the unprecedented manner in which, with respect to the workshop and the boiler room, Gropius 'discovered the art of the steel framed structure. His walls show clearly that they no longer carry and support the building, but that they simply depend from it – mere shields against inclement weather ... At one corner of the building the glass walls butt directly up against one another with no intervening column. This presents an unusual spectacle to eyes accustomed to the supporting wall'[3] (Fig. 9.1). Second, the whole project is organized according to a remarkable functional discipline: 'no volumetric element is accentuated more than any other, and the architectural tone is quiet and calm in the various bodies of the building corresponding to the various functions; even the general plan has no uncommon compositional features, the various parts being put together in the most simple and economical way possible'[4] (Fig. 9.2).

A part of the background to these features has been traced to the influence of the

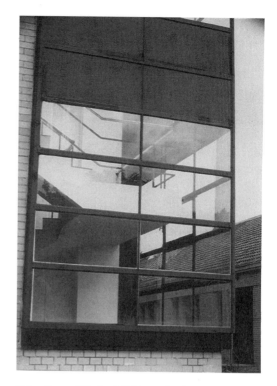

9.1 Fagus-Werk, Alfeld an der Leine, corner of administrative block. Gropius and Meyer, 1913

Deutscher Werkbund and, particularly, of the architect Peter Behrens upon Gropius's thinking. The Werkbund, initiated in 1907 to combine 'all existing efforts towards quality in industrial work,' had similar aims to those of organizations founded in other industrial countries of Europe about this time. Essentially, the Werkbund attempted, with considerable success, to put art and craftsmanship at the service of industrial production under the banner of *Qualitätsarbeit*. More to the point, it became the vehicle of transition between the pre-modern and often anti-industrial avant-garde, particularly the German Expressionists, and the eventual ascendancy of the Bauhaus in the 1920s. Thus, while some design experimentation outside the orbit of industry was being conducted, its antagonistic view of technology precipitated the avant-garde's quick demise: 'If architecture is the

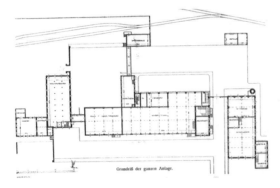

9.2   Fagus-Werk, ground-floor plan by Gropius and Meyer, 1913

system of controls on which the arrangement of the urban scene is based, one may say that the changes in supply, provided by artists and avant-garde groups, remained greatly inferior to the changes in demand.'⁵

The Werkbund, in contrast, counted designers like Hermann Muthesius and Peter Behrens among its members, men who were highly influential in established political and industrial circles. Given the then-current consumer penchant for whatever was *sachlig*, it is not surprising that the first alliance between a newly co-opted art and the manufacturing sector occurred in Germany under the banner of *Qualitätsarbeit*, against the aestheticist rivalry of the German Arts and Crafts Movement, the *Kunstgewerbe*. Because the Werkbund made a point of including all manufactured objects within its field of responsibility, Gropius himself, along with Behrens, accepted commissions to design locomotives, automobiles, and the fittings on warships. Architecture, then, was no longer seen by this group to possess a special nature, separable from other industrial objects. It is therefore hardly surprising that a factory would be the first building type to be about something other than architecture. More precisely, architecture had been about façades, but the Fagus-Werk possessed none that was recognizable as such. And, of course, the factory's internal organization, rather than

being axially arranged, followed and displayed externally the machine-like requirements of its internal purpose.

In a nutshell, this is the common explanation given for the background to the Fagus-Werk. Now the qualities described above were to have an enormous influence upon the course of building production throughout the industrialized world for the next forty years and more. Indeed, the innovations of Gropius at Alfeld are recognizable, with various mutations, in important industrial, residential, and commercial structures throughout the era of modern architecture. In the light of these widespread effects, an explanation based only on a fortuitous alliance of art and industry seems inadequate, limited as it is to discussion occurring in a corner of architectural culture in Germany eighty years ago; this suggests that the innovations were induced by factors that transcend, or underlie, the rather poor creative and interpersonal rapport that in fact took place between Gropius and his client. Some more durable imperative must have affected the development actions of German industrialists, an imperative that, in an evolved form, should be recognizable in the wide spectrum of actions that transformed the architecture and urbanism of this century.

The Advent of Industrial Science and Scientific Management

While a discussion of manufacturing procedures may seem distant from the subject of urbanism, it almost goes without saying that, to a large extent, the internal organization of an industry, its dependence on regional activity and infrastructure, the processes it uses, its profitability and societal status, and therefore the image it wishes to project, will be embodied in its architecture and its relationship to the city. Now the overwhelming fact about German industry at the beginning of this century is that it formed the world's most energetic crucible for the application of science and scientific management to manufacturing production. This extraordinary experiment accelerated the growth and concentration of industrial capital in that country from productive obscurity in the 1870s to world leadership by 1914. A Marxian analyst offers this explanation: 'The story of the incorporation of science into the capitalist firm properly begins in Germany. The early symbiosis between science and industry which was developed by the capitalist class of that country proved to be one of the most important facts of world history in the twentieth century, furnished the capability for two world wars, and offered to the other capitalist nations an example which they learned to emulate only when they were forced to do so many decades later.'[6]

In Germany, manufacturers were able to call on basic research then being conducted in the celebrated Technische Hochschulen on a scale existing nowhere else, which catalysed the chemical, metallurgical, and electrical industries particularly. The effects quickly spread from the production of capital goods to consumer goods, so that even small-scale enterprises were able to benefit from science as Germany's world markets continued to expand, propelled by their new competitiveness. This success at the expense of the nation's rivals has been attributed to the existence of a particular mode of German thinking: 'Hegel's influence on the development of science was both direct and indirect. In the first instance, there was his role in the reform of Prussian education in the second decade of the nineteenth century. And next, there was the pervasive influence of German speculative philosophy, of which Hegel was the culminating thinker, in giving to German scientific education a fundamental and theoretical cast. Thus, while Britain and the United States were still in the grip of that common-sense empiricism which stunts and discourages reflective thought and basic scientific research, in Germany it was these very habits of mind that were being developed in the scientific community.'[7]

Nor was science being used only in the discovery and invention of new materials and machines. The work of F.W. Taylor, conducted in the first decade of the century in the United States but never seriously adopted there until later, galvanized many German industrialists into investigating the techniques of scientific management of labour. The Germans referred to these techniques as *Rationalisierung*, after the pioneering work of Hugo Münsterberg at the University of Leipzig on industrial psychology. Later, in his book *Psychology and Industrial Efficiency*, published in German in 1912, Münsterberg reveals his dedication to the field of mental engineering: 'We ask how we can find the men whose mental qualities make them best fitted for the work which they have to do; secondly, under what psychological conditions we can secure the greatest and most satisfactory output of work from every man; and finally, how we can produce most completely the influence on human minds which are desired in the interests of business.'[8]

In short, by the time the Fagus-Werk was being designed, the new techniques of industrial production in Germany were already refined to a level that gave her paramountcy in the world. Emphasis in production began to be placed on the efficient organization of assembly in manufacture and on the productive potential inherent in an agreeable and healthy work environment. Good daylight and ventilation were seen to be an essential part of this environment, as they had been in the failed effort to reform residential standards at the turn of the century. Germany, indeed, was the first country, prior to the First World War, to subject every aspect of the industrial process to the close and detailed scrutiny of scientific managers and engineers, a fact which, within the space of a few years, was altering the architectural and locational requirements of the manufacturing process. Henry L. Gantt, the American disciple of Taylor, wrote in 1910: 'It is an economic law that large profits can be permanently assured only by efficient operation ... The supreme importance of efficiency as an economic factor was first realized by the Germans, and it is this fact that has enabled them to advance their industrial condition, which twenty years ago was a jest, to the first place in Europe, if not the world. We naturally want to know in detail the methods they have used; and the reply is that they have recognized the value of the scientifically trained engineer as an economic factor.'[9]

There is no doubt that, by this time, progressive industrial developers were devising stringent functional and cost programs which seriously constrained the initiatives and actions of their architects. Manufacturing assembly buildings were either large sheds, erected for their low cost and flexibility, or closely fitting cloaks for complex interior assembly functions. Architectural traditions were not permitted to get in the way of the high level of efficiency now required, by constraining the layout of machinery and ancillary equipment (Fig. 9.3). These imperatives in industrial processes no doubt affected the new ideology of functionalism in architecture,

but they also introduced, by precipitating an alteration of the city's internal and external boundaries, a new form of urbanism.

Architecture and Industry in Berlin before the Fagus-Werk

If the primary catalyst of German social and urban change during the last quarter of the nineteenth century was the transformation and fantastic productive success of manufacturing industry, these events did not quite begin with, but can be signalled by a particular decision made by Werner von Siemens, inventor of the dynamo and founder of the giant electrical firm that took his name. Until 1872 von Siemens had enjoyed inventing gadgets and improvising in the former kitchen of a Berlin house in the Markgrafenstrasse, surrounded by a few bright young mechanics from the shop floor. Over the previous three years his firm had experienced a sevenfold increase in production, a situation command-

9.3   Interior of a Berlin machine shop in 1910. A surveillance booth is located at the right

ing more and more of von Siemens's reluctant attention. Finally, he announced: 'I don't have time now for basic research, nor to coach the new lads; in any case I can no longer keep up with the whole scientific field.' He then hired a physics professor to set up the firm's first research department, strategically to be placed between the shop floor and the management wing.[10]

We have already seen how this kind of decision reflected two impending changes that were to make Germany at least the equal of the United States in the pioneering of scientific industrial management and industrial psychology by the beginning of the century. In 1899, *American Machinist* observed that 'the best American machine shop is in Berlin,'[11] referring to Ludwig Loewe's new establishment on the Huttenstrasse. The first change involved the functional compartmentalization of the whole production process, initially by shifting people around within the factory, then by determining the most strategic spatial relationships within a hierarchy of specialized tasks and machines. The second change involved the bureaucratization of production (the separation of mental from physical labour) by gradually increasing the ratio of technical/professional staff to shop-floor employees.[12] These innovations started an inexorable move away from the use of heavy discipline on the shop floor in favour of surveillance and standardized procedure. While similar changes were also happening outside Germany, their conjuncture with problems unique to Berlin was destined to give industrial-location decisions and factory design a special cast in Germany that had far-reaching consequences for urbanism.

Unlike those of the United States and Britain, the internal reorganization of industry in Germany was not accompanied – at least throughout the nineteenth century – either by the incipient suburbanization of production and the workforce or by the large-scale provision of suburban infrastructure. The indifference of the Prussian state, in particular to the needs of Berlin's industry, when confronting

the long-entrenched land-holding monopolies had virtually trapped the manufacturing sector within the municipal boundary, in close proximity to its employees[13] (Fig. 9.4). As we have pointed out, in Berlin the concerted pressure of an unlikely alliance of workers and industrialists would break the suburban monopolies only after the turn of the century, finally bringing some relief to the pathological overcrowding and inflated land rents of the capital.[14]

Prior to the break-up of the suburban monopolies, the cases of industrial decentralization were few, so that even the otherwise powerful, less labour-dependent firms were tied to the inner districts of the Oranienburger and Rosenthaler *Vorstädte*. Only in 1898, for instance, did the weapons plant of Ludwig Loewe and the Borsig locomotive works finally move to Tegel on the outskirts.[15] Then the few abandoned sites in Moabit and along the Chausseestrasse and Schönhauserallee were taken over by newer, but more labour-intensive firms, such as the burgeoning AEG complex, where the winding of electric motors was still largely a manual operation.

So even after the partial opening up of the urban periphery, the confinement of new development was predominant in Berlin up to the Weimar era of the 1920s. A combination of acute land shortages, low industrial wages, a lethargic Prussian government, and the continuation of archaic but highly profitable building practices had nurtured intensive mechanical relations whose outcome was the infamous Mietskaserne. All kinds of uses – production, commerce, and domestic life – were packed into this single generic building type. The form of constructed space was thus derived not from considerations of human activity and material flows, but from severe constraints imposed by the narrow lots and high land rents, a condition that inevitably induced the very antithesis of what was becoming known as architectural functionalism. As a general rule, the close spatial association between home and work meant that wherever industry happened to be labour intensive, architecture was non-functionalist and capital intensive, in the sense that each costly unit of land had to absorb large amounts of construction capital needed to accommodate the high population densities. There were few exceptions to this rule; those uses not so confined by tight site boundaries, such as the extravagant government edifices in the old Friedrichstadt, or the villas of the very rich out in Marienfeld, offered no relief to the ubiquitous mass of construction that burdened each plot of land (Fig. 9.5).

Clearly, circumstances such as those outlined above were ill suited to industrial rationalization. The need to shake loose from intensive mechanical relations and consequent boundary restriction, to mould space according to the needs of compartmentalization, efficient material flows, and the demands on the work environment of an emerging class of industrial bureaucrats, was essential to the further flowering of new techniques of production and control of the workforce. But equally as important, by the 1900s, was the ambivalence with which German society and industry perceived each other.

This ambivalence originated, on the one hand, from the dominant, almost patriarchal role played by industry in all walks of life but the land market as it established its economic hegemony in the final years of the century. It also stemmed, on the other, from the realization on the part of a few astute industrialists that an assertive image was neither propitious nor necessary to improve its position of authority in society and over the workforce.[16] The factory, once a great tourist attraction, had lost its popular appeal; indeed, its calamitous effects upon the Berlin community were bringing hostility from street mobs, urban reform groups, and inner-city developers alike.[17] Moreover, the fortress-like factory evoked expressive meanings of indifference and the rugged disciplinary control associated with coal, iron, and the industrial ascendancy. It hardly captured the more indulgent, although still manipulative spirit of *Partnerschaft* that formed the foundation of scientific

management; nor did it mirror the increasingly rapid shift to electrically driven precision machinery and the innocuousness that manufacturers now wished it to represent in the public eye. Nineteenth-century Berlin was not the place where either complete internal change or a more benign expressive meaning could effectively be realized by industry. The tightly knit, ossifying urban structure, entrenched and hostile property interests, and old-guard politics were hardly conducive to what was now required: the *hiding* of industrial power from society at large, and especially from the restless proletarian gangs who had taken over the streets. But how could such power become a secret, when colossal factories encumbered the city's boundaries?

Moreover, apart from a few far-sighted firms, the old ways still tended to prevail among many industrialists, so there was no concerted effort to conceal industrial authority and assertiveness. For instance, the views of many factory owners about shop-floor discipline were not only antiquated, but publicly announced. Heinrich Herkner proclaimed as late as 1908: 'The worker is, and by definition will remain, an uneducated man of limited understanding.' At Bergmann G.m.b.H., Bergmann himself had all the doors removed from the toilets, while in 1902 workers in the Greater Berlin Streetcar Company complained about the absence of daylight when the windows were covered with oil paint to prevent distractions.[18]

Despite the fervid debates that exercised the architectural salons, extreme conservatism still dominated architectural practice; the Social Democrat leader Karl Liebknecht was angered by the cost and gross monumentalism of the Royal Opera House, newly erected in the Tiergarten. 'This unfortunate, useless space for the narrowest of publics is the formal essence of court pomposity. If architecture tells us anything at all about economic and political circumstances, we see that efforts such as this are the concrete representation of the powerless mass against the privileged few.'[19]

9.4   Factory and tenement, Kreuzberg, Berlin, 1906

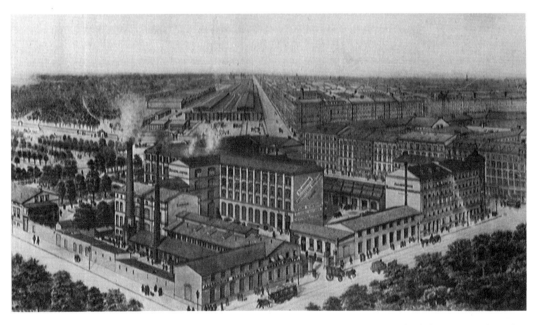

9.5   AEG complex on the Ackerstrasse, Wedding. The Humboldthain covers the far left. Drawing by Julius Pathé, 1889

Most of all, the insistence on maintaining old boundaries between classes in the larger Berlin region served to obstruct the industrial decentralization required to ease the increasingly problematic relations between factory and city. It was said of the Prussian interior minister von Dallwitz that it was essential for him to keep unruly Berlin in its place with the help of the suburbs. He could not rid himself of the fear that a Social Democrat majority would take over the whole region.[20] Industrial decentralization, indeed, was equated with political anarchy, and was therefore suppressed: 'How could the state, representative of private property interests in the age of imperialism, safely permit industrial development? Or the banks give free rein to their land companies? How much horsetrading had to take place over each piece of land needed for canal building, even though expropriation rights existed?'[21]

AEG *in the Inner City*

The position of the giant Berlin firm Allgemeine Electricitäts-Gesellschaft (AEG) was pivotal, when seen against this contradictory background. Their response at the time to the forces of extreme competition, political inertia, worker exploitation, and the dynamic shift to industrial efficiency seems remarkably sophisticated and 'modern.' Yet their factory architecture, although unique, suggested a forceful and intrusive presence within the society.

The firm's leader, Walther Rathenau, felt that 'modernity is foolish, but antiquarianism is rubbish; life in its vigour is neither new nor antique, but young.'[22] Quite unlike his chief rival, von Siemens, Rathenau was less an inventor than an organizer and production-process expert. Both he and Siemens had consolidated their market power by buying up the weaker competition at the turn of the century; however, by 1902, by using foreign patents, new small firms were eroding their lucrative monopoly in generators and lamps.[23] It was in 1903, when competition

between the two giants reached new heights, that F.W. Taylor's *Shop Management* was published in Germany, and its methods, first combined with the remarkable homegrown ones by Georg Schlesinger of Ludwig Loewe, were immediately taken up by AEG. But production efficiency was not enough for Rathenau and his colleague Paul Jordan. They were the first to sense that product appearance and a more understated image were important weapons in local politics and in the marketplace. Consequently, from 1907 to 1914, AEG undertook a massive program of design, building, and reorganization that combined the newly developed production techniques with a commitment to visually transforming the whole *Industriekultur*.

The consequences of this program, spearheaded by the architect Peter Behrens and inspired by the debates of the Deutsche Werkbund, are well known; product and factory design, graphics, letterheads, and symbols collectively represented the first serious push since William Morris's failed attempt to reconcile the contradictory demands of industry, society, and art. But whereas the new manufactured products – the famous lamps and small appliances – signalled a radical understanding of, and confidence in the machined aesthetic, the expressive meaning of the new AEG factories presented a highly assertive picture of industrial power. Here was evidence, despite Werkbund ideology to the contrary, that factory-produced items and buildings were not the same. Essentially, Peter Behrens's new large assembly plants – the Kleinmotorenfabrik, the Hochspannungsfabrik, and the Turbinenfabrik – like all buildings, were moulded by urban mechanical relations acting on boundary conditions, which in this case seriously constrained Peter Behrens's attempts to depart from the nineteenth-century tradition of factory design.

In particular, two factors of location, when combined with Behrens's inability or unwillingness to acknowledge the need to mask the inordinate power of the firm, marked the AEG factories. The first factor was the still-endemic

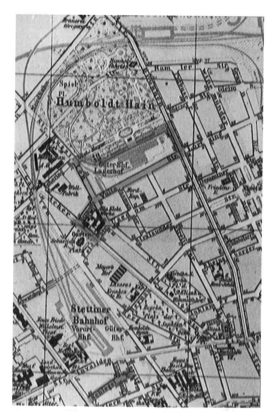

9.6 Humboldthain area of Wedding, 1896

scarcity of newly converted land around the periphery of Berlin. Very little progress had been made by 1907 in obtaining state sanctions and infrastructure to break the Prussian policy of containment, so the few available sites were both expensive and geometrically constricted. This was especially the case with the two locations chosen by AEG, each of which was surrounded by intensive housing and industrial facilities constructed in the 1890s. The Kleinmotorenfabrik (1910–13) and the Hochspannungsfabrik (1909–10) were to be built on the Voltastrasse in the working-class district of Wedding as extensions to the existing AEG complex south of the Humboldthain[24] (Fig. 9.6). This meant that each building had to be fitted between a narrow developed street front, existing nineteenth-century tenements, and crowded industrial facilities to the rear (Fig. 9.7). The famous Turbinenfabrik (1909) was planned for the corner of Huttenstrasse and Berlichigenstrasse in the even older industrial district of Moabit, where AEG had recently acquired an interest in Ludwig Loewe's Union Elekricitäts-Gesellschaft. The whole block was by this time completely occupied, necessitating the demolition of an existing

9.7 AEG complex on the Voltastrasse (foreground). View from the southeast about 1915

9.8   Sketch by Peter Behrens of his initial design for the Turbinenfabrik, 1918

turbine factory to clear a site that was destined to be enveloped to its boundaries by the new structure (Fig. 9.8).

The second factor of location seems almost paradoxical, given the progressive élan of the electromechanical sector and of AEG in particular, but it explains why the firm seemed so unconcerned about consolidating and ex-panding its inner-city facilities on difficult and expensive land. In spite of substantial improvements in machinery and procedure, the winding of electric motors and the assembly of the new AEG–Curtis turbines were still, in 1913, predominantly manual operations. The Ackerstrasse plant alone, in 1906–7, employed six thousand workers who were confined to a shop floor that provided less than seven square metres per employee.[25] A photograph of the interior of the old Kleinmotorenfabrik, taken sometime between 1910 and 1912, shows row after row of workers standing elbow to elbow at their workbenches (Fig. 9.9). In Moabit, by 1906, 1,600 men were engaged in the assembly of turbines in a single hall.[26] Given the pathetic state of transit facilities, a location close to their enormous labour pool, albeit crowded into the tenements of Moabit and Wedding, was essential to the AEG operation. So constraining were the mechanical relations and

9.9   Interior of the old Kleinmotorenfabrik, about 1912

excessive land rent that the new factories, despite their great areas of glass, could be little more than huge multi-storey sheds, overpowering in their bulk and urban intrusiveness.

The predicament faced by Peter Behrens, therefore, was to reconcile the mandate he received from Rathenau and Jordan with the inevitable monoliths that could only continue to evoke an expressive meaning of nineteenth-century industrial hegemony. Ironically, his ambiguous recourse, rationalized in several pronouncements about the conflict between nature and culture, was to instil his factories with 'corporeality,' an attribute that he felt elevated architecture above the realm of engineering.[27] Behrens argued that corporeality was the representation of 'cultural monumentality'; this led him to deal with the great bulk of the AEG factories by *emphasizing* their huge presence rather than reducing it (Figs 9.10 and 9.11). He therefore chose to add weight to the Huttenstrasse pylons of the Turbinenfabrik – against the vehement objection of engineer Karl Bernhard that they were structurally useless – and to distend the brick piers of the Kleinmotorenfabrik to form a colossal rhythm along the narrow Voltastrasse (Figs 9.12 and 9.13). Behrens's *Industriekultur*, in spite of – or rather precisely because of – its powerful signature, was already obsolescent, reflecting the old style of labour and social relations that many industrialists, if only out of self-interest, were already beginning to regret.

Carl Benscheidt: Self-Interest in the Suburbs

Modern architecture and urbanism could not blossom in the European city because the problems to be resolved were new ones occurring within the practically immutable context of expensive land and inflexible urban boundaries. Without some concerted action, necessarily on the part of the state, to bring about less restrictive development opportunities, the old heavy solutions persisted. It was not that the nineteenth-century city deter-

9.10   Voltastrasse front of the Kleinmotorenfabrik, 1916

9.11   Berlichigenstrasse side of the Turbinenfabrik

9.12   Brick piers of the Kleinmotorenfabrik on the Voltastrasse

9.13   Pylon and Huttenstrasse front of the Turbinenfabrik

mined architecture, but its constraining boundaries seriously hamstrung experimentation; the radical spirit of modernism, already beginning to thrive in other aspects of art and cultural life, had yet to make significant inroads into building design.

This pattern was finally broken, not in the industrial metropolis, but on the edge of the Saxon town of Alfeld an der Leine. It was here, beginning in 1910, that plans were made to build a modest precision machine and shoe-last factory, the Fagus-Werk. The events that affected the Fagus-Werk are an intricate weave of the talents, disposition, and ideals of those involved, as well as being a product of mechanical relations linked to the themes of urban boundaries and human motility. The unlikely character of the town, a cultural backwater, and of the client, a canny but tight-fisted conservative, only serve to emphasize the vision with which Walter Gropius was able to fuse crucial opportunities of location and emerging industrial instincts into this, his first independent work. But it was a vision nurtured in and transported from the political turbulence of Berlin.

Carl Benscheidt, the founder and owner of the Fagus-Werk, had been a long-time employee of the local shoe-last firm of C. Behrens AG (no relation to Peter) until he virtually took over as director in 1896. With little formal education, and plagued by ill health as a youth, Benscheidt possessed a complex personality. On the one hand, he decidedly belonged to the old school, displaying iron self-discipline which, through his rigorous vegetarian existence, enabled him to survive until the age of ninety.[28] He was in the habit of making stiff demands of his employees, and, as we shall see, was ambivalent about their welfare when it came to spending money on providing a decent work environment. He was, none the less, generous with words: 'Our wealth,' he proclaimed in an unwitting Marxian parody, 'will not be found in our property, but in the skill and know-how of our workers. Every man trained in the shop is our real capital.'[29]

On the other hand, when it came to matters of production, Benscheidt displayed a creativity belying his otherwise provincial traits. He constantly sought out, or personally invented, the latest in industrial techniques and machinery. His experiments while at C. Behrens, employing the most advanced technology, had transformed the firm from obscurity to world leadership in shoe-last manufacturing by 1900.[30] By this time, C. Behrens had embarked on a program of building expansion, for which Benscheidt was given the primary responsibility. It was he who, fatefully, approached an experienced industrial architect from Hanover called Eduard Werner to design the new factory, which turned out to be an efficient but unremarkable brick structure completed in 1902.

Then, after consolidating his obvious success, Carl Benscheidt left Behrens in 1910 at the age of fifty-three, under conditions that are not entirely clear but were probably crucial to what followed. It seems likely that he found his leadership eclipsed when the son of the founder became old enough to take over the firm, a matter that apparently caused some unpleasantness. In any event, Benscheidt was determined to set up his own rival company in Alfeld to compete with his old firm, which had been enjoying a virtual regional monopoly for some time. Over the years he befriended Fred Cox, a director of the United Shoe Machinery Corporation of Boston, who wanted to establish a shoe-last factory in Germany. So Cox invited Benscheidt and his son to visit the United States in the spring of 1910, promising the chance of some capital as well as an inspection of U.S. production methods and planning.[31] They took up Cox's offer and returned, apparently full of new ideas and with one million marks of venture money. This was not a great deal, considering the plans that Benscheidt had in mind, namely, to finesse his former employer through sheer technical and promotional superiority.

Benscheidt resolved to begin modestly, with respect to the size of his new operation, but to use only the best in precision machinery and to

expand when conditions permitted, later on. His first building was to house about seventy-five to eighty operatives and technical staff, which would have made it about a quarter the size of C. Behrens's factory. Nevertheless, given the intricate nature of the manufacturing process, a fairly sizeable technical-administrative component was to be incorporated from the start.[32] In searching for a site for his factory, Benscheidt did not have many alternatives if he were to invest as little as possible of his precious capital in land. The old town of Alfeld lay completely east of the river Leine, but the regional highway and railway ran along the west bank, serving a loose outer cluster of industries that included the C. Behrens factory and some scattered housing and institutions. This was the only feasible industrial area in Alfeld: close enough to town to afford convenient access for workers on foot or by bicycle, yet separated from the town by the river, and well served by regional transportation. (The official Alfeld Land Use Plan [1913] designated the area for 'mixed land use' – i.e., housing and industry [Fig. 9.14].) It was here that Benscheidt acquired three hectares of virtual swampland between the railway and the Hanover road, almost directly across the tracks from his old firm. He was apparently so concerned to save money that he bought only a few metres of road frontage, leaving the existing St Elizabeth Hospital to intervene between his land and the highway (Fig. 9.15).

Benscheidt decided to name his new venture after the *fagus silvatica* – the European beech – from which his shoe-lasts were to be made, and which grew profusely in the Leine valley. The manufacturing process itself was a difficult one, given the intricate shape of the lasts, requiring high-precision lathes; a well-lit, clean environment; expert operatives; and close supervision. Benscheidt himself had already devised a completely horizontal process while with Behrens, but was unable to exploit it fully in their old multi-storey shop. He commissioned Eduard Werner again, in October 1910, and worked closely with him to

9.14   Land use map of Alfeld, 1913. The Fagus-Werk site is at centre, between the railway and the regional highway

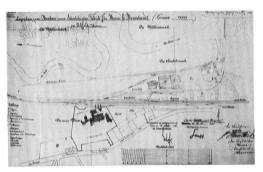

9.15   Fagus-Werk, Eduard Werner's 1911 site plan

prepare the new factory layout for the Fagus-Werk.[33] Quite unlike the AEG in Berlin, Benscheidt could afford to be lavish with land, having bought, for very little, sufficient to carry out his future expansion plans and to allow ample separation from the few adjacent activities. In effect, the factory, isolated as it would be from the street boundary, could be functionally and visually disengaged from the Alfeld community. Its major link was at the back, where a spur line could be joined to the railway, and the buildings informally arrayed along the prospect towards C. Behrens AG across the tracks.

Given this near absence of boundary constriction, Eduard Werner was free, in his consultations with Benscheidt, to deal with the factory requirements in an entirely programmatic way, sorting out the various compo-

nents of his layout strictly according to the division of labour and the flows of materials and products through the process (Fig. 9.16). The varied nature of the specialized spaces required, the stringent environmental needs of the drying room, the top lighting in the main workshop, and the non-industrial characteristics of the technical/administrative facilities precluded the use of a single, large, flexible space. Instead, Werner devised an informal horizontal arrangement of attached, rectangular, but externally differentiated volumes, to be situated close to the railway site boundary, and occupying in total only about one-eighth of the site. But Werner's layout was also affected by more than manufacturing utility; it was affected by the desired control over labour and the factory's relationship to the community.

The function, skill, and status of the employees roughly followed a threefold classification: labourers, warehousemen, and sawyers; precision-tool operatives; and technical-administrative staff. Each group had its own standardized procedures, supervisory personnel, and allotted place in the factory, which was spatially divided from the rest along the north-south axis of the complex. Thus, in direct accord with the principles of Taylorism, surveillance and control of employee activity could be decentralized to semi-autonomous zones. But Werner distributed the zones in such a way as to give visual

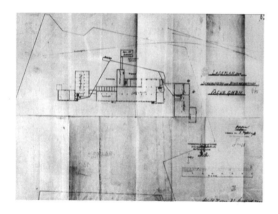

9.16   Fagus-Werk, Werner's 1911 layout

prominence to the technical-administrative wing, with respect to the views from the community to the south and east, and to the public entrance from the Hanover road. The manufacturing process itself, while not quite concealed from public view, he visually subordinated to the three-storey, L-shaped office building.

Benscheidt and Gropius: The Incubus Meets Proteus

Eduard Werner's competence seems to have satisfied Benscheidt with respect to the more straightforward programmatic aspects of the Fagus-Werk. The architect clearly knew what he was doing when dealing with supervision, machine layout, material flows, lighting, and practical construction matters. Even his elevational treatment was a departure from the traditionalism he had employed a few years earlier in C. Behrens's factory. With the exception of the proposed warehouse, to which Werner chose to give an unusual local timbered expression, the drawings display a rigour and unpretentiousness not apparent in his previous work (Fig. 9.17). But unfortunately for Werner, his client required more than he could offer in the way of architectural treatment. While Benscheidt was hardly motivated by a high aesthetic purpose, and was

certainly not prepared to lavish his limited capital on appearance, he wanted the Fagus-Werk to present a distinctive 'tasteful' image. It seems unlikely that he wished to show, in the appearance of his factory, his ostensible concern for industrial progress, or the well-being of his employees. For instance, he was not above contravening local regulations by insisting that his workers' eating room (it could not be graced by the term 'dining hall') be located in the basement.[34] In any event, by a chance decision, he asked young Walter Gropius to 'dress up' Werner's drawings.

Gropius had spent the first three years of his professional career in the Berlin atelier of Peter Behrens, where he worked on various industrial projects, including, possibly, the Turbinenfabrik itself. Deeply concerned, like Behrens, with the relationship of art to industry, he was influenced both by the Hegelian concept of the inseparability of artistic form and content and by Alois Riegl's ideas on the necessary connection between art and the *Zeitgeist*. Thus armed, Gropius was drawn into the vitriolic politics of the Werkbund and, while still an employee, became deeply critical of Behrens's approach to factory design.

The limited nature of the opportunity presented by Benscheidt – indeed, his working relationship with the young architect over the ensuing months – hardly matched the visionary enthusiasm Gropius was just then developing about the transcendent association of art, industry, and society. The day-to-day episodes of the Fagus-Werk contract were prosaic indeed, especially when compared with the grand scale and verve of the AEG enterprise in Berlin.

Gropius had encountered some difficulty in finding work during the first months of his independent practice, despite having sent hundreds of letters to prospective clients.[35] The first contact with Carl Benscheidt actually came, in December 1910, through Gropius's brother-in-law, who was an official in Alfeld. According to the recollection of Ernst Neufeld, a colleague of Gropius at the time: 'Werner's project was very orderly, but lacked

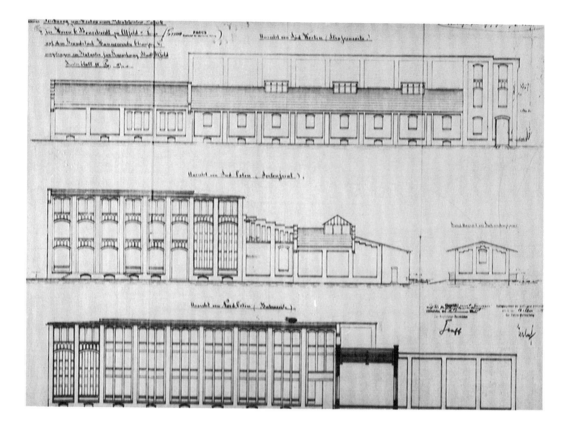

9.17   Fagus-Werk, elevational drawings by Werner, 1911

any architectural dash. Gropius somehow heard about this and said to his brother-in-law, "Tell me, couldn't I get a job like that? Could you perhaps do something for me?" So [the relative] went to old Benscheidt and said, "Herr Benscheidt, I have a young brother-in-law in Berlin who was an architect with [Peter] Behrens, the biggest man in Germany. Now wouldn't it be good for the sake of public relations if your factory had something special?" Benscheidt replied "Alright, I'm only just starting out, and every penny is important, but tell your brother-in-law to make me a proposition."[36]

Finally, after considerable deliberation, and with the virtual completion of Werner's drawings for the crucial first phase, Benscheidt wrote to Gropius on 13 March 1911: 'You are to undertake the architectonic, artistic design of our projected factory, for which the construction plans have been prepared by the architect Werner of Hanover. You should complete the plans and detailed drawings necessary for the construction and official approvals. In that regard you should respect the layout and structural proposals of Herr Werner, and do your best to give the whole project a tasteful appearance.'[37]

The subsequent correspondence between architect and client does not show Benscheidt to have been an accommodating patron, nor to have offered serious direction to Gropius about the kind of appearance he required. In fact, the young architect found it difficult to persuade the industrialist to accept his ideas, many of which had to be abandoned. There is

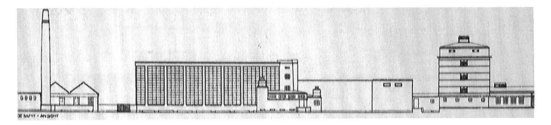

9.18   Fagus-Werk, northeast elevation. Gropius and Meyer, 1911

no record of inspired discussion about Gropius's new philosophy of the expressive potential in what he believed was an emerging industrial-social partnership. While Benscheidt seemed keen to build a factory that was up to date and efficient, his views about modernity were limited to industrial efficiency and public relations, and were coloured by a fear of wasting time and money. He was especially impatient with any suggested changes to Werner's layout and construction decisions. Ironically, the great glass wall that Gropius proposed to clad the three-storey administrative block, and which was to more than fulfil Benscheidt's narrow mandate, was especially contentious (Figs 9.18 and 9.19). In a letter dated 15 May 1911, the industrialist showed both his concern and general attitude: 'We have to consider that the maintenance of such big windows in a small place like Alfeld will present all kinds of problems. The local painters do not have the equipment, for instance, to deal with these kinds of windows, although you are aware that they will need painting every two or three years.'[38]

Benscheidt was shocked when a local firm gave him a cost estimate of five thousand marks for the windows. It was not until the Düsseldorf firm Fenestra submitted a lower tender, based on the advertising value of the windows, that the industrialist finally conceded.[39] Nevertheless, it is certain, given what we know of Benscheidt's personality and the correspondence between him and Gropius, that the Fagus-Werk was not to be sacrificed to a purely architectural cause. On the con-

9.19   Fagus-Werk, southwest elevation of administrative block

trary, it seems clear that Gropius's ideas were acceptable only in so far as they gave the impression of a benevolence and taste that did not in fact exist. The vehicle for such an impression was not so much the factory itself, the zone allocated for shop-floor employees, as the technical-administrative zone, to which

9.20   Fagus-Werk, main entrance

Werner's scheme had given public prominence. Here, for the first time, were assembled the weightless features necessary to purge industry of its authoritarian reputation, if not its actual authority (Fig. 9.20).

Words, Weight, and New Boundaries

Because Peter Behrens had chosen to seek the resolution of art and industry in *Korporealität*, whereby, perhaps unwittingly, the expressive meaning of industry was still one of assertive dominance, his factories already represented an archaic phase in the rapid evolution of German manufacturing from economic marginality to patriarchal dominance, to the emergence, with the final establishment of scientific management and industrial psychology, of a more complex, manipulative relationship with employees and society alike.

Social dominance, in a word, was succumbing, in the first decade of the century, to the essentially public-relations campaign of *Sozialpartnerschaft*, for which the fortress-like factory was hardly a corresponding metaphor.

Some early writings of Gropius show that he regarded this apparent shift in attitude, on the part of some industrialists at least, as a source of philosophical inspiration. Gropius and his associates were steeped in late-nineteenth-century aesthetic theory, which was devoted to the discovery of the metaphysical spirit of the times. This spirit, in the case of architecture, was deemed to lie less in the empirical study of social relations than in the transcendent artistic potential of form, materials, and purpose. Gropius seems, at first, to have adhered to this idea, even though he favoured, as did many of his contemporaries, 'practical simplicity' over 'false Romanticism.'[40] But then several of his papers and lectures, produced when he was designing the Fagus-Werk (between the beginning of 1911 and 1914) dealt directly with specific empirical and political questions.[41] The crucial theme – often couched in the same phrases – is pervasive: the avoidance of social upheaval depends upon the physical transformation of the workplace, a transformation from which industry could only profit: 'Work must have palaces constructed, that not only give the factory labourer, the slave of modern industry, light, air, and cleanliness, but also a sense of the value of the great concept that drives it all ... If this consciousness were to be awakened in the individual worker, then perhaps the social catastrophe that daily threatens us from the tumult of economic life can be avoided. Farsighted organizations have known for some time that work increases with the contentment of labour, thereby raising productivity in the factory. The sophisticated industrialist, then, will do everything possible to enliven the stifling drudgery of factory life, and to soothe the stress of work.'[42]

The 'new' industrialist, therefore, was not the culprit, but the potential saviour of a society in turmoil. By acting intelligently in his own interests, an alliance with the interests of labour could be forged, not by autocratic means, but rather by the subtle partnership that was the essence of scientific management. But Gropius was still faced with reconciling such conciliatory pragmatism with the high ideals of art that he refused to abandon: 'The field of art, that is the monumental art of genius ... begins where transcendental vision impregnates knowledge and representation. Art accomplishes nothing by representing the conscious world, with its naive impulses; it is rooted in spiritual needs and fulfils the spiritual needs of man. In principle it has nothing in common with material needs. The purpose of art is the representation of high transcendental ideals, by material means of expression belonging to the conscious world of space and time.'[43]

Like Peter Behrens, Gropius believed that *Zweckmässigkeit* – practicality – while essential, was certainly not enough. By contrast, the transcendental vision that was the well-spring of true art could not be alien to contemporary reality, but inspired by it; only thus would it be possible to adhere to the spirit of the times. But then, by insightful – and rather expedient – rationalization, Gropius seems to have transformed this spirit, at least in part, into the self-serving public image that industry wished to project, thereby deriving his own vision from the most compromised of motives. A few weeks before being appointed by Benscheidt, he wrote: 'The promotional responsibilities of the architect must eventually be recognized. His creative activities in particular must come to terms with the promotional intentions of the farsighted industrialist; they can lend a distinctive quality to the factory which mirrors the character of the whole enterprise.'[44]

It could perhaps be claimed that, if the Fagus-Werk represents the crucible of modern architecture, then it was born, not primarily out of avant-garde radicalism, but from pragmatic conciliation, an expediency that was to separate architecture from the mainstream of the artistic upheaval of European Modernism.

It was not, finally, only Gropius's adherence to prevailing theories of art, but also industrial power that led him to argue for proletarian well-being on the shop floor while promoting the interests of industrial capital, confronting Gropius daily in the forceful presence of Carl Benscheidt. The avoidance of social chaos (and therefore of the disruption of the old order) was apparently synonymous in his mind with his interpretation of the autonomous cause of art, which sought a grand reconciliation of the schisms in everyday life: 'From a social point of view, it is not a matter of indifference if the contemporary factory worker labours in the desolation of ugly industrial barracks, or in well-proportioned space. He would be happier to participate in the production of those things that benefit everyone in an artistically inspired workplace, confronted by an innate beauty that enlivens the monotony of mechanical labour. In this way both the spirit of the worker and the whole productive efficiency of the firm would grow.'[45]

Who could blame Gropius for not living up to his early words? As we have seen, if architecture is an art at all, it draws its special character from its impurity – from the contingencies of the world around. Giving voice to purely artistic intentions, as so many architects have done before and since, tells us little about actual consequences. So the eventual invocation of high artistic ideals anchored in practical and political reality did not distinguish Gropius from his older contemporaries in the Werkbund. Many of them held similar views, given their position as advisers to a powerful élite that was in the process of recognizing, on the one hand, the pecuniary merits of a decent work environment mirrored by a humane public image, and, on the other, the dangers of proletarian unrest. Moreover, the artistic theories of Hegel and Alois Riegl were widely regarded as the main conceptual weapons in a campaign by architects to dislodge the virtual monopoly held by engineers in factory design. *Zweckmässigkeit* – spatial efficiency, structural economy, air, light, and cleanliness

– were attributes of nature, rather than of culture; it was the material, not the essence, of the *Zeitstil*, and therefore fell short of the more spiritual demands of architecture. Nevertheless, while these views were widely endorsed in the architectural salons, they had not, until the Fagus-Werk, found convincing expression in construction. But now the factory – the object of protest, the laboratory of technical and economic progress, and the potential advertisement of ostensibly benign, cooperative intentions – became the first artefact of this cause.

Urbanism and Industrial Power

The Hegelian essence proclaimed by the members of the Werkbund could no more find expression in the mere assembly of new architectural leitmotifs than it could in straightforward practicality. Any iconographic analysis of the Fagus-Werk will reveal that none of the 'new' motifs – the flat, barely projecting roof; the curtain-wall membrane; even the open columnless corners – was without precedent. Instead, the factory depended for its breakthrough upon the inspired integration of constructed space and external space, an arrangement carrying a message of congenial symbiosis between the world of manufacturing and the world at large (Fig. 9.21). This impression is created primarily by the very absence of the characteristic that Peter Behrens sought to impose – corporeality.

Corporeal architecture, in a historical sense, is the architecture of inner city boundaries. Its expressive meaning is the unequivocal exclusion of the street mob from the proprietary domain that extends to the boundary between confined public activity and enclosed private territory. This is almost as true for Peter Behrens's Kleinmotorenfabrik on the Voltastrasse as it is for the Palazzo Strozzi, in the sense that the Berlin industrial hegemony had by that time nearly attained the assertive aura of Florentine aristocratic privilege. But architectural corporeality also carries a more subtle yet equally powerful message, one reinforcing the association between solidity and urbanness: the equation in the subconscious of façadal mass with capital intensity. The weight of stone, brick, and ornament occupying the site perimeter becomes a kind of metaphor for the great volume of construction that it encloses and conceals from view.

Suburbanity, by contrast, is essentially the substitution of construction capital by land;[46] one activity is separated from another less by sheer mass than by an unoccupied boundary zone that absorbs the outside shape of internal function and neutralizes the impact of external intrusion both upon and from surrounding activity. It had been sensed, long before Frank Lloyd Wright and Walter Gropius, that the villa and the factory, otherwise so incompatible, were identical in their need to occupy the kind of spatial cushion that is peculiar to the loose development of the urban hinterland. Only there is it possible to deal, simultaneously, with the customized demands of internal organization and the necessary amelioration of outside effects. But it took the intuition of Wright and Gropius to realize – apparently quite independently of each other – that the absorptive, neutralizing qualities of suburban space were the key to the invention of an architecture corresponding to that transformation in mechanical relations brought on by the impending invasion of the metropolitan hinterland throughout the West.

For Gropius, the corporeal façade was not only a redundancy in the context of suburban mechanical relations, or an artefact that excluded light and air. It also precluded, in a cogent symbolic sense, the essential cross-boundary mediation of industry and society that formed both the core of his own political philosophy and the promotional demands of industry itself. But these were merely his own rationalizations of a work whose expressive meaning is not only prerational but the reincarnation of protean urbanism with a vengeance. The kinetic life imprisoned in the Berlin streets was out of control to the point where further confinement in the oppressive city had become politically suicidal. The Fagus-Werk,

9.21   E. Pitsch, *A Scene in the Leine Valley*, 1925

however, far from impeding movement, was the model for building a *passe-partout* landscape – luminescent, self-effacing, insubstantial (Figs 9.22 and 9.23).

The immediate significance of the Fagus-Werk is therefore derived not from its status as a harbinger of modernism, but from the antiquity of its urbanism – its neutralization of the boundary between industrial and proletarian assertiveness, newly absorbed by the empty *poché* that surrounded and penetrated the transparent threshold, simultaneously disengaging, but not excluding, the factory from the wider community of Alfeld.

There seems to be a contradiction in the fact that Gropius's achievement occurred under such less-than-auspicious circumstances – a provincial environment, the limited scope af-

forded by Werner's drawings, and the intransigence of Carl Benscheidt himself – whereas all the resources and encouragement of the AEG were at the disposal of Peter Behrens in Berlin. It appears that, in these two cases at least, their corresponding urbanism was affected less by the financial circumstances and sophistication of the client than by the new imperatives and opportunities of extensive mechanical relations.

The half-hidden significance of the Fagus-Werk, nevertheless, concerns the appropriation of architectural ideals. The major social and political questions of the time were seriously addressed in the early writings of Walter Gropius, who believed that the deepening rift in German society could not be mended by material concessions alone. Spiritual unity,

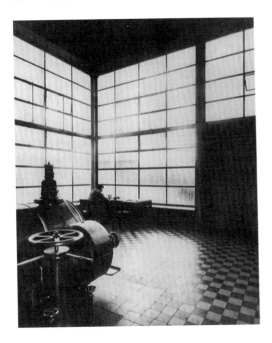

9.22   Fagus-Werk, interior of the machine room, 1913–14

9.23   Le Corbusier, interior of the Villa Savoye, Poissy-sur-Seine, 1929–31

fostered by an architecture that did not represent any special interest, but contained the sense of a higher order, was the key to social unity. Industry did not so much subvert this appeal, which was soon to become integral to modernist thought, as inspire it and put it to use from the beginning. It is conceivable that the eventual establishment of the new protean architecture depended upon its double role as a new-found instrument of urbanism and a decoy, which would explain why it would be disparately applied, first by the Constructivists and the Weimar architects, then, to this day, by corporate and industrial capital alike. Half a century later, however, what began as a benign near-absence would no longer obscure reality, but expose it, as urban renewal and economies of scale in commercial building turned the camouflage into a colossal badge. But the multiple, contradictory demands that urbanism places upon architecture still prevail, stirring further rounds of invention and new disguises.

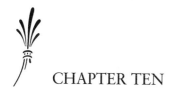

CHAPTER TEN

Retreat from a Magic Landscape

Empty Boundary Zones

But when you grasp him with your hands and
  hold him
In fetters, then in changing shape and forms
Of beasts he'll baffle you; for suddenly
He'll be a bristly boar or a savage tiger
Or a scaly serpent or a lioness
With tawny neck, or burst with a piercing hiss
As a flame, or slip his bonds, or melt away
Into insubstantial water, and be gone. – Virgil[1]

Urban theory, we have seen, proliferates whenever the boundaries of the city are in flux. Cities of the mind were not limited to the Dark Ages; they flourished throughout the Renaissance at a time of economic decline in Italy, and did so again during the suburbanization of neoclassical Paris. The metropolitan advent, too, has ushered in a century or more filled with theory-based prescriptions for embodying the public interest in the arrangement of urban space. The latter occurrence, like all its predecessors, seeks to suppress the old boundary dialectic through strategies of disengagement, seeing opportunities, in the spread of extensive mechanical relations, first in the suburbs, then in central cities, to assign separate zones to the static and

the protean in metropolitan development. But more than its historical counterparts, the twentieth-century phase has been embraced by planning institutions, which are deployed as an instrument of urban politics, and are part of another story.

Throughout most of this latter period, while events cannot be reduced to a simple formula, it can be said that theory and politics have combined to bring a factitious element to urbanism, which have placed moral reason in a state of semi-eclipse, although the passage from one state to the other has been everywhere uneven, and is still incomplete. We can detect how this passage begins by pointing, first, to Berlin, then, to the Alfeld story, where industrial power cast a penumbra around that ancient aspiration for the complementarity of things, turning this aspiration to use in metropolitan formation by degrading it to images. It is only one story, but representative, perhaps, of countless others as the self-interest of private clients, soon to be brokered by state intervention, captures the lion's share of architectural production and urban-boundary formation wherever the old dialectic, that precarious embodiment of self and otherness, begins to crumble beneath a contradictory ideology of individualism and rational order.

Much has happened to architecture and urbanism since the events at Alfeld, and many would claim that, if the themes discussed in this book were once recurrent, the character and magnitude of urbanization in this century have effectively severed the metropolis from all legacies of the past. Cities everywhere have been inflated and transformed by an unprecedented centrifugal movement, their outer regions expanding while the centres lose population. By 1910 the population of Berlin had peaked at two million; then the hinterland began to expand to contain more inhabitants than the old city thirty years later. This same process started much earlier in London, which had already been named 'the Great Wen' by Cobbett in 1822; in 1860 the City of London housed 120,000 people, but virtually none by 1939, while the Home Counties tripled their population to almost 3 million during the same period. The city of Paris between 1911 and 1941 lost 200,000 inhabitants, while the suburbs more than doubled theirs, to 2.5 million. The City of New York continued to gain, until plateauing at 7 million in 1940; thereafter the metropolitan region took over, and housed 19 million in 1970. The same trends continue almost everywhere.

Accordingly, twentieth-century urbanism is a complex story of coming to terms with extensive mechanical relations, in which investments for land and infrastructure predominate, a story of regions opened up at the periphery under the auspices of state subsidies for far-flung highways, sewers, and water-supply systems. The ensuing geography became one of single-use enclaves wherever institutionalized planning took over, partitioning ways of life, productive activities, and architecture into exclusive zones.

Those who followed Walter Gropius, and helped to pioneer the new style, did so on an empty terrain, believing it to be a metaphor of freedom, rarely confronting the intransigent boundaries of the old city but mentally sweeping them aside wherever its structures encumbered a rationality that ostensibly dealt in functions, pure geometry and mass produc-

10.1   Urban renewal in New York City, 1950s

tion, but that, in so doing, produced forms that were tailor-made for the urban hinterland. At mid-century, however, this same rationality began parachuting into the old centres, not to accommodate their existing boundaries but to erase them from the map in a problem-strewn crusade to impose extensive mechanical relations in domains where they did not belong. This suburbanization of the centre, also sanctioned by the state, brought an ambiguous landscape in its wake, one whose dialectic was stillborn, as architecture turned upwards and inwards, retreating from the old civic thresholds (Fig. 10.1).

So the outward shifts have been matched by other equally powerful changes in the geography of urban boundaries. Whole landscapes undergo transformation with the spectacular rise of the service economy, its ability to outbid manufacturing in the market for land and its continuing reliance on labour-intensive procedures. Industry, in turn, joins the migration to the hinterland, substituting its former spatial ties to dense labour markets with the locational independence that productive and transportation technology can bring. These mutations in the geography of work are matched too by the culmination of socio-economic segregation as, in the flux of migration, whole regions are reapportioned according to class, ethnicity, and race.

If the metropolis is being assembled from facts that have no precedent, then neither has

10.2   Downtown Houston

the manner in which we experience it. Gone are the days when whole armatures were traversed on foot, their minutiae absorbed at close quarters, as was possible during the famous walks by Horace and Martial. Now we navigate most of the public realm at speed, and the realm itself is arranged accordingly, voided of its carnivals and symbolism, usurped by signs and images, a hyperactive, unfocused conduit to some other destination (Fig. 10.2).

What, then, has happened to protean architecture, or to the boundary dialectic that animated the quarters and civic places? In the ongoing process of dismantling the industrial city and whatever preceded it, or of extending the commutersheds until they merge beyond the horizon, we inhabit a contradictory sea as unsettling to human life as it is to nature, mocking every attempt to cast the net of rational planning. But, as I have tried to show, reasoned acts have rarely figured prominently in the chronicles of city building. On the contrary, a river of impulsiveness crosses the foreground from its source in the myth-laden past, and the twentieth-century metropolis is fully immersed in it. We interpret its manifestations as the fruit of economic and political consciousness working at various individual or collective levels, and in so doing deploy a controlling mechanism of equivalently abstract measure, namely, a planning dialectic set in motion by the state to resolve competing local interests. But these interests, and the consciousness from which they supposedly derive, are just a sublimation of ancient impulses that, far from being kept in their place, spill out as never before and half-coalesce into the precarious shapes deposited in the wake of metropolitan formation. In this sense the technologies that catalyse the new formation, far from projecting it into the future, propel it backwards in time to a mirage of that binary condition where life vicariously oscillates once again between the worlds of Plato and Homer.

The narrative of city building in our century, of the illusions and actions that culminate in this return to primordiality, cannot be covered here. But familiar themes would animate such a narrative, and insights like that of Leroi-Gourhan remain a cogent part: 'The foundation of man's moral and physical comfort is the wholly animal perception of the perimeter of security, of the close refuge, or of the socializing rhythms.'[2] Much of the story, in other words, deals in the boundary dialectic, in the facts and expressive meaning of boundary architecture, as it always has. Nor can it really be said, as many have done, that the city was once an end in itself, the supreme embodiment of aspirations and the gift of human labour, whereas now we inhabit a contrivance engineered only to further the cause of material production. This simple package compresses history's ungainly shape, and that of recent events too. As we have seen, urbanism's compound spirit was nearly everywhere an uncompleted dialectic and so it remains, even as construction monopolizes every vista, even while the old practical ways lie dormant.

Again, such things cannot be part of our present story; and, in any case, the empirical narrative of metropolitan formation has been well told by others. It remains only to recall that our arena is that of the Western city, and in this regard, by way of a modest prelude to any thesis on the twentieth century, to glance towards two intersections where urbanism collides against the unprecedented. I refer, first of all, to the advent of cultural modernism, to its archaic roots and its strange alliance with the rootless men who have played no small part throughout the urban boundary chronicle. The alliance by its very nature excluded, then contested and won the day against this century's master builders who in turn, contrary to most accounts, were intent on replaying history's integrational theme. Second, I refer to the family; Plato's perennial enemy of the city is pushed into prominence as the flagbearer of an ideology that underlies the spread of extensive mechanical relations, as the foil to modernism itself in all its forms and, precisely as in Plato's sibylline words, urbanism's most formidable antagonist.

The Unsettlers

If Enlightenment reason failed to purge urbanism of its archetypal condition, were not those who followed Walter Gropius in search of the rational city more successful? While that search, the quintessential twentieth-century enterprise, also belongs to another story, it can be said that those who engaged in it, like the Enlightenment *philosophes* before them, essentially believed in miracles – in science purged of ideology, in ideology severed from the instincts. It can be shown, too, that their texts and plans rest on an unacknowledged stratum of old legacies, and that modernism never penetrated architectural and urbanist thought to its depths. On the contrary, the master builders of this century looked back in time, as their disciples still do, and like their predecessors, are intent on re-establishing a predictable universe by imposing structures around urban life with the same deliberation as Plato aspired to do. Where, then, does modernism enter the scene, if it did not drive the search for the rational city? In a sense, modernism too reincarnated the past, although one that is far more reminiscent of Homer's words than of Plato's. 'Whirl is king, having deposed Zeus' is a chorus from Aristophanes which has been repeated, in less cogent terms, down through the centuries. Whirl presides over a primordial domain, overseeing the destruction of every boundary in the civilized world, and his acolytes are the rootless young men who prowl the interstices of the city. They are the perennial *unsettlers*, intent on penetrating the last bounds of security and convention, and a hundred years ago their ranks were augmented by the modernist avant-gardes, who although none of them were builders, became the true harbingers of metropolitan formation.

Hermann Hesse's Kuhn inhabited an interior landscape that had already been shaped – or more precisely *unshaped* – by the apostles of Baudelaire: Mallarmé, Nietzsche, Kafka, Freud, Picasso, and several others. By 1902 August Strindberg could write in his preface to *A Dream Play*: 'Anything can happen; everything is possible and probable. Time and space do not exist; on a slight groundwork of reality, imagination spins and weaves new patterns made up of memories, experiences, unfettered fancies, absurdities and improvisations.' The characters in Strindberg's play 'evaporate, crystallize, scatter and converge.' There can be few more succinct descriptions of the modernist perception, of its fascination with the inchoate and its recognition of what we here have called expressive meaning, that 'area of expression which blurs the boundaries between rational and irrational, logical and illogical, intuitive and mechanical.'[3] A decade after Strindberg's play, Guillaume Apollinaire's Orphic poem *Zone* – surely a cogent title, chosen when *zoning* began to dominate planning, but also when the Fagus-Werk had just been completed – captures the indeterminacy of the boundaries between space, objects, and consciousness, a realm of in-between states made up of zones where things *absent themselves* or refuse to cohere. The modernist avant-gardes, taking their cue as much from Proteus as from Baudelaire, externalized not just some inner poetic voice heard by no one outside an aesthetic élite, but that kinetic, uncentred latency in the twentieth-century landscape.

The avant-gardes, in rejecting civilized history, focused their campaign against bourgeois Romanticism. Dialectics had been one of the intellectual obsessions of Romanticism, whose ideals were the harness, perhaps, to rein in a history threatening to accelerate beyond control. If events seemed to be swept along by their own momentum – witness the streets of Berlin – then the nineteenth-century mind refused to acknowledge their randomness, insisting on the weaving together of forms through syntheses, ultimate resolutions, organic relationships. Architecture and urbanism, continuing to cling to the dialectical idea they had shared since antiquity, thus never shed these transcendent ideals of Romanticism to participate in the cultural upheaval wrought by the modernist avant-gardes.

If action requires illusions, as Nietzsche maintained in *The Birth of Tragedy*, then the illusion of an integrated landscape propelled the work of Gropius, Adolf Loos and Otto Wagner in Vienna, then Le Corbusier in Paris, even the Moscow Constructivists; nor was Sant' Elia, whose drawings contain a monumental harmony the Futurist poets sought to erase from the world, exempt. The struggle of these builders against history was everywhere compromised, encumbered by the ballast of prior eras – an uneasy mixture of positivism and an integrative will. Both ran counter to modernism's disorganizing principle, which rejected habitual scenery of all kinds, displacing the familiar, the coherent, the rational with Fauvist unfinished canvases, white space, Joycean streams of consciousness, the negative landscapes of Albert Camus. To the modernists, the city was a *non sequitur*, atonal, a ship of fools. Giorgio de Chirico's paintings rupture the familiar linkage between people and objects, proclaiming an absolute disorientation that became the Surrealists' hallmark. To Kurt Schwitters, the city was a junk pile, a belief he rendered visible in his *Merzbau*, while André Breton, Max Ernst, and a host of artists, writers, and musicians externalized the weird shapes, prose, and sounds of an interior domain.

Architects and urbanists, unable to shrug off their historical mandate, refused this catharsis, countering it with monuments, boundaries, technology; their embrace of modernism was universally selective and limited to an ancient penchant for luminescent absences and kinesis, although never at the expense of a massive erosion in predictability. *La Ville contemporaine*, held together by

10.3　Le Corbusier, *La Ville classée, Les Villes pêle-mêle, La Ville radieuse*, 1935

forms employed since the days of Cardinal Richelieu, was designed as an antidote, not to nineteenth-century Romanticism as Le Corbusier believed, but to the self-same anarchy embraced by modernism that was shredding the shape and life of New York, Paris, Buenos Aires – *les villes pêle-mêle* (Fig. 10.3). Similarly, the other urban utopias of this century without exception reach back in time, espousing a life once led. They represent the opposite of a leap beyond progress, namely, a fear that the randomness that had infected the avant-gardes was escaping the garrets to permeate the streets.

If the master builders were replaying history, then the texts that influenced them, and that laid the groundwork for institutionalized planning, were also anti-modernist. The modern reincarnation of Plato's static, closed-end community has no single intellectual origin, although the 1887 publication of Ferdinand Tönnies's *Gemeinschaft und Gesellschaft*, and Georg Simmel's 1903 essay 'The Great Cities and the Life of the Spirit' were no doubt influential. Each was emphatically nostalgic, although presented in a scientific style that made them persuasive to the practical scholar who made up a large part of the architect's and the planner's self-image. A new element entered urbanist discourse, to accompany the old themes of art and technique, namely, the

oxymoron of the metropolitan community. The problems and scope of urbanism suddenly were inflated to expedite what was essentially mythical, but not recognized as such, and the unsettling effects of this most quixotic of all anti-modernist projects span the twentieth century.

Tönnies, a sociologist, also affected in a direct way the work of Camillo Sitte. Tönnies's theme was cogently expressed in his counter-position of the organized, institutionalized society: *Gesellschaft*, with the organic community: *Gemeinschaft*, whose form and structure are subject to a consensus of the human will. This consensus, the will itself, had been superseded by the social organization that he mistakenly thought is specific to metropolitanization. Organization, Tönnies claimed, is unnatural and inorganic, and undermines a primitive but essential social impulse, one manifested in traditional interdependencies, customs, and the collective memory. With the passing of these things, Sitte was to assert, in *City Planning according to Artistic Principles*, the intuitive basis for art and all cultural expression disappeared for ever. In architecture, he wrote, the 'lost' community principle had been replaced by rationalism, although one whose point of departure was the artificial re-establishment of classical or organic form whose meanings were now devalued beyond recognition. In planning, nostalgic optimism was to be even more striking, permeating the Garden City movement and the self-contradictory anti-urban bias that had existed for some time in America.

Georg Simmel's influence, and to a lesser extent that of Theodor Petermann, were felt in another direction – by German Expressionists like Erich Mendelsohn and Hans Poelzig, and by the Prague group of Josef Gočár and Jiri Kroha. Both Simmel and Petermann polemicized against the loss of individuality that was a consequence of metropolitan existence; unlike Tönnies, however, Simmel was more concerned about the effect of big-city life upon the human psyche than upon communal or cultural matters. Urban man, he claimed, constantly under new pressures from the metropolitan division of labour, from oppressive propinquity with others, and from the impersonality of urban institutions, responded by nurturing a blasé sophistication, a veneer of intellectuality to cover an emotional interior that had become an embarrassment. The world must be objectified, treated with cool detachment or even indifference, as the only way to adjust to constant nervous stimulation. Stable values had disappeared, and were replaced by abstractions of the same order as the monetary economy which was the very cause and foundation of the metropolitan phenomenon. However, Simmel's conclusion was not unequivocally against urban life, because cities were the place where the individual, in psychic self-defence, mustered 'the utmost in uniqueness and particularization.' Here was the place where the individual psyche and psychic freedom were most advanced, despite the rigours of incessant stimulus: 'For here as elsewhere it is by no means necessary that the freedom of man be reflected in his emotional life as comfort.'[4] Freedom, in Simmel's case, required a fluid, kinetic urban structure occupied by those who pursued, in Max Weber's words, conscious alienation. Here, just a trace of the modernist spirit surfaces, but only momentarily.

Given the ambiguous nature of Simmel's conclusions, the architectural and planning community wavered briefly; a few, like Ludwig Mies van der Rohe, were to *equate* sophistication with psychic freedom, and confront the metropolis by producing an architecture seemingly detached from pre-urban emotion and strongly attached to what Simmel had called the levelling of objects: 'All objects float with equal specific gravity in the flux of the monetary economy.'[5] In fact, the Werkbund was almost completely united in its frank acceptance of – and confidence in – its perception of socio-economic fluidity that reputedly underlay the metropolitan condition. August Endell, in his 1908 book *Die Schönheit der grossen Stadt*, just heralded the Futurists in extolling the quasi-natural beauty

of the metropolis, in contrast to his views about its individual buildings. Visual impressiveness should not be sought in the parts that were consciously ordered, but in urban dynamism. These new perceptions had transformed, as Endell comments, even 'Berlin, my city, into a miracle.' In a similar vein, another member of the Werkbund, the art critic Karl Scheffler, praised the money-based metropolis with an uncompromising fervour. His 1913 book *Die Architektur der Grossstadt* was essentially an apology of what was already largely taking place (although temporarily so) in the American metropolis. The city centre belonged to production, not just because it was more efficient that way, but for its symbolic authenticity. Gleaming towers of high finance should dominate the skyline, with manufacturing industry concentrated around. Scheffler prophesied and supported the appearance of a new internationally based style in architecture, as did many of his Werkbund colleagues at the time. For him, a *Weltnutzarchitektur*, the 'expression of the aesthetics of world-wide business and industrial enterprise ... a natural classicism'[6] would proliferate, to become the hallmark of the contemporary metropolis. The stable and the particular were already outdated.

One cannot but think that most of these ideas were rationalizations of industrialism itself. Such inclinations certainly were present in the Werkbund, whose most persistent project was the cause of German industrial competitiveness abroad. But even art tainted by monetary ambition can have some redeeming value. For the most part, the creativity, breadth, and seriousness of the Werkbund enterprise have a place in the annals of aesthetic accomplishment, if only because, for the first time, the tempo of production could be recognized in product shapes, designed to pass smoothly through machines. The Werkbund designers, like Scheffler, had grasped the kinetic future enthusiastically, but it was grounded in material self-interest, and required the organizational boundaries that were anathema to modernism.

So the great builders of our own time, in a
fundamental sense, tried to carry the themes
of history forward. Even the silence and isolation of Mies van der Rohe's towers are by-
products of his obsession with classicism; the
absences everywhere echo back to the dialectic that moulded the Domus Aurea and the
choir of St Denis. They *re-establish* propriety
rather than mock its necessity, and none
comes close, for instance, to the abrogation of
all expectation we read in Mallarmé's 'Un
coup de dés' – a poem of absences, in which
history's events are settled by a throw of the
dice. Of the builders, perhaps only two were
half-prepared to enter the subjective netherworld of modernism: Antonio Gaudi and
Hans Poelzig.

Gaudi, conservative in his ways, an advo-
cate of Catholicism and Catalonia, does violence to many – not all – expectations that
architecture deals in rational wholes, hierarchies of repeatable elements. But beneath the
contorted labyrinths of the Casa Batlló
(1905–7) and the Casa Milá (1905–10) lies a
discipline imposed by the mechanical relations of Barcelona: a development intensity
tied to profit, continuous street boundaries
occupied in the manner of the urban quarter
(Figs 10.4 and 10.5). Only in his design for the
Güell Park (1900–14) is Gaudi able to escape
this discipline (the unfinished Sagrada Familia
church also does, but fails to shed the recollection of a Gothic *summa*). The park is an
inspired canvas, but a canvas nevertheless,
where the artist is free to avoid the rigours of
urban-boundary formation; in so doing,
Gaudi sweeps away some habitual scenery but
only in a precinct sheltered from the problematic questions outside (Fig. 10.6).

Certain predispositions, perhaps, evoked
an entirely different response to the metropolis from Hans Poelzig. For him, Nietzsche was
far closer to the mark than Simmel in proclaiming the inevitability of an *Angst*-laden
future as the price of infinite technical dupli-
cation. Inescapable alienation blankets the
metropolis, where value perishes along with
singularity. There is no recourse anywhere, no

10.4 Antonio Gaudi, Casa Batlló, Barcelona,
1905–7

10.6   Antonio Gaudi, Güell Park, Barcelona, 1900–14

10.5   Antonio Gaudi, Casa Milá, Barcelona, 1905–10

conciliation in art; only anguish remains. What remains then, but to confront anguish, to grasp its horrors, to hold it before the unflinching eye? This is precisely what Poelzig did in a remarkable series of buildings constructed between 1908 and 1912. His Hamburg and Poznan water towers, and the chemical factory in Luban, not only capture all the gracelessness of the metropolis in architecture, but become containers of his own anxieties (Figs 10.7 and 10.8). Their biological references are especially telling: like the metropolis, each building is an insidious organism, rather than a rationally structured edifice. Even his sets for the expressionist film *The Golem* are less sinister in their capacity to chill the spine. They are, after all, a piece of theatre, while his buildings have a serious purpose, yet seem to mock our expectations of rationality and capacity for control over the urban destiny.

Poelzig's intensity and particularization would soon run their course, more rapidly

than it would have done in painting or literature, where expressionism was more at home. Architecture's commodity side usually prohibits the display of personal, or worse, widespread anxiety. How improbable, then, that the young Poelzig could capture the metropolitan netherworld in an uncompromising single act of construction.

If, for a moment, Poelzig, and perhaps Gaudi, could shed the mandate of history to join the ranks of modernism's avant-gardes, as builders they stood alone. Recently, Frederick Karl explored the fascination felt by the avant-gardes with the idea of the *comedian-wizard* as a persona of the artist. Baudelaire's main protagonist is the Dandy, who represents the 'greatness in all follies, a strength in all extravagance.' The figure of Pierrot the clown appears in many guises – on Picasso's canvases; in Arnold Schoenberg's *Pierrot lunaire*, Eliot's Prufrock; Stravinsky's Petruchka; and as Charlie Chaplin. Pierrot, like the medieval jester, points to an absurd world, noticing truths that others refuse to see.[7] But no one heard Gaudi, and Poelzig was too unpalatable, so urbanism had no Pierrot to call its own. The master builders may have warned of disintegration, but their advocacy of Pure Form never bridged the chasm between the modernists and themselves. To the builders, order, technology, and reason could never be a source of parody, and the illusions required by action made serious men of every one. A Pierrot, at least, could have played the harbinger, because the actions of these men were overwhelmed by the impending course of metropolitan formation itself, which could have been fashioned by some weird partnership of Marinetti and de Chirico, to become a binary parody of Futurism and Surrealism. So the ancient dialectic gives way to a volatile shapelessness in which we stand apart from each other, the whole sanctioned by the pursuit, not of freedom, but of self interest, embodied most of all in an absence of certain things – of the carnivalesque, of communal pleasures, of subversive laughter.

The Family as Metropolitan Hero

It may seem a far cry from *The Golem* to the planning of today, but if Hans Poelzig could compress into his architecture all the symptoms of a retreat into the self, the passage of time shows his work to have been an augury of what would happen to urbanism, which has been turned into a means of sterilizing all boundaries, of dealing with what economists now call *externalities*. But this poor word captures the opposite of what used to be urbanism's purpose.

For the most part, the old dialectic was played out reflexively, as in the Imperial cities of late antiquity, without people being fully conscious, perhaps, of the fact that towns were laid out and buildings raised according to their impulse to enter into or seek seclusion from the world. It is true, tyrants or institutions tended to subvert this process on occasion, and some now would say that such was always and everywhere the case, although we are not obliged to believe them. It is possible to sense, even in certain cities where civic liberties were hemmed in by rules, that the constructed landscape was carved into what Philippe Ariès called *domains*: 'neither public nor private, as these terms are understood today; rather [they were] both simultaneously.'[8] Consider once more the shaping of

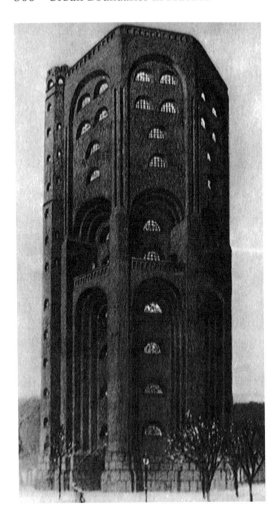

10.7 Hans Poelzig, project for a Hamburg watertower, ca 1910

10.8 Hans Poelzig, chemical factory, Luban, Poland, 1911–12

Rome; Giambattista Nolli's famous 1748 plan shows a palimpsest of styles reaching back two millennia, each bridge, square, lane, precinct, and avenue an embellishment to the city's remarkable *porosity* (Fig. 10.9). Rome served more than the aspirations of kings and priests; it was also shaped to sustain banal, practical cohabitation: 'The role of the family was to strengthen the authority of the head of the household, without threatening the stability of his relationship with the community. Married women would gather at the wash house; men at the cabaret. Each sex had its special place in church, in processions, in the public square, at celebrations, and even at the dance. But the family as such had no domain of its own; the only real domain was what each male won by his maneuvering, with the help of his wife, his friends, and dependents.'[9]

We do not need to admire this male-dominated existence to perceive that the city had a purpose that penetrated the thresholds of home and work, and was constructed accordingly. So while Rome had a few areas set apart for exclusive activities, the rest, including the stores, hovels, apartments, and workshops that lined the arteries and the processional avenues joining the basilicas, coalesced into a single, highly permeable domain. This city, long before 1748 and for almost two centuries thereafter, sustained and symbolized a particular way of life, one oriented outwards to a sea of interdependencies.

Any recognition that the way of life in eighteenth-century Rome might have been racked by narrowness, suspicion, and venality should not stop the curious from asking why it was swept away, nor from asking whether our way is any better. Most of all, we should wish to know whether the city was only an inert vessel, a passive manifestation of the life it contained, or whether it somehow worked back upon that life, refashioning it wherever touched by the city's contingencies. Must one be accused of old-fashioned determinism to question the validity of making an absolute distinction between urban life and urban form? To be sure, the analogy of art, in which

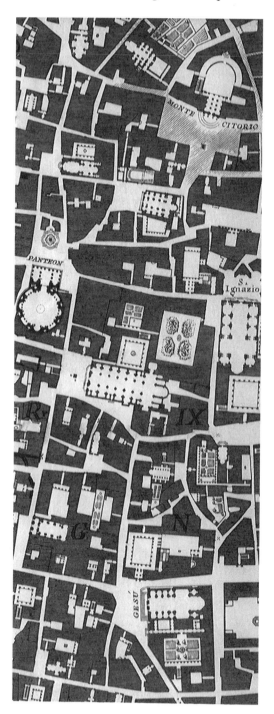

10.9   Giambattista Nolli, *Nuova Pianta di Roma*, 1748

form is completely fused to content, cannot apply to the urban condition, but like art, in the raising of cities do we understand what we are making, and are we not mostly innocent of how that creation alters life by creeping up on it from behind?

If the case of Nolli's Rome is too shrouded in nostalgia to provide any clarity, think of the contemporary American metropolis. That branch of modern analysis which sees metropolitan formation as the product of industrial and corporate capital is being outflanked by another, occupied by those who place the consumer, and above all the American family, at the helm. Whether or not the interests of production and consumption can really be separated, in the chaotic history of urbanism, modern legend attributes enormous status and cogency to the family in shaping the metropolis, which turns out to be everything that Nolli's Rome was not.

Just when the urbanizing surge in America gathered momentum a century ago, Frederick Law Olmstead observed: 'Probably the advantages of civilization can be found illustrated and demonstrated under no other circumstances so completely as in some suburban neighbourhoods where each family abode stands fifty or a hundred feet or more apart from all the others, and at some distance from the public road.'[10]

Yet during this same period, the urban rowhouse was still preferred even by the wealthy, whether in Boston, New York, St Louis, or much smaller towns.[11] But Olmstead's views began to be echoed by many others as the radial streetcar lines, then the automobile began to deposit countless numbers of households across the urban hinterland. Simultaneously, family life itself, which had until then been regarded as a necessary and desirable state, but no more, began to be an object of some piety, its alleged virtues expanding in pace with the spreading metropolitan landscape. By 1970, the United States became the first nation in history whose population was predominantly suburban,[12] while the veneration of family life has grown to a crescendo of eulogies given from pulpits and in advertising and social work, the popular media and political rhetoric.

As we have seen, through history the idea of each city was usually enmeshed with some founding mythical hero or other, around whom legends and ritual accumulated in a recurrent showing of the conviction that cities must be transcendentally ordained and protected. Etruscan Rome had Romulus and Remus, then St Peter to sustain its life force, and the city took its shape around their presence, her monuments, spaces, and boundaries a persistent reminder that the empirical world cannot be voided of mythic content. In the metropolis, the family has not so much taken on this role of founding hero as had the task thrust unsolicited upon it, for what else remains in the modern world as a persuasive object of veneration?

First, the family is deemed to possess a unique blend of innocence, strength, and durability. However corrupt and fractious we may know it often to be, the *idea* of the family continues to wax in the popular imagination as the last resort, an unsinkable island in a sea of trouble. Then, in a self-perpetuating cycle, as the porous city gives way to spatial fragmentation through the vicissitudes of suburbanization, the insularity of the household is itself deemed a blessing allegedly forged to serve family life, which has little choice but to adapt to further rounds of insularity. So the extensive mechanical relations of centrifugal development are handed a putative legitimacy that sustains and is sustained by the American dream.[13]

The sequence of events in a process which reversed the former outward orientation of the family to one of inwardness has been well scrutinized by Philippe Ariès. Unlike Rome, the metropolis has not been shaped around the presence of some reluctant hero, but according to a market logic which then is accorded legitimacy in the family's alleged need for complete insularity. 'When the city ... deteriorated and lost its vitality, the role of the family overexpanded like a hypertrophied cell.'[14] Whereas emotional attention used to be spread over a diversity of things – the natural world, supernatural objects, the communal domain, they are now focused on the immediate family, which exchanges an external system of politics for an internal one.[15]

The constitua of urban development are now assigned to their respective niches according to procedures dominated by the internalization of externalities, while the metropolis, far from being an inert vessel, works its way into the family psyche, propagandizing the values and forms of behaviour necessary to existence in an internally divided territory. Thus, closed boundaries are legitimized in the idea of the home-as-haven, in which emotional and economic self-containment find their confirmation in centrifugal urbanism and architecture. So only amid the symbols of the single detached house does the family come to rest. Because the suburban house cannot signify a world beyond itself, its finality suggests an end to the kinetic centrifuge of metropolitan formation; architecture, once protean, loses its historic momentum in order to proclaim itself as an anchor in a sea of human restlessness. Its boundaries are absolute, apostematic. Untempered by the socializing rhythms, by any connection to threshold zones, to special liminal places where life was once renewed and blessed as well in moments of epiphany; nor by connection to the once-great armatures, those festive seams that traversed the city and where urbanism's shapes and symbols were brought to an apotheosis in a spectacular denial of human insularity.

If the metropolitan family had indeed brought us to the end of Western urbanism there could be no talk of recurrence, nor of any stubbornness in that human aspiration for the complementary of things. Yet the industrial metropolis and its hero are already afflicted by an excess of nutrition, and the ideology that sustains them wears thin as the century nears its close. Here and there professional urbanism itself already shrugs off its servile mandate as a new generation enters its ranks, critical of a hundred-year legacy of administrative rationalism and of the part planning has played in extending, then partitioning, the urban realm. These young men and women reach back in time, to older legacies – not just to history's forms and styles, but to agreements about ways of doing things that are fixed in moral consciousness to transcend the politics that has denied a place for otherness. Only a fragile sign, a flicker of light in a professional corner, but it has been ignited by larger events that seem to shift the century from its axis, and may foreshadow an end to the metropolitan cycle in the West.

Notes

CHAPTER ONE

1 Hannah Arendt, *The Human Condition* (Chicago: University of Chicago Press 1958), 252

2 Homer, *Iliad*, translated by E.V. Rieu (Harmondsworth: Penguin 1950), Book XVIII

3 Ibid, Book VII

4 Ibid, Book V

5 Hans-Georg Gadamer expounds the Platonic and Aristotelian concepts of practice most clearly in *Reason in the Age of Science*, trans. by Frederick G. Lawrence (Cambridge, MA: MIT Press 1981), 75–92

6 David Gosling and Barry Maitland, *Concepts of Urban Design* (London: Academy 1984)

7 Louis Wirth, 'Urbanism as a Way of Life,' reprinted in R. Sennett, *Classic Essays on the Culture of Cities* (New York: Appleton-Century-Croft 1969), 153ff.

8 John Summerson, *Heavenly Mansions, and Other Essays on Architecture* (New York: Norton 1963)

9 Dimitri Porphyrios, 'On Critical History,' in *Architecture, Criticism, Ideology* (Princeton, NJ: Princeton University Press 1985), 16

10 Ibid, 17

11 Northrop Frye, *Words with Power* (Toronto: Viking Press 1990); Claude Lévi-Strauss, *The Raw and the Cooked* (New York: Harper and Row 1970), 139

12 Ernst Cassirer, *The Philosophy of Symbolic Forms*, vol. 3: *The Phenomenology of Knowledge* (New Haven, CT: Yale University Press 1957), 62–3

13 Ibid, 73

14 Ernst Cassirer, *An Essay on Man* (New Haven, CT: Yale University Press 1944), 82

15 Plato, *The Sophist*, translated by Charles Bernstein (Los Angeles: Sun and Moon Press 1987), 259

16 Ernst Cassirer, *Language and Myth* (New York: Dover 1953), 91

17 Ernst Cassirer, 'Mind and Life: Heidegger,' *Philosophy and Rhetoric* 16 (1983), 162

18 Cassirer, *The Philosophy of Symbolic Forms*, vol. 3, 448

19 Maurice Merleau-Ponty, *Phenomenology of Perception* (London: Routledge and Kegan Paul 1962), 127

20 Cassirer, *The Philosophy of Symbolic Forms*, vol. 3, 72

21 R.H. Hook, 'Fantasy and Symbol: A Psychoanalytic Point of View,' in *Fantasy and Symbol: Studies in Anthropological Interpretation*, ed. by R.H. Hook (New York: Academic Press 1979), 277

22 Alfred Lorenzer, *Kritik des Psycho-analylischen Symbolbegriffs* (Frankfurt: Suhrkamp Verlag 1970), 50–1

23 Cassirer, *The Philosophy of Symbolic Forms*, vol. 1: *Language*, 83–4; vol. 2: *Mythic Thought*, xv–xvi

24 John Michael Krois, *Cassirer: Symbolic Forms and History* (New Haven, CT: Yale University Press 1989), 85

25 Cassirer, *The Philosophy of Symbolic Forms*, vol. 2, 157

26 Ibid, 86

27 Cassirer, *The Philosophy of Symbolic Forms*, vol. 3, 72

28 John Ruskin, *The Seven Lamps of Architecture* (1849; London: George Allen 1903), 112

29 Ibid, 117

30 See, for instance, Colin Rowe's astute *comparison* of transparency in architecture and painting; his *attribution* of early modernist transparency in construction to Cubism, however, is misleading: 'Transparency: Literal and Phenomenal,' in *The Mathematics of the Ideal Villa and Other Essays*, 159–84 (Cambridge, MA: MIT Press 1976).

31 Jacquetta Hawkes and Leonard Woolley, *Prehistory and the Dawn of Civilization* (New York and Evanston: Harper and Row 1963), 206

32 Envico Guidoni, 'Artifacts,' in *Primitive Architecture* (New York: Harry N. Abrams 1975), 213

33 Ibid, 108

34 Rebecca Lok, 'The House as Microcosm,' in *The Leiden Tradition in Structural Anthropology*, ed. by R. de Riddler and J.A.J. Karremans, 211–33 (Leiden: E.J. Brill 1987)

35 J.P. Lebeuf, *L'Habitation des Fali, Montagnards du Cameroun Septentrional* (Paris: Hachette 1961). Anthropomorphism is a pervasive organizing factor in the well-known case of the Dogon settlements in Mali, best studied by M. Griaule and first explained in his *Dieu d'eau* (Paris: Editions du Chene 1949); translation: *Conversations with Ogotemmeli: An Introduction to Dogon Ideas* (London: Oxford University Press 1965).

36 Guidoni, *Primitive Architecture*, is exemplary in its global account of politics and meaning in primitive architecture. Amos Rapoport, *House Form and Culture* (Englewood Cliffs, NJ: Prentice-Hall 1969), while critical of the functional-material approach to architectural analysis, resorts to a rather ethnocentric 'possibilist' theory of house form in which 'choices' are made by builders from a wide context of variables (18–45).

37 Hawkes and Woolley, *Prehistory and the Beginnings of Civilization*, 705–9. Siegfried Giedion, in *The Beginnings of Architecture* (1964; Princeton, NJ: Princeton University Press 1981), refers to the great stele at Ur, depicting Ur-Nammu the king 'as a royal craftsman, carrying a pickaxe on his shoulder … Above him sits the moon-god (Nannar) upon his throne.' The god holds a measuring rod and line (p. 224). A builder-god, of course, apologizes to no one.

38 Samuel Noah Kramer, *The Sumerians* (Chicago: University of Chicago Press 1963), 137–40

39 Samuel Noah Kramer, *History Begins at Sumer* (London: Thames and Hudson 1961), 157

40 Kramer, *The Sumerians*, 81–3

41 Ibid, 82

42 John Gallery distinguishes the pre-autocratic 'towns' (pre-2500 B.C.), with their open-ended, organic structures, from the later 'cities': 'Town Planning and Community Structure,' in *The Legacy of Sumer*, ed. by Denise Schmandt-Bessarat, 69–77 (Malibu, CA: Undena 1976)

43 Hawkes and Woolley, *Prehistory and the Beginnings of Civilization*, 423

44 Claude Lévi-Strauss, *Structural Anthropology*, vol. 2 (New York: Basic Books 1976), 146–97

CHAPTER TWO

1 Marcus Aurelius, *Meditations*, translated by A.S.L. Farquharson (Oxford: Oxford University Press), 33

2 A. Leroi-Gourhan, *Le Geste et la Parole* (Paris: A. Michel 1965), 270

3 Erwin Panofsky, *Abbot Suger: On the Abbey Church of St. Denis and Its Art Treasures* (Princeton, NJ: Princeton University Press 1946), 24

4 Ibid, 51

5 E. Minkowski, *Vers une cosmologie: Fragments philosophiques* (Paris, 1967), 191; quoted in J. Rykwert, *The Idea of a Town: The Anthropology of Urban Form in Rome* (Princeton, NJ: Princeton University Press 1976), 195

6 Rykwert, *The Idea of a Town*, 190

7 Ibid

8 Susan Sontag, 'Against Interpretation,' in *Against Interpretation: and Other Essays* (New York: Farrar, Strauss and Giroux 1966), 1ff

9 Erich Auerbach, *Mimesis* (Princeton, NJ: Princeton University Press 1953)

10 J.J. Coulton, *Greek Architects at Work* (Ithaca, NJ: Cornell University Press 1977), 126–7

11 Walter Abell, *The Collective Dream in Art* (New York: Schocken Books 1966), 95

12 Ibid, 96

13 Andrew Robert Burn, *Pericles and Athens* (New York: Collier Books 1962)

14 Kevin Lynch, *A Theory of Good City Form* (Cambridge, MA: MIT Press 1981), 293–317

15 Henri Lefebvre, *Everyday Life in the Modern World*, translated by Sacha Rabinovitch (New York: Harper and Row 1971), 18

16 Quoted in Christopher Hussey, *Life of Sir Edwin Lutyens* (London and New York: Country Life 1950), 134–5

17 Andrea Palladio, *The Four Books of Architecture* (New York: Dover 1965), Book 1, ch. 2, 1

18 Ibid, Book 1, ch. 15, 12

19 A.J. Greimas, *Sémantique structurale: Recherche de méthode* (Paris: Librairie Larousse 1966)

20 Alan Colquhoun, *Essays in Architectural Criticism: Modern Architecture and Historical Change* (Cambridge, MA: MIT Press 1981), 132–3

21 Cf. Kenneth Frampton, 'The New Regionalism,' in *The Anti-Aesthetic: Essays on Postmodern Culture*, ed. by Hal Foster, 16–30 (Port Townsend, WA: Bay Press 1983)

22 Greimas, *Sémantique structurale*, 205

23 Paul Ricoeur, *Hermeneutics and the Human Sciences* (Cambridge: Cambridge University Press 1981), 285

24 Northrop Frye, *Anatomy of Criticism* (Princeton, NJ: Princeton University Press 1957), 97

25 Colquhoun, *Essays in Architectural Criticism*, 180

26 Ibid

27 Ibid

28 Ibid, 181

29 Nikolaus Pevsner, *The Englishness of English Art* (Harmondsworth: Penguin Books 1964), 18–20

30 Ibid, 79

31 Maurice Beresford, *The Lost Villages of England* (Oxford: Lutterworth Press 1954)

32 Penelope Lively, *The Presence of the Past* (Glasgow: William Collins Sons 1976), 91

33 Pevsner, *The Englishness of English Art*, 143

34 Cited in E.A. Gutkind, *International History of City Development*, vol. 6 (New York: Free Press of Glencoe 1964–7), 264

CHAPTER THREE

1 Allen J. Scott, *The Urban Land Nexus and the State* (London: Pion 1979), 28–54

2 Marcus Aurelius, *Meditations*, translated by A.S.L. Farquharson (Oxford: Oxford University Press 1990), 41

3 David Herlihy, *The Medieval City* (New Haven, CT: Yale University Press 1977), 13

4 Denis E. Cosgrove, *Social Formation and Symbolic Landscape* (London: Croom Helm 1984), 91

5 John Ruskin, *Unto This Last: The Political Economy of Art* (London: Dent 1968)

6 Plato, *The Laws*, translated by A.E. Taylor (London: Dent 1960), 779b

7 J. Rykwert, *The Idea of a Town: The Anthropology of Urban Form in Rome*

(Princeton, NJ: Princeton University Press 1976), 99

8　Ibid, 43

9　John Summerson, *Heavenly Mansions, and Other Essays on Architecture* (New York: Norton 1963)

10　Wolfgang Braunfels, *Urban Design in Western Europe* (Chicago: University of Chicago Press 1988), 314

11　Ibid, 117

12　Johann Wolfgang von Goethe, *Italienische Reise, 1786–1788* (Munich: Hirmer 1960), 556

13　Hannah Arendt, *The Human Condition* (Chicago: University of Chicago Press 1958), 292–3

14　Numa Denis Fustel de Coulanges, *The Ancient City* (New York: Anchor 1956), 252

15　Arendt, *The Human Condition*, 27

16　Fustel de Coulanges, *The Ancient City*, 63

17　Arendt, *The Human Condition*, 35

18　Arnold van Gennep, *Rites of Passage* (Chicago: University of Chicago Press 1960)

19　Robert L. Moore, 'Ritual, Sacred Space, and Healing,' in *Liminality and Transitional Phenomena*, ed. by Nathan Schwartz-Salant and Murray Stein (Wilmette, IL: Chiron Publications 1991), 22

20　Ibid, 16–17

CHAPTER FOUR

1　Friedrich Nietzsche, *Twilight of the Idols: The Problem of Socrates*, translated by R.J. Hollingdale (Harmondsworth: Penguin 1968), 1

2　J.J. Rousseau, *Essai sur l'origine des langues* (Paris: Hatier 1983), 111

3　Pliny, *Historia naturalis*, 12.1. Cited in Carl Boetticher, *Der Baumkultus der Hellenen* (Berlin, 1859), 9

4　George Hersey, *The Lost Meaning of Classical Architecture* (Cambridge, MA: MIT Press 1988), 11

5　Ibid

6　Ibid, 18

7　Walter Burket, *Homo necans: The Anthropology of Ancient Greek Sacrificial Ritual and Myth* (Berkeley: University of California Press 1983)

8　Hersey, *The Lost Meaning of Classical Architecture*, 21–43

9　Ibid, 23

10　Plato, *The Laws*, 302a

11　Vincent J. Scully, *The Earth, the Temple, and the Gods* (New York: Praeger 1969), 193–8

12　Homer, *The Homeric Hymns*: Loeb Classical Library (New York: Macmillan 1914), 456

13　Aeschylus, *The Oresteian Trilogy: The Eumenides*, translated by A.J. Podlecki (Warminster: Aris and Phillips 1987), 1007–13

14　Scully, *The Earth, the Temple, and the Gods*, 4

15　Ibid

16　Roland Martin, *L'Urbanisme dans La Grèce Antique*, augmented 2d ed. (Paris: Editions A.E.J., Picard et Cie 1974)

17　Ibid, 332

18　Pierre Lavedan, *Histoire d'Urbanisme* (Paris: H. Laurens 1966), vol. 1, 154

19　Martin, *L'Urbanisme dans La Grèce Antique*, 103–6

20　Scully, *The Earth, the Temple, and the Gods*, 43–5

21　Cited in J. Rykwert, *The Idea of a Town: The Anthropology of Urban Form in Rome* (Princeton, NJ: Princeton University Press 1976), 30

22　Ibid, 32

23　Ibid, 43

24　Ibid, 99

25　Ibid, 70

26　Scully, *The Earth, the Temple, and the Gods*, 13

27　Dora Konsola, in *Early Helladic Architecture and Urbanization*, proceedings of a seminar held at the Swedish Institute in Athens, 8 June 1985, 14–15. The period E.H. II also shows evidence of sophisticated regulation of construction and planning.

28　Joseph Rykwert, *On Adam's House in Paradise* (New York: Museum of Modern Art 1972), 166

29　William R. Lethaby, *An Introduction to the History and Theory of the Art of Building*

(London: Williams and Norgate 1912?), 10–19, 35–6, 201–2

30 Rykwert, *Adam's House*, 192

31 Scully, *The Earth, the Temple, and the Gods*, 50

32 Hippocrates, *Air, Water, and Location*, translated by Francis Clifton (London: J. Watts 1734), 389

33 Esther V. Hansen, *The Attalids of Pergamon* (Ithaca, NY: Cornell University Press 1941), 219–74

34 Martin, *L'Urbanisme dans La Grèce Antique*, 127–51

35 Ibid, 150–1

36 H.W. Parke, *Greek Oracles* (London: Hutchinson 1967), 47–87

37 Ibid, 84

38 John Boardman, 'The Parthenon Frieze,' in *Parthenon-Kongress (Basel)*, ed. by Ernst Berger (Mainz: von Zabern 1984), 210–11

39 Pauline Schmitt-Pantel, 'Collective Activities and the Political in the Greek City,' in *The Greek City from Homer to Alexander*, ed. by Oswyn Murray and Simon Price (Oxford: Oxford University Press 1990), 200

40 Xenophon, *Hellenica*, translated by Theodore Horn (Bristol: Bristol Classical Press 1978), 2.4, 20–1

41 Xenophon, *Oeconomicus*, translated by Carnes Lord (Ithaca, NY: Cornell University Press 1976), 4.203

42 Moses I. Finley, *Early Greece: The Bronze and Archaic Ages* (London: Chatto and Windus 1970), 30

43 Schmitt-Pantel, 'Collective Activities and the Political,' 207

44 Wolfram Hoepfner and Ernst-Ludwig Schwandner, *Haus und Stad tim Klassischen Griechenland* (Munich: Deutscher Kunstverlag 1985); T.D. Boyd, 'Town-planning in Greece and Rome,' in *Civilizations of the Ancient Mediterranean: Greece and Rome*, ed. by M. Grant and R. Kirzinger (New York: Scribner's 1988)

45 Michael Jameson, 'Private Space and the Greek City,' in *The Greek City from Homer to Alexander*, ed. by Murray and Simon, 178–9

46 Jean-Pierre Vernant and Pierre Vidal-Naquet, *Tragedy and Myth in Ancient Greece* (Brighton: Harvester Press 1981), 14

47 Pierre Vidal-Naquet, *The Black Hunter* (Baltimore, MD: Johns Hopkins University Press 1986), 159–248; see also Moses I. Finley, *Politics in the Ancient World* (Cambridge: Cambridge University Press 1983)

48 Vidal-Naquet, *The Black Hunter*, 147–8

49 Aristophanes, *Frogs*; Aelius Aristides, *Panathenaicus*

50 Vidal-Naquet, *The Black Hunter*, 108

51 Jean Pierre Vernant, *Myth and Thought among the Greeks* (London: Routledge and Kegan Paul 1983), 133

52 Ibid, 142

53 Aeschylus, *Agamemnon*, translated by Hugh-Lloyd-Jones (Englewood Cliffs, NJ: Prentice-Hall 1970), 965

54 Hoepfner and Schwandner, *Haus und Stad tim Klassischen Griechenland*. Refer also to a discussion of their claim in *Demokratie und Architektur: Der hippodamische Städtebau und die Entstehung der Demokratie*. Symposium of Constance, 17–19 July 1987 (Munich: Deutscher Kunstverlag 1989), esp. 63–8, 112–16

55 Jameson, 'Private Space and the Greek City,' 188–91

56 Ibid, 193

CHAPTER FIVE

1 Giuseppe Ungaretti, 'Sentimento del Tempo,' in *Selected Poems of Guiseppe Ungaretti*, ed. by A. Mandelbaum (Ithaca, NY: Cornell University Press 1975)

2 R.L. Scranton, *Greek Walls* (Cambridge, MA: Harvard University Press 1941), 21ff

3 F.E. Winter, *Greek Fortifications* (Toronto: University of Toronto Press 1971), 79–80

4 Axel Boethius, *The Golden House of Nero* (Ann Arbor: University of Michigan Press 1960), 96

5 *Epist.* i, 10, 22–5 (Loeb Classical Library), cited in ibid, 103

6 Lucretius, *De Rerum Natura*, translated by

Martin Ferguson Smith (Cambridge, MA: Harvard University Press), 5. 1370–7

7 Virgil, *The Georgics*, translated by L.P. Wilkinson (Harmondsworth: Penguin 1982), 4: 219–27

8 Cited in Miriam T. Griffin, *Nero: The End of a Dynasty* (New Haven and London: Yale University Press 1984), 129

9 Ibid

10 C.C. van Essen, 'La Topographie de la Domus Aurea Neronis,' *Medelingen der Koninklijke Nederlande Akademie van Wetenschappen* 17/12 (1954), 371f

11 Griffin, *Nero*, 129

12 J. Ward-Perkins, 'Nero's Golden House,' *Antiquity* (30 Dec. 1956), 209ff

13 Pierre Grimal, *Les Jardins romains* (Paris: Presses universitaires de France 1943)

14 Martial, *Liber de spectaculis* 2, cited in Griffin, *Nero*, 138

15 Ward-Perkins, 'Nero's Golden House,' 102–3

16 Ibid, 112

17 John Stambough, *The Ancient Roman City* (Baltimore, MD: Johns Hopkins University Press 1988), 90

18 Ibid, 185

19. Boethius, *The Golden House of Nero*, 179

20 Aeschylus, *The Oresteian Trilogy: The Eumenides*, translated by A.J. Podlecki (Warminster: Aris and Phillips 1987), 531–5

21 William L. MacDonald, *The Architecture of the Roman Empire*, vol. 2: *An Urban Appraisal* (New Haven and London: Yale University Press 1986), 1

22 Ibid, 5

23 Ibid, 18

24 Ibid, 139

25 Claude Lévi-Strauss notes how similar this definition is to certain Buddhist and Hindu doctrine, as well as to the principle which sustains 'illiterate' societies: *The View from Afar* (New York: Basic Books 1985), 283–4

26 Yvon Thébert, 'Private Life and Domestic Architecture in Roman Africa,' in *A History of Private Life*, ed. by Philippe Ariès and Georges Duby (Cambridge, MA: Harvard University Press 1987), vol. 1, 373

27 Cicero, *De oratore*, iii.46 (180). Cited in Boethius, *The Golden House of Nero*, 132

28 Wolfgang Braunfels, *Mittelalterliche Stadtbaukunst in der Toskana* (Berlin: Verlag Gebr. Mann 1966), 88

CHAPTER SIX

1 Hans-Georg Gadamer, *Reason in the Age of Science* (Cambridge, MA: MIT Press 1986), 33

2 Jean Hubert, Jean Porcher, and W.F. Volbach, *Europe of the Invasions* (New York: George Braziller 1969), 13

3 Michel Rouche, 'The Early Middle Ages in the West,' in *A History of Private Life*, ed. by Philippe Ariès and Georges Duby (Cambridge, MA: Harvard University Press 1987), vol. 1, 423

4 Ibid, 429

5 Hubert, Porcher, and Volbach, *Europe of the Invasions*, 34–5

6 Judith W. George, *Venantius Fortunatus: A Latin Poet in Merovingian Gaul* (Oxford: Clarendon Press 1992)

7 Peter Brown, 'Late Antiquity,' in *A History of Private Life*, ed. by Ariès and Duby, vol. 1, 287

8 Cited in Lorna Price, *The Plan of St. Gall in Brief* (Berkeley, CA: University of California Press 1982), 24

9 Victor W. Turner, *The Ritual Process: Structure and Anti-structure* (Chicago: Aldine 1969), 94–130

10 Ibid, 107

11 Mary Wolff-Salin, *The Shadow Side of Community and the Growth of Self* (New York: Crossroads 1988), 146

12 C.G. Jung, 'The Psychology of Transference Interpreted in Conjunction with a Set of Alchemical Pictures,' *The Practice of Psychotherapy*, 2d ed., trans. by R.F.C. Hull (New York: Princeton University Press 1966), para. 444

13 Wolff-Salin, *The Shadow Side of Community*, 143

14 Derwas J. Chitty, *The Desert a City: An Introduction to the Study of Egyptian and Palestinian Monasticism under the Christian*

Empire (Oxford: Basil Blackwell 1966), 22

15 Ibid, 54

16 *St. Benedict's Rule of Monasteries*. trans. by Leonard J. Doyle (Collegeville, MI: The Liturgical Press 1948), ch. 58

17 Possibly Benedict of Aniane, principal monastic reformer to Louis the Pious. Wolfgang Braunfels covers the monastic evolution admirably in his *Monasteries of Western Europe* (London: Thames and Hudson 1972).

18 Michael Dennis, *Court and Garden: From the French Hôtel to the City of Modern Architecture* (Cambridge, MA: MIT Press 1986), 73–87

19 Cited in Jeremy duQuesnay Adams, *Patterns of Medieval Society* (Englewood Cliffs, NJ: Prentice-Hall 1969), 14–16

20 David Herlihy, *Pisa in the Early Renaissance* (1958; Port Washington, New York, and London: Kennikat Press 1973), 35; Wolfgang Braunfels, *Mittelalterliche Stadtbaukunst in der Toskana* (Berlin: Vertag Gebr. Mann 1966), 178–9

21 Josiah Cox Russell, *Medieval Regions and Their Cities* (Newton Abbot: David and Charles 1972), 42. Russell, like Herlihy, relies on K.J. Beloch's *Bevölkerungsgeschichte Italiens* (Berlin: W. de Gruyter 1937–61) for many of his demographic sources.

22 Ibid, 63–4

23 D. Waley, *The Italian City Republics* (New York: McGraw-Hill 1969), 56

24 Ibid, 66. The classic work on the communes is J.C.L. Sismondi's *A Story of the Italian Republics* (1832; Garden City, NJ: Doubleday 1966)

25 Imre John Joseph Koroknay, 'Functional Differentiation of Medieval Main Squares in Northern and Central Italy,' unpublished MSC (P1) thesis, University of Toronto, 1972, 146

26 Braunfels, *Mittelalterliche Stadtbaukunst*, 146

27 Axel Boethius, *The Golden House of Nero*, 132ff

28 The few exceptions included, of course, the colonization programs conducted in Central Europe and, under Edward I of England, in Gascony and elsewhere. See F. Rörig, *The Medieval Town* (Berkeley and Los Angeles: University of California Press 1969), 15–16; M. Beresford, *New Towns of the Middle Ages: Town Plantations in England, Wales and Gascony* (London: Lutterworth Press 1967). Nevertheless, Beresford is of the opinion that the *Bastide* grid system was derived more from short-term commercial interests (like the pattern of American Mid-Western towns) than long-term vision (pp. 55, 60).

29 Diane Owen Hughes, 'Kinsmen and Neighbors in Medieval Genoa,' in *The Medieval City*, ed by Harry A. Miskimin, David Herlihy, and A.L. Udovitch (New Haven and London: Yale University Press 1977), 95–111

30 Jacques Heers, *Le Clan familial au Moyen Age* (Paris: Presses universitaires de France 1974), 149. The French term *compaignie* originally referred to such clans, as Philippe de Beaumanoir (1250?–96) recorded in *Coutumes du Beauvaisis*: 'For *compaignie* can be established, according to our customs, simply by dwelling together, from one bread and one pot, for a year and a day, after which the movable property of both parties is considered as one' (cited in Adams, *Patterns of Medieval Society*, 28).

31 Magni, *Bullarium Romanum*, IV, 717 (31 March 1425), cited in Braunfels, *Mittelalterliche Stadtbaukunst*, 91 fn. 275

32 Braunfels, *Mittelalterliche Stadtbaukunst*, 91

33 Ibid, 127 fn. 474

34 Walter Paatz, *Werden und Wesen der Trecento Architektur in Toskana* (Florence: Burg b.M. 1937), 81, 101

35 Cesare Guasti, *Santa Maria del Fiori* (1887: Bologna: A. Formi 1974), 9

36 Ibid, 185, 286

37 Braunfels (*Mittelalterliche Stadtbaukunst*, 116) refers to the municipal order of 1363, prohibiting extensions on the cathedral piazza, as characteristic of the stringency with which the authorities regulated growth.

But the final shape of the piazza tells a different story.

38 Carl Frey, *Loggia dei Lanzi* (Berlin: 1885), 195, cited in Braunfels, *Mittelalterliche Stadtbaukunst*, 118–19

39 Frey, *Loggin dei Lanzi*, 244

40 Braunfels, *Mittelalterliche Stadtbaukunst*, 120–1

41 Lando Bortolotti, *Siena* (Bari: Laterza 1982), 20

42 William M. Bowsky, *A Medieval Italian Commune: Siena under the Nine, 1287–1355* (Berkeley: University of California Press 1981), 17–18

43 William M. Bowsky, 'The Medieval Commune and Internal Violence: Police Power and Public Safety in Siena, 1287–1355,' *American Historical Review* 73 (1967), 1–17

44 Wolfgang Braunfels, *Urban Design in Western Europe: Regime and Architecture, 900–1900* (Chicago and London: University of Chicago Press 1988), 66–8

45 From an undated early fifteenth-century proclamation issued by the Sienese *Officiali de l'Ornato*: ibid, document no. 10, 254

46 Braunfels (*Mittelalterliche Stadtbaukunst*, 231) is of the opinion that the stone masons Donato, Lapo, and Gori had been granted similar privileges by Siena in 1271–2, although never recorded or confirmed by statute. Pisa gave Giovanni the same immunity when he migrated there in 1297 to work on the cathedral choir.

47 Bowsky, *A Medieval Italian Commune*, 266

48 Helene Wieruszowski, 'Art and the Commune in the Time of Dante,' *Speculum* 19 (1944), 14–33

49 F. Donati, 'Il palazzo del comune di Siena,' *Boll. Senese di Storia Patria* 2 (1904), 322

50 Recorded in Siena archives, 1309/10 statutes, Dist. I, Rubr. 83

51 Ibid

52 Braunfels, *Mittelalterliche Stadtbaukunst*, 121

53 Siena archives, Concistoro 2111, ch. 197

54 Ibid, 1262 statute, Dist. III, Rubr. 195

55 Braunfels, *Mittelalterliche Stadtbaukunst*, 124

56 Siena archives, Consiglio Generale, Deliberatione, vol. 160, ch. 37

57 Braunfels (*Urban Design in Western Europe*, 68) notes that the city employed officials whose sole task was to sell the disused towers and walls to private citizens.

58 Bowsky, *A Medieval Italian Commune*, 266

59 Bortolotti, *Siena*, 25

60 Braunfels, *Mittelalterliche Stadtbaukunst*, 257

61 Ibid, 157–8

62 Harald Keller, *Die Bauplastik des Sieneser Doms: Studien zu Giovanni Pisano und seiner Kunstlerischen Nachfolge* (Kunstgesch: Jahrbuch d. Bibl. Hertziana I 1937), 39–122

63 Braunfels, *Mittelalterliche Stadtbaukunst*, 159

64 Bortolotti, *Siena*, 38

65 Braunfels, *Mittelalterliche Stadtbaukunst*, 160–7

66 Ibid, 162

67 Bowsky, *A Medieval Italian Commune*, 292

68 For example, ibid, 292–3

CHAPTER SEVEN

1 Giovanni Villani, *New Chronicle* (London: Constable 1906), Book XI, 71–4

2 David Herlihy, 'Family and Property in Renaissance Florence,' in *The Medieval City*, ed. by Harry A. Miskimin, David Herlihy, and A.L. Udovitch (New Haven and London: Yale University Press 1977), 5–9

3 Jacob Burckhardt, *The Civilization of the Renaissance in Italy*, vol. 1 (New York: Harper and Row 1958), 53

4 Marc Girouard, *Cities and People* (New Haven and London: Yale University Press 1985), 116

5 Ibid, 119–20

6 Cited in Burckhardt, *The Civilization of the Renaissance in Italy*, 183

7 Ibid, 187

8 Jean Delumeau, *Vie économique et sociale de Rome dans le 2me moitié du XVme siècle*, vol. 1 (Paris: Hachette 1957), 230

9 Paulo Portoghesi, *The Rome of Borromini* (New York: George Braziller 1968), 382

10 Le Corbusier, *Creation Is a Patient Search* (New York: Praeger 1960)

11 Pierre Lavedan, *Histoire d'Urbanisme* (Paris: H. Laurens 1966), vol. 1, 228

12 Leonardo Benevolo, *The Architecture of the Renaissance*, vol. 2 (London: Routledge and Kegan Paul 1978), 722

13 Ibid, 719

14 J.F. Blondel, *L'Architecture française* (1752)

15 P. Goubert, *Louis XIV and Twenty Million Frenchmen* (Harmondsworth: Penguin 1970), 161

16 Anthony Blunt, *Art and Architecture in France, 1500–1700* (Harmondsworth: Penguin 1970), 237

17 Michael Dennis, *Court and Garden: From the French Hôtel to the City of Modern Architecture*, 91–5

18 Charles Oulmont, *La Maison* (Paris: Seheur 1929), 5

19 Fernand Braudel, *The Wheels of Commerce: Civilization and Capitalism; 15th–18th Century*, vol. 2 (New York: Harper and Row 1982), 50

20 Emile Mireaux, *Une Province française au temps du Grand Roi, La Brie* (Paris: Hachette 1958), 97

21 Louis-Sébastien Mercier, *Tableau de Paris*, vol. 3 (1782), 226–7

22 Ibid, 232, 239

23 Kevin Harrington, *Changing Ideas on Architecture in the* Encyclopédie, *1750–1776* (Ann Arbor, MI: UMI Research Press 1985), 22

24 Ibid, 25

25 Ibid, 26

26 Alberto Pérez-Gòmez, *Architecture and the Crisis of Modern Science* (Cambridge, MA: MIT Press 1983), 9

27 Ibid, 6

28 Ibid, 11

29 Ibid

30 Ibid

31 Ibid, 300

32 Ibid, 302

33 Carl L. Becker, *The Heavenly City of the Eighteenth Century Philosophers* (New Haven and London: Yale University Press 1932), 31

34 Braudel, *The Wheels of Commerce*, vol. 2, 308

CHAPTER EIGHT

1 Among the many excellent texts on pre-industrial Berlin, of particular note are: Paul O. Rave, *Berlin in der Geschichte seiner Bauten*, rev. by J. Rave (Munich and Berlin, 1976); and Hans Reuther, *Barock in Berlin, Meister und Werk der Berliner Baukunst, 1640 bis 1786* (Berlin: Rembrandt Verlag 1969).

2 Werner Hegemann, *Das steinerne Berlin* (Lugano: Jakob Hegner 1930), 196–7. Through the whole period of industrialization only a single boundary extension was undertaken. On 1 January 1861, 7,000 hectares were added to the municipality, incorporating parts of Moabit and Wedding in the north; Schöneberg, Tempelhof, and Rixdorf in the south; and Charlottenburg in the west.

3 Lothar Baar, *Die Berliner Industrie in der industrieller Revolution* (Berlin: Akadamie Verlag 1966)

4 Dorothea Zöhl, 'Die Randwanderung der Firma Borsig,' in Jochen Boberg, Tilman Fichter, *Exerzierfeld der Moderne: Industriekultur in Berlin im 19 Jahrhundert*, ed. by Jochen Boberg, Tilman Fichter, and Eckhart Gillen (Munich: Verlag C.H. Beck 1984), 140–7

5 Helmut Rogge, 'Zur Expansion und Selbstdarstellung der AEG Fabriken in Berlin,' in *Industriekultur*, ed. by T. Buddensieg (Milan: Gruppo Editoriale Electra 1978), 15

6 Heinrich Seidel, *Leberecht Hühnchen* (Boston: D.C. Heath 1901)

7 Peter Georg Ahrens, 'Neuzeitliche Entwicklung Preussens und Steuerung städtebaulicher Funktionen,' in *Berlin: Von der Residenzstadt zur Industriemetropole* (Berlin: Technische Universität Berlin 1981), 121

8 Hans Reuther, *Die grosse Zerstörung Berlins: 200 Jahre Stadtbaugeschichte* (Frankfurt-am-Main: Propyläen Verlag 1985), 58–9

9 Ernst Heinrich and Hannelore Juckel, 'Der Hobrecht-Plan,' *Jahrbuch für Brandenburgische Landesgeschichte* 13 (Berlin 1962), 40–58

10 Rudolf Eberstadt, *Handbuch des Wohnungswesens und Wohnungsfrage* (Jena, 1919), cited in Hegemann, *Das steinetne Berlin*, 337–8

11 Ibid, 367–8. Georg Haberland conducted a comparative study of housing in Berlin, London, and Paris at the turn of the century, and reported London to be better off than the other two cities, although they were roughly comparable in the congestion of low-income housing. Working-class rents in London and Paris, however, were twice those of Berlin, when calculated on a cubic-metre basis: *Der Einfluss des Privatkapitals auf die bauliche Entwicklungs Gross-Berlins* (Berlin: Sonderdruck aus der *Wochenschrift des Architecturvereins zu Berlin* 1913), 52–67. See also Miron Mislin, 'Die Entwicklung des Mietswohnhauses in der Industriestadt Berlin in Vergleich zu Paris, Wien und London,' in *Berlin: Von der Residenzstadt zur Industriemetropole*, 305–17.

12 Ernst Bruch, 'Wohnungsnot und Hülfe,' in *Berlin und seine Entwicklung*, Städtisches Jahrbuch für Volkswirtschaft und Statistik, vol. 6 (Berlin, 1872), 20ff

13 James Hobrecht, *Uber die öffentliche Gesundheitspflege* (Stettin, 1868). Reuther (*Die grosse Zerstörung Berlins* 63–4) points out that class segregation by district was well under way in Berlin at the beginning of the nineteenth century.

14 Hegemann, *Das steinerne Berlin*, 234. Faucher, a friend of Theodor Fontane, campaigned through the summer of 1863 in the pages of the *Abendpost*, a newspaper soon closed down by the authorities.

15 Annemarie Lange, *Das Wilhelminische Berlin* (Berlin: Dietz Verlag 1967), 148

16 Hegemann, *Das steinerne Berlin*, 202

17 Ibid, 206

18 Bruch, 'Wohnungsnot und Hülfe,' 12–18

19 Ibid, 39

20 Paul Voigt, *Grundrente und Wohnungsfrage in Berlin und seine Vororten*, part 1 (Jena, 1902), 90

21 Cited in Hegemann, 'Das steinerne Berlin,' 255

22 Ibid, 348–59

23 Paul Schmitt, *Die ersten 50 Jahre der Königlichen Schutz-Mannschaft zu Berlin* (Berlin, 1898), 87

24 Lange, *Das Withelminische Berlin*, 467–9

25 Rogge, 'Zur Expansion und Selbstdarstellung der AEG Fabriken in Berlin,' 9

26 Voigt, *Grundrente und Wohnungsfrage in Berline und seine Vororten*, part 1, 274

27 Lange, *Das Wilhelminische Berlin*, 61

28 Adeleid Dohne-Poninski ('Arminius'), *Die Grossstadt in ihrer Wohnungsnot und die Grundlagen einer Durchgreifenden Abhilfe* (Berlin, 1874)

29 Hegemann, *Das steinerne Berlin*, 352f

30 Annemarie Lange, *Berlin zur Zeit Bebels und Bismarcks* (Berlin: Dietz Verlag 1972), 593–4

31 Hegemann, *Das steinerne Berlin*, 280

32 Hermann G. Pundt, *Schinkels Berlin* (Cambridge, MA: Harvard University Press 1972); Eva Börsch-Supan, *Berliner Baukunst nach Schinkel, 1840 bis 1870* (Munich: Prestel 1977)

33 Lange, *Das Wilhelminische Berlin*, 92

34 Peter Klaus Kloss, 'Veränderung städtebaulicher Strukturen während der Industrialisierung,' in *Berlin: Von der Residenzstadt zur Industriemetropole*, 477–86

35 Lange, *Das Wilhelminische Berlin*, 94

36 *Statistisches Jahrbuch der Stadt Berlin*, 27 Jg. (Berlin, 1903), 670–1

37 Eberstadt, *Handbuch des Wohnungswesens und Wohnungsfrage*, 167

38 Reuther, *Die grosse Zerstörung Berlins*, 63–4

39 Lange, *Das Wilhelminische Berlin*, 89–90

40 Alfred Schinz, *Berlin: Stadtschicksal und Städtebau* (Braunschweig: Georg Westermann 1964), 171–2

41 Lange, *Das Wilhelminische Berlin*, 73

42 Richard Borrmann, *Die Bau- und Kunstdenkmäler von Berlin* (Berlin, 1893)

43 Reuther, *Die grosse Zerstörung Berlins*, 115

44 Lange, *Das Withelminische Berlin*, 95

45 Felix Escher, 'Siedlungsgeschichte Moabits,' in *Berlin: Von der Residenzstadt zur Industrienietropole*, 449

46 Lange, *Das Wilhelimische Berlin*, 75–9

47 Reuther, *Die grosse Zerstörung Berlins*, 108–9

48 Henri Lefebvre, *Everyday Life in the Modern World* (New York: Harper and Row 1971), 135

49 Hegemann, *Das steinerne Berlin*, 287

CHAPTER NINE

1 Henri Lefebvre, *The Production of Space* translated by Donald Nicholson-Smith (Oxford: Blackwell 1991), 189

2 Reyner Banham, *Theory and Design in the First Machine Age* (London: The Architectural Press 1960), 79

3 Siegfried Giedion, *Walter Gropius, Work and Teamwork* (London: The Architectural Press 1954), 23

4 Leonardo Benevolo, *History of Modern Architecture* (London: Routledge and Kegan Paul 1971), 386

5 Ibid, 375

6 Larry Braverman, *Labour and Monopoly Capitalism* (New York and London: Monthly Review Press 1974), 159

7 Ibid, 160

8 Hugo Münsterberg, *Psychology and Industrial Efficiency* (Boston and New York: Houghton Mifflin 1913), 23–4

9 Quoted in Braverman, *Labour and Monopoly Capitalism*, 163

10 J. Kocka, *Unternehmensverwaltung und Angestelltenschaft am Beispiel Siemens, 1847–1914* (Stuttgart: Klett Verlag 1960), 140

11 *American Machinist*, 28 September 1899, 1907

12 K. Hausen, 'Ludwig Loewe – Pionierunternehmen des Werkzeugmachinenbaus,' in *Berlin: Von der Residenzstadt zur Industriemetropole* (Berlin: Technische Universität Berlin 1981), 201–12

13 Werner Hegemann, *Das steinerne Berlin* (Lugano: Jakob Hegner 1930), 246 ff; H. Herkner, *Die Arbeitsfrage* (Berlin, 1908), 203

14 A. Sutcliffe, *Towards the Planned City* (Oxford: Blackwell 1981), 14–15

15 A. Schinz, *Berlin: Stadtschicksal und Städtebau* (Braunschweig: Westermann 1964), 162

16 H. Münsterberg, *Psychology and Industrial Efficiency*, 23: cited in Braverman, *Labour and Monopoly Capitalism*, 143

17 Annemarie Lange, *Das Wilhelminische Berlin* (Berlin: Dietz Verlag 1967), 73–4

18 Ibid, 142

19 K. Liebknecht, *Gesamte Reden und Schriften* (n.d.), 5: 315–16

20 Rudolf Eberstadt, 'Berliner Communalreform' in *Preussischen Jahrbücher*, vol. 70 (Berlin: Georg Reimer 1892), 577–610

21 Lange, *Das Wilhelminische Berlin*, 465

22 S. Anderson, 'Peter Behrens and the New Architecture of Germany,' PHD dissertation, Columbia University, New York, 1968, 198

23 Lange, *Das Wilheminische Berlin*, 127

24 H. Rogge, 'Zur Expansion und Selbstdarstellung der AEG Fabriken in Berlin,' in *Industriekultur*, ed. by T. Buddenseig (Milan: Gruppo Editoriale Electra 1978), 15–16

25 Ibid, 12

26 'Kraftwerkunion AG,' *75 Jahre Turbinenfabrik Berlin* (Berlin, 1979)

27 Anderson, 'Peter Behrens,' 202–5

28 Carl Barner, *Carl Benscheidt*, Niedersächsische Lebensbilder 3 (Hildesheim: August Lax n.d.), 3–11

28 Fagus, Publicity brochure (Alfeld an der Leine, n.d.)

30 H.W. Niemann, *Alfeld vom Werden einer Industriestadt* (Alfeld an der Leine: Dobler 1983), 17

31 Barner, *Carl Benscheidt*, 9

32 K. Wilhelm, *Walter Gropius: Industriearchitekt* (Braunschweig/Wiesbaden: Vieweg und Sohn 1983), 43–4

33 H. Weber, *Walter Gropius und das Faguswerk* (Munich: Baumeister-Bücher 1961), 3

34 Wilhelm, *Walter Gropius: Industriarchitekt*, 44–5

35 Weber, *Walter Gropius und das Faguswerk* 30

36 Wilhelm, *Walter Gropius: Industriearchitekt*, 134

37 Fagus, Letter of 13 March 1911 to W. Gropius, cited in Weber, *Walter Gropius und das Faguswerk*, 30

38 Fagus, Letter of 15 May 1911 to W. Gropius, Bauhausarchiv GN 2/10: 203–5

39 Fagus, Letter of 22 May 1911 to W. Gropius, Bauhausarchiv GN 2/11/2: 206

40 W. Gropius, [1910] Programm zur Gründung einer allegemeinen Hausbaugesellschaft auf Künstlerischeinheitlicher Grundlage, in H.M. Wingler, *Das Bauhaus 1919–1933* (Cologne: Bramsche 1962), 26–9

41 W. Gropius, 'Monumentale Kunst und Industriebau,' lecture given in Hagen dated 19 January 1911; 'Ausstellung moderner Fabrikbauten,' *Der Industriebau* 3 (1911), 46–7; 'Sind beim Bau von Industriegebäuden künstlerische Gesichtspunkte mit praktischen und wirtschaftlichen vereinbar?' *Der Industriebau* 4 (1912), 5–7; 'Die Entwicklung moderner Industriebaukunst,' *Die Kunst in Industrie und Handel*, Yearbook of the Deutsche Werkbund (Jena, 1913), 17ff; 'Der stilbildende Wert industrieller Bauformen,' *Der Verkehr*, Yearbook of the Deutsche Werkbund (Jena, 1914), 29ff

42 Gropius, 'Monumentale'

43 Ibid

44 Gropius, 'Ausstellung'

45 Ibid

46 Irving Hoch, 'The Three-Dimensional City: Contained Urban Space,' in *The Quality of the Urban Environment*, ed. by U.S. Perloff (Baltimore and London: Johns Hopkins University Press 1969), 75–138

CHAPTER TEN

1 Virgil, *The Georgics*, translated by L.P. Wilkinson (Harmondsworth: Penguin 1982), Book IV, ll. 406–14

2 A. Leroi-Gourhan, *Le Geste et la Parole* (Paris: A. Michel 1965), 270

3 August Strindberg, *Six Plays of Strindberg*, trans. by Elizabeth Sprigge (Garden City, NY: Anchor 1955), 193

4 K. Wolft, ed, *The Sociology of Georg Simmel* (Glencoe: The Free Press 1950), 418

5 Ibid, 415

6 Karl Scheffler, *Die Architektur der Grosstadt* (Berlin: Bruno Cassirer 1913), 46

7 Frederick R. Karl, *Modern and Modernism: The Sovereignty of the Artist, 1885–1925* (New York: Macmillan 1988), 418

8 Philippe Ariès, 'The Family and the City,' in *The Family*, ed. by Alice S. Rossi, Jerome Kagan, and Tamara K. Hareven (New York: W.W. Norton 1978), 228

9 Ibid

10 S.B. Sutton, ed, *Civilizing American Cities: A Selection of Frederick Law Olmstead's Writings on City Landscape* (Cambridge, MA: MIT Press 1971), 295

11 Kenneth Jackson, *Crabgrass Frontier: The Suburbanization of the United States* (New York: Oxford University Press 1985), 55

12 Ibid, 283–4

13 'The dream house is a uniquely American form because for the first time in history, a civilization has created a utopian ideal based on the house rather than the city or the nation': Dolores Hayden, *Redesigning the American Dream: The Future of Housing, Work and Family Life* (New York: W.W. Norton 1984), 7

14 Ariès, 'The Family and the City,' 227

15 Constance Perin, *Everything in Its Place: Social Order and Land Use in America* (Princeton, NJ: Princeton University Press 1977)

Illustration Credits

Illustrations by the author are not cited.

Imre J.J. Koroknay: 1.1, 1.2, 3.28, 3.36, 4.11, 4.21, 4.27, 6.14, 6.15, 6.17, 6.19, 6.20, 6.22, 6.24, 6.27, 6.29, 6.31, 6.35, 6.36, 6.37, 6.40, 6.41, 6.42, 6.43, 7.2, 7.3, 7.25, 7.26, 7.35, 7.54

Private collection: 1.5

Bildarchiv Preussischer Kulturbesitz: Berlin-Dahlem Museum: 1.8

Istituto Geografico Agostini, Novara: 1.12, 6.16, 6.26, 6.23

Musée d'Orsay, Paris: 1.13

Birmingham City Art Gallery: 1.14

J.P. Lebeuf, *L'Habitation des Fali* (Paris: Hachette 1961): 1.18, 1.19, 1.20, 1.24

Staatliches Museum Berlin: 1.21

National Gallery of Art, Washington: 1.22, 1.23

Academy Group: 2.3, 2.4

Andrea Palladio, The Four Books of Architecture, Isaac Ware edition, 1738: 2.5, 2.6, 2.7, 5.4

Michael Graves: 2.9, 2.10, 2.13

Tate Gallery, London: 2.15

A.F. Kersting: 2.16

Prestel Verlag: 2.17, 2.19, 2.21, 6.13, 7.6, 7.7, 7.62, 8.1, 8.2

Cheltenham Art Gallery: 2.18

Bibliothèque Nationale, Paris: 2.20

Regional Plan Association, New York: 3.1

Royal Architectural Institute of Canada: 3.7

Metropolitan Life Insurance Co. New York: 3.10

Ron Vickers: 3.11

Oscar Newman, *Community of Interest* (Garden City, NY: Doubleday 1981): 3.14

Electa Editrice Milan: 3.16, 3.17, 3.20, 7.32, 7.38, 7.39, 7.40, 9.5, 9.6, 9.7, 9.8, 9.9, 10.7, 10.8

Palazzo Pubblico, Siena: 3.22, 6.33

Uffizi Gallery, Florence: 3.29

Topographical Museum, Florence: 3.32

Edmund N. Bacon, University of Pennsylvania: 4.6, 4.7

Roland Martin, *L'Urbanisme dans la Grèce Antique* (Paris: Editions A.E.J. Picard et Cie 1974): 4.10

Wasmuths *Lexikon der Baukunst*, vol. 3 (Berlin, 1931): 4.16, 4.17

Edmund N. Bacon, *Design of Cities* (New York: Penguin Books 1974). Copyright © 1967, 1974, by Edmund N. Bacon. Used by permission of Viking Penguin, a division of Penguin Books USA Inc.: 4.18, 4.19

John Boardman: 4.20

Eugenio La Rocca, *Ara Pacis Augustae*. Rome: 'L'Erma' di Bretschneider, 1983: 4.22, 4.23, 4.24

D.M. Robinson, *Excavations at Olynthos xii. Domestic and Public Architecture* (Baltimore, MD: Johns Hopkins University Press 1946): 4.25, 4.26

Miriam T. Griffin, *Nero: The End of a Dynasty* (New Haven, CT: Yale University Press 1985): 5.1. Nicholas Purcell provided the draft on which the map is based.

William L. Macdonald, *The Architecture of the Roman Empire*, vol. 1 (New Haven, CT: Yale University Press 1965): 5.2, 5.3, 5.8, 5.9, 5.10

William L. Macdonald, *The Architecture of the Roman Empire*, vol. 2 (New Haven, CT: Yale University Press 1986): 5.12, 5.13, 5.14, 5.15

Barry Maitland: 5.16

National Film Archive Stills Library: 6.3

Stifts-Bibliothek, St Gall: 6.3, 6.8

Deutsche Staatsbibliothek, Berlin: 6.4

Victoria and Albert Museum, London: 6.5

Trustees of the British Museum; by permission of the British Library: 6.6, 6.10, 7.33

Lorna Price, *Plan of St. Gall in Brief* (Berkeley: University of California Press 1982). Courtesy of the estate of Ernest Born. Delineator, Carl Bertil Lund: 6.9

Wolfgang Braunfels, *Mittelalterliche Stadtbaukunst in der Toskana*, 6th ed. (Berlin: Gebr. Mann Studio-Reihe 1988): 6.21, 6.30, 6.32

Shoukry Roweis: 6.38

Leonardo Benevolo, *The Architecture of the Renaissance* (Boulder, CO: Routledge and Kegan Paul 1978): 7.5, 7.13, 7.14, 7.17, 7.19, 7.21, 7.23, 7.24, 7.43, 7.49

Vatican Museum: 7.12

H. Bier Collection, London: 7.16

Palazzo Ducale, Urbino: 7.18

Urbanistica: 7.27

Magnus Gabriel de la Gardie Collection, Royal Library of Stockholm: 7.28

Plino Nardecchia Collection, Rome: 7.29

M.G. Rossi, *Vedute della Chiesa e Convento di San Carlino alle Quattro Fontane*: 7.30

Musée des Invalides, Paris: 7.41

Musée Carnavalet, Paris: 7.44

Turgot Plan of Paris, 1734–9: 7.45, 7.59

British Architectural Library, RIBA, London: 7.47

SPADEM Paris/VAGA New York: 7.48, 10.3

J.-P. Blondel, *Architecture française* (Paris, 1752): 7.52

Atlas des anciens plans de Paris: 7.55

Michael Dennis, *Court and Garden: From the French Hôtel to the City of Modern Architecture* (Cambridge, MA: MIT Press 1986): 7.57, 7.58, 7.61, 7.63, 7.64, 7.65, 7.66

Marc Girouard, *Cities and People* (New Haven and London: Yale University Press 1985): 7.60, 9.4, 10.2

Staatsbibliothek Preussischer Kulturbesitz, Berlin: 8.3, 8.18, 8.30

Berlin-Museum: 8.4, 8.9

Verwaltung der Staatlichen Schlösser und Gärten, Berlin: 8.5

Niedersächsisches Landesmuseum, Hanover: 8.6

Landesarchiv, Berlin: 8.11

Rudolf Eberstadt, *Handbuch des Wohnungswesens*, 1909: 8.12

Hans Reuther, *Die grosse Zerstörung Berlins* (Frankfurt a. M.: Propyläen Verlag 1985): 8.16 8.20, 8.25, 8.27, 8.28, 8.29

Technische Universität Berlin: 8.17, 8.22, 8.26, 9.3

Archiv Klünner, Berlin: 8.19, 8.21, 8.23

Archiv Berliner Feuerwehr: 8.24

Der Industriebau: 9.2, 9.18

AEG-Foto, Berlin: 9.10

Stadtbibliothek, Alfeld an der Leine: 9.14

Bildarchiv Foto Marburg: 9.15, 9.16, 9.17, 9.22

Westermanns Monatsheft, photo by Henning Rogge: 9.21

Editoriale Escudo de Oro, s.a.: 10.4, 10.5

General Index

Index of Illustrations